By Gérard A. Besson:

History & Non-Fiction:

The Book of Trinidad (with Bridget Brereton)

From Colonial to Republic (with Selwyn Ryan)

A Photograph Album of Trinidad at the Turn of the 19th Century

Scotiabank, The First 50 Years in T&T

The Angostura Historical Digest Vols. I & II

The History of ANSA McAL

The Cult of the Will

Folklore:

Tales of the Paria Main Road

The Play Whe Diary of Dreams, Caprices and Charts

Folklore & Legends of Trinidad and Tobago

The Voice in the Govi

Historical Fiction:

From the Gates of Aksum

Roume de St. Laurent – A Memoir

Philippine – The Philip Family of Grenada, Carriacou, Petite Martinique and Trinidad & Tobago Vols. I & II

Philippine

The Philip Family of
Grenada
Carriacou, Petite Martinique
and
Trinidad & Tobago

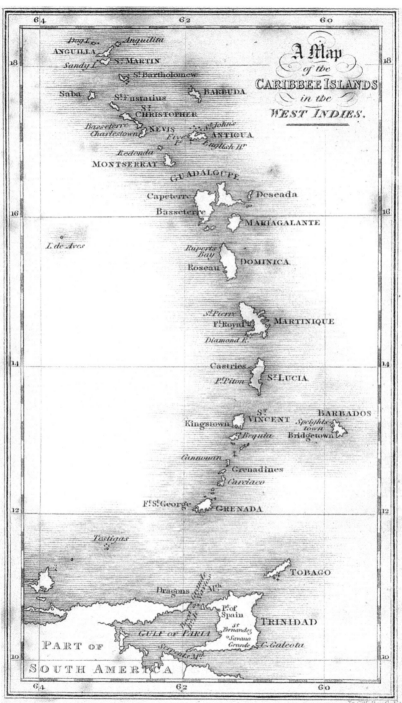

Gérard A. Besson

Philippine

The Philip Family of
Grenada,
Carriacou, Petite Martinique
and
Trinidad & Tobago

Book Second:
Souls on Fire

Book Third:
The Representative Man
The Servant of the Centurion

Paria
2024

Most of the historical images in this book are not actual locations or portraits, but meant to give an impression of what a certain scene or person may have looked like.

© Paria Publishing Company Limited, 2024

All rights reserved. Except for use in review, no part of this publication may be reproduced or transmitted in any form or by any means, electronic or mechanical, including photocopy, recording, any information storage or retrieval system, or on the internet, without permission in writing from the publishers.

 www.pariapublishing.com

Typeset in Poliphilus 12 point by Paria Publishing Co. Ltd. and printed by Lightning Source

ISBN 978-976-8244-51-2 (Book First)
ISBN 978-976-8244-55-0 (Book Second and Third)

To Bridget Brereton
Because I wanted to make them Heroes

THE PHILIPPINE TRILOGY

BOOK FIRST:

CHILDREN OF THE SUN 1788–1803

The love story of Jeannette, Free Negro Woman of Grenada and Carriacou, her husband the French baker Honoré Philip, and their children.

BOOK SECOND:

SOULS ON FIRE 1808–1829

The story of Dr. Jean-Baptiste Philip and his book *A Free Mulatto*, which I republished many decades ago.

BOOK THIRD:

THE REPRESENTATIVE MAN 1829–1870

THE SERVANT OF THE CENTURION 1870-1888

The story of Michael Maxwell Philip, famous 19th century barrister of Trinidad, after whom two streets in Port of Spain are named.

CONTENTS

BOOK SECOND

21.	Michel Maxwell Philip:	
	'In the midst of life we are in death.'	1
22.	Jean-Baptiste Philip M.D.	11
23.	The Alienist	29
24.	Jeannette-Rose Robin de Livet:	
	Love is like a red red rose newly sprung . . .	51
25.	Joyeux Vagabond	80
26.	East West, Home Best?	95
27.	A Stranger in a Strange Land	115
28.	And If Not Equal All, Yet Free	124
29.	Who Loves, Raves	143
30.	Wild and Wonderful	155
31.	The Free Mulatto	181
32.	Absence - that Common Cure of Love	199
33.	Long Ago and Far Away	215
34.	The Open Door	226
35.	The baton Is Passed	246
36.	A Soul on Fire	265

BOOK THIRD:

37. Michel Maxwell Philip:
    Nomen Est Omen   271
38. Meeting the Free Mulatto   277
39. Memory, Love and Eternity   297
40. Present, Past and Purpose   312
41. Conveyancing Clerk   327
42. Articled Clerk   347
43. In Pursuit of a Competency   360
44. Barrister at Large   374
45. Colonial Life   388
46. The Prodigal's Way   400
47. The Pied Piper   421
48. A Lie that is Half-Truth is the Darkest of all Lies   434
49. Captain Cipriani: A Time Bomb or a Time Capsule   441

BOOK SECOND

SOULS

ON

FIRE

1808–1829

"Yet he was jealous, though he did not show it,
For jealousy dislikes the world to know it."

George Gordon Lord Byron

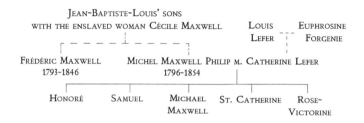

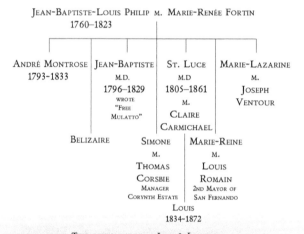

CUPAR GRANGE ESTATE, SOUTH NAPARIMA

21. MICHEL MAXWELL PHILIP
'IN THE MIDST OF LIFE WE ARE IN DEATH.'

*"Those who will not reason, are bigots,
those who cannot, are fools,
and those who dare not, are slaves."*

George Gordon Lord Byron

MY HALF-BROTHER JEAN-BAPTISTE WAS BORN IN 1796 AT CONCORDE ESTATE. He was my step-mother's, aunt Marie-Renée's, as I called her, favourite child and the second born into their family. He grew to become a precocious boy with a lively sense of humour. I recall him asking his mother, "Why did the farmer bury his money in the field?" Before she could think of an answer he said, "Because he wanted to make his soil rich!" Laughing at this little fellow's wit, she later said that she wondered if he had overheard the story of our grandmother, Jeannette, burying a bag of gold hidden in the magenta knots of a burnt hammock in her mother's grave, as the family here in Trinidad would often reminisce on how it was long ago.

Aunt Marie-Renée taught her sons André-Montrose and Jean-Baptiste, along with my brother Frédéric and me, to read and write good French as well as all the catechism that she could remember. She employed John Newbold, an Englishman, a veteran of the American War, as a tutor. He resided at Belle Vue estate as a permanent guest of Montrose Fabien. He came several times a week to teach us to read and write English.

I am a couple months younger than Jean-Baptiste and was fortunate to be influenced and guided by Mr. Newbold, as he taught me to speak and write the English language and become accustomed to being in polite society, where proper behaviour is expected along with the discretion to know my place in the order of things. He told me that it had nothing to do with my colour, it was simply the way of the world. Growing up at Concorde and spending a great deal of time at Philippine, where in both houses our grandfather Papa Honoré's fantastic trophies and prizes lay about, Jean-Baptiste, as we all were, was fascinated by their novelty. He wanted to know everything about Papa Honoré, his adventures and his travels. Everyone was happy to accommodate him, inventing lurid descriptions of sea-monsters that could swallow a brigantine, marauding buccaneers who sailed the Spanish Main, and pirate's gold buried in a dead man's chest. Which on one occasion prompted Jean-Baptiste to ask father, "What did the ocean say to the pirate?" Father, of course, couldn't think of an answer. Jean-Baptiste quickly piped, "Nothing, it just waved." He could make us all laugh or be fascinated by his displays of originality. One day Jean-Baptiste asked our tutor if womb is pronounced "woom" and tomb is pronounced "toom", shouldn't bomb be pronounced "boom"? We all agreed, English was a very funny language. Mr. Newbold told everyone that Jean-Baptiste possessed a talent for producing ideas that could only be described as original. All this caused father to say that Jean-Baptiste must be Papa Honoré returned, evidenced in his curiosity, his love of books and certainly his enjoyment of adventurous tales.

LOOKING BACK OVER SOME TWENTY-ODD YEARS, I can say that 1808 was an eventful year. I was then about twelve years old when a great fire ravaged Port of Spain, destroying our aunt Susannah's house and many others and importantly the warehouse where her husband kept both his and our goods for export. This disastrous event coincided with our aunt Judith's return from England, which to my mind, precipitated discussions as to whether or not Jean-Baptiste should be sent abroad for his education. Our uncle Josèphe was there and since his recall is vivid to this day, I shall draw on it to relate what transpired.

21. MICHEL MAXWELL PHILIP
'IN THE MIDST OF LIFE WE ARE IN DEATH.'

Aunt Judith, who had been living in England for some thirteen years, arrived in Trinidad in the aftermath of the fire and came directly to Concorde. She had decided to return to Carriacou and to make a life for herself at Gran'Anse. As uncle Josèphe recalled, aunt Marie-Renée had been assured by Mr. Newbold that Jean-Baptiste would benefit considerably if he were to be sent away for a formal education. Our father was convinced, however, that it would not serve his or the family's interest to educate Jean-Baptiste in England or France in such a manner that would lead him to expect to be treated by the English or the French people here in Trinidad with the respect that an educated person should expect. Uncle Josèphe recalled saying to aunt Judith that along with the age-old prejudices directed at coloured men, slave or free, the Fédon rebellion of thirteen years previously in Grenada and the other republican-inspired upheavals in the Caribbean, in which free coloureds had played a part were, when taken all together, responsible for that attitude. This caused aunt Judith to tell him rather forcefully, "Look here, Josèphe, don't you encourage Louis to think that there is no future for Jean-Baptiste if he is properly educated abroad. There is another world out there. Jean-Baptiste can be an educated man in England. He can have a life there that is free from colonial prejudice, free from being hated for his racial mixture or his skin colour, as is the case here. No one cares about that over there. And he is dark. You know what that means for him here."

Uncle Josèphe remembered aunt Susannah, who had come down to us from Port of Spain, joining in, saying, "In England, he can marry a white woman, Josèphe!" Going on to say to father, "He is a good-looking boy, Louis, he will have money, so he can be sure to get a white wife, and then he could live the life of a country gentleman. His children, whiter, would be free from all of this. That is what Judith is doing with her children and what I want for Jeannette-Rose and that is why we are leaving here as soon as we can."

Cousin Jeannette-Rose at sixteen was quite a tall girl. She was brunette, very fair-complexioned, and with the brightest, greenest eyes that I have ever seen. If you didn't know, you would not have guessed that she was of mixed blood. She had taken after aunt Susannah in her outspoken manner and had received an education from the Ursuline nuns in Martinique and was, in every way, a refined young lady. Her father had brought her up that way, very aristocratic, all her mannerisms were those of a superior person. Our other cousin Susanne, uncle Josèphe's eldest child, who was about four or five years older than Jean-Baptiste and I, was sitting next to Jeannette-Rose that day. I remember how different they were in appearance. Susanne was very dark-complexioned and did not possess the stylishness that came naturally to Jeannette-Rose.

Uncle Josèphe recalled aunt Susannah telling father, "Let the boy thrive, Louis—he is what, ten? He already knows, or shall soon understand, that he is not stupid. It would be worse for him if he stays here, his nose pressed forever against the windowpane of ambitions that will never be realised. What do you think that will do to him?"

Aunt Susannah had spent a short time in Napoleonic France, where her husband, uncle Guillaume, had attempted, without success, to regain ownership of property abandoned by his relatives as a result of the revolution. They were now planning to return there. My aunts brought with them the touch of that other world, that other reality, one that spoke with confidence of attainment and freedom, the opportunity to live free from "all of this": the boredom of plantation life, the risks and dangers of slavery, the stupidity of the blacks and having to unendingly deal with them as well as with the English people, here in the colonies.

Uncle Josèphe remembered aunt Susannah saying, "Louis, the world *has* changed. When a young girl from an ordinary white family in Martinique could marry a Corsican soldier and become the Empress of France, how was it father used to say, 'Atlas has shrugged!'"

21. Michel Maxwell Philip
'In the midst of life we are in death.'

Neither my father nor uncle Josèphe had experienced life abroad; to them this was all a lot of highfalutin humbug. But they knew that another way of living existed. "My children shall never live in these islands, Louis," said aunt Judith, taking both of father's hands gently in hers, going on to add, "My boys are being educated, and they shall find employment with the firms with which Edmund has business dealings. They may become merchants themselves and make a living that way, and marry English women. The girls, with handsome dowries, they too shall marry Englishmen. I will leave them all, when I am gone, more than enough to live by. They will have investments and own properties in London."

I remember pricking up my ears when aunt Susannah said to father, "Louis, you should let Michel go to London too!" She was being, in her usual brisk manner, provocative. "He too, is bright. Allow him to make a man of himself over there. Eh, what you say, Michel? With money in your pocket, you would." Uncle Josèphe told me that she went on to say that while I was not fair-skinned, she thought that I was very good looking, and with what is called good hair I could even pass for a Hindoo! As for Jean-Baptiste, with his remarkable intelligence, she believed that he would be successful in England, and happy in a way that he never could be here. Well, this apparently led to a quarrel, with father saying something like, "What are you saying, that only stupid people could be happy here, is that what you mean, Susannah? Stupid people with bad hair?"

Uncle Josèphe told me that aunt Susannah replied impatiently, saying, "Yes, Louis, that is exactly what I mean. If they have the brains, they should go, and get away from this place. How long do you think that all this will last? We are already feeling the financial effects of the abolition of the slave trade, and that was only enacted last year. No more recruits coming in from Africa. This way of life is coming to an end."

I knew that as far as father was concerned, I would be staying right here in Trinidad. Uncle Josèphe said that father answered, "It will not end as soon as you think, Susannah. From the moment it was announced that the Atlantic slave trade was to be abolished, Africans from the coast were brought into this colony at a rate and sold on credit of many years to all and sundry. There are now about twenty thousand slaves in Trinidad." To which aunt Susannah replied with a dry laugh, "Fortunately, mother's scheme for making them marry and breed on Carriacou has more than borne fruit for us, but soon, very soon, the abolitionists in England shall have their way. The people over there in England, they do not want slavery to go on, Louis. More and more people see it for what it is, an evil nightmare, inhumane, and a thing of the past." To which my father replied angrily, "Well, I hope not, we have four hundred acres apiece in both Concorde and Philippine under the plough, we have invested heavily in the new boiling house machinery, and as for the steam engine that we purchased from your husband, I haven't even started paying for it."

At that point uncle Josèphe recalled Susanne asking him whether they would be getting one of those for Paraclet. She had only just returned from Concorde where she had gone with Frédéric to see how the new Scottish drivers were handling our blacks. Uncle Josèphe told her no, at least not right away—he couldn't afford it, and in any event the economy was unlikely to improve. This was when Susanne, who from young had shown an interest in estate life, expressed the wish to go to Carriacou with aunt Judith. Uncle Josèphe said that he had no objection and aunt Judith appeared very pleased to take Susanne away with her to Gran'Anse.

Everyone has said that Susanne takes after our grandmother Jeannette in her manner and looks and certainly in the way that she has involved herself in estate work. My father thought that she had taken after our aunt Marie-Magdelaine in that she too had what they called "the gift." Which I took to mean the uncanny ability to anticipate future events.

It was, however, when aunt Judith spoke to our father privately that he relented. To let Jean-Baptiste depart for what would be a

21. Michel Maxwell Philip
'In the midst of life we are in death.'

long time was a very difficult decision for him to take. I remember him saying to aunt Marie-Renée, "I may never see him again, Marie, never, I may be dead by the time he comes back. If he ever comes back."

"You shall be alive and healthy, Louis, no fear of that," she told him.

But it was also the manner in which the family worked in those days. Everything was already underway, and father didn't really expect to get his way. My aunts were in support of the idea and so quietly, without too much fuss, letters were dispatched to uncle Edmund Thornton in London and plans were put into place for Jean-Baptiste to travel to England where he would be under Edmund's care and be a part of the household at Great Coram Street, which was presided over by aunt Judith's eldest daughter, Anne-Rachael and her brother, Louis-Edmund, both named Thornton even though aunt Judith and uncle Edmund had never married. His leaving, as I recall, did make me sad for quite some time.

KNOWING THAT I AM EXPECTING AN ADDITION TO OUR FAMILY, my brother Frédéric has arrived to join me in my vigil beneath the samaan tree.

"Frédéric, I am so glad you've come. I feel that I am standing on the cusp of worlds—one life has ended with Jean-Baptiste dying just a few months ago, and Catherine, God willing, is giving birth to a new life this night."

"Ah, I see we are being philosophical this evening," he replied, handing his reins to the stable boy who had come running on hearing him drawing up his mare.

"You know, I was just thinking, it is so strange that after going head to head, poor Jean-Baptiste and his adversary Woodford would have left this world just a year apart, each one before his time."

7

"But were they really adversaries?" Frédéric mused. "Or were they more like, if you could imagine it, the sides of the same playing card? The Jack of Diamonds on the one side of the card, and the Jack of Spades on the other? They had so much in common and were at the same time so different from each other."

"That's an interesting way to look at them." Frédéric always had an original way of seeing things. "I know little of Sir Ralph's background, his people, his education, his raison d'être, as they say, but as a governor he was certainly different from the previous English ones who were simply interested in suppressing us, while Woodford was about reducing both our economic potential *and* our self respect. He pretended that he couldn't distinguish between those of us with culture and education and those who had neither. Jean-Baptiste, Mr. Hobson and the others strove to accomplish peacefully what our uncles Joachim and Honoré had attempted in war."

"Who tried to force the English to return to their original undertaking in Grenada and lost," said Frédéric, sitting down beside me. "What Joachim and Honoré were attempting over there was not cast in law, while Jean-Baptiste, Mr. Hobson and all those others upon whose shoulders he stood, were aiming to force the English here in Trinidad to keep their legal obligations—those that were first made under Spanish law."

"Yes, under the heaven-sent Cedula of Population that brought us here, which was accepted by them, the English, in the Articles of Capitulation of this island," I answered.

"Jean-Baptiste had to face Woodford's arrogance and his manipulation of the laws," he said, lighting his pipe. "As governor, Woodford was a very powerful man. Fortunately, Jean-Baptiste was equipped with an education and the experience of dealing with men like him. Jean-Baptiste also inherited our family tradition—the pursuit of liberty at all cost, which made him a worthy opponent of the governor's will."

"Exactly. Jean-Baptiste fought a different kind of war, Frédéric. A war that was indeed won. If he and Jean Congnet had not fought, the English would have systemically reduced us to slaves without masters, as they did in Grenada."

"Jean-Baptiste became quite close to Fr. de Ridder towards the end. I was surprised to see that."

"Were you? I wasn't. They were both educated men. De Ridder's background wasn't so different from our own."

"It was when Fr. de Ridder delivered the oration at Jean-Baptiste's funeral that I realised how close they were."

"Yes, we learned a lot about Jean-Baptiste in that sermon, incidents in his life, people he met, things that he never spoke about. Their friendship, I think, was based on the principles that they shared. It grew from there."

"Yes. He may have both encouraged and inspired de Ridder to take a stand against the Catholic Church that was getting closer in its views to those of the Colonial Office, which worked against the free coloureds. You were not there the evening that Jean-Baptiste told him about some of the atrocities committed by Woodford. I think the one that concerned the women and children who drowned, because Woodford had turned back the boats in which they were, was the one that really touched him."

"What was that sad business?"

"You were too young to know. Jean-Baptiste told de Ridder that after Fédon's fall, and in the wake of the public hangings in Grenada, many of the wives and mothers, sisters, female companions of the men who had stood by Julien and our uncles, fled Grenada in a small flotilla of sloops in the hope of finding refuge here in Trinidad. A tragic turn of events came about when they were turned away at sea by an English sloop of war sent by Woodford. Rough seas overturned some of the sloops, and a lot of them drowned. Some women were landed in Tobago, others were never heard of again."

We sat quietly for a while, I admiring the way that the full moon, as it rose, brightened the surrounding cane fields to silvery shafts of wavering light. A limpid quiet, quite warm and still, had settled over the fields.

"Have you heard that this estate may be sold to someone called Burton Williams from the Bahamas?" I had kept this rumor to myself as I didn't want to alarm him or any of the others.

"I wasn't going to say, but yes, I have. What are you going to do?"

"I haven't made up my mind, actually. What do you advise?"

"I think that you should go to Champ Fleurs. Things are not getting easier either there or here, for that matter. Either way I could use a hand, think about it."

From the house we could hear shouts and laughter, the domestics were calling the news. Lights were coming down the path and here came the good news, Catherine has safely been delivered of a baby boy.

"Congratulations old man! You haven't asked, but I expect to be his compère. Let us name him Michel Maxwell Philip, after yourself!" said Frédéric, taking my hand and then embracing me heartily. "This one must be a proper little Englishman! Look at you, three boys! Now I must be off. You go to Catherine and your newborn, give her my best. I must get back to Concorde, as mother and aunt Marie-Renée will be expecting me there tonight and I want to give them the good news— aunt Marie-Renée needs to be cheered."

"I'll have one of the grooms ride with you, wouldn't want you to get lost in the dark."

"Chuts, boy, you were with father and me when we cut those canebrakes, what happen, you still learning to read and write, or what."

Already a groom was coming, leading a fresh horse.

22. Jean-Baptiste Philip M.D.

"Sorrow is knowledge, those that know the most must mourn the deepest, the tree of knowledge is not the tree of life."

George Gordon Lord Byron

SCOTLAND 1810: HUDDLED IN THE CORNER of the lurching coach he clutched to his chest a thick medical textbook. Bound in Moroccan leather and blocked with gold-leaf, its title read, *Outlines of the Anatomy of the Human Body*. It was the work of the Scotch anatomist, physician and medical educator Alexandre Monro, *tertius*. A page was marked by a slip of paper. On it was an address, 58 Nicolson Square, off Marshall Street, Edinburgh. He was to be the guest of the surgeon and sometimes banker, John Borthwick Gilchrist, a long-time acquaintance of Edmund Thornton.

Jean-Baptiste knew nothing of Edinburgh, other than that it was very far from London, and that it was said to be colder, wetter and even more cheerless than Bloomsbury, where he had lived with his cousins at Great Coram Street for the past two years. Their father, Edmund, whom he was told by his father to address as uncle, was not in residence at Great Coram Street. When not in the country, at Whittington Hall, uncle Edmund lived a short distance away at Compton Street with his wife Jane and their young son Butler.

Jean-Baptiste, who had survived the sea voyage to England remarkably well, found it difficult to settle down in his new environment. His cousins Anne-Rachael, Magdalaine-Judith and Louis-Edmund were all in their late teens and early twenties. They appeared to him as marvellously accomplished and intimidating beyond comparison. There was the strangeness of the house itself,

Jean-Baptiste-Louis Philip with Cécile Maxwell

Frédéric Maxwell
1793-1846

Michel Maxwell Philip
1796-1858
m.
Catherine Lefer

Honoré
b. 1820

Samuel
b.1822 d.1847
Edinburgh

Michael Maxwell
Q.C. b. Cupar Grange estate 1829
d. Trinidad 1888

St. Catherine
male b. Carriacou

Rose-Victorine
b. Carriacou

Before the end of the year Jean-Baptiste was put aboard a merchantman that sailed from San Fernando.

its rituals, the remoteness of the people who worked in it and his cousins, who were kind, even loving, but remote as well. He missed home, and, even to his own dismay, displayed his desperation with fits of temper mostly directed at Anne-Rachael, who wanted only to console him. These outbursts would be followed by crushing bouts of chagrin, expressed with elaborate apologies. Anne-Rachael was kind. She understood that being so young he was at a difficult time of his life.

Jean-Baptiste was to be tutored at the Thorntons' residence at Great Coram Street by Vincent Wanostrocht, a young man who was eating his dinners at Lincoln's Inn. Slight, pale and myopic, Wanostrocht taught him English, arithmetic, the rudiments of Latin and Greek, while instilling in the boy's imagination a life-long appreciation for English literature and the classics. Firm, even strict, his manner always formal, he was supportive of his charge. Weeks, then months went by. Jean-Baptiste read, studied, memorised and repeated to his teacher what he learned, as this very different world opened before him.

Vincent came from a family of educators. Originally from Belgium, they had lived in France before relocating to England, where Vincent's uncle, Nicholas Wanostrocht, was appointed tutor to the children of Henry Bathurst, 2nd Earl Bathurst, and at another time to those of William Cavendish-Bentinck, 3rd Duke of Portland. Vincent introduced his young charge to where he lived and where he studied law. Lincoln's Inn was a Spartan environment. The Inns of Court disallowed all modern fashions, "including all new-fangled comforts", Jean-Baptiste was told. There were indeed no comforts to be seen.

Vincent lived with his widowed mother, his sister, her husband, who was also a teacher, and their young family at Lincoln's Inn Fields, between the Strand and Drury Lane. One day, they were on an outing to London's East End, a ragged boy ran up to Vincent and whispered something in his ear. He had received word that he must go to his mother immediately. It was in this way that

Jean-Baptiste was introduced to a world that he could hardly have imagined. Stepping from a busy street they entered a labyrinth of narrow alleys that stank of rancid smells and dirty washing and into a winding lane which was lined by a shamble of dilapidated, soot-blackened buildings. A narrow passage opened onto a flight of wooden stairs that led to a small, lamp-lit apartment that was modest but tastefully appointed. Jean-Baptiste's attention was drawn to the restrained distress of those who were there, and standing at Vincent's side he observed his tutor's mother who was so obviously in the throes of departing this life.

The silent weeping of the women and children, their helplessness, touched him, even as his tutor's gentle kindnesses to his dying mother moved him deeply. It was his first experience of death. To see Vincent surrounded by his young nieces and nephews, their affection so sincerely demonstrated, filled Jean-Baptiste with such a heady mixture of emotions that it was all he could do not to burst into tears himself. He came away feeling very sad for Vincent's loss and very much alone. These poor people, they so loved one another.

He was happier with the sights and the distractions of the city centre. Its tumultuous traffic. The corpulent crowds, the cobbled streets, so noisy, where ancient, soot-crusted stone buildings seemed to lean towards each other in archaic conspiracies whispered through thick, muck-stained glass windows. He enjoyed accompanying Vincent to the Inns of Court. He discovered a round church where crusader knights, cast in stone, lay recumbent, clutching swords, their feet resting upon their dogs of war. Its winding lanes, its grounds, gardens and quaint buildings, the little gate in a long low wall that opened onto the river Thames. The river's traffic. The cold, vile-smelling fog. Yellowish. Fishy. Winter came, bringing an icy drizzle with the fog. Cold, too cold, it blanketed London. Walking with Vincent along the snow-covered streets between Blackfriars Bridge and London Bridge, Jean-Baptiste looked at his breath as it froze before his eyes. He wrote, upon returning to Great Coram Street, a long and descriptive letter to his father, not realising that he would not be able to read it without the help of his mother or Mr. Newbold.

Vincent also took him to his favourite haunts and watering holes in what he called "the city within the walls". Jean-Baptiste sampled the conviviality of the public houses where his tutor met with fellow diners of the Inns of Court. These places, dark and smoky, boasted specialties such as toad in the hole, bangers and mash and warm beer in pewter tankards. The Tower of London. He saw the Yeomen Warders of His Majesty's Royal Palace, the Beefeaters, on parade. The magnificence of St. Paul's cathedral. The most amazing sight of all was of the River Thames Frost Fair, where he saw an elephant being led across the frozen water below Blackfriars Bridge. At the fair were tradesmen of all types. Booths selling everything imaginable. Peddlers, pickpockets, whores and mad people circulating through the shivering crowds. Regimental bands performing in formation. The Hindoostanee Coffee House! Delicious-smelling and warm. Gas street lighting. He attended Sadler's Wells Theatre, where he saw the white-faced clown character "Joey". The London Beer Flood: a gigantic vat of porter in Meux's Brewery burst, demolishing buildings and killing nine women! He attended a concert with Anne-Rachael, Magdalaine-Judith and Louis-Edmund and a party of their friends.

Jean-Baptiste enjoyed listening and learning. Vincent, wanting him to improve his diction and enlarge his vocabulary, would have him recite the arguments and precedents concerning the rights of persons, the rights of things, of private and public wrongs contained in Blackstone's *Commentaries on the Laws of England*. The British class-based social structure appealed to Jean-Baptiste's imagination in much the same manner as the heroic works of Horace and Virgil, Pindar and Homer.

They drove by coach from London to the village of Whittington in Lancashire, and sojourned at Whittington Hall for the summer. Uncle Edmund's style, as he would come to know, was typical of retired West Indian planters. It was altogether different from Great

Coram Street, where in the first place all the servants were English. The great door at Whittington Hall was opened by a black man dressed in blue and gold livery with a powdered wig. There were any number of green parrots in a huge cage in the morning room, and a great many stuffed creatures from the tropics lurked in glass cases in various places throughout the house. It was, however, the food that surprised him most. He had grown accustomed to the fare at Great Coram Street. Uncle Edmund's cook at Whittington Hall was a coloured Créole woman from Grenada. When told who he was she overwhelmed him with embraces, kisses and incomprehensible endearments. Uncle Edmund was pleased with his polite, respectful and considerate manners. Jean-Baptiste no longer threw temper tantrums. But he still missed home quite a lot.

Vincent reported to his uncle that Jean-Baptiste showed great promise and was ready to enter a grammar school, which would prepare him for matriculation at the University of Edinburgh's medical school.

Edmund forewarned him, saying, "You will be going to Dr. John Gilchrist in Edinburgh. He is an eccentric fellow, rather quarrelsome. Met him in Grenada in '88. He had an interest then in the growing of indigo. Spent some time in India. I think you may like him, fancies himself a republican, of all things."

On his arrival at Nicolson Square, to Jean-Baptiste's relief, the old gentleman greeted him with surprising conviviality. He had feared, from how Edmond had spoken about him, that Gilchrist would be taciturn, even unsociable. On the contrary, the old doctor was curious and wanted to know all about him, his parents, their interest, what language they spoke amongst themselves and why a young man from the West Indies would want to embark on a medical career. Even before Jean-Baptiste could come up with a studied response, the old gentleman was already enthusing on the climate of the tropics, the mysteries of the indigo plant and the excitements of foreign travel. Bewhiskered, portly and garrulous, Gilchrist explained that he was first and foremost a philologist, and went on to demonstrate this with an amazing fluency in an incomprehensible language that he later described as Hindustani. His voluble versatility was as astounding as it was exhausting. As a surgeon, he had studied under Alexandre Monro, *secundus,* the father of the author of the book that Jean-Baptiste had been gifted by his cousin, Anne-Rachael, upon his leaving Great Coram Street for Edinburgh.

"Not as fine a man as his father was, and as a surgeon hardly accomplished, smelly old devil, what!"

Jean-Baptiste, with hardly anything to say, blurted, "My cousin gave it to me as a farewell gift."

"*Cras mane,* we go to the Royal High School where *ab initio, et incipe tuum Latine gradus ad Parnassum! Et non fecit ibi intellegere necesse est ex principiis Latine admittendae ad universitas* Edinburgh Medical School, and don't you ever forget, *castigat ridendo mores!*" declared the venerable gentleman cheerfully.

Jean-Baptiste had enough Latin to grasp that he would be attending the Royal High School from the morrow where he would learn Latin, comparable only to the peaks of Parnassus, to be prepared to enter the Edinburgh Medical School, and that he should have a sense of humour when it came to dealing with customs that may appear strange. He went to bed and dreamed that he was going home to Concorde.

He was at first awed, then intimidated by his surroundings. The sheer antiquity of the place, the echo of his footsteps in the wet and cobbled courtyard, the shadowed hallways, the gloomy presence of ancient lives, well-worn ideas, thoughts and theories. Flashes of genius long lost in the gloom of abandoned cupboards, eternally rooted in the slow-moving pendulum of time, unimaginable, appeared to haunt this very old place.

Without realising it, he had moved away from the mystifying rituals of the Catholicism of his childhood and was absorbing, quite consciously, the more exacting Presbyterian ethic in both

Kirk and school. Then there was the egalitarian spirit of Scotland of which he had heard from Vincent. It originated, Vincent had explained, from a classical tradition that he could not imagine. In the coming months, he was made to understand that the school's culture spoke of a fresh movement, one that embraced, for example, the study of classical Greek and Roman literature, over the obscurity of metaphysics. The school's emphasis was on simplified logic that elevated languages and the sciences to the same status as philosophy, allowing accepted ideas in all areas to be challenged, and encouraging the spontaneous overflow of powerful feelings. With those he was more than well equipped. All these notions crowded close, so strange, so forbidding, yet as beckoning as the bony finger that pointed at the new and restless spirits in literature and the arts, who were seeking, at times violently, to burst through old and cramping forms of understanding to a newer meaning of things.

The underlining of the meanings of words—which held mysteries yet to be unravelled in those dusty classrooms of panelled wood that were more like stage sets or courtrooms—became for him a habit. He grew to appreciate the school, its smell of boys, of unwashed woollens, armpits, crotches and feet became for him familiar and even cosy. The stupor of study. The realisation of understanding, at last, what was said by men who wore gowns that were blacker than black. The undecipherable accents of masters who had little patience with the misunderstandings of those who came from Demerara, Trinidad, France, Germany, the United States of America, Switzerland or Barbados, as well as those from England and Ireland. The time spent learning Latin and the art of remembering, saying over and over words in a language described as dead, but very much alive. Latin. It was the language of the elite of all professions. Every student at the Edinburgh Medical College was required to produce a thesis in Latin in order to graduate.

Jean-Baptiste was fortunate to be there at that time. Perhaps he knew it, or sensed it. A German boy, a classmate, older than he, spoke to him enthusiastically of an artistic, literary and intellectual movement taking shape in Germany, *Sturm und Drang*. It spoke of the significance of the free expression of the feelings of artists. It was an effort, in the aftermath of the wars and upheavals generated by the French revolution and the ongoing Napoleonic conflicts, to return to the forgotten sources of life. Truly idealistic, it was at the very heart of the Romantic Movement, which of course had nothing to do with feelings of love or even a strong attraction towards another person.

Jean-Baptiste read *The Adventures of Peregrine Pickle*, a picaresque novel that depicted the adventures of a roguish, but somehow appealing character of lowly origins, who gets by with wit and charm in an unscrupulous society. And was moved by Robert Burns' *A Man's a Man for A' That* and his *A Red, Red Rose*. As for love, the poet reached into his heart with the words:

> O my Luve's like a red, red rose
> That's newly sprung in June;
> O my Luve's like the melodie
> That's sweetly play'd in tune.

He knew nothing of romantic love but understood that Romanticism was a literary movement, yet the last few lines of that poem brought tears, as they spoke of the unreason of fate and circumstance:

> And fare thee weel, my only Luve.
> And fare thee weel, a while!
> And I will come again, my Luve,
> Tho' it were ten thousand mile.

Ten thousand miles! He missed home. He missed his mother and his father, his brothers, André-Montrose, Belizaire, Frédéric and Michel. And St. Luce, who was only a very little fellow when he left for England, and only heard of in his mother's letters which were kept beneath his pillow.

He bought books and started a journal because it was fashionable to refer to it. He made a friend at the school, Marc de Beauvau. Marc was a gloomy egoist, who, in France, lived in a château with three hundred and sixty-five windows, fifty-two fireplaces, twelve towers, and four bridges crossing a moat. He drank single malt whiskey and enjoyed it. He read Lord Byron's *Hours of Idleness* because Marc said that it had received a terrible review in the *Edinburgh Review*. They were delighted by Byron's response in his *English Bards and Scotch Reviewers*. He read *Waverley* by Walter Scott, having read *The Lay of the Last Minstrel,* and welcomed an invitation to visit the Highlands over the Christmas holidays, for which he bought a kilt but couldn't bring himself to wear it.

Jean-Baptiste spent his first winter in Scotland at Craigston Castle, an invitation arranged by Edmund with William Urquhart of Craigston. Edmund was, until his final departure for England, the Urquhart family's attorney in Carriacou, managing the Craigston and Meldrum plantations. Jean-Baptiste thought the idyllic atmosphere of the Highlands mysteriously attractive. The swirling icy mists, the haunting wail of bagpipes at dawn, the clan's chief being in residence, the morning's dew still upon the hydrangeas. Then there was the sight of lovely ladies cantering side-saddle on palfreys and country gentlemen in kilts, keepers with hounds, terrier at heel, and everywhere a profusion of fallow deer, pheasants and hares. All of which served to further excite his imagination even as he read Byron's *Lachin y Gair,* which was all the rage at school.

Not having brought a servant with him he was assigned a valet, an elderly fellow who assumed responsibility for his clothes and timely appearances. He introduced Jean-Baptiste to the tales and folklore of the Highlands. There were witches in the wind, he was assured. These stories, the man claimed, were related by the old woman who lived "up there" with a white dog. Everyone said she was a figment of the man's imagination, for no one had lived up there since Sir Thomas Urquhart who, upon his return from the continental wars, having translated the work of the French poet François Rabelais, died from laughter while celebrating the Restoration in 1660 and, in any case, "up there" didn't even have a floor! Jean-Baptiste's imagination was further fired when he found a copy of James Macpherson's *Fragments of Ancient Poetry* on his bedside table. On its frontispiece was a lithograph of Ossian, the legendary bard, evoking ghosts on the edge of the river Lora. He wrote in his journal that he had entered a world yet to be disclosed.

Jean-Baptiste regaled his hosts with stories of his home, a home of which his actual memory was already almost erased, but in his imagination was peopled by a quantity of kin-folk, all strong, adroit and industrious. He described in detail the fields of sugarcane and the enslaved Negroes, whom he could not actually recall ever seeing at work, and told them of his lovely cousin Jeannette-Rose, his aunt Susannah's daughter who lived in Trinidad, intimating that he was in love with her and she with him. But alas, it was not to be. They understood—consanguinity—it had always been a problem for the gentry.

He did remember that once, at Philippine, Jeannette-Rose and he had listened to the haunting cry of a jumbie bird nesting in a calabash tree. He told them that he was preparing himself for her. They would meet one day, he said, soon, to plan a future that would escape all convention and carry them both away to Rome, perhaps, or even to the Levant, whence the sun rose. At home, in Trinidad, there was a place called Levantille, he assured them, this was where his people had plantations and it was so named because it was from thence the sun arose, to shine upon a bright city that overlooked a Dragon's Mouth.

What he was hardly prepared for was the curiosity of a red-haired kitchen maid, who guided him away from confusion and ineptitude, leading him towards both the sublime and the passionate natures of Eros, whom he knew as the son of Aphrodite, the ancient Greek goddess of love, beauty, pleasure and of course passion.

Mary Arbuthnot, who he took to be maybe William Urquhart's sister or cousin, he wasn't quite sure, saw him as errant. A person who had broken away from his origins. She put into his hands the very popular *Childe Harold's Pilgrimage,* a narrative poem in four parts written by Byron. He was at once fascinated by Childe

Harold, a world-weary young man who was disillusioned with a life of pleasure and revelry, and believing himself alienated from human society, sought distraction in foreign lands. She explained what the word "childe" meant, saying that in days of yore, "a young Lord, who was a candidate for knighthood, was called a childe." She told him of Childe Horn in the tome King Horn; the library at Craigston Castle possessed a rare copy of this chivalric romance. He would see himself, for some years to come, as Childe Jean-Baptiste Philip, preparing himself for an important quest or mission, and his lovely cousin Jeannette-Rose as Ianthe, Byron's sobriquet for Lady Charlotte Harley, to whom *Childe Harold's Pilgrimage* is dedicated:

> *Oh! let that eye, which, wild as the gazelle's,*
> *Now brightly bold or beautifully shy.*

Mary Arbuthnot called him Othello because he was tall, dark and daring. She made a handsome study of him in crayon and introduced him to the works of Joannes Leo Africanus, who had travelled as far as the city of Timbuktu, and to his book *Descrittione dell'Africa*.

Byron's *Lara, A Tale* affected him especially. The idea of returning home altered, reserved, haughty, and apparently palled with pleasure and fame caused him to strike a private pose before a dark mirror in one of the castle's deserted halls, there muttering to himself:

> *That brow in furrowed lines had fixed at last*
> *And spake of passions, but of passions past.*

His complexion, darker than the Mediterranean's olive, was slightly tinged with rose madder. Tall, he had that lissome height and way of carrying himself that came from his forebears. His thick mat of tightly curled black hair was cropped close. His handsome features were distinguished by a long oval face, a high forehead, a strong brow and brown eyes. He, not knowing it, bore a telling resemblance to his father. Taken altogether, his form and features went well with his elegant tailoring, charming smile, easy manner, graceful demeanour, not to mention the warm Scottish accent that shaped his conversation. He did not at all see himself as a freedman of colour from Trinidad as he entered, with confidence, the Edinburgh Medical School.

LETTERS FROM HOME WERE OFTEN IGNORED. This was not intentional, but the days just seemed not to possess sufficient hours. Dr. Gilchrist allowed him the use his extensive medical library and was pleased to sponsor an apprenticeship. Jean-Baptiste was very grateful, as an apprenticeship to a practicing physician was vital to both his admittance and to his actual studies. The library occupied almost an entire wing of the house and opened onto a conservatoire which, Jean-Baptiste was delighted to discover, was heated. Through the palms, ferns, fig trees and other tropical blooms flew green parrots and a colourful variety of exotic birds collected by Gilchrist during a sojourn in the West Indies.

He discovered that his host, now in the role of guardian, much as Edmund Thornton had described him, was a man of many parts. Something of a polymath, Gilchrist, apart from being a surgeon, was also a linguist, a philologist, a banker, a botanist and Indologist and was once a surgeon's mate in the Royal Navy. It would appear that he had spent many years in India, as there were several tiger skin rugs about the place. Their huge heads, containing staring, evil-looking glassy eyes, appeared to Jean-Baptiste to follow Gilchrist around the massive rooms.

It would seem that everywhere Gilchrist had travelled, he made a fortune. By nature argumentative, the worldly doctor enjoyed controversy and delighted in the telling of his successes in putting people in their places. Jean-Baptiste found him distracting, even tiresome, yet sufficiently entertaining and informed on a wide variety of subjects that there was always something to be gleaned in their late-at-night, after-dinner conversations.

Gilchrist introduced him to the writings of David Hume, the Scottish Enlightenment philosopher who advanced a system of philosophical empiricism, scepticism, and naturalism. He heartily encouraged him to think well of himself, adding, "Explore your full potential, my boy!" And then there was politics:

"Res publica, a thing of the people, that's the ticket to the future, my boy," shouted the old gentleman, startling the Borneo long-tailed parakeets to squawking wakefulness and the blue-fronted lorikeets to delirious flight. "The order and character of the just city-state, and the just man."

"What does that mean, Sir?"

"A republic, my boy, is a state in which supreme power is held by the people and their elected representatives, and which has an elected or at least a nominated president, rather than a monarch. Read Plato's *De Republica*, when you have the time. Kings and all of that are a things of the past!"

Jean-Baptiste had neither the time for, nor an interest in politics. The outcome of the wars being waged across the length and breadth of Europe held little meaning for him. Living in Edinburgh, he could not help but be aware of the thrilling martial air that inundated the city. Yet the battalions of kilted warriors, the pipes and drum-majors, their twirling batons, the robust men who embodied the very meaning of 'Scotland the Brave', who were marching away to certain death in distant countries, did not mean a thing to him.

He was introduced by Gilchrist to the physician who maintained an anatomical lecture-theatre at Surgeons' Square. To these lectures he eagerly went when not attending classes given by the University's distinguished, world-famous doctors. He accompanied them on their rounds of private cases, whenever they had an inclination to invite him. He walked the wards of the Royal Infirmary of Edinburgh— the courses in practical medicine and obstetrics required this—and he became dresser to one of the principal surgeons, who would later be president of the Royal College of Surgeons of Edinburgh. The University's apothecary befriended the young man and was pleased to instruct him in the therapeutic properties of substances used for healing. The conservatoire at Nicolson Square contained tropical botanicals with known and undiscovered medicinal properties. Gilchrist was eager to invite the apothecary to inspect them all. The Latin learned at the Royal High School served Jean-Baptiste in good stead even when pronounced by Masters with the broadest of accents. It came easy to him as he read by lamplight, late into the night, Alexandre Monro's *Outlines of the Anatomy of the Human Body*.

A dingy public house on Infirmary Street, near Surgeons' Hall, was where Jean-Baptiste ate his haggis while toying with a warm pint, writing up his journal and reading letters from home written by Mr. Newbold or his mother. These increasingly complained of the disagreeable nature of a new governor whose name was Woodford. Sir Ralph Woodford. A baronet.

His friend at the Royal School, Friedrich von Fürstenberg—whose father, he was informed, considered psychiatry, which was a new field of medicine that focused specifically on the mind, an essential scientific discipline that should be taught at universities—introduced him to the works of Gottfried Leibniz. These were written in German, a language Jean-Baptiste thought he should become familiar with because much of the new scientific thinking was in that language. This study of the mind caused him to read John Locke's major work, *An Essay Concerning Human Understanding*. The notion that nothing is in the mind without being first in the senses, except for the mind itself, was the thought that sparked his interest in mental phenomena, moods, frames of mind, dispositions and the private freedom of his own imagination.

Friedrich, enthused by his friend's enthusiasm for his father Franz's work, wrote to him. Franz von Fürstenberg, who was, at that time, the curator of educational institutions at Münster, responded, suggesting that his son's young friend communicate with Ferdinand Ueberwasser, a professor of empirical psychiatry and logic at the University of Münster. Which Jean-Baptiste did. As a result of the correspondence between himself and Dr. Ueberwasser, the topic for his doctoral thesis began to take shape.

It was in his final year that he returned to the highlands, once again the guest of William Urquhart. Mary Arbuthnot presented him with a copy of Byron's *The Corsair*. He stayed awake that night and read it. At breakfast, he entertained them all with totally invented tales of the corsairs of the Caribbean. This led to his reading Samuel Taylor Coleridge's *The Rime of the Ancient Mariner*. He was thrilled by its sense of danger, the subtle unease evoked by the writer in descriptions of the supernatural and the varying moods introduced in different parts of the very long work. The poem's central idea of an old gray-bearded sailor, the Mariner, stopping a guest at a wedding ceremony to tell him a story of a sailing voyage he took a long time ago, evoked for him feelings of home and family, much as Byron's *The Corsair* had done. This was followed by his discovery of *Lyrical Ballads* and William Wordsworth's *Lines Composed a Few Miles above Tintern Abbey*. He liked the poet's memory of those "beauteous forms" and how they worked upon him in his absence from them: when he was alone, or in crowded towns and cities, and how they provided him with "sensations sweet, Felt in the blood, and felt along the heart." So utterly elegiac, it filled him with the timeless pain of sweet nostalgia that brought tears to his eyes.

Yet he would return to Byron's man of loneliness and mystery, as seen in his *Childe Harold's Pilgrimage,* where the hero of the poem is alienated from human society and sees this as a restriction of his liberty.

> *Adieu, adieu! my native shore*
> *Fades o'er the waters blue;*
> *The night-winds sigh, the breakers roar,*
> *And shrieks the wild sea-mew.*

Jean-Baptiste appreciated these lines from the vantage point of someone inside the canvas of his own imagination. They appealed not merely to his romantic sensitivities but also to his academic interest. He read about the European thinkers, those who treated mental alienation and were called 'alienists', who were seeking a 'medical treatment of the soul'. Their logic inspired him to form the view that hysteria, which was, at that time, mostly associated with the perceived erratic mood swings, contrariness and irrational behaviour of women, a view shared by most scientists in those times, was more than likely associated with the workings of the human brain itself, rather than an obscure feminine eccentricity. It was, however, in 1816, when the German physician and phrenologist Johann Spurzheim visited the Edinburgh medical school and lectured on his craniological and phrenological concepts, that the final decision for the subject of his dissertation was made.

These influences, taken all together, led to his preparing for submission a thesis that he first thought of calling 'Nervous Melancholia', eventually settling on 'Hysterical Moods'. Writing in Latin, he worked every day sitting at a table close to a window that just managed to allow the dreary winter's sun into the stone-cold library of Craigston Castle, until his task was complete. An early spring brought out the gorse, its bright yellow flowers brightening the hills and valleys, and primroses flourished on the bluff that overlooked the still, icy Banff Bay.

His hostess presented him with a copy of Byron's *The Giaour*, which at the time was gaining in popularity, telling him that the sentiments contained in the poem's title—an offensive Turkish word for infidel or non-believer—was a prejudicial term, and race prejudice may be applied to him by some people, because he, being both an outlander and a man of colour, should be prepared for this as he went forward in life.

He replied that if he had to think about that sort of thing at all, he would, like Locke, subscribe to the idea of the individual as a tabula rasa at birth, shaped later by experience and education. He went on to say that he considered himself more an Abyssinian type of man coming from the French islands in the West Indies.

He pointed out that he was told that his grandmother had been of the Fon people of West Africa. His grandfather, on his father's side, had been a Frenchman, and his mother's father was also mostly French.

"I am an individualist," he told her, his eyes wide open as if searching to see himself.

As for his complexion, he explained that the work of a distinguished professor, a scholar at Göttingen University, demonstrated that from a scientific point of view he counted the inhabitants of North Africa among the Caucasian race, grouping the other Africans as of the Negroid race. In this context, the professor named the Abyssinians and Moors as peoples through which the Abyssinian race gradually "flows together" with the Caucasian race. She replied that she was pleased that he had given the topic such considerable thought and wished him every success in life. He promised faithfully to read *The Giaour* upon his return to London.

23. The Alienist

"Sincerity may be humble, but she cannot be servile."

George Gordon Lord Byron

RETURNING TO LONDON IN 1815, Jean-Baptiste was excited to discover that Jeannette-Rose would be soon arriving. She, being on her way from Whittington Hall, was to stay a week at Great Coram Street before leaving for France with the family with whom she had travelled from Trinidad. She was to meet her parents in Paris. He had but a vague memory of her but imagined her as beautiful, elegant and as sophisticated as Byron's Ianthe.

His long-manufactured idea of being 'in love with a cousin who lived on a distant island' was now a part of his life's story as told to strangers. It fascinated him in an inexplicable way, as it allowed him to create for himself an intriguing past. His cousins, Anne-Rachael, Magdalaine-Judith and Louis-Edmund, whom he had not seen regularly, as he had returned to London but twice in all his time in Scotland, were eager to take him everywhere. It was the London season, they explained, and invitations to receptions and balls were being handed around in their circle and he, grown lean and handsome and with a Scottish accent that charmed his speech, together with his affected air of bored melancholy, seemed to them as not simply 'ton', but verily 'haut ton'.

He was to be received by Edward Utterson, a friend of the Thorntons, "an uncompromising Tory of the old school," as Edmund described him. Going on to add that Utterson was a barrister and one of the Six Clerks in Chancery, "he is also a fellow of the Society of Antiquaries and is possessed of an astonishing

Philippine • Souls on Fire

. . . EVERYWHERE A PROFUSION OF FALLOW DEER.

23. THE ALIENIST

collection of books, drawings, prints and objets d'art. He was one of the eighteen members who founded the Roxburghe Club, an exclusive bibliophile and publishing society."

Jean-Baptiste was introduced to Utterson's circle, who in spite of their being conservative bibliophiles, imagined themselves to be radical thinkers and progressive liberals. His reception into this company surprised his cousins. They could not imagine their cousin, who appeared to them as vain and excessively concerned with his manners and appearance, so fashionably dressed, not to mention his lugubrious manner, would be possessed of the intellectual prowess to be at ease in the company of such men and women, people whom they saw as their superiors and whom they had long characterised as social and intellectual snobs.

Jean-Baptiste noticed neither their wealth nor social standing, merely appreciating that they appeared to enjoy the same forms of leisure, style and taste as he. He was far more interested in their conversation and was more than a little pleased to be at the very centre of their attention. That he was a student of a new science, psychiatry, he explained, and was what was called an alienist, and that he had defended a thesis entitled *Hysterical Moods* before the medical faculty at the University of Edinburgh, was of interest to them all. He related, after some moments of pretended bashfulness, that in French, the adjective aliéné, 'insane', gave rise to the noun 'alieniste', referring to a doctor who treated the insane. He was such a charming novelty.

OLAUDAH EQUIANO, THE AFRICAN WRITER AND ABOLITIONIST. Although they were acquainted with Equiano's writings, they had never met a Negro as educated and as well bred as he. It came as no surprise to him that Equiano had penned the story of his life. The book, *The Interesting Narrative of the Life of Olaudah Equiano, or Gustavus Vassa, the African*, which contained a lithograph of the well-dressed author, did not seem to him an achievement beyond comparison. He was not surprised at its existence, but he discerned that his present company expected him to be.

He had no idea of the conventional image of the black man as an ignorant savage, soulless and subhuman. Because arriving in England at such an early age, he knew not of colour prejudice and thought nothing of the realities or the travails of the enslaved Africans at home on the estates which were owned by his family, nor anything of the true nature of plantation slavery. He had experienced merely a curiosity about his skin colour and hair texture at the Royal High School. While attending the medical faculty at the University of Edinburgh he realised, early on, that he was slighted by some professors in a way that he believed himself insulted, and knew that he was ignored by others in a manner that he understood to be a form of debasement that suggested that he was possessed of a lesser mental capacity than others. There were some doctors who were frankly surprised at his intellectual capacity, referring to him as a remarkable Negro. Saying this in such a way made him feel he was being disparaged. As time went on and he came to know them better, he was not surprised at their prejudice. But, on reflection, he became aware that many of his fellow students were also treated by their teachers much in the same manner and, in a great many instances, even worse.

On leaving the company of Utterson and his friends, after explaining that, to him, Africa was as mysterious as China, he promised that he would read Equiano's book. Sitting in his uncle Edmund's study that evening, looking at the engraving of the author on the book's frontispiece, he became conscious that he was seeing a man who was, in appearance, not dissimilar to himself and that, in truth, he knew very little about Africa or Africans except for what he had read in the work of Joannes Leo Africanus. In the memories that he cherished of his home, of when he was a small boy, of his parents and those around him, he never thought of them as black, as Africans or as having parents or grandparents who were once enslaved.

These recollections had long been reduced to mere shifting fragments pictured vaguely. Less than vague, they were more like moon shadows, formless and faceless but accompanied by feelings, which were for the most part nostalgic. Except for his mother's dark face and Mr. Newbold's old, white, speckled hand as it held a white quill from which words appeared in black on a sheet of vellum, there was so little that could be called to mind. He remembered André-Montrose holding Michel Maxwell's hand and how they appeared when he looked back at them standing on the shore. There was something about his father's expression that he could almost see plainly in his mind's eye. However, his recall of his cousin Jeannette-Rose was more than a shard of memory. She, to him, was the personification of home, of Concorde or perhaps of Philippine estate house. There was a feeling that came to him when he thought of home, it was always about her, about them at dusk, sitting on the front steps of a house in a lilac light, listening out for what she said was the call of the jumbie bird. The memory of this both excited and frightened him a little after all those years.

That Equiano as a boy of eleven was snatched and sold into slavery touched him. That had been his own age when he was sent away from home to England. The terror described, the feeling of being lost, forever, so simply put; the nightmare journey aboard the slave ship, my God, he thought; the candle's flame flickering above the book's yellow pages, this boy, he must have been so afraid. Then his displacement. So many masters. So many places. He felt that he could identify with Equiano's pilgrimage, his life as a sailor, seeing Virginia, Gibraltar, Holland, the Caribbean, he even had been in Grenada! Then to the polar regions. With his reason for writing this work, to "excite in the reader's august assemblies a sense of compassion of the miseries which the Slave-Trade has entailed on my unfortunate countrymen."

It came to Jean-Baptiste, while reading Equiano, that he had never thought of himself as a slave owner, which, in fact, he was not, but he was in truth a beneficiary, a recipient of money earned as the result of their enslavement. Working as a deckhand and later as a valet, Equiano earned money and in just three years made enough to buy his freedom. Equiano's fear of being sold again into slavery after working so hard and saving so diligently to purchase his freedom came as a surprise. He had somehow believed that once free, a slave could not ever again be enslaved. It struck him that must be every free black person's greatest fear.

The story told of this black man's pursuit of self-improvement, his search for knowledge and an understanding of himself as a whole person. How he came to be baptised and learned to read and write. Before reading this work, Jean-Baptiste had had no idea of the struggle, of the superhuman effort, required for a black man to be seen for his own worth in this world. As a man with the same potentialities, blood and bones, skin and heart as other men. The condition of the African in the context of European consciousness, that was a revelation. This man's mind, the profundity of his insights, his compassion. His attempt to demonstrate the contrast between civilisation and barbarism and how he argued against the prevailing attitudes that Africans, especially the enslaved Africans, were uncivilised and barbaric compared to Europeans. Equiano lectured against the cruelty of British slave owners and spoke out against the English slave trade. He condemned them and it so eloquently, so movingly, so meaningfully. Jean-Baptiste was forced to consider his own work of little consequence compared to this man's insights and certainly his eloquence, not to mention the clarity of his thinking.

The early morning sunlight, as it streamed into the room, made him realise that he had read through the night. The fire had long dwindled away and a chill was making its way into his bones. What an amazing person this man was, this African, he thought, looking at a reflection of himself in the looking glass above the washstand in his bedroom. Falling into bed he told himself that he must know more about the slave trade because its mark was upon his features, and the colour of his skin spoke plainly of his past. So strange. He

23. THE ALIENIST

had only recently stopped seeing himself as "Abyssinian" and had started to describe himself in his journal as French.

He returned to Utterson's circle the following afternoon. His verbosity curbed, he was more thoughtful than before, spoke less and listened more to what was being said with regard to the question of slavery and the possible emancipation of enslaved Africans in the colonies. A London newspaper had recently reported on the cruelty meted out to slaves on the plantations in Trinidad. It especially mentioned plantations in south Naparima. This report had rekindled the fire in the anti-slavery movement in Parliament. It alarmed him. The family's plantations were in south Naparima. He was now, as the result of reading Equiano's story, more aware of his family's position as plantation owners and possibly, heaven forbid, guilty of, as the newspapers reported, 'working slaves to death so as to make a profit before emancipation laws are passed'.

He would know more. Edward Utterson obliged. He said that the slave societies of the Americas and in the Caribbean were out of date, originating in less enlightened times. Utterson spoke to him of a change in moral values in British society. Particularly, purity-based morality, which was rooted in ideas of compassion, sanctity and piety. When standards of purity were violated, the reaction in certain religious communities was disgust, and violators were seen as unclean and tarnished. Jean-Baptiste had no idea of this. They discussed the efforts of Granville Sharp, Thomas Clarkson, Josiah Wedgwood and the struggles of William Wilberforce and the difficulties experienced in bringing about the Slave Trade Act, which had been passed by the British Parliament eight years ago in 1807, making the trans-Atlantic trade in slaves illegal throughout the British Empire. Utterson explained the influence of the West India Committee, a lobbying group formed in 1780 to represent the interests of the planters in the British West Indies, and its desire to perpetuate the African slave trade. The discussion warmed as various ideas were presented concerning the virtues and vices in society, the ideals of a fairness-based sense of morality, which stood in opposition to an authority-based morality. And the manner in which a society judged right and wrong using values of equality, impartiality and tolerance, and disdained and condemned bias and racial prejudice as it happened to suit it at any point in time.

He understood that he personally was not being condemned as a slave owner or even as a supporter of slavery, but the discussion brought to both his heart and to his mind the nature of his origins and the source of his family's wealth. The difference between him and the others in the room was that he was there *because of* slavery. His unease perceived by his hosts, the conversation was gently turned to his favourite topic, the works of Lord Byron, the poet's latest work, *Darkness*, having been recently published. That it was viewed by the company, notwithstanding the tens of thousands sold, as simply a popular fad, he thought shocking. Jean-Baptiste averred that although merely positioned in the common vogue, the poem told of several spectacular events which were occurring in different parts of the world; these resembled in no small way the biblical signs of the apocalypse. Utterson, who was not a fan of Byron's, suggested that volcanoes were a natural phenomenon and that if sufficient dust was spewed into the air the sun's rays would be dimmed in distant places, even as another in the company quoted Matthew verse 24 saying, "Immediately after the tribulation of those days shall the sun be darkened, and the moon shall not give her light, and the stars shall fall from heaven, and the powers of the heavens shall be shaken," declaring in closing, "you will agree, my boy, that there's nothing new under the sun." He was about to argue that inspiration, drawn from nature, came easily to the poet, notwithstanding whether he be an apostle or a lyricist, when Jeannette-Rose Robin de Livet was announced and there she was at the door of the Uttersons' drawing-room.

Quite overwhelmed by the sight of her, yet pretending that they had parted just the day before yesterday, he took her hand and presented her to the company. She, very much at ease, was all charm and grace. He could not wait to be alone with her and as the conversation waned, they made the appropriate excuses and left the Uttersons to join their cousins.

That afternoon they strolled out into the summer evening's lingering light towards Bloomsbury Square. She would hear all his news and he had her to himself, as far away as possible from their enthusiastic relations. At twenty-three, she was three years his senior, and possessed her own bright eyes and carried well her mother's lithesome loveliness and playful flirtatiousness. So fair-haired and vivacious, he could hardly look at her as she teased him for his Scottish accent and laughed at his stories while listening closely to his ideas. She wanted him to tell her of his academic work and paid close attention to what he postulated in his thesis, which was that hysteria, a general term for a variety of mental disorders, ultimately sprang from the fear of being alienated from the world. She thought him brilliant. He found her wise.

She listened, fascinated, as he spoke passionately of his literary interest, describing the poetic works of Byron with an intensity that suggested he knew the poet personally. Particularly so with the narrative poem called *Childe Harold's Pilgrimage*. She could not help feeling that he identified with this fictional character. Or was he modelling himself after the poet, whom she understood to be a Scottish Lord? Scotland, it would appear, had made an enormous impression on him. The Urquharts, their castle, his outings into the Highlands, seemed to her like visits into the past, a very ancient past from the way he spoke of it. And so emotionally.

His mother's letters had brought sadness and concern where they told of the passing of his old teacher, Mr. Newbold, who had taught him English, of his father's recent illness, and of the difficulties with obtaining labour for the plantations. He was puzzled. Jeannette-Rose explained that an Order in Council, passed here in England, introduced in Trinidad three years ago in 1812, prescribed for the compulsory registration of slaves.

"The bloody abolitionists," she snapped. "They are attempting to stop us from bringing in our people from Petite Martinique or from Gran'Anse. It is intolerable. Gone are the days when you could buy an adult male slave for fifty or sixty gallons of rum. First they abolished the trade, now they want to prevent the movement of our property. This has upset your father no end! It's coming at a time when it appears that the new Commandant of the Quarter, a man named Mitchell, is not at all sympathetic to the free coloured planters. It is hard for the family."

"What can we do?" Jean-Baptiste asked, apparently not having any notion of the circumstances.

"We do what we have always been doing, Jean."

"Which is?"

"Oh for God's sake, don't you know anything! We bring them in from Carriacou and land them at the embarcadero at the Fortins' estate, your grandfather's plantation on the point above Guapo Bay. Then, we move them discreetly in the dead of night, and bring them to Philippine or to Concorde. If Michel Maxwell needs hands, he does the same." She could see that he hardly understood their predicament.

"Listen, the law is arranged to suit the governor. Labour, Jean, is the issue. It is a problem. We have had losses. Slaves die from all sorts of things. All the time. I sometimes think that they *want* to die, the ungrateful wretches. You have no idea what it takes to maintain them."

He didn't. Neither could he remember or find the words to express the condemnation of African slavery that he had recently read in the work of Equiano. She was so authoritative!

"Jean-Baptiste, you haven't heard of the eruption of the Soufrière in St. Vincent two or three years ago?"

"I did. To some here it marked the end of times."

"Not at all. These things explode all the time. What it did do was destroy the entire cotton crop on Petite Martinique. The ash, the darkness, the terrible heat. This has affected your father's income. In Carriacou, our crops have suffered. We have had losses, terrible losses. That is another reason why we have had to move our people to Trinidad, to work there—and damn the governor." She regarded him crossly. "You can't continue feeding them if they are idle."

He thought that he should commiserate, and taking her hand, he asked about his mother. She looked at him as if seeing him for the first time, thinking, 'He does not understand that slaves cannot be left to idle.'

"She is very well. Aunt Marie-Renée is a strong woman and looks good for her age. She worries about you. Your brother St. Luce is going to a school in San Fernando that is preparing him for his entry into the same medical school that you attended in Scotland." She regarded him closely, the late afternoon sunlight slanting through the tall trees revealed his thoughtful, worried look. 'He has no idea of what is taking place at home,' she thought.

"Uncle Josèphe's eldest, Susanne, she has returned to Trinidad. I don't know if you knew, but she went with aunt Judith to Gran'Anse in 1808, the year you left to come here. Well, Susanne and her brother Louis, they now own half of Philippine. They bought those shares from my mother and your father. The estates in Trinidad are being run by your brothers, your mother and cousin Susanne. Susanne is very capable. She was able to bring the entire acreage of Champ Fleurs to full production and has made it very profitable. They have thirty-five slaves on that estate."

He nodded. She saw that he could not remember Susanne. Nor did he know that Susanne had a brother named Louis. 'He doesn't understand that wealth in the Caribbean is only meaningful when it is represented by the number of slaves owned,' she thought. 'Not land. Land is meaningless without slaves.'

"They bought up those shares in 1813. Did you not know that St. Luce has decided to become a doctor, like you?"

"No, I had no idea. I've not heard from home for a while. I have only recently discovered how I get the money that I live by. That has given me an education. When my letters home went unanswered,

I thought that something must have happened to mother or to Mr. Newbold. I am sorry to hear that he has passed away, very sorry."

"Can we sit for a while?" she asked. "There's a bench with some sunlight. I'm glad that I remembered the gloves, my fingers are like ice, feel them."

He blew on her cold hands, holding them in his. "Thank you, I am cold, let's sit. Jean, your father and aunt Marie-Renée are comfortable, financially, at Concorde. It is free of debt and very productive. Your brother André-Montrose is doing well. He is a bright man and Belizaire, well he is a little strange, but St. Luce, now, he is extraordinary."

St. Luce was nine years his junior. This would make him eleven.

"Is he learning to read and to write English?" he asked.

"Yes, of course. Your father hates the idea of him leaving, but aunt Marie-Renée wants it and so does aunt Judith. You can imagine what my mother has to say about that?"

He couldn't. There was hardly a memory of his aunt Susannah or of any of the family, really. She could see from his expression that what she was telling him was remote, even removed from what mattered to him.

"And you, tell me about yourself," he asked. She smiled, taking her hands away, saying "I am to meet my parents in Paris. The family with whom I travelled from Trinidad, the du Pont du Vivier family, had estates in Carriacou and are returning to France. With the second restoration of the monarchy they have a hope of regaining their property. A slim hope. The return of the kings to France does not mean that the country will be as it was in 1789. The best they can hope for is that their property was not sold. Failing that they shall travel to America. Father is also making plans to return permanently, for the same reason as well. The wars are over. Thank God the Emperor has abdicated, again. I hope they have sent him even further away, or put him in some deep dungeon and forgotten about him. Father does not see it that way, he believes that Napoléon, although defeated, restored glory to France. They have been in France since last year. Life is very hard there now, I understand. Oh, look, a cavalcade of carriages and outriders, come."

Already a crowd was gathering at the square's iron railing. It was the Prince Regent and an elegant entourage. "England is so rich, everything is covered in gold, don't you find?" she asked, standing on tiptoes to look over the heads of the women and girls who were waving and calling out to the swiftly passing coaches.

"Yes, this is a rich country. I think I have just begun to understand something about the source of that wealth."

"What do you mean?"

"Well, the institution of African slavery and the sugar. The vast amount of treasure that it generates. For people like us and for the government, the kingdom, for them."

"Yes. So what of it? Are you an abolitionist, Jean-Baptiste?"

"No, or maybe I am. I don't know. I have only recently come to understand something about the slave trade and its effects on the minds of both the slave and the slave owner. It seems to be horrendous. Cruel. There is a move against it here in England which, according to my friends, shall end slavery. I read recently that in Trinidad, in the Naparimas, where we are, there has been great cruelty inflected on the slaves. Great cruelty that amounts to murder. Is that true?"

"I don't know what you have been reading, Jean-Baptiste, but I can tell you that the ending of the trade, the blockade in the Atlantic Ocean mounted by their Royal Navy, has brought about the unavailability of new blacks. That has made life very difficult for us. We must get more out of them. There are planters who have invested large sums, very large sums, and what do they face? Ruin. If they do not get a return that covers their outlay, they shall be ruined. And I have heard that they want to stop the whipping of black women on the estates."

"Whipping women, my word! It is reported here that the slaves on the estates are being worked to death. Surely that is wrong, Jeannette-Rose, tell me, we are not like that. Are we?"

"No, of course not. Our people are valuable. Your father is kind; so too are aunt Judith and uncle Joséphe. As for Frédéric and Michel Maxwell, they are saints. Jean, slavery is a reality, a terrible reality. From what I understand from history, it has always existed. The Jews were slaves in Egypt, and in Europe the Slavic people. Their name was derived from their condition when they were captured by the Romans."

"How do you know that?"

"Father educated me at home. And I spent some time in St. Pierre at the convent of the Ursulines. His opinion is that slavery shall end sooner rather than later. His concerns, if he has any, for he is a happy man, are for the future of the free coloured people in Trinidad, people like us. What he fears is what the governor, Sir Ralph Woodford, is up to."

"And what is that?"

"Woodford is intent on reducing us, the free people of colour, no matter how we appear or behave, whether we are rich or poor, educated and cultured or not, to the same level as the blacks. He would, if he could, stop you from inheriting Concorde estate, for example. When your parents pass away, God forbid that this happens any time soon, you would receive its worth in cash when it is sold to an English planter for next to nothing. Then he would tax you on what you have received. Make it impossible for you to survive in the style that you presently enjoy. You have no idea, Jean-Baptiste, no idea, of the kind of man he is."

"No, I'm sorry, I don't."

"He would not receive my parents. He received my father, but not mother. And when he saw my father, he was rude to him. He did not allow him to sit."

"Why?" he asked.

"Because she is a coloured woman. And because father is married to her. That is one of the several reasons why they are looking into leaving Trinidad. That is why mother sold her shares in Philippine to your mother, who sold them to cousins Susanne and Louis."

"Really. I hope you don't mind my asking, but what would one receive from such a transaction? I ask because I have no notion of the value of things in the colonies."

"I do not mind at all, Jean. This is the family's business. Mother received £23,654 in all for those shares." She smiled coyly and glanced at him. "It may become my dowry."

He had no real idea of the value of anything or what she meant by that remark and thinking it indelicate to inquire further, he asked about Sir Ralph's method of governance. She told him of a young Frenchman, a person of her acquaintance, a resident in the island who was desirous of espousing a virtuous coloured woman, but was refused permission to do so by the Catholic Church, and was obliged to take her to Grenada to be married. She spoke of the governor's manner in dealing with people, all people. He was haughty and disdainful. She described how Sir Ralph would summon an individual and interrogate him in such a way that he could incriminate himself with some triviality, which would be held against him.

"He intercepts and opens letters addressed to persons in the town, and demands a sight of those that people may have received. Jean-Baptiste, he censors the newspapers. No one knows what is really going on. He searches houses and breaks open locks to obtain possession of papers at his own will and pleasure." Taken aback, he asked how this had affected the family. She told him of the new taxes, imposed by the governor's sole authority, the commandeering of the estate's slaves for public works. Going on to say that "If an angel from heaven were sent down to administer the government of Trinidad in its present form, he would find it impossible to give satisfaction."

"The most oppressive action of his, so far, has been the issuing of a proclamation that strikes at the root of the titles of all the landed property in the island. It calls upon the inhabitants to hold their estates in future by a new tenure, to pay enormous fines besides annual quit rents forever as well as huge fees to himself and his associates. We could lose everything, Jean. This man has no regard for the law. He is after the articles in the Cedula of Population of 1783 that gave us the same property rights and legal privileges with regard to the ownership of land as the white people in Trinidad, which were upheld in the Articles of Capitulation to England. In the Cedula's twelfth article we are protected by law as the white people are. He wants to annul them. What do you think would happen?"

He said nothing, because he had no idea of what she spoke. White people? Did she mean the English? 'Does he not know of this,' she thought. 'Uncle Edmund Thornton must have apprised him of these developments in the colony.'

"What Woodford is doing, Jean, is making sure that when the slaves are emancipated, in what, the next ten or fifteen years, we are in the same boat as they. That is what he is after. It shall be all of us niggers together, free as birds to flock together. But there are men, our people, who oppose this, like Mr. Hobson. He and others, in 1810, went to the then governor, Hislop was his name, for permission to approach the King with a petition."

He couldn't think of asking what the outcome was, but was only interested because he delighted in her earnest manner, her grave and serious expressiveness, the hard look that came into her eyes that served to enhance her beauty. He would know of her plans and why she was in London. She was on her way to Paris, she told him, he thought with an air of bored resignation, to meet her parents. He would be delighted, he exclaimed, not being able to imagine a moment without her company, to accompany her to the French capital. She was gentle but firm when she told him no.

Then she was gone. It seemed to him that the whole world had become silent. All voices came as if from a distance. Insights were

23. THE ALIENIST

no longer possessed of surprises. The weather that brightened with the summer did not shine for him. He suspected that his cousins thought that he was a bore, a stick in the mud, especially when it was discovered that he had not learned to dance. They and their circle of gay and noisy friends would teach him if he dared. He did. They, the friends, were all the children of merchants or of planters who had made their fortunes in the West Indies. There were two coloured families from Barbados, born to the mixed-race side of families connected to the Byams and the Codringtons. Very rich and almost white, they lived round the corner in a mansion where they maintained the most formal of styles. He thought them amusing and more intelligent than his cousins. He would befriend them but was disappointed by their polite but firm rebuffs.

"They are after English husbands," he was told by his cousins, all of whom, he soon understood, were about the very same thing.

He sought out Vincent Wanostrocht, his former tutor, and was pleased to find him busy. Having passed his Bar examinations, Vincent was well set up with both wife and children, living comfortably at Camberwell Green where his uncle Nicholas had established a school. Vincent was engaged in a body of work, evidently of a legal nature and voluminous, judging by the quantity of books and papers that filled the small room of his modest cottage. It was meant to be an epitome, a summary of Blackstone's *Commentaries* on the laws of England.

"What I have attempted here is the tracing to its source the origins of that free Constitution, which is the boast and pride of every honest Briton, the real foundation of true liberty, admired by all the world," Vincent explained.

"My word, you are ambitious," remarked Jean-Baptiste.

"It is for the use of schools," said Vincent, smiling modestly. "You arrived just when I was putting the final touches to the manuscript, which is to be presented to my uncle's former charge, a peer, Henry Bathurst, third Earl Bathurst, with whom I am on familiar terms." Resting his palm on the pages on his desk, he continued: "My uncle Nicholas was his Lordship's tutor at Cirencester Park and later on at their residence Apsley House in Hyde Park. He was being prepared to enter Eton College. The Earl is of a humane spirit, a year or so older than I. I knew him there at Apsley House. I was schooled there by uncle Nicholas together with him and his half-brother, John. His endorsement of what I undertake here is of great import. I am to see him on the morrow. Would you care to meet him? He would be very pleased to meet you, I'm sure. Especially so as he is at present the Secretary of State for War and the Colonies."

The following day Vincent introduced Jean-Baptiste to Henry, Earl Bathurst, in the rooms of the Teller of the Receipt of the Exchequer at Great George Street. It was a convivial meeting. The noble Lord, a handsome man with an engaging manner, was pleased to offer his endorsement to Vincent's endeavour. He appeared familiar with it, and upon Jean-Baptiste being presented, his surprise and interest were obvious. He had heard of his people, the Philip family of the Naparimas, from Woodford, the colony's governor.

"Your people are landed of quite great property, I understand."

"We do own sugar plantations in Trinidad. I, alas, have been abroad these several years."

"Oh, I see, and what brought you here, to England? And in Vincent's company—was it in the pursuit of a legal profession?"

"Not at all, my Lord. I was fortunate to have Master Vincent as my tutor while I lived at my uncle's residence in Bloomsbury. Master Vincent prepared me for medical school, at Edinburgh University. I have only recently graduated."

"A medical doctor, no less. Are your plans, Sir, to return to your island to practice physic, or will you be a planter like your father and uncle? From Sir Ralph's correspondence I understand that your people are amongst the leading free Negroes in the colony. Done very well by us, what?"

"I believe we have. I would do both, if I could manage."

"Careful my man, *labitur enitens sellis herere duabus.*"

"*Auxilio sit in manu affligit me inimicus,*" answered Jean-Baptiste. "If I am fortunate, with a willing friend."

"I say, I am surprised to find a person such as yourself so, how should I say, so well brought up. You are doing your old schoolmaster here proud."

"Hardly so," murmured Vincent.

"Oh! but it did have to do with you, Master Vincent. I was a boy of eleven when I was put in his charge."

"You said you had an uncle, came to an uncle. Who is your uncle, the one that lives in Bloomsbury?"

"Edmund Thornton, of Whittington Hall in Lancashire."

"Oh yes, Thornton, did very well for himself with sugar in Guiana with James Baillie."

"In Guiana?"

"Why yes. Don't you know?"

"I had no idea. In truth I know little of the family's affairs."

"Your style and manner, Doctor, with whom were you when you were at Edinburgh? For I must say, you have all the characteristics of someone to the manner born."

"I was fortunate to be apprenticed to Dr. John Borthwick Gilchrist, of Edinburgh during my studies there. A very fine gentleman, perhaps something may have rubbed off. And I was a frequent guest of William Urquhart of Craigston Castle. Both of these gentlemen were acquaintances of my uncle Edmund. He knew Dr. Gilchrist in Grenada where he acted as attorney for the Urquharts. Looked after their affairs on Carriacou island. Cotton plantations, as I have recently come to understand."

"And you have acquired the manner of a gentleman by imitation. My word. How outstanding!"

"By inclination, I would hazard, as it came easily, perhaps more honour'd in the breach than the observance, I'm sure, Sir."

"What, what? Hamlet! Learned his Hamlet. I say, Vincent, you did a fine job. Now doctor, tell me how come you have Edmund Thornton as your uncle?"

"My aunt Judith is a free woman of colour, she lived in concubinage with uncle Edmund, as is common in the West Indies, I understand. They raised a family together who are now here, in London."

"In Bloomsbury?"

"Why yes, at Great Coram Street."

"And your studies at Edinburgh University, how did you manage?"

"I managed quite well actually. I found it an enlightening experience, on the whole."

"How so? What was your specialty, if I may ask?"

"I wrote on the subject of the mind, perhaps following in the footsteps of Dr. William Battie, who wrote a thesis on the subject of treatments for mental illness. His *Treatise on Madness*, published in 1758, was in large part a critique aimed particularly at the Bethlem Hospital."

"Yes, it created quite a reaction, I am told, in some circles."

"A debate that still continues, in some circles."

"'We of the craft are all crazy. Some are affected by gaiety, others by melancholy, but all are more or less touched!' So sayest the bard."

"Lord Byron, I am sure, would be pleased by your remembering him thus, but you should have no fear of that sad malady."

"It is the burden of genius, I am told, and you are familiar with the works of Byron as well! Well, well. This has been most informative, a pleasure meeting you, Dr. Philip. Most informative. I have heard a great deal of the free mulattoes of Trinidad. I commend you on your progress. If you have a mind to, send me a report, after you have studied the conditions under which your people live and thrive in Trinidad."

"It would be a privilege. You are too generous, I'm sure."

"By Jove, I say, you could be an Englishman, except for your accent! What you say, Vincent?"

"Indeed, and thank you for your approbation. The manuscript shall be at the printers by Monday week."

"Excellent! And very pleased to have made your acquaintance, Dr. Philip, my regards to Governor Woodford on your return, he is a great friend of my brother John. In Woodford you may find the willing friend who would lift you up from betwixt the stools."

"Thank you, my Lord, you are most kind."

Great George Street was shrouded in an icy fog as they made their way to St. Stephen's Tavern.

"I say, Jean, you certainly made an impression on his Lordship," said Vincent. "Will you send him a report about the free mulattoes, as he referred to your people in Trinidad?"

"I may," said Jean-Baptiste. "But I am sure he has a great many reports to look at and my own would be of little consequence."

"You may find him welcoming," Vincent said. "He is of a liberal and candid character. His is a calm and moderate spirit."

Jean-Baptiste smiled, adding thoughtfully, "I will bear your words in mind, Vincent, I may just do so."

"And your plans? What shall you do, return to your home in Trinidad?"

"No, not immediately. I have a mind to travel. I would visit my cousin in Paris, where she is joining her parents. I don't remember them, it would be useful for me to hear what they think of the world, what it is like in Trinidad and then, I would wish to see the famous surgical theater at Leiden. Most of all, Vincent, I would prefer to keep up my studies on the human mind, the imagination, especially in the context of this present craze, the Romantics. Its causes, its effect on myself, on our generation. I am fascinated by its emphasis on sensation and individualism and the scientific rationalisation of nature. I must, with careful observation and scientific method, experience all of this myself."

"Self-experimentation! You would be the experiment?"

"Isn't that always the case, Vincent?"

24. Jeannette-Rose Robin de Livet
Love is like a red red rose newly sprung . . .

*"Man's love is of man's life a part; it is a woman's whole existence.
In her first passion, a woman loves her lover,
in all the others all she loves is love."*

George Gordon Lord Byron

I DID NOT WANT A DOE-EYED DEVOTEE HOVERING,
AND NEITHER WOULD MY PARENTS.

1817: JEANNETTE-ROSE: CHÂTEAU DRACY LE FORT. In the aftermath of the terrible fire of 1808 that destroyed our home in Port of Spain, the family moved to a small plantation in the Sainte Anne Valley. It was a special place for my parents, as this was where they had met and fallen in love. Mon Repos estate, long planted in coffee and cocoa, was cradled by thickly forested mountains that received the coolest of breezes all year round. It was especially charming in the late afternoons, as the light of the westering sun illuminated the valley with a Midas touch. Everything would turn to gold.

Susannah's Children & Grandchildren

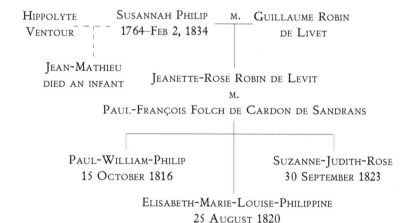

Hippolyte Ventour — Susannah Philip 1764–Feb 2, 1834 M. Guillaume Robin de Livet

Jean-Mathieu
died an infant

Jeanette-Rose Robin de Levit
M.
Paul-François Folch de Cardon de Sandrans

Paul-William-Philip
15 October 1816

Suzanne-Judith-Rose
30 September 1823

Elisabeth-Marie-Louise-Philippine
25 August 1820

24. JEANNETTE-ROSE PHILIP
LOVE IS LIKE A RED RED ROSE NEWLY SPRUNG...

As I left there that morning to take ship on this fateful journey, a feeling swept over me that I would never be seeing this heavenly place again.

Both my parents are ambitious; my mother in her pragmatic manner certainly is, and so too is papa, in his own careful way. They have been preparing me for a propitious marriage since I was a child, both subscribing to the thinking of the French philosopher Rousseau, whose view was that a woman's entire education should be planned in relation to men: to please men, to be useful to them, to win their love and respect, to raise their children, and to care for them in sickness and in health. These, they both believe, are a woman's duties from time immemorial, and this was impressed upon me from my childhood.

Upon their arriving in France, my parents took a very small house on Rue de Reims in the hamlet of Gentilly just outside of Paris and, as father likes to say, away from the noise of the restoration. I joined them there. The return of the monarchy in the person of Louis XVIII, the former king's brother, brought internal and external peace to France and the sort of stable economic prosperity that allowed for science, as father said, to move forward. My father is not a Bonapartist. Papa is a monarchist, through and through, but he has, as maman maintains, a patriotic view of the Emperor as a warrior prince whose armies had carried the banners of France from Madrid to Moscow, and who, as a modern man, has introduced into law, ideas "born in fires of liberty". By that he meant the Code Napoléon that has given France a logical and uniform legal system. Josèphe-Philippe du Pont, with whose family I had travelled from Trinidad, suggested that father keep those ideas to himself, especially as the armies of the Sixth Coalition, encamped in various parts of the city, may take objection to his liberal views.

In declining my cousin Jean-Baptiste's offer to accompany me to France I knew that I had disappointed him. His infatuation was obvious and became more so as the days at Great Coram Street went by. Jean-Baptiste is a lovely man. He is intelligent but removed from the day-to-day realities of life. I suppose this is so because he has spent so many years at his books. Just to imagine a medical doctor in our family, in our kind of family, is thrilling; it is a rarity. He may be the first one in Trinidad, that is if he ever returns.

I, however, did not want a doe-eyed devotee hovering and neither would my parents, so it was a sad parting. He appeared as a person displaced. I could see that the news given to him about conditions at home in Trinidad had brought about some semblance of reality, one that had previously eluded him. At least he now has an idea of the serious danger we face from the new governor, Woodford. But there was also the impression left on him by his reading of that book, the one written by the educated Negro, Equiano. As he spoke of it, of him, I discerned that he was completely unaware of the plantation economy and the sugar estates that gave him a living. Jean-Baptiste is a naive man to be taken in by some over-educated black. He appears to be entranced by the works of the British writers and romantic poets. I am unacquainted with and not interested in that sort of writing. To me, it is an escape. A way to avoid the realities of life. Jean-Baptiste's experiences in Scotland, vacationing with the Urquharts in some dingy old castle, have to do with it somehow, and so does the German friend he met at school in Scotland.

Papa is to meet Pierre-Josèphe Amoreux, a distinguished physician and naturalist, with whom he corresponded over many years. Father is actually here in France to attempt the recovery of his ancestral property in Puy-de-Dôme where, he assures us, there is fine château in which his people have lived from the time of Charles the Bald. But first we go to the Royal Garden of the Medicinal Plants to meet Monsieur Amoreux.

The Royal Garden is, from mother's point of view, the only reason why we are in Paris. It was always father's dream to return there and to present his portfolio of drawings of medicinal plants from the tropics and have them accepted by some august gathering of horticulturists. Amoreux shall endorse his efforts, Papa's portfolio will be published and he can live happily ever after.

24. Jeannette-rose Philip
Love is like a red red rose newly sprung...

These beautiful gardens on the left bank of the Seine convey the impression of being a perfectly laid out and carefully arranged Eden where there are neither sins nor serpents. There is only order and care. Every flower, shrub, tree and bush is labelled. There is also a ménagerie, founded, papa said, in 1795 from animals taken away from the ménagerie royale at Versailles. This was of course during the revolution. Alas, there was no question of us going to see the animals. We were for the great salon where the horticultural delights were on display.

As we crossed the crowded park, maman and I were attracted by the sight of a huge tent that was decorated with amazing illustrations of fabulous creatures, fantastic portraits, grotesque images, flags and banners. As I looked at it, an astonishing sight began to unfold. As if by some magic, a large round shape seemed to be emerging from the top of this huge tent, rising up like an enormous bubble. We all stood and stared as slowly the great shape ascended, soon leaving behind the beflagged rooftop of the tent. It was a hot air balloon, launched from behind the tent, and it was as gaily decorated as the tent itself. Hanging from it was a little wicker basket in which were men who doffed their hats and waved at the crowd that responded with hurrays, with many men throwing their own hats into the air. It was a mesmerising novelty.

But Papa had no time for novelties. We were for the great hall where at the very entrance stood Pierre-Josèphe Amoreux. They had never met, never laid eyes on one another, yet, in some mysterious way, even at a distance, they recognised each other, and upon vigorously shaking hands immediately fell into a deep discussion regarding the scientific attributes of *Achillea millefolium, Adonis amurensis,* and *Bougainvillea.* The first two, I gathered, deriving from figures out of Greek mythology, and bougainvillea, a lovely vine with terrible thorns whose name was constantly mispronounced and often misspelled, named after Louis Antoine de Bougainville, a French admiral and explorer whom they had never met, but were well aware of. Maman and I were not at all bored. She was excited, there were so many handsome men about and I, well, one could say that I too was curious.

Father and Monsieur Amoreux were about to start off arm in arm like old comrades when they were joined by an imposing man who had, with some difficulty, extracted himself from a crowd of what appeared to be students. He seemed to be Amoreux's acquaintance as there was little formality in their greeting, and we were straight away presented to him. This was Alexandre von Humboldt who, I was to learn, was a famous geographer, naturalist and explorer. He had not long returned from the Americas, both north and south, and had recently published a book based on an ancient manuscript discovered in a library in the German city of Dresden. It was apparently all the rage.

Mother and I were about to follow the three when one of the young men from whom Monsieur von Humboldt had fled came running up to us. He would have a word with the distinguished gentlemen—well, in a way that I have come to understand was customary to these men of science, he was not sent away, and after some discussion he was presented to mother and me. He was Paul-François Folch de Cardon de Sandrans.

JEAN-BAPTISTE ARRIVED AT OUR HOUSE on the Rue de Reims quite unexpectedly some weeks later. He was sitting in the tiny parlour with my parents when we, Paul-François and I, returned from a visit to the devastated Bois de Boulogne. This was where forty thousand soldiers of the British and Russian armies were encamped since the banishment of Bonaparte to St. Helena. Paul-François was much dismayed at what had happened to this beautiful forest, as were many Parisians. Thousands of trees had been felled for firewood and to build shelters. It was a terrible sight, nothing but a bleak and ruined landscape covered with the stumps of ancient oaks.

Paul-François was a retired army officer and thirteen years my senior. I could understand that he felt ashamed that his country was occupied by foreign armies. As a boy, he had seen his father depart as a deputy of the nobility for the Estates General held at Versailles, and then came the revolution, a time of uncertainty and fear. This was followed by his military service and the fall of the Emperor, which, he told me, had been in his opinion as theatrical as his rise.

I had no idea of what he spoke when he said that after the Spanish war, the Moscow campaign and the battle of Leipzig, all of which followed in rapid succession, the imperial structure, which had been brought into existence after the revolution by Napoléon Bonaparte, cracked, swayed and fell like a house of cards. I of course agreed, repeating "Yes, just like a house of cards." The idea of a house of cards collapsing on itself I found very disturbing. It could happen to us, our family, I thought, with what was taking place in Trinidad as a result of the machinations of this new English governor, all of which could reduce us, if not to poverty, to a very uncomfortable position.

Paul-François' interest in nature was a hobby, an all-absorbing one, but a hobby all the same. Like papa, he was dissimilar to the many other returning noble émigrés who wanted to take revenge against the revolutionaries and turn back the clock to before the revolution. Like father, he wanted to move ahead, and to regain some or all of the properties which his relatives had abandoned at the start of the revolution.

Mother was not at all surprised to see Jean-Baptiste standing, hat in hand, at our front door. She said to me later that after my telling her how he had greeted me in London, his amour so obvious, she knew he would appear. She was, however, pleased to receive him. She had not seen him since he was a boy of nine or ten when her sister, aunt Judith, had returned to the West Indies in 1808.

Jean-Baptiste was much as he had been when last we met. Discreet, urbane and so devoted. Paul-François was naturally pleased to meet a relative of mine. He immediately engaged Jean-Baptiste in conversation, wanting to know about his medical studies, his experiences in Scotland and his future plans. It was plain that

Jean-Baptiste was taken aback by the obvious familiarity displayed by Paul-François, in the way he appeared to be on intimate terms with my parents and with me. I must say, so was I.

It then came to me that he viewed Jean-Baptiste not merely as a relative, but as a possible rival for my affection! Mother noticed this as well and initially appeared to be delighted, while papa, unaware of the subterranean tensions, was genuinely curious. He wanted to hear more from Jean-Baptiste.

"Hysterical moods, eh? What made you think of that as your topic?"

"I wanted to explore, amongst other things, feelings, ideas, mind–body dualism, as René Descartes did in his work, so as to gain an understanding of what is awareness, and why we have what is called imagination. And there is Hume's work, his examination of the psychological basis of human nature. But most of all I was thinking of intelligence." Jean-Baptiste appeared to be speaking somewhat rhetorically. "What is intelligence?" he asked dramatically, lifting a hand. "Why is that faculty so difficult to harness when we are faced with circumstances that are, for example, unexpected or even frightening?" He appeared to be out of breath, as he sat bolt upright in a straight chair, his hat, which was new, still in his hands on his lap. He had not parted with it since his arrival.

"Yes, it takes discipline to deal with fear," said Paul-François reflectively. "For a person as yourself, a civilian, that requires the creation of new habits of thought. Becoming accustomed to being afraid, I suppose, is important."

"Yes, of course, fear causes physiological changes and ultimately behavioural changes," said Jean-Baptiste, his Scottish accent shaping his French in a most amusing way. "These escape control, the control we imagine that we have over our feelings," he concluded, smiling brilliantly. "Yes, feelings."

"Fear occurs in anticipation or even an expectation of a future threat perceived as a risk to oneself." Paul-François stroked his whiskers, adding, "It could be caused by seeing or thinking that an object or even a pattern in nature could be dangerous."

"Trypophobia, I believe it is called," said father. "I once saw a man terrified at the sight of the holes in lotus seed-heads. They appeared to have elicited feelings of discomfort at first, and then for some reason, terror in this man, who was a distinguished man of science. A botanist."

"How very strange!" Maman sounded amused, but I could see that she was puzzled.

"Yes, trypophobia, it is an abhorrence at the sight of irregular patterns or clusters of small holes or lumps," said Jean-Baptiste. "To most people this would be unreasonable, unthinkable, but it exists." An awkward silence followed, during which I experienced a kind of delight. I had been quite captivated listening to Paul-François and Jean-Baptiste discuss fear. It made me wonder if they were both afraid of losing me!

Then, suddenly, Jean-Baptiste stood up. "Aunt, I wonder if I could have a word with you. It is about what is taking place at home. This is why I came, I . . . please, Jeannette-Rose, do excuse me. Sir?"

"Of course, Jean-Baptiste," said maman. "Come, and you too, Guillaume, as I am sure that these two have other things to talk about."

Mother told me later that evening that Jean-Baptiste did not really want to have a better understanding of what was taking place in Trinidad, on the plantations or with the family. Rather, he wanted to know about their plans and about me. "I ignored that. I patiently explained that he should go home, at once. That this lingering in Europe was a waste of time. That is was selfish." She admitted that by now, she had become quite impatient with him.

"Why?" I asked.

"Because of his affectations, his lack of interest in the family, and I suppose this idiotic infatuation with you."

"How did he react to you telling him to return to Trinidad?"

"He just looked as though he hadn't heard a word. I said to him, look here, boy, you are over here posing as a gentleman of leisure, making a grand style, keeping company with people who have country estates the size of Trinidad. Go home and mind your business. The government is trying to take away your inheritance. Your father is old, he is not well, your mother is doing the best she can, dealing with the danger we face with this man, Woodford."

"How did he take that?"

"He listened, but he was more interested in telling me his immediate plans. I wouldn't let him. I said to him, look here, do you know what it costs to keep you here? In money? In sweat in the cane field, in the lives of the slaves who die working to make money for you? What it takes out of your mother? Every cent you spend costs something that is paid for over there, in Trinidad, on those estates. Go home. Be responsible. He didn't say anything, he listened, nodding, all the while looking at me closely. I could see his eyes as they travelled across my face, scrutinising me, taking me in."

Mother said that Jean-Baptiste did not care about plantations or sugar or gave a damn about the new English governor. He really had come to see me and was surprised to find that I had company. This, she said, was difficult for him to hide. "I think he believes that he is truly in love with you," she said, her face showing both amusement and dismay. "It appears that you excited in him a strange, un-childish passion. He has carried a memory of you in his heart for many years. It may have sustained him in his loneliness. And the poetry of this British lord, Byron, whoever that is, that you told me about, has shaped his imagination. He does not know who or what he is, really. In his mind he is a white man. That he is in a black man's body has not yet occurred to him."

Jean-Baptiste told us that he was on his way to Leiden, in Holland, where there is a medical faculty and a famous surgical theatre. A cabinet of curiosities, he said, in which ancient Egyptian mummies and Roman antiquities may be seen. "Why would he be interested in such obscure people?" Maman wondered. "I told him that it sounded like a waste of time and money"! Jean-Baptiste didn't agree. He said he needed to know more about the human condition. I think that he has had too much education and it has gone to his head.

I KNEW ONLY TOO WELL WHAT WAS TAKING PLACE between father and Paul-François. They too had a long talk, after Paul-François had proposed marriage, some days later. He was a straightforward man. I liked that about him. He was also handsome, fair-haired and steady. He came to the point. The wars were over. A king was once again on the throne of France and because the privileges of the aristocracy had now and forever been abolished, it was time for him to move on with his life. He said that he thought me beautiful, intelligent, amusing and, he was sure, passionate. I kissed him for that. He had no idea at the time that like mother, I too was ambitious.

He promised he would be true to me and could not think of moving ahead without me at his side. He also admitted that he was poor. He probably had no idea just how well off we really were, but I was certain that he suspected that we were wealthy. I can't say that I was in love with him. But as a woman, I have come to understand that men simply fall into one or the other of two categories, either you would not let them even touch your toes, or you could see yourself becoming close, very close, and Paul-François was one to whom I could become close, very close. He was relieved when papa gave his consent and I said that I would be delighted to be his bride.

CHÂTEAU DE SANDRANS, NEAR TO CHÂTILLON-LES-DOMBES, which had become Châtillon-sur-Chalaronne after the revolution, is in the picturesque Rhône-Alpes. It was modest, to say the least, compared to the grand castles that I had seen as we drove there in a rented carriage. Abandoned by his family when his father had died at Sandrans in 1797, the château was left more or less untouched by the revolutionaries, his father having been a man much revered by those who knew him. Arriving in the week following our wedding, I could see that Paul-François was very embarrassed by what he found.

Apart from the chickens that had deserted the poultry yard to live all over the place, there was an astonishing accumulation of broken furniture, torn up papers, broken books, destroyed statuary and paintings, dirt and cobwebs in every room. The entire house was cold and damp. Damp oozed from the bulging walls. Damp created weird shapes in the plaster that in the flickering lamplight appeared to shift, ghostlike, with macabre faces and spectral-appearing hands reaching out.

For me, these were mere nuisances that paled when compared to the hundreds of bats that flew about the rooms, and to what they left behind. I was always terrified by bats, convinced that they would become stuck in my hair. The place was unlivable! The peasants had stolen the beds and all the linen, and there was hardly any usable furniture left. The kitchen had been looted. There was nothing useful in the old place, except the title deeds and the family's Letters Patent which were kept in a secret closet that he had to break into. Finding these was, according to him, a godsend.

We settled in as best we could, encamped in the main hall around a very large fireplace. As the days went by the villagers, most of whom had been in the family's employ or were once their tenants, came to pay their respects. They were helpful. They started to clean the rooms and repair the broken doors, windows and furniture. First the kitchen, then the rooms upstairs. With the autumn rains coming on, the roof was attended to and finally the chimneys were repaired. I was assured that the damp would vanish with the spring. Mother joined us at Château de Sandrans as the first snowfall commenced.

24. JEANNETTE-ROSE PHILIP
LOVE IS LIKE A RED RED ROSE NEWLY SPRUNG...

I came to understand that Paul-François belonged to an old and quite distinguished family. His people were originally Spanish nobles from Cardona in Catalonia and were thought of as second only to the royal family of Aragon in their antiquity. As such they were directly descended, in ancient times, from both the Spanish and the French royal families. Because of this, they were called "kings without crowns". They had fought for Henry, king of Navarre, who became the first monarch of France from the House of Bourbon after the Wars of Religion in the 1500s. In return for their loyalty and service, when he became King Henry IV, he granted the brothers Horace and Folch Cardon the barony of Sandrans in Ain. Paul-François' relatives in Spain were dukes and grandees and rich beyond anyone's imagination.

All this he confided in an offhand way. I, myself, was thrilled to become a baroness. Don't talk about mother, she was already trying on the title, thinking that she could borrow it from me, calling herself Susannah, Baroness Robin de Levit, much to papa's amusement.

Father was, in truth, enormously impressed, as this marriage was well beyond his aspirations. For my part I must say I always believed that I would marry not just a white man but a nobleman like my father. It would appear that with the return of the nobles, much to the discomfort of the former revolutionaries, all unsold or unconfiscated property would be returned to its former owners. Father, who was in Paris, was waiting for an opportunity to present his claim at the court of the restored Bourbons. Paul-François, because of his family's Spanish connections at court, largely in the person of one Madame de Cayla, was to be ahead of father with regard to establishing his right to regain his family's properties. These were the château itself, three farms and an extensive vineyard. After an interminable and agonising wait, documents came to hand. We were allowed to keep the château but were denied access to the vineyard and the farms, as these had already been bought from the state by peasants from the nearby village.

My Paul-François, a hobby naturalist but at heart a vintner, was of course disappointed. I could not share his chagrin because I was expecting our first child and was quite pleased with myself. Maman was not dismayed either. Never enervated and ever propelled by her ambitious nature, she encouraged Paul-François to take heart and seek out another opportunity, inasmuch as he was now in control of my dowry.

Poor Jean-Baptiste. It was ironic, I thought, because my dowry, all twenty-three thousand pounds sterling of it, came from what his mother, aunt Marie-Renée, had paid to my mother for her shares in Philippine estate, and would now be at Paul-François' disposal. I did not mention this to Paul-François, but it was a tremendous amount of money in France in those days. It meant coming into a vast fortune, but as I was to learn, this was not at all unusual for a family such as theirs, as in a previous century they had been saved from bankruptcy by marrying into the Strozzi family, a dynasty of Florentine bankers. It was the way of the nobility. To maintain it, you had to marry an heiress and in so doing you could add another escutcheon to your quarterings. Because of my father, I too possessed a splendid coat of arms that was, because of its antiquity, quite respectable.

Paul-François did take heart and with the spring he went in search of a place where we could reestablish ourselves. Some months later we were driving in our new barouche with a handsome pair of grays through rows of old poplars which were all waving respectfully over the dusty roadway, towards a large but unfortunately quite rundown château close to the village of Dracy Le Fort in Burgundy. Its magnificent vineyards, occupying acres upon acres, stretched across a most beautiful rolling countryside. The estate came with wine presses and thousands of empty bottles and hundreds of huge barrels that vanished into the underground gloom of an enormous cellar. Such a large cellar was extremely important, I was told, in that it provided the required darkness, constant temperature and humidity for the grapes to turn into fine wine. Luckily, the estate came with

24. Jeannette-rose Philip
Love is like a red red rose newly sprung...

a family of vintners. The cellar-master assured us that they had been there, in that domain, from before Louis IX became a saint! It was perfect.

I was brought to bed when still at Château de Sandrans in the spring of 1816 and, with mother in charge, gave birth to a baby boy. Paul-François was over the moon with delight. He was christened Paul-William-Philip. Paul-François had insisted that the name Philip be included in his baptismal names in honour of mother's family. By summer, we were in residence in our new home and I was pregnant again.

ONCE AGAIN JEAN-BAPTISTE ARRIVED UNEXPECTEDLY. I had just put little Paul-William-Philip in his cot and was closing the drapes of the window that overlooked the courtyard when I saw a carriage approaching. At a pace, it was coming up the driveway that curved towards the château's main entrance. Curious, I stood at the window and looked as the driver pulled up the horses, and before the carriage could actually come to halt, its door was flung open and out jumped Jean-Baptiste. Standing in the brilliant morning light, a cloud of dust swirling around him, I could hear as he gave instructions to the coachman, who answered something that I could not plainly understand, but to me sounded impertinent. As this was taking place, another man clambered out of the carriage. Eventually, Paul-François appeared. He had been up before dawn and was returning for his breakfast. Then came what appeared to be much explaining. Eventually the coachman, with the assistance of one of our grooms, took down their baggage and led the foaming horses towards the barn. After being introduced to the other person, Paul-François, taking Jean-Baptiste by the arm, walked towards the château's entrance. With a final word to the nursemaid I, by this time quite curious, hurried downstairs to greet them.

Jean-Baptiste had been making his way to us for some time, he explained, after kissing my hand and both my cheeks and doing the same to mother. Presenting his companion, whose name was Amédé Pichot, he recounted that they had travelled through the night. Paul-François recommended food, rest and a change of clothes. Later that afternoon they joined us, mother and me, who were waiting, indeed looking forward to hearing what had brought them to us.

Departing Leiden, Jean-Baptiste related, they had journeyed on horseback in a leisurely manner, stopping at wayside inns and hostelries. They were making their way to the German city of Aachen where in its ancient cathedral were kept the most holy relics of the dark ages and those of the famous king and emperor, Charlemagne.

"Who?" both mother and I asked in unison.

The greatest king and emperor of the west after the fall of the Roman Empire, we were assured. It was there in a church called the Palatine Chapel that thirty-one German kings and twelve queens had been crowned. Assured that mother and I were impressed, Jean-Baptiste went on to say that amongst the marvels held in the cathedral were the white robe that the Virgin Mary had worn when she gave birth to Jesus, and the linen that covered Jesus' body after being taken down from the cross, with marks from Jesus' precious blood still warm and wet after eighteen hundred years.

For some reason I instantly thought to make the sign of the cross, but didn't. The cathedral also held the right hand of Charlemagne, his head and his hunting horn, which was made from an elephant's tusk. This was where the *Noli me tangere* casket was kept. This was Latin and meant Don't touch me. "No one knows what is in it," they both assured us. Then, there was the skull box of Saint Anastasius, whoever that was, and a great collection of reliquaries containing foreskins, femurs, oracular jawbones and various saintly body parts that could only interest those who were enraptured by the most distant past. It was a place, they said, for the Romantics, where myth met up with history.

24. JEANNETTE-ROSE PHILIP
LOVE IS LIKE A RED RED ROSE NEWLY SPRUNG...

Jean-Baptiste had remembered Paul-François saying that he was originally from the village of Sandrans. They had arrived at the château some days before, only to find it deserted. On getting our new address from the mayor, he was finally able to find us. Jean-Baptiste seemed now different from when last we met. His self-assuredness was as obvious as his reinstated charm. They had hired a coach and a driver upon arriving in Dijon with whom he had quarrelled for every mile that they travelled.

Amédé Pichot, also a medical doctor, was reserved and one could even say, a diffident individual. Having had some experience of the French, I suspected that his origins were simple. They had quite an extraordinary adventure before finding us, being detained by a party of German officers who thought them spies. Eventually their credentials were believed by the officer in charge and they were directed to the quickest route that would take them to the city of Aachen.

We listened as they spoke of the awesome antiquity of the place, more fascinated by their obvious rapture than anything else. It was the cradle of western civilisation! we were made to understand more than once. The birthplace of chivalry and knightly honour, where whispers of the legend of the grail were first discerned and echoes of the footsteps of Siegfried and Brunhilde, whoever they were, could still be heard in the naves and clerestory's of this marvellous church. He was breathless, they both were.

But that was not all, not all at all. For in the cathedral's garden there was a grotto. Sitting in the sunlight, close by the stream that encircled a huge stone, was the most beautiful maiden that they had ever seen. At first they believed her to be a vision, but as she rose and came towards them, they saw that she was human. But more than human, for her beauty shone about her, a halo of fine light. They thought to fall at her feet as she stopped to gaze at their amazement. Her shower of golden hair falling about a pure white lace collar, she turned her bright blue eyes on them. On him, Jean-Baptiste corrected. It was to him that her first glance was directed.

He took her hand. She let him. He believed that he was chosen. He said his name. She hers.

"What was it?" Mother asked, her heart beating in her throat, I could see it there, thumping.

"Lieselotte Petzold."

"Lieselotte Petzold," we both whispered.

"Yes. The cathedral's cryptkeeper's daughter," whispered Amédé tremulously, I thought he would cross himself.

We sat in silence for a reverential while. Then mother asked, whispering, "So, what happened next?"

"Her father came up, he seemed to have materialised out of the cathedral's stonework, or perhaps he was there all the while," whispered Jean-Baptiste, we were all whispering for some strange reason.

"We presented ourselves to the old fellow," said Amédé. "He appeared an agreeable person, Günter, he said his name was, and invited us to his lodging. Literally a shelter that had been built into the outer wall of the cathedral by the original masons who had constructed it a thousand years ago."

"He was proud to show us the Palatine Chapel and throne of Charlemagne and the magnificent Barbarossa chandelier, which had been donated to Aachen cathedral by Emperor Frédéric I in the twelfth century," breathed Jean-Baptiste, going on to add in a stronger voice and with very little modesty that it was because of his bearing and overall demeanour that he was, from the start, treated as a gentleman by Monsieur Petzold. They were offered hospitality and were glad to accept it.

"The old man, who was a widower, gave us beer, bockwurst and freshly baked bread, all served by the increasingly beautiful Lieselotte." Clearly, Jean-Baptiste was stricken by Cupid's arrows, mortally or mentally, as it would appear. In the days that followed, he saw a great deal of her. "I think I would like to marry her."

24. Jeannette-rose Philip
Love is like a red red rose newly sprung...

"You think what?" gasped mother.

"I thought I would ask her father for her hand in marriage. Aunt Susannah, Jeannette-Rose, I have come to ask you, you are my family here in Europe, to receive them. Her father is a kind and simple man. She is a saint. I would like to marry her here and take her back with me to Trinidad. What do you think?"

Quite surprised, I looked across the room at Amédé, he caught my eye and shrugged, a Gallic gesture if there ever there was one.

"Isn't this all a little quick?" wondered mother.

IT WAS FASCINATING, INSTRUCTIVE AND ALARMING all at once, to have Jean-Baptiste and Amédé with us. In conversations with them, my father and my husband over the next few days, I learned a lot about France, my new home, the way it was before the revolution and how it was now. A different France by all accounts—even though to those nobles who returned after having been in exile for over twenty years, it looked much the same: the peasants were in the fields. The walled vine, fruit and olive orchards, the open fields of wheat, rye, clover, the fallow fields resting a year before they were replanted, all appeared much as they had before the world had heard about the "Rights of Man". The difference was that the men and women in those vineyards now owned them. Lands that had once belonged to the Catholic church as well as many of the great seigneurial estates were now in the possession of the ordinary people. Great fortresses like Bourbon-l'Archambault were being turned into stone quarries, and the Laws of France were now framed by the Napoleonic Code. A world had ended.

One particular conversation was especially enlightening. It started when Jean-Baptiste, no doubt excited by the prospect of meeting his Lieselotte Petzold again, and enthused, as ever, by the Scottish poet Byron, regaled us with:

Man's love is of man's life a part;
it is a woman's whole existence.
In her first passion, a woman loves her lover,
in all the others all she loves is love.

I could not help noticing that my mother had to turn away as he expressively recited those lines. She took a deep breath and shut her eyes for a moment. This made me wonder if the poet's words had struck a chord, a note that chimed in some half-forgotten hall of her memory. I had not imagined her as being sentimental. We Philip women, and I was brought up by her to be a Philip woman, were famous for being cool, calculating and pragmatic. Glancing at Jean, I perceived that he too had seen her reaction. He smiled; it was though he had vanished and all that was left was the smile.

"It is from his *Don Juan*," he said. "He was not a womaniser, but a man easily seduced by women."

Maman nodded, sighing and saying that she understood the true meaning of those lines.

"Ah, we are in the company of the Romantics!" exclaimed father, clapping his hands excitedly. Looking at me, his eyebrows raised in exclamation, he added: "The Romantics are not like the troubadours of long ago. They are not about love, requited or otherwise. Romanticism is artistic, even intellectual. It concerns itself with the inspiration of the individual. Am I not correct, Jean-Baptiste?"

Jean-Baptiste beamed in wordless concurrence. I could see that my Paul-François was not taken in at all. Don't get me wrong, he is a Frenchman with roots stretching all the way back into the steamy soil of the Iberian peninsula and was passionate, very, in all sorts of clever ways. But I knew that he had no use for the Romanticism that was all the rage with the return of King Louis XVIII, after Napoléon's defeat at Waterloo. The conversation must have got under Paul-François' skin in some irritating manner, as he said sharply: "A sham world, this fortress of Romanticism. It merely serves to save you fellows from contemplating your fate in this emerging age."

This, of course, brought heated denials from both Jean-Baptiste and Amédé. "We are men of science!" "We are about the future!" they exclaimed. Amédé was indeed a trained surgeon, and Jean-Baptiste had a special interest in the modern sciences of the mind. Amédé's view was that yes, the world had changed, but wasn't it the rationalism inculcated by the philosophers, the likes of Voltaire and Rousseau, which was patronised in the 1780s by an aristocracy that began to see themselves as the children of the Age of Reason? It was they who had produced the likes of the Marquis de Lafayette and Comte de Mirabeau and all those other aristocrats who had been prominent in the early days of the revolutionary era.

"It was your class that produced the dilettantes who toyed so lightly with reason and rationalism," Amédé said. "It was the nobles who furnished the admiring audiences for the philosophers who were actively manufacturing the intellectual gunpowder for Robespierre, Danton and Saint-Just to blow up the world!"

"And it was us who led the armies that held the Saxon Brunswick and that other one, Hohenlohe, at bay at the battle of Valmy," said Paul-François. I could hear in his calm reply that the temper in him was rising.

"You are bred for war, Baron," said Amédé in an unctuous tone, no doubt backing away. Having sensed a harsh response to a point of view that, to me, seemed sound, he added: "I think that you would have fought for any noble cause. Like yourself, I believe that there are inequalities between men. Society must be organised in hierarchies of social order, so that each may know his responsibility, his rights, and his place. That is what the king should be making plain."

"I fought for France, Monsieur," said Paul-François, rising. "The violence of the revolution, the terror, became the logical climax of the Age of Reason. It has produced in the hearts of men like yourselves a yearning to invent a wonderful and exotic past in which your imagination may be exercised. It has converted you to this new-fangled vice."

I knew that he was going to leave the room, lest his honour be offended. He once told me that as an officer of the Royal Army he had been taught that if he saw a drunk or a madman approaching, he should immediately cross the street, lest he be insulted and forced to defend his honour against an unworthy opponent.

"I must now say goodnight, Messieurs, but before we leave you, I would make my position clear," he said. "I am of the émigré nobility that has returned to France, but I do not support those of my kind who would return to the past. The ones who ride through the countryside with the white flag have found common ground with you, the Romantics and the religious fanatics, the ones you follow. It shall come to nothing." And so saying, he bowed and departed.

"Yes," said papa evenly, sensing that a clash of political ideals had overtaken the evening's conversation. "After the revolution, rationalism went out of style and freethinking became bad taste."

"Jean-Baptiste," I hazarded, "your taste for the Romantic idea was not born in the tumult of the streets of Paris or in the shadow of the guillotine, as Amédé's was. Yours came about as a result of reading the work of the British Romantics in a castle in Scotland, where you said that there were witches in the wind. Not so?"

"It is no less real, cousin," he replied. "The works of Lord Byron sell tens of thousands of copies. *The Corsair* sold ten thousand copies on its first day of publication, as was the case with his other works. Different roads could lead to the same destination. As a rational person, I can embrace both worlds. I can be a man of science by day and, as the evening shadows fall, I can lose myself in the dreamworld of long ago, where gallant knights and beautiful ladies, like yourself, graciously rule a charming countryside, and young men such as ourselves, can manufacture our own version of reality, or hear at the close of day the call of the jumbie bird, remember that? and thus change the world around us, if only for a short while." He said this, looking at me with an ingratiating smile that I did not return with a reassuring one.

"The wish France could return to a state that resembles the France before the revolution," said father in a serious tone of voice, "where the king would rule supreme. The government, so decentralised that the landed aristocracy, preserved by primogeniture, could be the driving force behind the running of the country, that has become a preposterous notion. Those days are past."

"Primogeniture? Never heard that word before. What is that?" asked mother.

"It means, Madame, the right of succession belonging to the firstborn child," explained father in the kind voice he used when instructing mother.

"Oh! Well, I am glad that we didn't have that in Grenada, otherwise we would have had my half-crazy brother Honoré running the show, or, failing him, poor Nicolas-Régis," said mother non-chalantely.

"It is the wisdom of women in your family, my dear, that is the source of everything that we hold dear," said papa. "How is it said in scripture? A wife of noble character, who can find her? She is worth far more than rubies. Her husband has full confidence in her and lacks nothing of value. She brings him good, not harm, all the days of her life."

And money too, I thought to myself.

JEAN-BAPTISTE AND MAMAN spent the following day together. According to her, his interest in the family's situation in Trinidad was not as vague as it had been when last they spoke. "He was just dazzled then by your beauty, my dear," she said in a tone that somehow conveyed the impression that my attractiveness was entirely her doing. "He is uninformed, but he wanted to have an understanding of how the money is made. How much money is needed to make the money that we make, that supports him, and what it costs in labour. His interest in the slaves, from what he has read in the writings of the African man, I forget his name, appears to me to be merely one of curiosity. He very much appreciates the extensive role that Edmund has played in his upbringing and in our monetary success. He has a partial understanding of the significance that we, as a family business, have never been in debt to the merchants or to the money lenders."

She said that she told Jean-Baptiste of long ago, about life on the estates and of the dangers faced by his father, his uncle and herself, in going into that backwater, Trinidad. Its diseases, its awful people, the rottenness of its governments. She also told Jean-Baptiste about our origins and about our grandfather and grandmother, Papa Honoré and Jeannette, Free Negro Woman. How Papa Honoré had become wealthy. The pirate stories! The type of woman Jeannette was and her origins in the Fon nation. He was surprised. He had no understanding, just half remembered stories, and he found it hard to believe how Honoré fils and Joachim had faced the English in Grenada, how it caused the deaths of his uncles, and that what was taking place in Trinidad now was the same thing all over again.

"It is the same fight that your uncles died for. Grenada is ruined. That is the reason why we went to Trinidad. And that is what we have to deal with there, again," she said. "Jean-Baptiste is a dreamer, but he is not unrealistic. I think the years of arduous study, the isolation, being so far from home, have propelled him into this make believe world that seeks to idolise the importance of the whole person, body and mind, the glamourising of the past and the goodness of 'the old ways.' It shall pass. It is a fad of youth. He said that he had no idea that his brother St. Luce would be going to England. I am sure that his mother would have written to him, telling him this. But marrying that German girl would be a disaster for him, and for her. I told him so. He has to marry up, I said, at least find an equal partner, someone with whom he would share similar interests after this absurd preoccupation has passed. He listened. I thought, at times, that he was more fascinated by me than truly appreciating what I was saying. He is a strange boy." She paused, appreciating the memory. "He paid attention when I said that of the free people of colour of Trinidad, our family is the wealthiest in slaves and land. We are among the most privileged in all of the West Indies. The distribution of land between 1783 and the present has given us an advantage in land ownership that is incomparable to anywhere in the west. This is what we must hold on to at all cost. There is a struggle for civil equality taking place that is winnable, because unlike the free coloured people in other British islands, we are not after the bestowal of *new* privileges, but the restoration of *eroded* or even *lost* rights. Go home, boy, I told him—east, west, home best."

The following day, following luncheon, we all walked out into the herbal garden that adjoined the greenhouse, ostensibly for Paul-François to show Jean-Baptiste the botanicals. All was in full summer bloom and teemed with bees and butterflies and all manner of birdsong. In the middle of the shrubbery was a little pavilion, totally overgrown, that looked like a funerary chapel. It was built of marble and made to look like a ruin.

"Is it possible that your attachment to the German girl springs from your ruminations about Europe's glorious past?" Paul-François asked just as we sat down in the brilliant sunlight. He went on to add, I thought sarcastically, "For a person with an education such as your own, she must appear a fascinating study."

Jean-Baptiste smiled, saying, "She is beautiful and very amusing, and . . ." here he paused as if reaching for the word.

"Not too bright?" said mother. "My dear Jean-Baptiste, as I said to you yesterday, since your announcement I have felt a concern, a serious one, about your plans. Forgive me. You are my brother's child and I shall speak plainly. It will be most unfair to take a silly, uneducated girl, whom you imagine to be a figure out of a fantastic past, to a place like Trinidad. The reality of life there would appall her. It will appall you too, if or when you ever return."

"Aunt Susannah, I would prefer to say that she is a *simple* girl, not a *silly* one. I appreciate your candour and your concern but this is my affair, my life, my future. Lieselotte will be my wife. We shall live as all married people do. I shall protect her and love her." He said this in a quiet, conciliatory tone while looking closely at her. "She is simple," he went on, nodding as if in agreement, "that is her most salient virtue. She is not possessed of states of mind that complicate her understanding of the meaning of things. She is like a commonplace book. Her pages are blank. We shall write our lives across its pages. A journal of wonderful events of love and children." He spoke as though implying that it might be a conspiracy.

"Trinidad," said Paul-François, "as I understand it, is on the frontier of the New World. It is where the fox tells the hare goodnight, as we say. It would be difficult, nay, impossible, for a simple German girl to liver there, and find happiness."

Maman said, "What you propose is exactly what the English government is against: the marriage of Europeans to people as ourselves. I fear that you will find yourself and Mademoiselle Lieselotte on the pathway to the sort of difficulty that destroys marriages."

"Is it not always such a case?" replied Jean-Baptiste in a voice that conveyed mild sarcastic amusement. "The unknown? Life's adversities. If we decide to stay in France or Germany I would set up a practice, see patients, work as a physician. Yes, because of my colour and appearance, there are some who would see me as an aberration, even as abnormal. Those would be the uneducated ones. For the rest of society, the educated, the cultured, I would be like Jeannette-Rose, or the Russian poet Pushkin, who is a man of colour, a charming novelty."

"Never heard of that one," said maman somewhat archly. "Jeannette-Rose is much fairer than you, Jean-Baptiste."

"Or more specifically, aunt, like the famous Chevalier de Saint-Georges."

"A Grenadian chevalier? Is he black?" she asked.

"Not Grenadian, I believe he was from Guadeloupe," said Jean-Baptiste. "He was a mulatto, the son of a planter, a former gentleman of the King's Chamber. His mother a slave. He became a renowned composer, a conductor of the leading symphony orchestra in Paris. And a champion fencer."

"I heard of him. He was made the Commander of the 13th regiment of Chasseurs, called Légion St. Georges," added Paul-François.

"And there is the equally famous Olaudah Equiano, the African of whom I spoke to you, aunt," said Jean Baptiste. "In England he was taken seriously by the abolitionists. Who appear to be getting their way. The world is changing."

"Not in Trinidad," I said to him. "And I hope that you are not in support of freeing the slaves. You will be a laughing stock. You will be ostracised. And Lieselotte too."

"And the English will be even more convinced that the free coloureds must be controlled," maman said impatiently. "But Jean-Baptiste, a white wife for a person like yourself, from our family, would be extremely impolitic. It will fly in the face of everything that your father and his friends and all the free coloured people there are trying to achieve."

"On the contrary, it will demonstrate that we are free, independent to do as we please," said Jean-Baptiste. "And you, aunt, you have married a European person, so has Jeannette-Rose. Both your sisters, married Europeans. Why can't I?"

"It is not the same thing at all. For women like us, it is different." I could see that mother was warming to the topic. "A drop or two of African blood in the veins of a thousand year-old, noble family does not change or reduce their status in any way in Europe."

I decided to speak up and asked, "Jean-Baptiste, why would you want to marry a simple peasant girl, a German of all things, and from a society, a background so unlike your own? Do you imagine that such a relationship could endure? After the first blush of emotion, and passion, what would be left? Boredom, that will turn into resentment? Think well, cousin. The family may not take to her. You will need them. And you will have to return to Trinidad, perhaps sooner than you think."

"Yes," maman continued, "Your mother, who is now, with the support of your cousin Susanne and half-brother Frédéric Maxwell, running the estates, she cannot afford to keep you here, living in the style that you have enjoyed. The cost in these changing times is much greater than you imagine. The slave trade has been abolished. Deaths on the estates are rising. Deaths that keep you posing as a gentleman of leisure."

Jean-Baptiste was listening but appeared indifferent to our entreaties. Even as he paid attention to our pleas for reason, to me he seemed more interested in the way we expressed ourselves, expressed our feelings. Our choice of words. Our emotions. It crossed my mind that he was testing us, examining us, in some sort of way.

"It is now time for you to go home, Jean-Baptiste, to put your shoulder to the wheel, for the family's sake, for the sake of our people. Before it is too late."

"Maybe, aunt" he answered, frowning. "But first I shall go to Montpellier. There is still much I have to learn, new techniques, the classification of mental disorders. I shall study with Professor Philippe Pinel at Montpellier."

"Why do you want to study with this professor?"

"Because, aunt, I have specialised in what is presently called psychiatry."

"And what is that, pray tell?" asked mother.

"It is a new medical specialty that is devoted to the diagnosis, prevention, and treatment of mental disorders."

24. Jeannette-rose Philip
Love is like a red red rose newly sprung...

"Madness? You know that you must spit on yourself if you see a mad man."

"I shall remember that in the future, aunt, yes, thank you, I will."

"Yes! That's for the mad man to think that you are mad too."

Jean-Baptiste laughed at this, and although I thought the conversation had ended unpleasantly, I could see that he was not in any way offended. But I was. "What a shallow man," I said under my breath. He must have heard me, I suppose, from the way he looked at me as we rose to leave the pavilion.

The morning after that day's contretemps dawned apparently without hard feelings. From the nursery's window I saw Paul-François, Amédé and Jean-Baptiste joking with their coachman. There was much excited laughter there, the loudest was from Jean-Baptiste. He was preparing to return to Aachen and Amédé was bound for Montpellier. They were to meet there later in the year. Mother and I came down to say goodbye. I felt sad to see them leave. I knew, somehow, that I would not see him, ever again.

25. Joyeux Vagabond

*"Sorrow is Knowledge: they who know the most
Must mourn the deepest o'er the fatal truth,
The Tree of Knowledge is not that of Life."*

George Gordon Lord Byron

Theatrum Anatomicum, Leiden

MONTPELLIER 1817: I MET AMÉDÉ PICHOT IN LEIDEN IN 1816. He had received his medical training at the famous school of medicine at Montpellier and like myself had recently graduated. The anatomical lecture theatre at Leiden was a disappointment. We had arrived much too late. A hundred years too late, said Amédé. He was sitting next to me as we looked on at what was obviously a show that pretended to be an examination of the liver and spleen of a cadaver by a person who was not a surgeon. Leiden was recovering from a catastrophe. The year before a boat loaded with gunpowder had exploded in a canal that ran through the middle of the old city. The blast killed hundreds of people, including several

25. JOYEUX VAGABOND

medical practitioners. It left thousands injured and maimed, while destroying a great many buildings, among them the medical school.

We passed what remained of the day at the city's famous university recounting our medical school experiences. Amedé thought my use of the French language highly amusing. I was happy for the company. We toured the university's botanic gardens, which were founded in 1587, and visited the museum of primitive antiquities, a fantastic collection of oddities from the world over. I was immediately attracted to a case that displayed African female beauty with bronzes and masks from the kingdom of Benin. They appeared primordial yet exquisitely beautiful, and disturbing in an indefinable way. Then, there was a hall in which an eclectic collection of armor and trophy weapons was displayed, relics of wars and Viking raids that had been left behind on battlefields after the foe had fled. This was where Amédé and I discovered that we shared a common interest in Romantic literature which tended to glorify Europe's heroic achievements. Its valorous past, its valiant individuals, heroes and artists, whose example, we agreed, could raise the present quality of society.

We had both heard of Goethe, the German poet and playwright, but had not yet read his work. Amédé had heard of Robert Burns but knew only the poem, *A Red, Red Rose*. He had not yet read Byron. I had with me two of Byron's more recent publications, and was pleased to introduce him to the bard's other works. It was reassuring to meet someone with whom I could share my faible for Romantic poetry, which was occupying the imagination of young people in the western world, and my scientific interest—psychiatry.

Already seeing ourselves as colleagues, we concurred that the great object of life was *sensation*—feelings. By the following day we were like old friends. Amédé was an admirer of William Blake, but it was François-René de Chateaubriand who had fired his imagination. He was at the time reading *René,* which was a part of Chateaubriand's *Génie du christianisme,* along with another novella, *Atala.* He was planning a visit to the château de Combourg in

Brittany, Chateaubriand's family residence, as this was, from his point of view, the birthplace of Romanticism in France. But not before meeting up with Anna Hurault de Sorbée, a young lady, much younger than he, to whom he had pledged his eternal devotion, whose father, Colonel Louis-Marie Hurault de Sorbée, a hero of the Peninsular wars, was encamped with his regiment just outside of Leiden.

The family, as Amédé remembered, was at the village of De Vink and he could not imagine leaving Holland without seeing her again. It was a daring adventure, as the family would be closely guarded.

In the early morning light, on rented sorrel geldings, we approached De Vink. At this hour the Dutch countryside had about it a mind-numbing neutrality, which was as bland and as cold as blancmange. You could taste the boredom. Huddled around a very large windmill, the little village held two houses that a family of the status of the Hurault de Sorbée could reside in. Of the sentries, and we had seen them earlier relieving themselves at the rear of one of the houses, there were two.

With not many trees about, we tethered our mounts a short distance away from the village, in a deep ditch behind a long hedgerow. From there we could secretly observe without being seen by either the village people or the sentries. From behind the thorny hedge, we watched as a curl of smoke emerged from the chimney of the larger of the two houses. The sentries were at the gate. For a long while nothing happened. No one appeared, anywhere. By mid-morning, as I was nodding off. Amédé grabbed me by the arm. "Look, here they come!" Peeping through the hedge I could see a group of children, five or six little ones all dressed in yellow smocks, white stockings and little red clogs. A taller girl, dressed in white, was obviously in charge. She was herding them along like geese. Amédé was about to emerge when a woman appeared at the door of the house. She was calling, beckoning and saying something. Then the children, all together at once, ran back into the house, leaving the tall girl standing at the gate.

25. JOYEUX VAGABOND

"There she is," he gasped, "I must go to her."

"No, wait. The sentry, the fat one, is coming round the side of the house, wait," I warned, holding on to his coattail. Just then I was grabbed from behind by the neck. A strong grip that wrenched me to my feet and shook me like a rag, while a voice growled something unintelligible in my ear. I thought that my head would fall off. Amédé, who had started off, turned about, I could see, for a brief moment in the shaking, his startled face, just as a man dressed in black grabbed him by the arm. Amédé, with a yelp, tried to wrench his arm away, this caused them both to slip and then slide backwards into the ditch. I felt as if my neck would snap, already I was on my toes. To my amazement I saw a flash of steel, as Amédé, taking a scalpel from his waist, plunged it into the man's thigh and breaking free, began punching the red face, as the fellow falling over, took Amédé with him to land on his chest! They struggled. Suddenly I was flung aside as the thug who had grabbed me was in the ditch delivering several blows to Amédé's head. Well, I jumped on him and we all rolled in the mud trying to gouge out each others eyes even as the horses stomped, reared, snorted and neighing shrilly, bolted away.

The ruckus brought the sentries running and after much shouting, blows and kicks, which were delivered indiscriminately, we were released and the two held at bayonet point. In the meanwhile a crowd had gathered. It would appear that these two were well known by the villagers as chicken thieves. Amédé, and I hadn't thought him capable of such falsehood, quietly explained, in almost sotto voce, that we had caught them in the act of something or the other. Then the children were there. I must tell you they really looked like a flock of little ducklings in their yellow smocks. The tall girl, Anna, was smiling proudly and as for Amédé, he seemed to have grown taller. We were given breakfast. Our horses were captured and the villains were marched off complaining all the while that *they* had caught *us* in the act spying on the family.

No one paid them any attention. Madame Hurault de Sorbée was, however, suspicious. What were we doing lurking about the countryside at that hour of the day? Amédé at once confessed. He loved Anna. He had seen her at Leiden. She had not taken notice of him. Really. Only sensed his existence and had smiled. Later that morning in a haberdashery he had whispered an endearment. What endearment? Well, after much blushing:

> *"And fare thee well, my only love!*
> *And fare thee well awhile!*
> *And I will come again, my love,*
> *Though it were ten thousand mile."*

Madame Hurault de Sorbée was touched. I could see her heart melt. I caught her eye, we smiled conspiratorially. Amédé and Anna held hands and we all sat quietly for a long moment. Love needs to linger silently on the edge of eternity. It is its nature.

Suddenly there was a commotion in the garden. Colonel Hurault de Sorbée had arrived! Tall and rapier thin, his head almost touching the low ceiling, his very presence wordlessly demanded an explanation. It was all revealed. He was not impressed. I could hear him saying in his mind as he glared at us, "bloody scalawags."

He was more interested in me, actually. Where did I come from? Why was I here, in Holland? He had seen Negroes, he said, there were a few in his regiment, Martiniquans, he thought. Rough bunch. We were doctors, we explained, furthering our studies. Seeing the sights before setting ourselves up to practice medicine. We were heroes, he was assured by Madame Hurault de Sorbée and the servants. We had captured the praedial larcenists. He was still not impressed. Amédé was not allowed a moment alone with the lovely Anna, but their eyes promised each other a lifetime. We were put up for the night and as morning broke we were on the road to Aachen.

Upon departing Holland we entered the zone of occupation in north-east France, close to the German Confederation, and becoming lost in a rainstorm somewhere in the vicinity of Aachen we met a

25. JOYEUX VAGABOND

party of German officers, elements of the Prussian force that had served under von Blücher at the battle of Waterloo.

The weather was bad and night had come on suddenly. We were about to seek shelter in what appeared to be a farmhouse when we heard the sound of horses, a great many horses, approaching. Fully aware that there were marauding bands still at large in the countryside even after the restoration of the monarchy, we urged our mounts off the road into a copse of trees in the hope of avoiding the riders. To our utter consternation, we soon became aware that this was where the main body of horsemen was heading, even as others, no doubt their leaders, were making for the farmhouse. In moments we were surrounded by Germans.

In attempting to explain that we were on our way to Aachen and thence for France to visit relatives, we were misunderstood and accused of being spies. The arresting officer immediately gave orders that we be detained in a nearby barn. I thought their behaviour outrageous. I felt insulted. Amédé, of course, was as meek as a snail. It was a miserable night, as we had to share lodgings with several cows in a stall that was at least warm.

The following morning we were brought before the German officers. Questioned, I explained again, speaking in German, that we were medical doctors who, having attended lectures at Leiden, wanted to visit Aachen cathedral, and then would be on our way to a relative at Château de Sandrans, near to Châtillon-les-Dombes.

To our dismay we were not believed by the officers who had taken turns in the interrogation. We were on the point of being placed in irons and put into a waiting cart when I demanded that we be proved medical practitioners. Surprised by this suggestion, it was reluctantly agreed that we should meet a member of their party who was also a doctor and had served with them at Waterloo.

After waiting for some time, a young man came into the room. He was from Silesia. We had a talk, in German. I told him under whom I had studied at Edinburgh and what I thought of the lecture theatre at Leiden. We both agreed it was a farce, a grotesque leftover from medieval times that should be done away with. It did not take long for our credentials to be established. The young doctor, whose name was Siegert, along with the officers, was preparing to depart for South America where they were to join the army of Don Simón Bolívar in an ongoing war for the liberation of the world. Dr. Siegert had been appointed to act as the secretary to the leader of the party.

I was pleased to give my father's name to the young German doctor, Venezuela being so close to Trinidad, in the event that he would be in need of visiting there, as one never knows which way the wind blows in the foggy battlefields of war. Released from detention, we were directed to the quickest route that would take us to the city of Aachen.

If castle Combourg, Chateaubriand's home, was for Amédé the cradle of the Romantics, Aachen meant the same to me. I suppose that was so as a result of having met Wilhelm von Fürstenberg and having been introduced to the culture that underlined the Germanic character, which draws copiously from an imagined, even mythic origin. From Wilhelm I heard of the Valkyries and the *Nibelungenlied*, and of the historic events and individuals of the 5th and 6th centuries. That Snorri Sturluson the Lawspeaker gave the world the *Prose Edda*. And that Charlemagne was made in the mould of the legendary kings.

On those boyhood treks that had taken us across the Scottish countryside from Edinburgh past Dalkeith and Gorebridge into that beautiful Border country, Fürstenberg's enthusiasm, his depth of feeling for his homeland's heroic past, seemed to me to be a fitting dialogue for such a magnificent countryside. For if there were witches in the wind, the wind also carried the battle cries of the clans-men, fighting, dying, their souls rising to a forgotten Gaelic Valhalla. I tried to evoke in my journal their ghostly voices echoing in those ruined castles that stood on holy hills, imagining hearing the wind as it whistled through their gaping Gothic windows,

25. Joyeux Vagabond

and the play of light and dark in the shifting shadows of their abandoned courtyards. It takes one away into a vast and terrible past that contains just the flavour of memories captured in their myths and folksongs.

All this I had absorbed. It struck a chord that resonated in my imagination. The study of imaginative thought had become for me a preoccupation ever since the writing of my doctoral thesis. The very idea that memory, imagination, and prediction could be distinct cognitive functions, I was finding terribly exciting. The idea that memory and imagination were intimately linked allowed me to explore a past that I had never imagined. That this coincided with the popular Romantic poetry that was presently sweeping Europe off its feet was, to me, not coincidental at all.

Jeannette-Rose was right when she said that my taste for the Romantic writers was not born as a reaction to the murderous tumult of the streets of Paris during the revolutionary terror or in the shadow of the horrifying guillotine, as Amédé's was. My own came about as a result of reading the work of the British Romantics in a castle in Scotland. The idea that nothing is in the mind without being first in the senses, except for the mind itself, was the thought that had sparked my interest in the mental sensations of moods, frames of mind, dispositions and my own emotional state. Psychiatry was widely regarded as a branch of philosophy. I was convinced otherwise. It is a science of the mind in its own right. To me, this idea, expressed in art, music and drama—and particularly in poetry, the molten larva of the imagination—is closely linked to my scientific inquiry in the human mind. It has to do with the instinctive, the emotional and the intuitive, because, undoubtedly, the great object of life is *sensation*.

EVEN AS WE RODE OUR WEARY MOUNTS THROUGH AACHEN'S ancient gateway, the crowds of busy people bustling, the noise of wheeled traffic on the cobbled streets, the iron smell of foundries, the rank of tanneries, the calls and shouts of journeymen, the cries of fishmongers and of baker's boys which were carried on a cool air, to me all came from a distant past. I could feel time unravel, curling back to previous epochs. I did not need to close my eyes to imagine the mounted, mail-clad knights, their pennants fluttering in the breeze, the sunlight glittering on their armour, winding their way through the narrow streets. A glance upwards, caught in the woodwork of the timber-framed houses that lined the street, I imagined the girls and women leaning out of windows, they were throwing blossoms on the departing armies who were riding out to conquer time, to capture lost opportunities and to return with the shackled trophies of mastered lands.

The vast cathedral was our goal, all the while I endeavoured to maintain the mood that upheld this vast landscape of the mind in which I now lived and moved. My thesis had explored hysteria, which is ungovernable emotional excess, theoretically. I wanted to experience this in reality in the context of my literary, cultural and historic interests. In truth, it was an all-absorbing preoccupation.

It was fortuitous that I came upon her at the cathedral. She was washing clothes in a swift-running canal and was as I had hoped she would be. Pale-skinned, blue-eyed, thick blond plaits wound round a shapely head. Tall, full-bosomed, a Germanic Valkyrie. A chieftain's daughter, a child of nature. And I am that wandering hero who falls into a melancholic reverie to become a victim of *amour courtois,* as the knight-errants and troubadours had done five hundred years ago.

I took her hand as she stepped from the stream. "What is your name?" I asked, after murmuring my own. "Lieselotte Petzold," she answered with a wide smile. It did not matter that her dirty linen lay in a rumpled heap. I hardly noticed that she was older than I. We spoke a while of this and that, her dialect, quite strange to me, was very different from the high German that I had learned, first from Fürstenberg and later as I undertook my studies. I could see that she was curious. She had never seen a man like me except as when portrayed as one of the Magi in the Yuletide pantomimes. Saint

25. JOYEUX VAGABOND

Balthazar, I was to her, the black King of Abyssinia who gave the gift of myrrh to the Christ child. Some silver coins were all it took and she became our guide, first in the great cathedral itself and its grounds and later she was happy to show Amédé and me the town, in truth its taverns where the ordinary folk enjoyed themselves.

As the evening grew late Amédé discreetly withdrew from our company. I would see her naked beauty, she knew this and was as curious about me as I was of her. Returning to the cathedral's grounds I found that we were in an old outbuilding where processional paraphernalia and ceremonial objects were kept. I called her Ianthe, as in the dedication to *Childe Harold's Pilgrimage* by Byron. It was his term of endearment for Lady Charlotte Harley.

I undressed her in the shifting gloom and released her golden locks to let them fall about her magnificent white breasts. She was magnificent. Even our breaths echoed, as did our sighing, groans and small screams as our bodies found each other. All was captured in the static stares of the retired medieval statuary that watched over our lovemaking, which was not hurried, with languid knowing eyes. Of course I wanted to make her mine, discovering the falsity in the Giaour's claim that "the cold in clime are cold in blood." The mood must be made flesh, and mine was like the lava flood that boils in Ætna's breast of flame... This pilgrimage must never end. I pledged my troth. Amédé was much amused to hear this. He had returned in the early morning and saw us emerge from beneath the grimacing gargoyles and waved and pointed to her old father who was sweeping the gateway. I approached him and asked permission to see his daughter again, he appeared to understand and was hospitable. We joined them for their morning meal. It was a week in which I experienced much, both in the physical sense and in the deeper, more profound emotional realms, but there was still a lot more to do and to learn.

Upon departing Aachen we made our way to Château de Sandrans, only to discover that Jeannette-Rose and aunt Susannah were presently somewhere in Burgundy where they had acquired a château and a vineyard. I am not at all like Byron's Harold, the Childe, who is cloyed and sickened with the pleasures of the world and reckless of life. He must wander around Europe in pursuit of sensations to distract his mind. No, I am a scientist. The experiment was on myself.

It was amusing to see the reaction of my relatives when I said that I would marry Lieselotte Petzold. Their prejudices, disguised as admonitions, their cautions, which were even a sort of scolding, revealed a great deal of their temperaments, their fears and their ambitions. It was, however, instructive to listen to them discuss the situation in Trinidad and the present politics of France. I was gratified to learn that both Guillaume and Paul-François are not of the same mettle as those hidebound aristocrats who, upon returning to France, would turn back the clock to a time before Cardinal Richelieu was born.

My attraction to my cousin Jeannette-Rose had edvolved. I must say that I like her mother, my aunt Susannah, better. Her lively originality, such a spontaneous relationship to life, to change, so optimistic and lovely still in her middle age. I was not sorry to leave them, it was becoming boring and repetitious, although I appreciated their concern for me.

Amédé and I parted on the Dijon road, he for Montpellier and I to return to Aachen to see Lieselotte Petzold once more. It was important for me to see if I felt the same as when we met. She was where I saw her first. Washing clothes in the canal that empties into the river Pau. All was simpler now. We were as old friends, well met, all passion spent, curiosity quite satiated. I had some small treasures for her, a silken scarf, a marcasite brooch, a little gold pin with small gemstones and handkerchiefs of fine linen. I had to make this journey. To return to where I had trembled in the strong and lovely arms of this Brunhilde. But as a journalist wrote when satirising Byron, "Sated abroad, all seen, yet naught admired; The restless soul is driven to ramble home." But first to Montpellier medical school where I would meet up again with Amédé.

25. JOYEUX VAGABOND

I HAVE LIVED ABROAD FOR MORE THAN TEN YEARS. I came to the United Kingdom as a boy of eleven in 1808 and that being the case, my formative years have been shaped by the circumstances of my schooling in London and by my education in Scotland, along with the experiences that I have had with the people with whom I have kept company, and, of course, by my travels on the continent. Oddly, of Trinidad I remembered only isolated incidences that stand out like islands of the place where I was born.

However, this changed somewhat when meeting my aunt Susannah, first in Paris and then again in their new home in Burgundy, my eyes were opened to the realities of my origins, the people from whom I came. In meeting her I saw the true beauty of my race. The elegance with which she carried herself, how she shone. Her grand style, flaunting what she said were the family's jewels, amongst these a magnificent pearl collier. I could see from whence her daughter's beauty springs. I could understand now, having lived at Montpellier, where her mode of dress originated, their style of life. My grandfather was of that place. This was from whence he came, the south of France.

Aunt Susannah spoke to me about our family, of her brother Jean-Pierre, who had been the first to return to the land of our forefathers. He journeyed to France in 1789 where he became the voice of the free mulattoes amidst the storms of the Revolution. She told how he travelled into the Haute-Provence to carry a bequest to our relatives and sojourned there for several years. She told me many things about our family; of the islands that we owned in the Antilles, the several plantations of cotton and sugarcane, of the black slaves, our chattel, who labour there, and the investments that were made in England by her sister Judith, with whom she was very close; and of her eldest sister Marie-Magdeleine who lived in a state of permanent premonition. I wish I had known her, those experiences would have been of enormous value to me in my present work.

Aunt Susannah spoke about her father, my grandfather, who sailed down the Spanish Main, from Cuba to Colombia, with the

French Corsairs. Papa Honoré amassed a fortune in treasure and died a dreadful death. Of her other brothers, the handsome Nicolas-Régis, the trials of my own father and uncle Josèphe-Michel in their attempt to set themselves up as planters in the wilds of Trinidad in the 1780s. She spoke emotionally of Honoré, her eldest brother, who was named for his papa, and Joachim, the fearless one, both of whom gave their lives in the cause of liberty. I felt proud to come from such a line of brave men and remarkable women.

It was with passion that she told of the betrayal of the people of Grenada by the English, and more especially, of us, the free coloured people. This led, she said, to the uprising and to the ruination of fair Grenada and to our family relocating to Trinidad. That we faced the same chicanery in Trinidad, she said, was the most serious danger. There were men there, in Trinidad, men like John Hobson and Désir Fabien, who were rich planters, who would oppose the English. Others from all over Trinidad had put their names to a petition and addressed it to the King in England.

In speaking of her mother Jeannette, the proud warrior woman of the Fon nation, I admired how my aunt's eyes glittered with pride as she described that indomitable figure. Her will to be as good and as great as any European man or woman. Her striving to leave behind the terrifying experience of slavery and its ignoble past, to make a future that to this day transmits ambition, success and wealth.

I am not especially concerned with what they, Jeannette-Rose and her husband Paul-François, my aunt Susannah and her husband think of me or my ideas, or of what forms, shapes or inhabits my imagination. They know nothing of my personal life. In much the same way I know nothing of theirs. They have no idea how, as a lad, as a wee boy, alone at school in Scotland, I had to create a world in which I could move and thrive, without anyone familiar, with no bosom to weep upon, nor arms to hold and comfort me when I was overwhelmed by the daemons of the night. In those years of unfathomable loneliness, when I felt like I was slipping, losing the contours of my remembered self, believing that I had

25. Joyeux Vagabond

lost something in the transplanting of my previous world into the reality of this new life, I think I must have made up a personality to watch over the vulnerable me, even as I wondered, is this the real meaning of getting an education? I undertook to feed my brain, to nourish my mind and to build a fire in my awareness that could steer fearlessly into the enormity of humanity's potential. My friend Amédé said that I was a soul on fire when I spoke, I suppose with some excitement, to him of these experiences and ideas. I know that there is more to the human race than the limited peripheries that are manufactured to constrain us. These are all man-made and self-inflicted.

The past is deep. It contains in its inscrutable vastness more than merely an echo of human frailty and greatness, it holds the seeds of the future. The present as well as the recent past here in Europe demonstrate an end of things. A branch, long withered, has fallen because of its dead weight. We, who are ridiculed as Romantics, as being unrealistic, of living with our heads in the clouds, are in search of a new cutting from that old tree from which may spring a future full of wonder. We do not sit upon the ground and tell sad stories of the death of kings merely to relish in an exotic nostalgia that emphasises emotions and notions of individualism for their own sake. We do not glorify the past because we seek to escape the present. It is the present generation that must be glorified, for it is the present that we occupy as the thinkers of today.

In my journal entry I wrote that I see myself first as an alienist-cum-physician in the company of the avant-garde: with scientists like Ephraim Chambers who prepared the famous *Cyclopædia; or, An Universal Dictionary of Arts and Sciences*. Dr. Edward Jenner, with his work on what he calls vaccines that could eradicate smallpox. Dr. Franz Mesmer who theorises that a natural energy transference occurs between all animated and inanimate objects, while exploring the imagination of his patients by producing in them trance-like states. André-Marie Ampère, the mathematician and physicist, and his work on electromagnetism. These are the sciences of the future, they shall define the modern.

Montpellier medical school was all and much more than I expected. We worked, Amédé and I, to advance our medical knowledge, as we had done when we first embarked on our studies, but much harder. There was so much more to learn, so much to do, so very much more to participate in, that I did not have time to think about anything but medicine, its practice, its goals.

Amédé's interest in the Romantics has only deepened even as he has shifted his focus away from the world of Chateaubriand to the writings of Lord Byron. He has commenced the translation into French of what he hopes would be, over time, Byron's complete works, with a view to having them published as soon as possible.

A letter arrived from Aachen. She, Lieselotte, had died. A cloud of darkness descended upon me, which only work made bearable.

Another letter arrived, from aunt Susannah. I couldn't bring myself to open it. I was, I suppose, hoping that it would become lost amongst the books and papers that overflowed my desk to the floor. It, however, seemed to reappear as if by magic whenever I least expected. I opened it eventually and my eyes fell upon the lines, "Your father is very ill, Jean-Baptiste, your mother is in charge of Concorde now. The new governor's interference with the former grants of land by the crown of Spain during 1783 has her very worried. Guillaume may have to return to Trinidad to help her if you do not. Would you consider returning to Trinidad?"

With Lieselotte gone, that was the question which was to alter the course of my life.

26. East West, Home Best?

*"How much would novels gain by the exchange!
How differently the world would men behold!"*

George Gordon Lord Byron

TRINIDAD 1818: THE SPAN OF OVER TEN WEEKS spent traversing the vast expanse of the sea was endowed with a certain degree of excitement, as we journeyed on the swift *Amphitryon*. This unexpected novelty elicited a sensation within me that I could scarcely have imagined, bringing to my mind the rousing verses of *The Corsair*:

*"O'er the glad waters of the dark blue sea,
Our thoughts as boundless, and our souls as free."*

Yet, as we departed from Barbados, my spirits took a turn for the worse. A vague and disquieting apprehension crept over me, persisting through the night. Roused from slumber before dawn, I ascended to the deck, greeted by the sight of a sky still adorned with gleaming stars, the crisp air and the unwavering course of the *Amphitryon*. I stood by the ship's railing, entranced by the eerie apparition of a crescent moon resembling a phantom ship, sailing through a mass of glistening clouds. And yet, amidst this moment of awe-inspiring beauty, I was struck with a sudden realisation that I would arrive at my destination unannounced, with no one there to greet me.

As the ship's pilot made mention of Tobago appearing on the larboard beam, a pale grey figure gradually emerged on the horizon, enveloped by a mass of pinkish clouds. In unison with the rise of hundreds of flying fish from the waves and their subsequent submersion, I sensed a shift in the cool wind. The cadence of the

I FOUND MYSELF BETWEEN A CROWD OF UNSHOD WOMEN, ALL AS
BLACK AS NIGHT, AND DRESSED IN DIRTY, SMELLY RAGS.

26. East West, Home Best?

Amphitryon in relation to the ocean had transformed, and the sailors were clambering aloft, their voices bellowing out orders. "Strong head winds," someone noted. "They may delay our arrival at the Bocas del Dragon," another interjected.

We were detained for almost the entire day, the coast of Trinidad at times so close that I could see the forest rising, towering up from bare, black, wave-washed rocks towards where a rolling mist concealed the mountaintops.

We made several attempts to enter this fantastically named passage, the Bocas, which appeared hazardous because of the several small forested islands that rose above what looked to me like a conflict of rushing tides and contrary winds. Seen on the map, these islets appeared as unsafe stepping stones between Trinidad and the Spanish Main.

I was below decks when we finally entered the Gulf of Paria and did not need to be told that it was a placid sea. There was a stillness. A sense of stop that was distinct. Coming up, I found the air warm and moist. I could smell a difference in the atmosphere. Something tepid, dank and sluggish. Above, the sails were being taken in. We were at rest as twilight fell.

With the morning's breeze we weighed anchor and stood down gently before its refreshing breath. I was fascinated by the changes in the light, as the sun, slow in making an appearance, turned the cloudy sky from gentle tones and milky pastel shades to red, even as masses of water fowl, some more magenta than the sky itself, overtook the dawn.

"That is Chaguaramus Bay," the ship's quartermaster was saying to a passenger while lighting his pipe. "This is where a Spanish admiral burnt and scuttled his squadron. You might see them. The water is shallow here, quite clear and almost fresh."

I could see many boats about and all sorts of crafts on the glass-like surface of this sea. Some, in the distance, because of the haze on the horizon, looked like they were in the sky. As we skirted the shore, I gazed at the mountains. Their soft shades, like vaporous sapphire rising, were quite picturesque, as were the deep valleys, so verdant and welcoming. In one of those lovely glens, standing out far above the forest cover, was an exceptionally tall tree. It was catching, in its uppermost crown, the morning's first slant of sunlight. "That there is the estate of James Martin," said the ship's quartermaster, pointing. "It was granted to an Englishman by a king of Spain, they call it here Diego Martin."

The range of mountains rolling westward now appeared a gentle backdrop to a day that seemed reluctant to begin. Smoke rose to twirl here and there in the quiet air behind a thickly forested shore. Passing sails, as the sun came out, appeared bright white, against the blue of the sky and the brilliant green of the sea. Already the heat was becoming unbearable. Some people, passengers, were dressed as if they were attending a church fair. The sailors and some men wore shirts and blouses with nankeen trousers and sported wide-brimmed straw hats. As we dropped anchor some distance from the quay I heard someone say: "Dress down, this is the tropic zone, if you wear woollens you shall broil." Too late for that, I thought, as I took the accommodation ladder, which was mounted parallel to the hull. I was wearing a cropped riding coat, woollen, a linen shirt with a high collar wrapped in a cravat and tied as fashionably as I could manage, with snug leather breeches tucked into my newly purchased boots. Stepping onto the waiting boat, I realised that I was perspiring profusely.

With the ship's motion still with me I was walking on dry land. We were at a fort, small and round, five rusting culverins pointing towards the sea. It was some distance from the shore, connected to the mainland by a crumbling mole. There was a tin-roofed customs house, the worse for wear. A quantity of people, mostly blacks and others of various shades, the women richly attired, milled about in fanciful costumes, speaking very loudly in French Patois. An auction of slaves, it would appear, had recently ended. There were soldiers as well, in red tunics, smart officers, and what appeared

26. EAST WEST, HOME BEST?

to be gentlemen. Here and there were my fellow passengers. Boxes, barrels and heady odours overflowed this small hot space. Where to go? A man in uniform with an air of authority stopped me and barred my way, "Now where do you think you're going, Sambo?" Obviously an Irishman. "Get in line, that line, over there, that's for the likes of you." I was about to tell him something, I can't remember what, when he bellowed "Go on, what are you staring at? Move!"

"I beg your pardon?"

"Beg my pardon? Beg my pardon! Who do you think you are? The bloody Prince Regent? Get in line, over there! You black monkey, move!"

He was so adamant that, quite shocked, I immediately complied. Looking around I saw that people were laughing. Amongst those were some with whom I had recently shared the trials of the voyage, not a few to whom I had been of assistance. I felt ashamed, insulted and I experienced a vexation rising. I looked about me, I felt that I could seize a weapon and strike this man. He had already walked away and was speaking to another man, glancing over his shoulder; obviously they were talking about me. They were laughing. A black woman was telling me something that I could not make out. She was guiding me away. Frustrated, and experiencing a strange feeling of confusion, I found myself between a crowd of unshod women, all as black as night and dressed in dirty, smelly rags. Burly men were shouting, all rolling eyes in hideous black faces. I took them to be sailors. My God, I thought, trying to control my breathing, this place is hell. There were people arriving, gangs of men, all carrying something on their heads. Shouts and bursts of laughter, some directed at me I could tell, although I could not understand in what language they spoke. Already quite anxious, I was almost overtaken by an attack of panic as I watched those with whom I had travelled being attended to by the port's officials. I was being left behind. Suddenly, it came back to me: this was what Jeannette-Rose had spoken to me about! This was how people of colour were treated in Trinidad.

Where were my things, my boxes, books and instrument case? How would I get them off the ship that I could see, out there in the shimmering heat? I wished I were still aboard. I felt to flee this place, sweat drenching my clothes inside and out. It was all I could do to restrain myself. It seemed to take hours to get to where the officials sat at a table overflowing with ledgers and papers. I gave my name and profession and was told to wait. I waited. The delay was having mostly to do, I realised, with my saying that I was a medical practitioner returning home. This appeared to be unbelievable. I understood. It was my colour, not to mention my clothes and manner. People, all black, crowded round. I suppose that advice was being volunteered, but I could not understand a word. The noise, the confusion, the heat. I must not faint, I thought, as I felt a dizziness rising.

"A black Scotsman I have here, Sir, says he's a doctor, Sir." A person who looked like a gypsy with missing maxillary lateral incisors and a sickening breath was shouting over my shoulder. "Says he's a doctor, Sir."

"What's this?"

I could see at once that here was an Englishman. Just seeing a recognisable figure was a huge relief.

"A doctor he says he is, a black doctor, Sir, fresh off the *Amphitryon*, there she is at anchor, Sir."

"Doctor?"

"Jean-Baptiste Philip, Sir, doctor of medicine, late of the university of Edinburgh, at your service."

"Ah! Really?"

"Yes, actually. I say, can you help me please? I have been here for hours."

"My word. Yes, come. Let him pass."

Paul Reinagle was the first person I met upon arriving in Trinidad. He was about my age or perhaps a bit older, elegant in the way that

26. EAST WEST, HOME BEST?

well-bred Englishmen sometimes are, and dressed, obviously, in the appropriate manner for the tropical climate: nankeen trousers, white, a light-weight dark coat over a loose cotton blouse and the wide-brimmed straw hat that appeared to be the most typical headgear for men. I fell in naturally with his use of language, the English of the educated, which carried those invisible diacritical marks, the expressions of caste. He was unabashedly curious.

"You studied medicine at Edinburgh. By Jove, how did you manage?"

"Very well, thank you."

"And you are a Philip?"

"Yes."

"Jean-Baptiste-Louis Philip of Concorde plantation, is he a relative?"

"Yes, he is my father."

"And you studied medicine at Edinburgh. My word. You must have lived abroad for several years. I must say, you sound and act almost like a, ah, like a. . ."

"A Scotsman?" I looked him over carefully, adding laconically, "to the manner born."

"Exactly! I say, by Jove, yes! You must meet my brother-in-law Philip Souper, he knows your people, all your people, down there in the Naparimas." Reinagle was helpful, amused and certainly very interested in me. "I must say, I have never met anyone like you."

Well, I was not surprised. He said this several times over as we walked away from the quayside and into the town, while assuring me that my things would be safe and I would see my parents on the morrow, as there was a steam-driven vessel that made a regular journey to the south of the island.

I looked about as we made our way through the riff-raff. Swarms of black vultures that looked ludicrously like barristers in wig and gown were hopping about. The encounter with the rude Irish official was still a pounding reality in my head. I thought to speak of it to Reinagle, but didn't. I felt too ashamed.

My first impression of the town was that it was a ramshackle affair. There were buildings, once under construction, that had long been abandoned even as others were being built. The many vacant lots around were overgrown with weeds and large trees. I could see evidence of where a fire had destroyed what may have been stores or dwellings. One could almost taste the stench of cesspits and offal energised by the heat. The sound of iron-wheeled traffic, the clatter of galloping hooves, the crack of whips became louder as free-running animals, push carts and very noisy people, many hideous, some hurrying, others standing about, all talkative, laughing hilariously at God alone knows what, crowded a tree-lined park. The curiosity of a few was obvious as Reinagle and I came along.

I was given a room on the ground floor of a wooden, two-storied boarding house that overlooked the park. There was a cot and a small table. It opened onto a pig sty!

"I say, Reinagle, I can pay for something better. Surely there must be another room in the house." I felt at my wits' end. It was all I could do not to scream at the stupid woman with whom he had been speaking.

Apparently not. It required some insistence on his part that I was given even this accommodation. Fighting off an encroaching feeling of dismay, indeed regret, I had a meal in the room of something dark brown which was hot and tasty, along with what I was told by the surly black woman who brought it was "provision." I later discovered that I had eaten a lizard. The entire thing, including the room and the iguana supper, had cost two dollars and tuppence!

Night came on quickly. I was afraid to go outside into the street. The small space became unbearably hot and the redolence of the pig sty overwhelming. I felt myself indescribably alone. It was the first time, I realised, that I was actually by myself since those days of my first arrival in London. I sat on the cot close to the table where

26. EAST WEST, HOME BEST?

there was a smoky lamp and tried to read from a satirical book by Jonathan Swift. This proved to be impossible as I was attacked by swarms of mosquitoes. Cowering beneath the smelly sheet, as sweat poured from every part of my body, I lay exhausted. I was falling off to sleep when a deep and awful rumble commenced, a drumming that was accompanied by a howling chorus that continued into the night. I awoke when the surly woman entered without knocking and without a word pointed at a latrine, close to a small area enclosed by dry branches, through which I could make out a bucket. I understood, it was where my ablutions may be performed in private, except for the pigs. Actually dismayed, I still tried to be amused by the way that I was being treated.

I was so relieved when my boxes were brought into the room! Reinagle had also arranged this. A short time later there he was, in company with another Englishman.

"Dr. Philip, may I present my friend and colleague, David Lockhart. He is the man responsible for those trees being planted out there in our Plaza del Marina. Philip here has returned home from Edinburgh and is no doubt anxious to meet his parents, eh, what you say, Doctor?"

David Lockhart was a short, round, balding man with a broad north country accent. Having been a gardener at the Royal Gardens at Kew he was in charge of the Colonial Gardens here in Trinidad. Reinagle was a surveyor and also an architect. It would appear that he was the man responsible for the construction of a large church, which was taking place close by. I understood that I was a curiosity. They had come to see me in daylight and to observe my behaviour. It would be interesting, I thought, to study theirs, to pay attention to the nature of their curiosity, as this could prove instructive. As we sat together in the common-room of the boarding house and breakfasted, I saw that we were being watched by the other guests, even as one or two nodded a reserved greeting to Lockhart and to Reinagle. I understood. This was apparently an unusual event. This was what my aunt talked about. This objectifying of me. My word!

Setting out towards the waterfront where I was to board a steamer that would take me to Petite Bourg, which I gathered to be another name for the town of San Fernando, and then on to Concorde estate, a violent commotion erupted almost in our midst. A man, black as night and of huge proportion, came running towards us through the crowded street. Another man, a European, of an equal size and weight, was after him. As the black man came abreast, I saw that he carried under his arm what appeared to be the side of a slaughtered animal. The white man, evading attempts to bar his way, lunged at the fleeing one, just managing to bring him down almost at my feet.

All this was, of course, the work of a few seconds. Between the quickly gathering crowd and the stamping and rearing of nervous animals, the two men struggled on the muddy ground. Even as the white man gained the upper hand, the side of meat was snatched up by another black who instantly vanished into the swirling mass.

The black giant was howling and writhing, apparently in great pain. Pushing through the noisy throng I saw that in the rough process of pulling him down in order to secure him, he was all but being throttled by the rupturing of a goitrous swelling in his neck. A diseased carotid artery it was, in which an incipient aneurysm had ruptured. Pushing aside the curious and then restraining the arm of the white man, who by this time was covered in blood and pus, then catching the eye of two burly blacks, I ordered that the man be lifted from the ground and taken to a place where he could be treated. With considerable effort, the black man, who was in a state of insensibility, was taken into a nearby store and placed upon the counter.

Reinagle in the meanwhile, acting on instinct, had retrieved my medicine bag from between my boxes on the cart that was already on its way to the quayside. There was nothing to do but dress the rupture and revive the patient. My concern of course was that a stroke might be an imminent event. Even as the patient regained his senses, I could hear coming from all quarters shouts both in

26. EAST WEST, HOME BEST?

English and French that a white man had killed a black. The store was by this time invested by a noisy crowd, causing its manager to order them out and to bar the doors, bolting them shut. This caused an even greater uproar, as it would appear from what was being shouted in my ear that the patient's wives, he apparently had several, were outside and were madly inciting the blacks to take vengeance. The young man, who turned out to be an American seaman, was beside himself with fear, being certain that he was about to be lynched by the angry mob.

My concern was for the patient who had by then regained awareness and by the look of him was somewhat improved. As I was ordering that he be given something to drink, a crashing sound was heard and looking up I saw that the roof above was being ripped open. Men were climbing onto the rafters and swinging to the ground, all claiming, speaking in a combination of French and Patois, to be related to the sick man and demanding that the young man be handed over to them. There was nothing for it but to stand about the American, which was what Reinagle, Lockhart and I did. Then some officers from the regiment arrived through a back entrance, together with what I took to be members of the local constabulary. It was with some force that the intruders were subdued, and with the protection of the officers and the assistance of the policemen the young American was taken away, ostensibly into the safety of police custody.

The injured man, in my opinion, should have been made to lie quietly to allow his system to settle itself, but because he appeared to be recovering, those who had come in through the roof encouraged him to sit up. Much against my urging, he was dragged into the street by the gang of gabbling relatives and friends. He was plainly unable to speak and obviously quite exhausted. I was appalled, as all the while the excitement was kept up amongst the blacks by women who to me appeared all quite crazed. We were about to move away when I saw him fall. Upon examination, I found that he was dead. At this, the furor amongst the people achieved a fresh pitch of excitement. It would seem that the entire town was in the streets and I was becoming the object of their attention.

"Come away, Philip, you have done more than most would have, come, let's make haste, your things are all aboard and the boat is about to shove off," said Lockhart, taking me by the arm. Reinagle, holding his stick high in warning, was clearing the way through the clamour. We were soon at the waterfront. After a negotiation of some sort with officials on the dock my accommodation was arranged by my new-found friends. A ship's boat was waiting, and in the distance I could see the steamboat. The strangest contraption, it was rigged like a schooner with both main and mizzen, but with huge wooden wheels on either side and a tall chimney in the middle. It made one wonder at its ability to stay afloat. As we came closer, I could see painted on its side the name *Woodford*. Clambering aboard, I was immediately struck in the face by a heat wave. Above me, the tall chimney was sending up a thick curl of black smoke, and from somewhere below, a bell was rung, a rumbling shudder came from everywhere and we were away.

I was placed amongst several people of colour who were seated around the smokestack, some on fixed benches, others on crates amid bundles, barrels and boxes. In between the crates and boxes, I could recognise my things. There were a few pretty young women, quite refined and fashionably dressed, and one or two young men of fine appearance and handsome bearing, and we all sat between some who were plainly labourers and others who appeared wretchedly poor. There was a larger crowd of people, European by their appearance, who were crowded in the stern of the steamer. I soon understood why. The heat generated by the steam engine below the deck came through the flooring to where I was seated. It was quite great, and the vibration was unnerving to say the least. Taking off my hat, I made myself comfortable on a crate that held chickens, and judging by the loud complaining squawks they were as uncomfortable as I. After the recent excitement I felt the need to compose myself.

As the *Woodford* picked up speed, it engendered a refreshing breeze which was calming and evidently welcomed. I was perfectly aware

26. EAST WEST, HOME BEST?

of being the object of attention by both my companions amidships and by those who sat in the stern of the vessel. I concentrated on the scenery to port, which I found flat and uninteresting as it was comprised of what I would later learn to be the vast mangrove swamp created by the Caroni river and its estuaries. To starboard extended the vastness of the Gulf of Paria, with the mountains of the Spanish Main in the distance, reminding me with a pang of the Highland lochs.

I was on the verge of nodding off when I heard someone say in French, "Pardonnez-moi, monsieur, I couldn't help noticing the care that was rendered by your good self to the injured man. Are you a physician?"

Looking round, I beheld an elderly man, pale, yellow-complexioned, with a mass of grey hair and negroid features. He was as well dressed as I.

"Yes, I am a doctor. How may I be of help?"

"Not at this present moment, thanks be to God. May I, Sir, present myself, I am Alexandre Congnet, at your service, and may I be so bold to ask your name?"

"Jean-Baptiste Philip, at your service," I replied, leaning towards him to hear him better.

"Upon my word, you are Louis' son! I am most pleased to make your acquaintance. You were the first to go abroad to study medicine. Your brother, St. Luce, how is he? Has he settled in over there?"

His saying this made me remember my brother St. Luce. Had he already left for England? I had no idea. After mumbling, I can't remember what, I asked him about himself. Mr. Congnet was the senior member of a family whose circumstances, I was to discover, were not dissimilar to my father's. He too was a planter who as a young man had come to Trinidad from Saint Lucia, having been enticed to do so by the attractive terms of the Cedula for Population, and he was now the owner of several plantations in both north and

107

south Naparima with his principal holding, St. Magdelaine, not far from my father's at Concorde.

"We often see your parents," he was saying in French. His accent and intonation, not to mention the noise of the paddle-wheels, made it difficult to understand him clearly. "Your father is a fine man who has done a great deal for our cause. And your mama, ah, she is a marvel. I do so admire her. They shall be very happy to see you. As we all shall be. These are trying times."

"Yes, I have recently experienced something of a rude awakening, although I had been told, I think even warned, of what to expect."

"An example of which we are presently experiencing, even as we sit here vibrating in this heat. The authorities are intent on creating a divide, indeed on expanding the historic divisions that will only alienate, perhaps for all time, one segment of the population from another."

"And what is being done to address this? Surely there must be a recourse, an appeal to the law. My aunt Susannah explained that we free people of colour were protected by the laws of both Spain and England. Why then is this injustice tolerated? As I understand, it is people such as ourselves, free from slavery, who are in the majority here."

"We have never tolerated this situation. But Trinidad is a British Crown Colony. The governor wields absolute power. He will re-engineer this society, the fabric of which was an experiment launched by an enlightened Spanish sovereign for the benefit of all. We could have been a light shining from the west, an example of tolerance, all beneficiaries of an enlightened age." He shook his head sadly. "My son Jean, he too has had an education in England. We anticipate his return shortly, praise God."

Sitting on the chicken crate, in the shuddering heat, watching the coast going sullenly by, it was all that I could do not to despair. My God, this place is hell on earth. What an affront! Because of our colour, we must endure the indignity of sitting with the lower

26. East West, Home Best?

classes, while several among us, well-dressed young women and elderly and cultured persons like Alexandre Congnet, should clearly be placed with the Europeans in the stern where the air was cool and there was less vibration. This was an atrocity.

There were tall chimneys beyond the mangrove shore from which black smoke rose. An odour came. I sniffed the air.

"Warm rum and molasses. Sugar factories," Mr. Congnet was saying, "the plantations line the shore. With few roads, most of which are impassable for half the year because of flooding, there is a difficulty in taking out produce. Your father has built an embarcadero at Petite Bourg. We ship our sugar from there as well. He has done a great deal for us, for people such as ourselves, a very great deal."

"Petite Bourg? I thought it was called San Fernando."

"It was originally known as Petite Bourg, the Little Village, then Governor Chacón, the last Spanish governor, declared it a town and called it San Fernando in honour of a Spanish prince. But we mostly still use the French name."

Because of the sounds made by the whirling paddle-wheels, the discomfort of the vibrations, not to mention the insufferable heat, it became impossible to speak further. I closed my eyes, the journey appeared to be never ending. When I opened them again there were schooners, drogers and a great many canoes about. The vessel was slowing. In the distance I could see a tree-covered flattop hill that I gathered to mark our destination. There was no harbour, only a shallow roadstead that extended far out to sea where heavy vessels, and there were five or six at anchor, stood off more than a mile.

A row of black and dirty gray shacks lined the sea front where fishing boats were beached. From there a short jetty sagged into the water. A strong smell of fish now mingled with the smoky air, as the *Woodford* came about to put her bow into the wind that suddenly dropped. This caused those of us who were amidships to be engulfed in a hot cloud of acrid smoke. The sound of the anchor told me that we were finally at rest. The European passengers were the first to go into the waiting longboats. There were none for us!

Once again I experienced a frightening desperation. A sense of being out of control of things. My word, how helpless I was.

"There are our pirogues. They are coming. Your things shall be taken care of. Never mind. I have a cart standing by. There are my people, over there." Mr. Congnet was waving his hat. There was a crowd on shore, some were waving in return. "You shall be home soon. Don't worry."

The coloureds, there were about fifteen or more of them, were being helped into the boats, their "pirogues" as Mr. Congnet had called them, by the men who had brought them alongside. I followed Mr. Congnet into one, being handed in by a black fellow with a wide smile. There was a profound feeling of relief as we pulled away. I shall never set foot on the *Woodford* again, I vowed to myself. There were black men coming out into the shallow water, taking people off the long boats and helping them onto their shoulders. They were being taken ashore. My word. What a place. Now it was my turn. I climbed onto the shoulders of a large man who waded away from the boat and out of the water with me holding on to his head, then, bending over, he deposited me on the beach. Before I could thank him he was away, back into the sea and briskly making his way to another boat. My word.

"Come this way, Doctor. Here is the carriage, yes, up you get. It looks like a shower of rain is coming our way. Not to worry, your things shall be at Concorde perhaps even before you arrive there." As we moved off I could see evidence of what must have been a fire.

"Yes, there was a very bad fire. Nearly all the newly built houses were burnt. It was in May, the 1st of May this year. The flames spread far and wide, as the houses were entirely built of wood."

Carried in the warm air, the briny smell of fishing nets contained the odour of decomposition. Huge black vultures were devouring

26. EAST WEST, HOME BEST?

something, they barely gave way to our carriage. San Fernando was hardly more than a collection of wooden houses between large trees, a quantity of shacks, a store or two on the mangrove shore and what looked like a church. A cart with a massive hogshead, drawn by a team of oxen, and a boy leading a donkey came towards us, it was followed by another and then another. There were handfuls of people, all black, speaking loudly in Patois. White men were supervising something or other under a shed. A mule cart dashed past us, sending the vultures flapping into lazy flight. It was followed by a pack of curs barking frantically in its wake.

We left the shadow of the flat-topped hill just as the rain started, but with the sun still out, it became quite a beautiful sight. We were soon surrounded by fields of sugarcane that sparkled with raindrops in the bright afternoon sun. Along a winding hilly track we drove, the black coachman clicking his tongue and snapping the reins, the pair of high-stepping mules smartly trotting. The well-worn earthen trail was called the Royal Road, it wound its way up and over a rolling countryside and through what appeared to be an endless sea of sugarcane fields. Here and there I could make out a homestead. A large house isolated on a hilltop. A row of enormously tall palms. A factory, smoke rising from its chimney. The rich smell of turned earth and fresh air came to me. The sky, so blue that one could be made dizzy gazing upwards.

At my side Mr. Congnet had fallen asleep. It was all so strange yet familiar in an odd manner. Was it coming back to me? I was just eleven when I had come along this road that morning so long ago. What do I remember? Mother. It was more of a feeling than an actual memory of when I was put into the boat that took me to the ship, all to be confused with the frightful loneliness that I was to experience in London. Father. A stern face like an old portrait came to mind, that too produced a feeling of being sent away. I suppose I experienced abandonment, being left behind, in much the same manner that those who have been orphaned do. When I recalled my time at Great Coram Street, I think I must have been miserable. And the others. My brothers. I have brothers and sisters who are all now grown. As these and other thoughts and emotions passed over me, the carriage was turning into a wide driveway.

I hadn't noticed that the cane fields had given way to pastures which were fringed by long hedgerows. Animals grazed in them. A great many horses. White-painted fences and several very large, wide-spreading trees. Cattle, resting in their shade. Neat, even picturesque, a house stood on a small rise, its roof high-pitched and thatched. It appeared wide, low, wooden and was raised from the ground on brick pillars. There were other buildings nearby. And people, a quantity of people. I could see a cart being offloaded. My things had indeed arrived before us.

"You are home, my dear boy, you are home. There is your dear mama and your father, see, there."

Mr. Congnet was beaming, there were tears in his eyes. Children were running, dogs barking. Men on horseback and a large crowd of people, all black, were gathered together beneath an enormous tree. These must be the estate's slaves, and in the midst of them all were my parents and brothers and sisters. It was only by their dress that I could make out the difference. That came as something of a shock. I had thought of them as very old but they were not. I was home. This was home, as I remembered it. It was not entirely unfamiliar, just strange and quite exciting.

Everyone would have me, hold me. My mother, her large eyes weeping, held me close. My father shook my hand and in saying welcome, burst into tears and hugged me to his chest. We stood together, clinging, weeping, it was all such an emotional moment. André-Montrose I knew at once, but had to be introduced to Belizaire, and to Frédéric and Michel Maxwell. I was really meeting them all for the first time.

My sisters, these must be my sisters.

"I am Simone," said a pretty one. "I am Marie-Reine," said another.

"And this is Marie-Lazarine," said Simone, "she is Mrs. Ventour now."

26. EAST WEST, HOME BEST?

"She soon will be Mrs. Corsbie," laughed the little one who had introduced herself as Marie-Reine, "and this one here is hoping to be Mrs. Romain."

"Oh shut up."

"Who are you?" I could hardly understand them.

"Me? I am Lucille."

It was overwhelmingly emotional and all so confusing. I could hardly tell the girls apart.

So, this is what it feels like to come home.

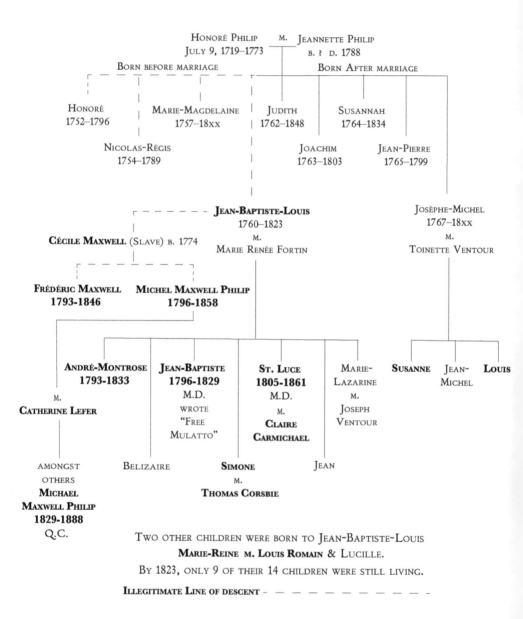

27. A Stranger in a Strange Land

"The mind that broods o'er guilty woes,
Is like the scorpion girt by fire."

George Gordon Lord Byron

TRINIDAD 1819: I HAD BEEN WARNED BY AUNT SUSANNAH that father was not at all well, but it was on meeting him that I saw both the physical and mental decline that is associated with advanced old age, which at fifty-nine, I found a little surprising. I understood from mother that he had not recuperated well from a tropical fever of some years ago, but quite apart from his physical weakness, his mind had a way, often charming, of wandering off from what he was attempting to say. So much so, he could become puzzled and lost for words. Mother and my brothers André-Montrose and Belizaire, together with our cousin Susanne and of course, our half-brother Frédéric Maxwell, have made all the important decisions with regard to both estates over the last two or three years.

Our relatives in France had also told me to expect an untenable situation, this was endorsed by Mr. Congnet who suggested that I should avoid engaging the English authorities on contentious issues, as this would be fruitless and could provoke an unjustifiable response. This last has proved to be so. I was ordered to fall in as a private soldier in the Quarter's militia. This indignity finally came to pass after several months of sly and roguish correspondence. I had no interest in military affairs. However, as a licensed physician I expected to be granted a commission by the governor as others here have. He did approve my application to practice medicine, but refused my request for an audience. I later learned from Reinagle that the Medical Board was only granted permission by Woodford to examine me because my parents were married and our family were in possession of landed property. So even this came with all sorts of indignities.

Mother said that the life expectancy of an slave was hardly more than nine or ten years. In the estate books I saw that an outbreak of smallpox some years before my arrival had taken the lives of almost half the work force. Clabba-yaws was endemic in the slave population, caused by the organism treponema pertenue, so too was dracunculus medinensis. They called this guinea-worm. This too was endemic. One found it in all strata of the society. An adult worm could be as much as a foot long! I understood that the larval form was spread by the ingestion of aquatic crustaceans. Yellow fever took a terrible toll on everyone in the colony. There was much malaria in Trinidad and typhus icteroides. Those fatalities can only be compared to the deadly effects of what is called new rum.

I had not set up a practice but already I had patients. A great many were poor. They arrived, almost all were mixed race or black, at all hours of the day or the night. I treated them in a small front room off the verandah as discreetly as I could, as this drew the attention of the entire household with both family members and domestics offering advice. They had little or no money to pay me but would come to the house bringing fish, game, eggs, ground provisions, whatever they had, even oysters, which they would leave with mother. There was a vast disparity in the fees paid to medical practitioners for services to coloured and white patients. According to the published schedule for a visit in town or the suburbs to a white person during the day, the sum of eighteen shillings may be charged. A visit to a coloured person would be twelve shillings and to a slave, six shillings. It was like this from a tooth extraction to bleeding from the jugular vein on through to setting a fracture.

Mother explained that on Concorde and Philippine the family worked over one hundred and sixty slaves on eight hundred acres, almost entirely planted in sugarcane. We owned four lots of land in San Fernando. Two of those were rented to English merchants,

27. A Stranger in a Strange Land

while the others, which were on the waterfront, provided basic accommodation for overnighting travellers and were used as a wharf. The family's sugar was shipped from there to England. There was as well a parcel of land in Port of Spain. Mother has built a modest house there in the event that any of us would take it into our heads to live in such a hellish place. She assured me that there was another parcel of land on Carriacou, she was not sure of the acreage, and in St. George's, Grenada, where father had inherited, or had been gifted, a property on Gore Street. We were also possessed of gold and cash, well in excess of several thousand pounds sterling. This was kept in an iron chest chained to a massive slab of stone in my parents' bedroom.

The estate house at Concorde, very much like the one at Philippine, was covered by a high-pitched, neatly thatched roof. The carat palm provided the material. They were constructed on small rises, surrounded by undulating fields of sugarcane. Built on platforms, they had vast rectangular hardwood floors supported by stone pillars that stood about six to seven feet high. If seen from their rustic rafters, the various rooms and many corridors, with their seven foot high, unpainted cedar-wood partitions, would appear much like a maze. Concorde's central drawing and dining rooms had four bedrooms on either side, all opening onto a wide verandah that surrounded the entire structure. The principal idea was the circulation of fresh air. The houses were thought of by the family as large ajoupas, the Amerindian name for a hut.

I found Concorde and Philippine picturesque, full of exotic oddities, eclectic collections of furnishings, objets d'art, and nostalgic keepsakes. In each, a massive mahogany dining table, along with their ten ferociously carved chairs, was at the very heart of the family. Reflected in their dark sheen were brightly burnished silver candelabra of a heavy Spanish style. Scattered around the drawing rooms were home-made stools, chairs and occasional tables, rustic to say the least, these stood in contrast to elegant gold-leafed Louis XIII masterpieces.

Veneered cabinets in the Rocaille style at Concorde displayed obscure objects of perhaps Amerindian make alongside superb examples of Vincenne porcelain. The many mahogany monstrosities, euphemistically called sideboards, in both houses, that appeared to have been carved from the imaginations of Barbadian joiners, displayed in antique gilt and solid silver some of the astonishing trophies taken by my pirate grandfather. Over a beautiful rococo commode at Concorde was a shocking collection of framed, mezzotint erotica, entirely pornographic. This occupied almost an entire partition. There were tall corner cabinets that contained golden objects that mother said had been looted from the graves of long dead native chieftains. The great bed at Philippine was once the prized possession of a Dutchman who became, through the generosity of Louis XIV, Baron of Tobago!

It was a pleasure to awaken to bird-song and a thrill to hear the lambi-shell trumpet-call that summoned the hands to labour, the dawn just breaking. From my window I would see a vision full of exotic charm. A chanting caravan of young girls, some black, many lightly coloured, several with their breasts exposed, all barefooted, transporting in wide trays—which were elegantly balanced on their heads—a variety of fruit and vegetables and what were called here provisions, all the produce of this estate. They would be on their way to neighbouring estates that did not have vegetable or provision gardens.

There were at any point in time members of the extended family as well as itinerant travellers overnighting or, in some instances, staying on for indefinite periods at Concorde or Philippine. To accommodate this, the kitchens, which were some distance away from the houses, were never idle, and maintained great cauldrons of something called pepperpot—a repulsive stew, kept permanently on the boil since 1796, into which whatever meat left over from any occasion was added. It was highly spiced, flavoured with cassareep, a thick black liquid that was concocted from the juice of the bitter cassava root, which I understood to be poisonous, but which, if used in the right amount, served as a preservative.

27. A Stranger in a Strange Land

On both estates the sugar-mills were worked by mules. The rhommeries, that is to say the sugar-houses, with their tall chimneys were surrounded by little villages of thatched slave-cabins surrounded by neat vegetable gardens, quite picturesque. Each slave was allowed a small patch of land to, as it was said, "make garden". Half-days were allowed once a week for that purpose. They were permitted to keep all or most of the proceeds. Legally a slave could own nothing, yet several of our hands were known to have saved creditable sums.

Cooperage, stables, smithy and other appurtenances were adjacent to decent housing for the overseers. The small hospitals on both estates were in almost derelict condition, though. These contained when I arrived an assortment of medicinal herbal preparations, crutches, piles of cotton bandages, stocks for hands and feet, bed stocks, a tin collar with a huge padlock, which, I was informed, was used for drunkenness, and tin face masks that were applied when treating slaves afflicted by geophagy, the habit of eating dirt—a practice that was brought by them when they were shipped to the New World. I could not help thinking, however, that this condition was more likely to be caused by the mental despondency brought about by their condition.

The morning inspection of the feet of the enslaved children was an amusing scene. Up to the age of four or five, they have nothing to do but eat and play. At Concorde they were under the charge of the infirmière: the gentle, always smiling Cécile, the woman with whom my father shares his love, the mother of my half-brothers, Frédéric and Michel. She would have all the children sit on a long bench and on command hold up their little feet, and aided by her helpers, they would be inspected for chiggers with much tickling and laughter. Cécile's practiced eye would not miss that small round swelling between their wiggling toes: the child would be sent to the infirmary for immediate treatment, and the child's mother would receive a severe reprimand for not spotting it earlier. I understood this—it was important that the children, the future hands, should not be afflicted by a form of scrub typhus, a disease caused by the mite larvae that could become crippling.

Mother, when asked about Cécile Maxwell's presence, in truth her position in the household, gently explained that she had been a part of father's family from the time she was a child. "She grew up with your father, his sisters and brothers on their estate in Carriacou. Both Frédéric and Michel are your father's sons, they are your half-brothers."

I could not bring myself to ask at what stage Cécile and father became lovers, as I thought it would embarrass her, because of the obvious similarity of our ages. Michel Maxwell Philip, as he has become, and I were born in the same year, 1796, and my brother André-Montrose and Frédéric Maxwell were also of the same age, born in 1793. In Europe it would be said that Cécile was father's mistress and there would be a scandal. Out here in the Caribbean and as I have come to understand also in New Orleans, there was a word for this arrangement: "plaçage", which appears to be a recognised albeit extralegal arrangement that seems to exist in all of the French islands. It found its way to Trinidad with other customs that shaped Créole life in this colony. As for her position in the household, mother explained that Cécile had been for several years the family's eyes and ears at Gran'Anse in Carriacou during the time that aunt Judith was abroad in England. "When your aunt Judith came back home in 1808, Cécile continued at Gran'Anse, helping Judith with the estate. Susanne went to them as a girl, she grew there with Cécile and Judith. They taught her everything about estate business."

I found mother's attitude strange but fascinating, and it caught my attention because I was interested in not merely what people thought about things, but how things made them feel, how those feelings affected their lives and charged their future actions with meaning and consequence. Here, on the estate, Cécile did not live in the same house with my parents, as I came to understand was the case in other families, both black and white. She had her own house, modest, with a lovely garden in which a startling variety of medicinal plants thrived. She was knowledgeable of their properties and, importantly, she had a subtle, almost uncanny way

27. A STRANGER IN A STRANGE LAND

of diagnosing the multitude of complaints that were brought to her by the slaves, the free coloured planters around and our French Créole neighbours. As time went by, I would often consult her for an insightful second opinion.

Cécile and mother have raised their children together. My half-brothers grew up with my brothers and sisters with few distinctions made between them. The manner in which mother spoke of Cécile gave the impression that they were like sisters who went about the complicated business of the plantation, dealing with the large, ever complaining slave population and, increasingly, their shared grandchildren, with mutual understanding.

I made the acquaintance of Thomas Corsbie, my sister Simone's fiancé. He was a fair-complexioned man from Barbados who, according to mother, has had a great deal of plantation experience. St. Luce, who sailed for England the year before my return, was constantly on mother's mind and I am sure in her prayers. She missed him and would speak of him as though he was still at home. His things still lay about the house. I noticed that she would make a display of discovering them—his fishing gear, or bits of clothing, books, or his favourite pillow—putting them away only to discover them again another day.

Work began in the fields at dawn and was performed with song, at times to the music of the drum, and there were days and evenings when the slaves were given the privilege of dancing. I noticed that adult slaves, both men and women, were thought of and, at times, treated by family members like children. I did not see them as such. Nor did I believe them to be happy, lazy or stupid, as many coloureds did. I saw them as whole human beings caught in a terrifying situation. It was with a degree of surprise that I saw the slave women, old and young alike, go bare-breasted into the cane fields, but I was shocked to see them so appear in the house. It seemed to be a family tradition to sell only those slaves who could not be controlled without physical punishment, although in the estate yards of both Concorde and Philippine there were whipping posts where corporal punishment was administered by the overseers. This was a most disturbing sight, one I avoided, especially as it was followed by the application of a concoction of ground pepper, rum and heaven only knows what else which was rubbed into the wounds left by the whip, to prevent infection.

At Concorde, the lambi-shell trumpet call at six in the evening summoned all from the fields and the mill buildings. There, at the gate that opened onto the sugarcane fields, a patriarchal scene would unfold. My father, gray-haired and frail, supported by my brother Belizaire, the Scottish overseers standing behind them, would wait for all hands to assemble. My father would then call, in a shaky voice, for the evening prayer. The slaves, all bearing a bundle of forage for the animals, would remove their hats and kneel to recite the Lord's prayer, the Creed, a prayer for their master and one for themselves. In the fading light and at times against glorious sunsets, the heat of the day giving way to the cool evening breezes of the dry season, this ritual appeared to me biblical and deeply moving. I came to understand that it was instituted by mother. It had been the practice on her father's estate on the island of Marie Galante, as was another, where once a year all the slaves on the estate would celebrate with bamboulas and kalendas and be received by mother on the verandah. Each slave in turn would kiss her hand and would find in it a sliver of a silver coin. I recorded in my journal that it was with a mixture of surprise and delight that I watched these feudal incidents of colonial life, so full of exotic oddities and unconscious poetry.

Then there were my sisters. I seemed to have such a quantity, especially when they were all here being entertained, along with their numerous Ventour cousins and friends, which was almost daily. The northeastern corner of the verandah, which captured best the refreshing easterlies, appeared a hammock-strung harem of Spanish shawls, scented Martiniquian fans and languid beauties, who would all fall silent the moment that one approached.

"They are talking about husbands," said mother in passing, "and what to wear on their wedding night,"

27. A Stranger in a Strange Land

"Ah, I see." I actually understood. I had heard them singing in Patois, very prettily, something that went like this:

"I am dimpled, young,
Round-limbed and strong,
With sapodilla-skin
That is good to see.
All glossy-smooth
Is this skin of mine
And the most serious of men
Like to look at me!"

They also sang another that raised shrieks of laughter and riotous applause. This would bring mother demanding decorum and promising damnation. The chorus of that one sung in Patois when translated to French went something like this: "Depuis que ma mère me fait, aucun homme ne me donné jamais de bois, sous la maison!" Which may be loosely expressed in English thus: Since my mother make me, no man ever give me wood, under the house! "Anba kay-la!"

28. And If Not Equal All, Yet Free

*"It is not one man nor a million,
but the spirit of liberty that must be preserved."*

George Gordon Lord Byron

Cabins neatly thatched

Having heard of Governor Woodford's deplorable acts—the censoring of the press, the manner in which he intercepted private correspondence, his invading of homes, the breaking of locks so as to gain access to the private papers of individuals, and importantly, his actions with regard to land tenure, which could only be described as nefarious, all these from my cousin Jeannette-Rose—I now wanted to gain an understanding of the present state of mind of people like ourselves in the first instance, before moving on to speak with the common free people.

I listened first to my parents. My mother's view was that the governor, in appearing to want to dispossess those who held lands by virtue of the Cedula of 1783, had created distrust of the government, generated communal fear and had set in motion,

28. And If Not Equal All, Yet Free

once again, a dangerous and accumulating discontent. On the other hand, she was pleased that he had curbed gambling, that awful vice that destroys families and fortunes, and that he was able to control the ruffians who plagued the towns and the countryside. On father's advice I sought out Mr. Congnet, but first spoke to my brothers Frédéric and André-Montrose who jointly managed our affairs. Their concerns were more immediate. These had to do with the manner in which the estates' slaves were mandated to engage in extensive unpaid public road building and maintenance works at times when they were most needed in the factory or in the fields.

The slaves from our plantations, with their drivers, were required to be at work on the public road by six in the morning, failing which we would be fined. The corvée, as it is called, a system of unpaid compulsory labour for the state, ended in France shortly after the beginning of the revolution, when it was abolished along with other feudal privileges. However, here in Trinidad, it was imposed by Governor Woodford as a duty to which all landowners had, by law, to adhere. I thought to myself that they should not put too much emphasis on it being abolished in France at the time of the revolution, because the free people of colour in Trinidad, I had heard, were held in suspicion of harbouring republican, even revolutionary ideas.

Governor Woodford's policy had been to concentrate on the development of the island's road system, to abandon the distribution of Crown lands, and to encourage all planters to become more productive. These measures appeared to me to be good and useful, as I had come to see for myself that a road system hardly existed here, and that some planters, free coloured and European, whether they possessed large acreages or small, often had to let their lands lie fallow and in some instances still covered in virgin forest for want of roadways. It came to me, as I listened to my family members and their friends, that they had formed, or perhaps inherited, the habit of resisting *all* government directives, whether these were justified or not. I thought it best to listen and not to form or to voice opinions. Frédéric and André-Montrose gave me an understanding of how unjust the system of the corvée actually was, and the manner in which people like us were being affected by it, in terms of productivity and of course, financially.

Frédéric, who bore I thought a somewhat unnerving resemblance to Belizaire, explained, "Jean-Baptiste, year before last, our slaves from Concorde built, with gravel that had been taken unpaid for from our land, three hundred French paces of the Mission Road. It was laid out and rounded off, high in the middle and sloping to the verge. This work included the widening of the road and the digging of box drains along its entire length. This was followed by work, this year, during crop time, that reopened the road through the St. John estate!"

I nodded, not quite understanding the volume of work implied, or even the lay of the land. André-Montrose went on to add: "And not to dwell on every other task performed by the estate's slaves, Jean-Baptiste, we contributed no less than nine hundred and seventy-six days of free labour in filling up the public wharf at San Fernando. Those tasks, on the most moderate calculation, may be computed at one thousand pounds sterling per annum!"

"And for this year we have already contributed a very large share in repairing the Pointe-à-Pierre road," added Belizaire, who had joined us. "It had a very deep chasm to fill, and a portion of road to repair," he went on to explain, "this was after the deluge of mid-October, remember?"

I did remember the storms, but had no idea of the movement of labour from the plantation, as to me, the work had gone on as usual. I would come to understand that our plantations contributed above one thousand three hundred and eighty-nine French paces of roadway, gravelled by our people during a period when it was important to have those gangs at work here on our lands, because of the quick regrowth of weeds and bushes in the cane fields. A thousand pounds per year for several years! That appeared to me as grossly unfair.

28. And If Not Equal All, Yet Free

"Every planter, coloured or white, has to deal with this," said André-Montrose, "but it affects us especially in the way that we, the black and coloured estate owners in the Naparimas, are singled out by Mr. Mitchell, the Commandant, who is Woodford's creature, to perform these works at a time when it is most disadvantageous financially to do so." His outrage appeared justified as he continued, saying, "Why on earth must we be singled out and be treated in such an unjust manner? We, who have a bona-fide right to be protected under the laws of this land!"

What I saw was an injustice being meted out on the one hand and an ingrained resistance to English rule on the other. I wondered why the free coloured people here in Trinidad believed that they were a specially privileged group, and thought of themselves as unique in the Caribbean.

"Why do you feel you deserve protection?" I asked André-Montrose.

"We see ourselves as being subjects of an occupying power, the English," he answered. "We came here by the invitation of the king of Spain, and for fourteen years everything went well enough, then the English arrived. They cannot see, or pretend that they cannot see, that there are differences in intelligence, education and upbringing amongst us, and as a result of this, we are all treated in the same disrespectful manner. We resent them for this and naturally resist all their injustices."

"Having said that," added Frédéric, "the behaviour of a great many of us in the early years of colonisation was dangerous, even murderous in the other islands. The revolution in France inspired the republicans out here."

"You must have heard of our homegrown republicanism!" laughed André-Montrose, adding, "Now, with regard to believing ourselves privileged, this is because of article four in the Cedula of Population, which specifically refers to free blacks and mulattoes. Our titles to land were to be equally legal and granted in the same manner as to whites. The twelfth clause of the Capitulation document when Spain surrendered Trinidad to the English in '97 also specifically refers to us. We are not seeking new privileges, we merely want to keep the ones we have."

"What does that twelfth clause of the Capitulation say?"

"It says that we are protected under the laws of Spain in our liberty, person and property, like other inhabitants."

"Do you know anyone who has actually seen these documents?" I asked, having heard of them from almost every person that I had spoken to with regard to these vexing subjects.

"No, Jean-Baptiste," André-Montrose answered. "I must tell you, I have never met anyone who has actually seen either of them, far less read them. But we all have come to know what is in them, by necessity, as they are being undermined by Governor Woodford."

An example of this deep-seated and far-reaching animosity that resides in the hearts of the so-called republican element here in Trinidad was given to me by Mr. Congnet. This concerned a man named Antoine Protain who, encouraged by a notorious planter called Begorrat, was able in 1799 to influence Napoléon Bonaparte, then First Consul, to use his powers, at the time significant at the royal court in Madrid, to overturn the Spanish court-martial's verdict that exonerated Governor Chacón for having surrendered Trinidad to the English. It was through a relative of Protain, a certain Jean Protain, one of the savants in Bonaparte's train in his attempt to conquer Egypt, who was able to represent to the First Consul that republican France had lost the opportunity of taking Trinidad as a result of Chacón's decision. The result of this was that on the recommendation of Bonaparte, Chacón was brought before a hostile judiciary in 1801, and retried. The court-martial's honourable acquittal was overturned and poor Chacón was banished to Portugal, where he died impecunious.

Over time, I appreciated that beneath the veneer of patriarchal beneficence an iron fist, the threat of physical violence on a scale

28. And If Not Equal All, Yet Free

that approached actual murder, all fortified by the whip, permeated plantation life. It was driven by fear, an all-pervading fear that necessitates the creation of terror. The slaves must be kept perpetually terrified, either subtly or overtly. The fear was mutual. It was inherited in all planter families from birth. It came with the isolation of plantation life and from being outnumbered by the slaves, who might be mobilised by any of their number to rise up and instantly take the lives of their tormentors with fire and blade, rape, torture or some terrible and lingering illness caused by poison.

This fear was kept alive by the almost ritualistic repetition of stories of slaves on other islands who had risen up, murdered or poisoned, planter families. Rebellion, unspoken of, was a reality. Every planter's child, coloured and white, was inculcated from birth to command. Every slave was conditioned to obey. Every plantation was a prison camp where men and women were worked, under guard, at hard labour in perpetuity. An accommodation that waxed and waned was precariously balanced, it was maintained in an atmosphere of suspicion, poised between the potentiality for panic and a watchful form of familiarity.

If anything disturbed this artificial equilibrium, anxiety was the consequence. We experienced this in January of 1819. I was awakened in the middle of the night to the yowling call of conch shells and the ringing of the estate's bell. Standing in the verandah I could see in the distance southward what appeared to be a fire, in fact several fires. Cane fields were on fire. From the estate yard came the sounds of horses and the shouts of command. Around and about there was a great hue and cry. People with torches, my brothers and the overseers were all armed. Mother was at my side, she too was armed with a flintlock that was almost as long as she was tall.

"Fires have started on Bienvenue and La Fontaine. The estate bells have been ringing since midnight. You didn't hear them?" There was alarm and also fury in her voice. Her fury was, I felt, directed at me. "You hadn't heard them. Look!"

"What must I do?"

"Nothing. Just watch these here, all of them. Can you use a gun?"

"Yes." I had handled fowling pieces. She appeared stern. I could never have imagined her this way. "Take it. Go to the other side of the house. You have to look to see if any one of them would start a fire. This," she lifted her arms to indicate the thatched roof, "could go up in flames. Go and do not hesitate to shoot dead any one of them you see with a torch or a flambeau."

I took the old-fashioned piece, which I saw was loaded, with a flint in position in the lock but not cocked, and walked around to the other side of the house. All was quiet. There were women about. Some men and boys. They all seemed to be waiting to be told what to do. The dawn was still far from breaking, they were up too early. As it turned out the fire at La Fontaine had been accidental, and the one at Bienvenue deliberately set soon after the other appeared. Within days the alarmists were able to manufacture a monstrous plot meant to generate excitement and fear that all the slaves on the island were planning to rise up in revolt, this was when I understood that this island actually possessed a subversive element.

Some weeks later, I was invited to luncheon at St. Madeline estate, the home of the Congnet family. I had already made the acquaintance of Mr. Congnet's eldest son Jean, who had recently returned to Trinidad having been educated in England. Jean Congnet, like myself, came from a large family. Like us, they had made their money a generation before their arrival here, and like ourselves were the proprietors of several large cane estates. I found him to be cultured, well read and an excellent companion who was interested in what I had to say concerning the emotional effects of the Woodford administration on people like ourselves.

It was arranged that I should meet, on that occasion, John Welsh Hobson and Désir Fabien. These men, I came to understand, were the leading personalities behind the concerted movement to oppose

28. And If Not Equal All, Yet Free

Woodford in his unrelenting endeavour to use locally contrived laws to degrade our community and deprive us of our legal rights. In order to suit my own scientific interest, I desired to hear from them how they were affected mentally by Woodford's persecutions, and what impact these were having on the minds of free people of colour generally. But first, I inquired about the existence of copies of the Cedula of Population of 1783 and the Articles of Capitulation of 1797.

"Several copies of the Cedula were made by Monsieur Philippe Roume de Saint Laurent," said Alexandre Congnet. "We all shall speak French here today, my boy," he said with a smile. "Our colleague, my great friend John Hobson, who shall soon be joining us, is in possession of copies of both these documents. They came to him through John Nihill, the former Chief Judge of the colony. The provisions in both those documents that refer to us, the free blacks and people of colour, are our guarantee for fair treatment. This in itself is significant," he explained, "as such a generous endowment does not exist anywhere else in the Caribbean."

I had heard this. I asked if he knew of the condition of the free coloureds in the other islands. He explained that in the other islands various situations, all onerous, existed. In St. Vincent, for example, free Negroes and mixed-race people were limited to the ownership of just eight acres of land, and under no condition could be deemed freeholders, as this would carry political privileges. Adding, "That act went further and required all free Negroes and mulattoes to select some white master to live with, so that their lives and their conversations might be known and observed. The difference between us here in Trinidad and the free coloureds in the other islands is that while they are fighting to *get* rights, we are struggling to *retain* the rights granted to us by a sovereign government, which were guaranteed by another under the law, in the name of the British Crown."

"Have we," I asked Mr. Congnet, "the free coloureds, ever approached the government here in Trinidad in the hope of addressing all of this?"

"Oh yes. First in 1810, when a group of us attempted to tackle these issues in terms of an equitable constitution, but we were threatened with prosecution by the governor of the day, General Hislop. I actually ventured to attend a public meeting that was called by the white planters who would be affected by these changes, but was asked to leave. It was then that we decided to act on our own and to eventually petition the King in England."

It had taken me some time to get even a meagre understanding of the political machinations at play in this place. In asking about the political future of the colony, I was told by Mr. Congnet that in the following year, 1811, two motions had been introduced in the House of Commons, one to give this island British laws, and the other to grant Trinidad a British constitution. Both were lost without a division. Mr. James Stephen, then Master in Chancery and a supporter of Wilberforce, expressed the view that what was proposed was that the House should accede to the wishes of five hundred and seventeen white inhabitants, in opposition to the wishes of twenty-two thousand. He was, of course exaggerating. Or perhaps he was anticipating the emancipation of the slaves. The free blacks and people of colour at the time numbered hardly more than six thousand.

"They would want to exclude us from taking part in an elected body?" To me, that seemed farcical.

"Oh yes, they would indeed," replied Mr. Congnet.

"Is this generally known?"

"There is a great deal of misunderstanding about these issues, depending on to whom you speak," replied Mr. Congnet. "We, Hobson, Fabien and the others, who have formed ourselves into a committee of sorts, have gathered hundreds of names and signatures from people in the town and from all over the countryside. We hold no public meetings, and make a point of never staging any sort of protest. What we do is talk to people in their homes. We encourage them to have all their documentation in order, especially

28. And If Not Equal All, Yet Free

manumission papers and title deeds. We ask them to be prepared to join in the signing of a petition which we intend to submit to the Crown, as is our right to do under the twenty-eighth Article of the Spanish Cedula. When you see the names, you imagine that we are all one and the same, but you would see for yourself, if you examined the individuals, that we are not at all the same. The coloured society in Trinidad has different levels, although we do as a group tend to have the same circumstances or even experiences. We may all have the same dark origins, but through life's circumstances, I assure you we are not all the same."

"The twenty-eighth article of the Spanish Cedula? What does it state?"

"In a nutshell, it states that leave is given to both the old and new inhabitants of the colony to remonstrate through the governor. All free citizens have the right to petition the Crown. It goes to say that in case the business should be of such a nature as to require a person to solicit it, they should ask permission to do so and this would be granted, if their demands are just. Our petitions did not go through though, because they had to go through the governor."

I had heard as much from Frédéric and was about to ask if such a person had been selected, when he was told by a domestic that the company had arrived. "Ah, my son and the others are here," said Mr. Congnet, rising to greet them.

John Welsh Hobson was a large, fawn-coloured man with pale blue eyes and almost handsome European features. Soft-spoken, he greeted me, to my surprise, in an almost deferential manner. Both Fabien and Jean Congnet were younger men and of dark complexions. Fabien's features were refined and there was about him a somewhat delicate grace of the sort that I have seen in England in solicitors' clerks, while Congnet was well-built, athletic-appearing, and exuded the manner and confidence of an educated person. After the formalities of meeting and inquiring after each other's well-being, I guided the conversation towards my learning more about the feelings of the free black and coloured community here in

Trinidad, inquiring, in general terms, about the conditions under which they lived and how they were being affected mentally.

"The free people of colour here in Trinidad are on the whole mostly Catholic, otherwise they would not have been admitted under the terms of the Cedula," said Hobson. "They consider themselves French, having arrived here from islands which were originally settled by France, with two or three families originating in Saint-Domingue."

"They come from a variety of backgrounds," added Fabien, as he helped himself from a pitcher of sangria. "Would you like some?" he asked, looking at me with a wide, friendly smile. He hadn't noticed that I already had a glass of this deliciously spiced wine, placed on a small table. Returning his smile I declined, asking him please to continue.

"Yes. Notwithstanding the basic similarity of all our origins," he said, "the enslaved woman and the European man produced, over the generations, different levels, partly determined by shade and, interestingly, hair texture. Obviously, people with large plantations, people like ourselves, in spite of our various complexions, who possess many slaves, fifty or sixty to one hundred, are seen by ourselves and perhaps by some others to be of a higher class."

I understood that the quantity of human beings owned was a greater determinator of wealth and prestige than the amount of land that one possessed.

"Yes, quite so," added Hobson. I sensed, however, that he did not quite approve of the way the other had put that distinction, as he went on to continue from where he left off, "Amongst these families there are two or three men with attainments, professional men like yourself, who have been educated in Europe and, like you, were received in polite society in London and in Paris. And there are several young ladies who have attended convents and are seen, at least by their families, as being 'finished', that is, having been taught the social graces and cultural rituals necessary for entry into

28. And If Not Equal All, Yet Free

polite society and, if fortune smiled on them, for acquiring well-off European husbands."

I had to think of my cousins and the Codrington sisters, our neighbours in Bloomsbury, and contrary to what I had been told by my relatives in France, apparently European wives were all the rage here. It gave me a pang to think of fair Lieselotte... But I understood them. It was all about getting fairer complexions and becoming wealthier. My aunts had cohabited with Europeans. Aunt Judith even continued to have children with uncle Edmond after he had married an English person.

"Women of colour preferring white men? Does this have a deleterious effect on the psyche, the minds, of black men?" I wondered. "Plainly, this way of life, although it seems desirable, even enviable, to some black men, could appear to be a rejection of them, affecting their self-worth, while others could see it as parasitic, some would even call it a form of prostitution." I felt that perhaps I was being too provocative.

"Call it what you may," answered Congnet, I thought uneasily. "It does have an effect on the minds of men of colour, if that is what you are getting at. Partly as a result of this, women of colour have become very wealthy. They own slaves and not a few inherit substantial properties, both in the town and in the countryside." He shrugged. "In the end we men still benefit."

I thought he might have said that the coloured men could be jealous, but I understood, free black and coloured women made possible the transference of wealth and property to their relatives.

"On the other hand," said Hobson, "free coloured women, who are by nature virtuous, modest or even shy, especially if attractive, fair-complexioned and having what is called good hair, must be extremely discreet, failing which she could become fatally conspicuous and attract insults or even assault by white men who would want to simply debauch her. It is us, the free mulatto men who are on the outside of this false world."

"How so?" I asked.

"Free black and mixed race men live a different life here in Trinidad," Jean Congnet opined after a pause where he appeared to put his thoughts in order. He went on saying, "I think, very likely because we are perceived as aberrations, human anomalies, there is actually no real place for the mixed race man in the white man's world, and as a consequence we are held in contempt and deprived of every opportunity of demonstrating our true worth."

"Many men of colour accept this role and shy away from any demonstration of ambition in fear of ridicule," added Hobson. "They are terrified of demonstrating abilities and talents, because they would be considered dangerous deviants from the conventional white image of us. It takes a mixed race man of extraordinary moral strength to continue to distinguish himself."

"Yes," I answered, I could see that special talent and distinction would alarm the authorities here, bearing in mind the political upheavals that this community was involved in during the previous century. "I can understand that living under such conditions we are condemned to lose all ideas of dignity. Producing an awful form of mental slavery."

Fabien replied, I could see that he had become emotional as he went on saying in a louder tone, "We live under a social system that discourages virtue, talent and education. As a consequence, our people, the men, if they do not fall prey to drinking, gambling and dissipation, steal through life unobserved and creep with timid caution, seeking obscurity."

"Many hope to live and die in the bosom of this small society, here in the Naparimas, only knowing each other, fearful of shame or any social disgrace," Hobson said calmly, but with such a note of compassion in his voice that I regarded him, wondering if he was on the verge of tears. "I can tell you the slaves would pounce upon any perceived weakness. They are not stupid, they know that we are easily compromised."

28. AND IF NOT EQUAL ALL, YET FREE

"All the while consuming immoderate quantities of rum," added Congnet.

"Drunk on cacapoule rum and rightly terrified we are!" shouted Fabien, slapping his thigh. "Being imprisoned by the governor is where any one of us could meet our end, starving to death, while hanging in chains in his newly built prison on rue des Anglais. Do you know that the governor has gone to far as to threaten to commit to prison people who do not salute him as he passes on the street?"

I had no idea. However, I had noticed that alcohol consumption was very high and its deleterious effect on the health of many was evident. Everyone called it "daemon rum", but consumed it all the same. "Mental despondency," Hobson thought was the cause of alcoholism.

"We are shunned, insulted, often physically attacked here, Jean-Baptiste, by both the local whites, the French Créoles, and by the English people," said Congnet. "It is enough to drive a man to drink. Many, if not all, of the Englishmen here come from the poorer classes, the sons of shop-men, chimney sweeps, farm workers and domestic servants. They know nothing of racial discrimination when they first arrive. They start off as labourers or servants or low-paid overseers, but they learn quickly. Take a person like Mitchell, the Commandant of this Quarter. The governor refers to him as his 'old, able and honest officer,' but he is neither old nor honest. He is a coquin! A rogue. As for being able, you have only to pay a visit to his plantation to see for yourself his lack of competence."

"Sir Ralph has done his duty with regard to enforcing the laws of the colony for the protection of the slaves," said Hobson, "but regarding slavery and the colonial prejudice of caste, he is by no means in advance of his times."

They then spoke among themselves of the manner in which the governor had surrounded himself with a degree of splendour previously unknown in the colony. The discussion then turned to the European planters, land owners, not a few being Englishmen,

137

some from the time of the Chacón administration of fifteen years past, who were also seeking to have Woodford's local laws revoked as the strictures being imposed with regard to land ownership and the inheritance of estates would also be applied to them. This was the first that I had heard of this. I wondered if they had sought an alliance with these planters.

"They, the white planters, would have nothing to do with us. They see us as a mongrel race," said Fabien with a frown, and regarding me closely added, "You have not received a commission in the militia, have you, Dr. Philip?"

I admitted that I had not, but I did not want the conversation to become mired in a round of complaint and recrimination. I wanted to know more about the free coloured class, their feelings, what gave them a sense of self-esteem, what in their minds defined them, made them take courage in the face of what was plainly a highly organised attempt to diminish their resolve.

"A thing that Woodford has done that has really affected the young men is forbidding their holding commissions in the militia," Hobson said. "In Governor Chacón's time, several held commissions. When Colonel Picton assumed command, he dismissed all of them. Some were given non-commissioned status, becoming sergeants and corporals, the others were reduced to the ranks."

"To hold a commission, to be an officer," added Fabien, "is to be respected. Woodford does not want us to be respected. Peletan de Carriès, when they broke him to the ranks and later when he lost his estate, committed suicide. His grandfather was a count in France. He had been educated there at a military academy, where he was treated as a white man."

"Perhaps he should have stayed over there," I mumbled to myself.

I had come to understand that amongst the free coloureds were the children and grandchildren of French aristocrats. Some were wealthy and fair-complexioned, others were darker or poorer, but all believed that they deserved a special respect from anyone who did not have a count or a marquis somewhere in their family tree. Amongst themselves, when they addressed each other in writing, they employed the term "esquire". The governor put a stop to that. Privately, I thought them vain and showy with many of them living beyond their means. I wondered about this and spoke of my half-brother Michel, who had recently adopted the Philip name, giving up Maxwell, upon being manumitted by father.

"He has married a descendant of a French artistocrat, I have been told," I said, "and in a previous generation there was a relation of ours who was connected to the Empress Josephine in some mysterious way!"

Hobson said, "Those who are connected by blood to the French nobility and appear European, with their fair complexions and proper manners, are especially shunned by the French aristocrats here, to whom they are in many instances related. There are a few exceptions. As in your half-brother Michel's wife's instance, the Lefer family's white relatives, her father and uncles, have always taken an interest in her and through them, others have extended a helping hand to Michel. Perhaps because your people were helpful to her father during his business reversals.

"Then there are the ordinary Europeans. As Jean Congnet said, these whites, crofters' sons and children of the slums of London or Glasgow, are prompted by Woodford's instituting of official racial prejudice to assume a superior attitude soon after their arrival here in Trinidad and proceed to lord it over us all. We are not granted the courtesy of using the term 'esquire' or being addressed as 'mister' by any white person, even the likes of them. Now I hear that it is being passed into law that we must carry a lighted lantern at night so as to be recognised by the police or any white man."

That the conversation should be returning to this rebuke, one that I had heard several times over, was making it plain to me that these well-off men of colour, owners of slaves and plantations, wanted not only to be *protected* by the law, but also to be *recognised* as part of the colony's polite society and accepted as gentlemen by

English gentlemen so as to distinguish themselves from the lower classes, both European and free coloured and black. An ideal so well expressed in Milton's *Paradise Lost*:

> *"And if not equal all, yet free,*
> *Equally free; for orders and degrees*
> *Jar not with liberty, but well consist."*

Plainly, the political and social aspirations of the free coloureds who possessed wealth and status were increasing, even as the Woodford administration was treating them even worse than the previous English governors. Their notion that they should be seen as gentlemen, and hold commissions in the militia, had been based solely on the Spanish governor's generous interpretation of the Cedula of Population, on their possessing wealth and, more recently, on their being au courant with certain European social graces.

Having experienced disgrace myself at the hand of Governor Woodford, I felt sympathy for these men. They were ignorant of the fact that from time immemorial in England and on the continent, there were two qualitative terms, "gentle" and "simple", which were applied to the upper and lower rungs of society respectively. I recalled from Vincent's Latin tutelage that the word "gentle" was derived from the Latin *gens,* that is, *gentilis,* meaning belonging to the same family or caste. This meant that a person or a family was known to be as such, and to be known, which in old French was pronounced *noble,* from Latin *nobilis,* meant being accepted in that caste or that extended family, hence the notion of being "of noble birth". Everyone else, no matter their wealth, calling or profession, were merely the simple folk, that is to say, the commoners.

The free coloureds here in Trinidad had no understanding of the rigidity of rank. Vincent, in his unflagging attempt to have me leave behind what he called my "native creolised French accent", made me recite from Blackstone's *Commentaries on the Laws of England*. In that tome it was made clear that the rank of gentleman comprised

28. And If Not Equal All, Yet Free

the younger sons of the younger sons of peers, and the younger sons of a baronet, a knight, and an esquire, in perpetual succession.

As such, the connotation of the term "gentleman" captures the common denominator of *gentilis,* gentility, and often came with a coat of arms, indicating the ownership of property, a right shared by the peerage and the gentry, the constituent classes of the British nobility.

These men, here in Trinidad, had no idea that gentlemen were born into the gentry, their people having been made *noble,* having become "known" at some point in the past by Letters Patent issued by the monarch. They, or ordinary Englishmen, for that matter, could not necessarily become gentlemen by simply being wealthy slave owners with large plantations in the West Indies or, as in their case, by having lighter complexions and nice manners, or even by acquiring European wives. Their wanting to be called "mister", and to be received at Government House and be recognised as officers and gentlemen, was against everything that the class of people to which Sir Ralph aspired stood for. To allow such a thing would be to diminish his own recently attained status. For Woodford, the idea of a black or coloured man being both an officer and a gentleman was a contradiction in terms. That a man of colour could be gilded with epaulets and carry a sword was preposterous. Swords from time immemorial were for the knightly class, who were from birth gentlemen. I personally tended to take the view that the appellation of gentleman is never to be affixed to a man's circumstances, but to his behaviour in them.

In any event, being merely a baronet, Sir Ralph was at the lowest rank of the peerage. His connection to the peerage of England, as I was able to gather from Vincent's correspondence, was that a relative in a previous generation had married a daughter of the 3rd Duke of Gordon. The Woodford baronetcy was rather freshly hatched. It was created on 28 July 1791 for his father, Ralph Woodford, a former ambassador to Denmark. Sir Ralph's mother was a "simple" Dutch person, one Gertrude Reessen.

My impression of Sir Ralph was that he was first a parvenu who felt the need to give structure to the island's society so as to preserve his own distinction, and by structure he meant only in the context of contemporary English society and selected individuals from the French community. It had already crossed my mind that the governor could be afflicted by some undefined mental disorder.

I was told by mother that Europeans often fell victim to colonial customs and habits. I felt certain that Woodford had not been a racially prejudiced person before his arrival in Trinidad. However, he soon became a victim of the all-engulfing vileness and the criminal manner in which race prejudice was embedded in the society, reinforced by the French Créoles, several of whom were married to the children of St. Hilaire Begorrat. Like the vampire in Byron's *The Giaour,* they shall suck the blood of all our race.

I asked Hobson if I could have the list of names that formed the petition that had been presented to the English government. As a student of the science of psychiatry, I felt compelled to gain an understanding of the true nature of their complaints and importantly of the effect on their mental states that Sir Ralph and his creatures were causing. I wanted to interview them. I had in mind to accumulate and to organise, in an scientific manner, the evidence of this alienation that so obviously contravened the law, and to write a paper on the subject. There was no objection to my taking away the list, everyone agreed, and after some discussion of a general nature, we were called to luncheon.

29. Who Loves, Raves

"She walks in beauty, like the night
Of cloudless climes and starry skies;
And all that's best of dark and bright
Meet in her aspect and her eyes."

George Gordon Lord Byron

WE MET THEM IN THEIR CANE FIELDS AND IN THEIR HOMES.

TRINIDAD 1820: IN MAY OF THAT YEAR, INFORMATION WAS RECEIVED that runaway Negroes had joined together and formed a camp in a distant part of the island. It was determined to surprise them, and a detachment was ordered out for that purpose. Fearful that some mishap might occur, Mr. Mitchell, the Commandant, resolved that a medical man should accompany the expedition. Both North and South Naparima had white surgeons attached to their corps and in common justice, one or the other of them should have received notification to accompany the detachment.

Whether they represented to Mr. Mitchell how detrimental that could prove to their practice, or what injury they might experience

All who held commissions were reduced to the ranks.

29. Who Loves, Raves

in point of health, it was immaterial to know; but he had the injustice to order me by letter, the only coloured practitioner in South Naparima, to accompany the detachment on its march from Savanna Grande in my medical capacity; this, although I was enrolled as a private in the militia.

I was not taken by surprise at this command and because I had been on exhausting route marches before I had prepared myself for this one, both mentally and physically. First, a stout pair of boots and a change of clothes was packed. I had with me food, what is called *pasteles* by the Spanish peons, this was meat, well seasoned, cooked in cornmeal and wrapped in plantain leaves. These were good for a day or two. I had as well ground coffee, some bread and of course tasso, meat that had been smoked, spiced, and cured. Together with a small skin of wine, I hoped these would be sufficient comforts to see me through what was going to be a gruelling time in the bush.

The quarter's militia company was already in formation when I rode into the compound on the Mitchell estate. Anticipating rebuke, I tethered my mount and, shouldering my home-made portable medical kit, fell in among the smelly black and mixed-race men who comprised the majority of the company.

"I see Philip has finally seen fit to join us. Step forward, Philip. Attention!" Assuming a military air, I stepped forward and stood to attention.

"Look well at him. He pretends to a medical degree. Claims to have seen the world. Poses as a gentleman! What you say we put him to the test?" All this was bellowed by a burly grocer's clerk, in the uniform of a lieutenant, in an accent that I recognised as what is called Cockney. Spitalfields perhaps, or I would hazard Shoreditch in east London, even.

I could hear chuckles coming from the mounted officers and a shuffling of feet in the ranks. After several such remarks, too boring to recount, we started off. The expedition, I gathered, would take us along the Mission Road south and then eastward towards the border of the vast forest in which it was reported the band of escaped slaves had marooned themselves.

As it turned out, it was a pointless affair. The Negroes had decamped long before our arrival to make their way through the forest to the east coast of the island.

IN THE MONTHS AHEAD I MADE AN EFFORT NOT TO PLACE excessive emphasis on my own moods, attitudes and state of mind. Instead, I paid close attention to what the people in the area had to say and what they felt about such outrages, and I took copious notes.

By that time I had come to understand that, as sometimes happens to those who do serious study of a scientific nature, I had become, in a manner of speaking, "colonised" by my doctoral thesis, which was on the study of the human mind. I couldn't help being obsessed, for here in Trinidad was the perfect opportunity for a case study. More than two thirds of the free population, itself a society in formation, that had arrived here with every hope and wish for peace and prosperity, were being made an alien nation in a land to which they had been invited. Once taken over by another power, they were subjected to a governor hell-bent on alienating them not only from their legal rights, but also from the other segments of the free society. The method he employed was the systemic reduction of their self-worth.

Over time, I discovered that the majority of the French-speaking, free black and coloured people lived in Port of Spain, and were by and large owners of almost all the small lots and ramshackle town properties. These townsfolk numbered in the vicinity of perhaps six or eight thousand. Of those, not a few were idle and vagrant. A handful were well off, while many were modest but productive and earned a living as craftsmen: shoemakers, carpenters, blacksmiths, coopers. Some were brothel keepers, stick fighters,

29. WHO LOVES, RAVES

cockfight aficionados—that sort of thing. Almost all owned two or three slaves. Almost all were illiterate, and had no idea from whom they came. If there was a feeling of estrangement as a result of English rule in my family and among their friends, there was also a flame of rebellion lingering in the minds of those who lived "beyond the diameter" or sphere of polite society. Some of these even called themselves *diamètres* which, when pronounced in the Patois, sounded like *jamet*.

As for the very poor free mulattoes, they squatted in the hillsides that surrounded the town, some worse off than the abandoned slaves. Not a few cohabited with slave women simply to obtain subsistence. Others lived in the interior, in the mountains, eking out a desperate life, hunting and fishing, near naked figures, some diseased, perhaps leprous, or ill with ringworm or diabetes. They stank, with matted hair and overgrown beards.

In the Naparimas, north and south, a distinct sense of community had been formed among the plantation owners. They were second only to the French Créoles, the "big whites", as my father referred to them, when it came to wealth and to style. That there should be in Trinidad a veritable aristocracy of skin was utterly ludicrous to me. As long as the difference in skin colour was used to distract us from the relentless pursuit of liberty for everyone before the law, we would be forever a deformed society.

The notion of self-esteem, to value and think well of oneself, is of immense importance to all men, because it serves a motivational function that enables people to explore their full potential. What was being endured by les gens de couleur was plainly a grievous miscarriage of natural justice that in the long term would have a deleterious effect on us all.

Free men of colour were being deprived of their defining roles as men, both in their personal lives and in how they functioned in the wider society. They—including myself—were virtually enslaved to a system that did everything in its power to diminish all notions of self-worth. The Europeans here in Trinidad, the English, French

147

and other foreigners, were obviously doing all in their power to demonstrate, physically and mentally, that we, as a people, were of no value whatever.

Divesting one segment of the society of its most human characteristics will be the cause of us becoming strangers to each other. This is obvious in the self-deprecation and lack of ambition that is passed off as a sad joke, or even worse as a self-fulfilling prophecy. Failures of every sort imaginable have come to pass because the free, mixed-race people *believe* that they cannot succeed at anything. In conversations with those from the Naparimas who have an understanding of the situation, I gathered that we numbered in 1820 some thirteen thousand taken all together, the majority of them Patois or French-speaking, as compared to the European population that amounted to hardly more than three thousand, the French people being in the majority. If this sense of self-deprecation is allowed to continue, the accumulative effect, over time, will be disastrous for this colony. No good will come of it if the majority of the free people of this place believe that they are worthless and good for nothing.

Among the wealthy coloured planter families and those with a claim to nobility were several marriages during the first year of my return. In every case a special license had to be granted by Mitchell, the Commandant of the Quarter, costing some fifty dollars, because coloured folk were forbidden to hold a wedding celebration or give a ball without paying this sum and having his written consent.

I attended a marriage of a coloured Montrichard to an almost-white Angeron, and another when the free coloured Nolly Beaubrun married the equally free Sophie Fabien. These were all grand affairs, held on plantations where every effort was made to convey their aristocratic connections. At the sumptuous wedding reception of my sister Simone to Thomas Corsbie I came to know my cousin Susanne, my uncle Josèphe-Michel's eldest daughter. Dark-complexioned and older than I, there was about her, in her physiognomy, something that I recognised or remembered seeing

29. WHO LOVES, RAVES

somewhere before. Her eyes, a little aslant and clear, were frank, her smile showed her front teeth quite white and a little spaced. I was immediately attracted to her. She was dressed in a voluminous red silk petticoat over what may have been a black sateen shift, with a sort of gypsy blouse, and wore a high turban, black, with a white diagonal stripe. She was a full-bodied woman, perhaps as tall as I, who even in repose, as she sat amongst the others, had a dancer's grace, like a ballerina waiting for her cue. She appeared, because of her costume, to be a person from a previous time and seemed disconnected, removed, quite separate from the noise, the frivolity, indeed the shared lightheartedness of what was a joyous family occasion.

As the gaiety swirled in noisy commotion, and Thomas Corsbie, the bridegroom, was attempting to make a toast against the noise of an excruciating string quartet that screeched and scratched out an indeterminable melody and the waltzers twirled, I watched Susanne closely. She sat at the far end of the head table and I could not help noticing how several of the wedding guests approached her with respectful deference. Mother told me that she had returned from Carriacou some time ago, where she had lived for almost as long as I had been abroad. Everyone said that she, Susanne, who is close to aunt Judith, had returned to Trinidad to save us.

She had been aunt Judith's right hand on the family's estates on Carriacou and was once the chief overseer of our holdings on Petite Martinique. Susanne had also bought in her and in her brother Louis' name a half share in the Champ Fleurs plantation from uncle Josèphe-Michel and purchased, also in both their names, a half share in Philippine from us, all with money that came from aunt Judith, and she has made a success of these investments. She commands in excess of one hundred and seventy slaves and several hundred acres, all under cultivation. There is no wild bush or forest standing on any of our plantations.

It was quite dark, the fairy-lights in the branches of the great spreading trees were casting a rosy glow upon the company who had already dined and drank to a hundred toasts and were now settled into noisy groups and cosy couples around the tables scattered on the lawn, when I approached her.

"You had to wait until it was night to hide your true intentions, eh?" she said in Patois.

Somewhat surprised I replied in French, "Well, I dare say there is a modicum of truth to that." I had to laugh. In truth, I could feel the blush as it rose past my eyes.

"You think you 'fraid me. I wouldn't be surprised."

"What is there to be afraid of? You are my first cousin," I said, moving about to stand in such a manner that the lantern lights would illuminate her and hide my confusion.

"That I might take you 'way and not bring you back like a La Diablesse."

"My word! What a thought! Do you have such powers?"

"You have to sleep with fowls to know if they snore."

I found that I was holding her hand. I couldn't recall taking it. It was a hard hand, rough, like a labourer's. Her voice, there was a timbre to it, not deep but enriching the quality, the value of what she was saying. What was she saying?

"Come, let us sit down over there. Sit down here, with your back to them, so they don't see you and come and bother me."

I followed her to sit in the shadows at a small, candle-lit iron table on the edge of the lawn. It was laid for two.

"You like curaçao?" she asked. "Here, take some."

I hadn't noticed the bottle, small, brown and oval in the middle of an old tarnished silver tray. There were some shot glasses there. I had heard of this potent mix of spirits, a heady liqueur flavoured with bitter orange peel.

"Here, fire one!"

We fired several in quick succession. My word, what a strange woman.

29. Who Loves, Raves

"You're thinking I strange. You never meet anybody like me yet?"

"Well, no. I find you are, well, quite sensational."

"Yes I am. Look here, I watching you too. I think we should start something. You want to sleep with me?"

"To see if you snore?"

"I could snore. You?"

"I have no idea."

"You ever sleep with a black woman?"

"No, I have never."

"But you not a virgin, eh? You look sly, you only watching, watching. What you watching?"

"I have an interest in people."

"Well, come and watch me."

We left the wedding party and walked slowly in the clear milk-white moonlight hand in hand, down and away through the shadows towards where I could make out a horse. It was tethered to the main gate. Without a word she was in the saddle.

"Come, get up behind me. Hold on good eh?"

And we were away. I held her by the waist as the beast took the road, its hoofs pounding, the wind in my ears.

"Hold this," she cried over her shoulder, as her turban left her head and her full shock of hair became loose to fly about my face in the rushing wind. The night became pitch black, as the stallion bounded through a criss-cross of cane breaks. It was like entering a labyrinth, or a giant maze. It appeared, as if by some magic, that time and distance had folded upon themselves, because it seemed to me it was in moments that we were through the gates of Philippine and before us the great house loomed.

There were no lights to be seen and no one came to take the steaming horse. From somewhere close came a haunting cry that

I remembered so well. "You were here before," she said, "the memories that you took away with you have left a stain. They were worthless. She was the wrong cousin, come, there is nothing to the call of the jumbie bird that you need to be afraid of. It's only a stupid owl and I have had that calabash tree cut down."

My word, how could she have known? I followed her, as if in a trance, up the front steps and into the deserted hall that the half-finished moon was illuminating darkly, and along a corridor of many doors. It appeared an endless procession of doorways. It must be the curaçao, I thought, as we passed between a velvet drape, and there before me was the legendary bed with its elaborately carved headboard and four magnificently turned bedposts, a trophy from a previous time. Without haste in the slanting light but with a rising passion we kissed. Her mouth tasted of something that reminded me of a pistachio-flavoured delicacy from long ago, or perhaps it was not my memory at all, but hers.

With trembling hands I removed the red and black that covered her, she wore nothing beneath, my own clothes had somehow already fallen away. I could feel her heat and smell the passion on her breath. Her eyes were shut but I knew that she could see me in the astral light that shone about us. I entered her even as she clung to the great spiral bedpost and groaned. We made love all through that night and with the dawn pale but coming on, I lay beside her, the delicious agitation of the nerves spent, and I elated yet not a little confused. Was this a sin, an act that was an abomination on a biblical scale? It has to be a secret, surely. Mother must never know. No one must ever know. I left Philippine on the borrowed stallion whose name I was to learn was Toné (Thunder in Patois), with the strongly flavoured sentiments of a half forgotten dream, echoing a mad confusion of words that came from Virgil's *Aeneid* as if in beat with the stallion's hooves:

> *Do the gods light this fire in our hearts*
> *or does each man's mad desire become his god?"*

29. WHO LOVES, RAVES

I guided the animal through the rustling, sunlit cane breaks, overwhelmed by this sensation. Why was I reciting Vincent's Latin tutelage? Did I dream of Dido and Aeneas because I had made love to my first cousin? Will she be fated to kill herself, as Dido did? What an alarming association of ideas. Altogether what a strange woman! On the one hand she certainly was a commanding figure, possessed of a superior type of confidence that one finds in men who are in charge of affairs. On the other, there was her sensuality, her femininity in the act of love, so beautiful, the eroticism that she evoked quite maddening, so compelling. I had felt as if this lovemaking must never stop, and it lasted all through the night and even into the dawn. As she lay across the great bed, she appeared to become even more alarmingly beautiful. I felt drained, weary as if I had been engaged in some Herculean feat of mythic proportion. Her last words to me before turning over and pulling the sheet over her head were: "Don't think that this will become a habit or that we are going to become secret lovers, or anything of the kind. I just wanted to know what kind of a man you are."

"And, what have you discovered?"

"You are conceited and immoral. And brave, perhaps. You like women and you have some experience. I like you. You smell nice and you are well made."

In a curious way, I straightaway felt absolved from all responsibility for my personal feelings. I suppose being brought up a Presbyterian, I did not have the same highly developed sense of sin that haunts the conscience of all Catholics when it comes to sex. I have had very little exchange so far with free black women. Those who are mixed and of French or Spanish heritage, I have found pleasing. They affect an air of confidence, even as they pretend to be disdainful. The wealthier ones have a style, sensual and playful, perhaps even innocent, possibly deceitful, but charmingly so. Not so cousin Susanne. She was different, most individualistic, but then I have come to understand that the women of my family all appear to be somewhat singular.

It was not until April of 1822 that a detachment of more than one hundred militiamen, commanded by a Captain Taylor, came upon the main maroon encampment. Storming the flat-top mountain Tamana, the militia, upon receiving fire, shot three blacks and captured twenty-three others. Moving eastward towards Manzanilla, another band of runaway slaves were encountered and engaged, leaving several dead and many more to be returned to servitude.

The counter currents of resistance by the slaves and by the subversive element which had planted its revolutionary roots during the Spanish governor's time and which, according to my brother André, blossomed under the stewardship of the first English governor, Colonel Picton, continue to radically characterise the culture of this small, hardly populated place.

Now, with Governor Woodford, a new element is being added: the shaming of a community because they are biracial, mixed black and white. In the mind of Woodford, an abhorrent, detestable people are in the majority here.

My word, what sort of society was in formation in Trinidad? What could possibly be its future?

30. Wild and Wonderful

*"There is a pleasure in the pathless woods, There is a rapture on the lonely shore,
There is society where none intrudes, By the deep Sea, and music in its roar:
I love not Man the less, but Nature more."*

George Gordon Lord Byron

Enormous vegetable cables, thick and unbelievably entangled

Philippine 1821: The yellow glow of tall wax candles in our old-fashioned Spanish candelabra shone softly upon the white napery of the dining table, sparkled among the slender stems of half-empty wine glasses while making wavering reflections on the heavy, old-fashioned cutlery, elegant entree dishes and massive gravy bowls. It would appear that this evening we were dining off of the family's heirlooms. Michel Maxwell Philip was saying: "Had you told me that you were laying out your antiques, I would have brought along the silver plates that our father gave to my mother." I had never seen those solid silver dining plates but was not surprised because fabulous objects, at times of considerable value, were passed about in the family as gifts, casually given at birthdays, christenings or at weddings.

"Before people like us and the others came, Trinidad was empty, a place in waiting," said Susanne, signalling to the domestic to serve the steaming bowls of chocolate with a sprinkling of grated nutmeg. This was considered a digestive, enjoyed with brandy. "I brought the nutmeg with me from Grenada," she said solemnly, as if it were myrrh or frankincense that she was speaking of. "You'll like it, Jean, it is good for your bad digestion."

"Is it? Thank you. Ah, it is delicious, exquisite," I answered, taking a careful sip after inhaling its fragrant aroma.

"Because of the Cedula, in the space of ten or fifteen years the foundations for a population were laid," added Michel, smacking his lips. "Our parents, along with many of their friends, came here in the 1780s, together with the Grenadian French people, who all arrived with Créole slaves aplenty, first from their own estates, then when those were dead, they brought in the Africans."

"Who are preserving important aspects of their traditions," I said, taking another sip of the delightful brew. "I met such a one, a Mohammedan, Jonas Bath was his name, a striking personality."

"A prince or a sheik or something, I hear," said Michel. "Woodford has made him a magistrate for his people. Imagine that?"

"Yes, quite. But Michel, father said that when it came to opening up our lands, we did the reverse of what the French planters were doing," I said, adding, "He told me that he and aunt Susannah bought new slaves at Fort St. Andres in Port of Spain. Only *after* the land had been cleared of the high forest and ready for planting did they bring in our people from Gran'Anse."

"By that time all the African slaves were dead. We do not deserve those memories at all," interjected Susanne, suddenly rising to stand behind the chair in which she had been sitting. "They should pass through the prism of time to children not even born yet." The candles, I noticed, were lighting her mysteriously. "Our blood, yours, his, mine, like the silver laid out on this table, is haunted by dark memories. The past is quite alive in the forest of all our minds. It is not even past. Look at the two of you, and me. We are prisoners of devices which were in place before we were born. We are trapped... trapped in a past that, if it had a future, it would be a dead end."

She appeared to be reaching inside of herself for something abstruse, finally adding with a toss of her head, "Yet we speak ambiguously through them. His mother," she said, pointing at Michel, I understood that she was referring to Cécile, "brought me up to be the woman you see me here today. She was a slave, he was a slave, just last year he was a slave. Our grandparents were slaves. People owned them. Now we own slaves... what kind of destiny do we create for ourselves, for them?"

Saying nothing I regarded her more closely, realising that her words may not have been actually addressed to either of us but were more a conversation that she was having with herself.

She was dressed that night all in white with large, gold, oval-shaped earrings that glowed in the candlelight, illuminating her dark beauty. A high lace collar framed her sharp features to black and white. She wore her hair piled untidily on top of her head and had several gold rings, embedded with gemstones, flashing on almost every finger. I glimpsed some thick gold chains made of irregular nuggets half hidden in the lace of her blouse, and her heavy golden bracelets could be seen through the lace of its tight-fitting cuffs. All this gold produced a nimbus-like quality that seemed to vibrate and glow darkly about her. Seeing me admiring her, she said softly in another voice, "Put that out of your mind, cousin. What you think you are looking at is not for you tonight."

"What do you see for him?" asked Michel.

"If I were to tell you what I see, you would start crying for him from now."

I couldn't get over the thought that in this island so full of lovely women, it was she whom I desired. I then remembered reading somewhere that the aetiologies of love and madness were identical, except in degree.

I heard Michel saying, "Of course, for us it was less land." His Patois that night was more nuanced, more French-sounding, while hers was broader than usual. Typically, the way she spoke often lacked the pleasing, lilting inflections that one hears in Trinidad. Neither of them spoke French well, in truth very few free coloureds of their generation did.

"And with the conquest in '97, the English arrived, along with a lot of very rowdy Scotsmen," I added, wanting to distract myself.

"I see Hessian apprentices now become merchants, setting up shop in Port of Spain," he continued. "And Corsicans too, who I think are all vagabonds."

"Irish peasants as well," I added. "I understand that they are invited, and someone told me even Chinese are here. I suspect that Woodford, with the contrivance of the planters, may be thinking of bringing in these people as a counterbalance to us." This was when I noticed that she was wearing a strange pendant on a longer chain, much longer than those made with the irregular gold nuggets. I couldn't help wondering if Michel knew about Susanne and I.

"That's possible, but interestingly, there are a lot of people here from Venezuela," he said, adding, "New World Créoles who were actively involved in fomenting a revolution to overthrow the Spanish Crown, over there, in South America."

"This is a place where every extreme of race and class could meet, have intercourse, marry or not, where destinies originating from anywhere on this earth could intersect." She glanced towards a shadowed corner. "How much of all this do you want to know, Jean, how much do you really care to know? You're not even really from here."

I didn't answer. Michel, perhaps sensing that she would speak of my isolation or even of my loneliness, was saying, "Plainly, there is no society here or a single culture, merely segments. The French

Créoles maintain an aristocratic tradition and marry, quite rightly, only among their kind."

"White women see to that," she said, sucking her teeth.

"We coloureds merely mirror them in a ludicrous way. Oh, I have come to understand that there is a literary circle in Port of Spain that revolves around an English Jew by the name of Joseph. After that, nothing surprises me anymore." He feigned indifference.

"Everyone tells me that Trinidad is so different from Barbados," I added, wanting to encourage to them speak more generally. "They call it 'little England'. There are only local whites there now I hear, the children of the original masters and the servant class, the itinerant ordinary English people having left. And of course the inevitable blacks."

"They don't have a lot of mixed-race people over there," said Michel. He had never been 'over there', but, like so many things in Trinidad, it was common knowledge. Susanne was to the point when she implied that it was the white French Créole women who saw the very existence of mixed-race people as a living reproach to the morals of their sons and brothers, husbands and fathers, and a threat to the stability of white family life.

"Their hate is mostly directed at the red-skinned woman who is perceived as sprung from the couch of corruption. White women decide who can pass and who cannot pass. You could never pass, Jean, you too dark. And on top of that, you sound like a Scotsman, more confusion in their heads." She laughed derisively, the candlelight picking up the highlights of her face and flashing jewelry. Pointing at Michel, she said to me: "Your brother here is even darker than you, but he has white friends. He can't pass, but he is in with them. Ask him, he can tell you a lot of what is going on in official circles."

She helped herself generously from the brandy decanter and settled back in her chair as if expecting Michel to hold forth on his connections to the important people with whom he had formed acquaintances, she smiled, I thought derisively.

As he seemed to gather his thoughts, I noticed that what I had taken to be a pendant of some sort was actually an amulet, small, dark and carved. It seemed to be perhaps African, and as primordial as the objects on display at the museum in Leiden. She held it between her thumb and finger, and tilting it towards the candlelight, looked at it closely, then she glanced at me. Her face was as still as a mask, her slanting eyes a sightless stare that strangely suited her. I had to think of Pliny's *Natural History* where amulets are described as objects that protect a person from the evil eye.

"I know how to behave around them, Jean," Michel eventually said with an unapologetic grin. "I know that I am not in any position to pretend to be on familiar terms with these people. I accept their superior attitude and at times their stupid behaviour, even their bad remarks. But when, for instance, we talk estate business or meet to discuss an expedition into the high woods, well, that's a different matter. You see, out in the forest, on an extended hunting trip, all differences vanish. Like the time when we went into an area called Bush-Bush to find a maroon camp, that was dangerous, every man becomes his brother's keeper. Folks like the Garcias, and I have met some of their friends, see themselves as true Trinidadians. The English people, who come and go, see England as home, but Jean, these local whites, French or Spanish, they have no home over there anymore. Trinidad is home to them. That is what I have in common with them.

"As far as the women of these families are concerned, in private I am well treated, like a favourite servant who has grown up in the family. I take those roles as they come. My wife Catherine is the half sister of Olympe Lefer. They are not strangers to each other, Catherine looked after her when she was a child. The Lefers love her. When Catherine's father, Louis-Christopher Lefer, was in financial difficulties, I helped him as best I could. They didn't want me for her, but they were glad for the money. In public, I am never familiar. All of that does not bother me, as I prefer their company, Jean. Intelligent conversations about the world and history. The coloured people have nothing to offer me. I cannot stand the endless round of stupid talk, the complaints, fault-finding and the depressing hopelessness."

"What he not telling you is that in private he has his way with the hypocrites, eh, tell him about the Spanish woman!" Which of course he did not. He had assumed the Philip name, becoming Michel Maxwell Philip, when father manumitted him, his brother and Cécile last year. He was presently the manager at Cupar Grange estate, and he conducted himself as such.

My earliest impression of Michel was that he was of the sort who yearns to be invited to ride to hounds. In truth, he was simply possessed of bien-séance, nice manners. He was a tall man, dark-skinned, quite slim, with fine European features. He carried himself well, dressed elegantly, had "good hair" or, as they say here, "good grass". He was certainly cleaner than most men I had met here, and, best of all, he exuded a relaxed, unobtrusive confidence. I noticed, while in his company, that he showed consideration for others and generally kept things light and on an even keel. He was surprisingly well read. Mother described him as a charmer, going on to say that as a planter his only success lay with his handling of labour. Father thought that he reminded him of an older brother, Nicolas-Régis, who died as a young man.

Like myself and mother, Michel benefitted from being taught to read and write English by Mr. Newbold, who brought him to the attention of James Anderson, a Scottish doctor, the proprietor of Cupar Grange estate. Mother said that because Michel got the slaves there to work hard for him, Dr. Anderson was grateful. The price of sugar being high, the doctor was able to keep his sons Henry and Alexander at school in England. In return, Anderson helped defray the cost of educating Michel's son Samuel in Scotland. Dr. Anderson also took Michel into the company of families like the Garcias, Venezuelans who settled in Trinidad around the time of Woodford's arrival. Marrying Catherine Lefer, an almost white-appearing woman, whose father's people had not turned their backs on her, and who were closely connected to the Andersons, Durutys and the Garcias, Michel, now a Philip, was able to ease himself into a unique situation in the colony's white upper-class society. When I asked about his being in the white people's company, he simply shrugged.

As the conversation changed, I related that some weeks before, when going through father's papers and his small collection of books, I found Père Labat's *Nouveau voyage aux isles de l'Amérique*. On opening it, my eyes fell on a passage that described mulatto men in a most derogatory way, claiming that they were inherently immoral. I wanted to hear what they had to say to that.

"Yes, well, morality, rather like beauty, is largely in the imagination of the believer," Michel said with a dismissive laugh. "The superficial character of race prejudice is demonstrated by the amount of white men who have black mistresses."

"And white women who take black lovers in secret," said Susanne, looking meaningfully at Michel. "Is that why your father said that you reminded him of uncle Nicolas-Régis? I heard a story about his romantic attachment to a white woman, quite hopeless and sad. Anyway, it is in the bed that the proud tyrant's true character, his strengths and his weaknesses, are revealed." She smiled conspiratorially. "The irresistible fascination of the mulatresse gives the open lie to pretended hate. This is never mentioned in their polite society, but it is known." I could see that she did not want to discuss this further and wondered if she had been, or possibly was presently, the occasional lover of a white man, especially when she added as if offhandedly: "Having an outside woman eases up the wife, or so they say."

For the briefest of moments I struggled, caught in the stranglehold of an implacable spasm of jealousy.

"A whole new strain of half-breeds is in the making here in Trinidad. They are not like you, Jean, they don't want to change anything, they like it so," said Michel, sighing and taking a drink

30. WILD AND WONDERFUL

from the brandy glass that he was holding between his hands. "They like to be vex, up against everything, it makes them feel important. Their generation wouldn't want to be reduced to the same level as the blacks when emancipation happens. But, outside of that, they don't give a damn, all they want is to drink rum, fête and fornicate."

Remembering the words of Olaudah Equiano the African, I attempted to evoke a sense of compassion for the enslaved on the estates, reflecting on the macabre unreason of fate and circumstance. But there was no sympathy here and no question of any discussion concerning their eventual emancipation. I reiterated the views of Wilberforce and Buxton and some others, pointing out the obvious cruelty and the negative mental effect that slavery had on us all, especially those who enforced it. I even ventured to suggest that slavery in the Caribbean had been too narrowly identified with the blacks, as un-free labour in the New World was known to have been brown, white, black and presently even yellow, as well as Catholic, Protestant and pagan.

"Plainly," I said, "a racial twist has thereby been given to what is basically an economic phenomenon. Slavery was not born of racism, rather racism is the consequence of slavery." That was shrugged off with Susanne saying scornfully, "You, you see you, you really not from here!"

I knew what she meant, it was not the first time that she had said that. I have felt like an outsider. They had much the same attitude as André-Montrose and Belizaire, who were only concerned with maintaining the productivity of the estates. The same could be said for Louis, Susanne's brother, who was definitely of the generation that Michel spoke about. They all saw themselves as rich. In their opinion, yes, slavery will end but by that time 'we all will be out of it and the money will be there.' I wondered what my young brother, St. Luce, was like, as a person and as a medical doctor. He will be here with us, if all goes well for him, in the next few years.

Susanne must have read my thoughts as she said in a softer voice, "Do you think that he will follow in your footsteps, Jean, and be the kind of doctor who studies the heart and mind?"

"I don't know, the rigour of the work can take a person into fields of research where he feels challenged or just to where his imagination carries him. In my case it was my imagination that made me inquire into the workings of the mind. Your pendant, Susanne, is it a charm or a decoration?"

My saying this appeared to startle her. I held her gaze for a moment and then let my glance wander down to where this dark object was nestled between the white lace of her blouse. She reached for it and held it in her fist.

"Why do you want to know that, for what? This is not your business."

"I beg your pardon, Susanne, it is just that it caught my eye earlier and I wondered if it was an African charm of some sort."

"You got that in Carriacou, didn't you, Susanne? I remember aunt Marie remarking on it when you came back from aunt Judith's."

"Yes Michel, it is from Ti Guinée, but I don't want to discuss it with you and Jean, you all will pick it apart and reduce it to an absurdity."

She was clearly annoyed and I let the conversation fade into the silence of the candlelight until Michel asked:

"So, what are you going to do, Jean? What do you have in mind?"

"I go with Jean Congnet, beginning next week, to commence the interviewing of people who have signed the petition. I want to hear what they have to say about Woodford and his man, Mitchell. I want to gather evidence and to eventually write it all down."

The evening ended pleasantly enough with Susanne inviting me to ride with her on the morrow and Michel, assuming the discretion that came naturally to him, left us alone.

IF IT HAD NOT BEEN FOR MR. CONGNET, HIS SON JEAN AND MY FAMILY, I would have been in Trinidad much like an ignorant near-sighted stranger traversing a European city's inner life. Through them, I was able to glimpse some of the more salient features of this society while not losing sight of its finer shades, or perhaps perceiving them inaccurately through the prism of my own imperfect imagination.

What clearly came across was governor Woodford's intention, which was firstly the Anglicisation of the Spanish laws, beginning with the court system and the property laws. He would consign to the dustbin of history the Spanish Cedula, which specified for all colonists the terms of settlement as well as the Articles of Capitulation, which implicitly retained them, and which General Sir Ralph Abercromby, as the representative of the British Crown, had endorsed when he affixed his signature, thus plainly demonstrating the Crown's intention to maintain the status quo in Trinidad. In discussing them with many people, I learnt them by heart. Article IV of the Cedula stated that the free negroes and mulattoes who settled in Trinidad should have half the quantity of land granted to the whites, and their titles should be equally legal and granted in the same manner as to whites. Article XII of the Capitulation enshrined that the free coloured people should be protected in their liberty, persons and property like the white inhabitants.

But then there was Woodford's apparent commitment to creating a polarised society, white and black, without acknowledging the existence of a multiracial class of free people, which had come into existence in these Caribbean islands over the past three centuries.

As free people, whose settlement in Trinidad was defined in law, the "free mulattoes" as Lord Bathurst had referred to them, had developed a culture within the general society. They identified with each other on the basis of shared attributes that distinguished them from other groups in the colony. They possessed a common set of traditions, a shared religion, Catholicism, the French and Patois language, similar ancestry and a shared history of being free people, in some instances for three or four generations. Taken all together, this made them obviously different from the enslaved, many of whom had only recently arrived in Trinidad from Africa, and certainly from the English and from the other Europeans who, like many of the slaves, had only just come to this island.

Because there was a legal basis for their existence in Trinidad, and because they formed the majority of the free people of the colony, some twelve thousand four hundred and eighty in 1819, far outnumbering the Europeans who amounted to three thousand seven hundred, they had a legal and moral right to differentiate themselves, not only from those who were still in bondage, approximately twenty three thousand four hundred, but also from those who had been endowed with authority and were seeking to demean them.

As a trained professional, an alienist and a medical doctor, I intended to expose the nature of the organised disenfranchisement of the free mulattoes of Trinidad and their emotional experiences. I wished to convey a vivid sense of the unseen or dimly seen— vivid, yet fitful, and characterised by darkness, the darkness of the psychological and sexual complexities created by the established convention of race prejudice.

I decided to make a record of all this, starting here in the Naparimas. There were thirty-eight free coloured planter families in the Naparimas; ten in North Naparima and twenty-eight in the South. Of these thirty-eight proprietors, seventeen owned sugar estates, the other estates comprised a variety of coffee, cocoa and ground provision plantations. A few of the sugar estates were like our own, large, with fifty or more slaves, the majority of the others were modest, with ten or twelve slaves. The total number of slaves on those estates amounted to approximately nine hundred. In the entire Naparimas there were ninety-one estates and two thousand eight hundred and fifty or sixty slaves. The free coloured planters in the Naparimas possessed about thirty-five percent of the estates and about thirty percent of the slaves.

Susanne and mother, together with Frédéric Maxwell, were very successful as sugar planters. We had no problems with our labour and no indebtedness, being able, as we had always done, to finance

30. Wild and Wonderful

ourselves in the purchase of modern machinery and new blacks as the need arose. The estates, Concorde and Philippine, had also benefitted by having Thomas Corsbie, my sister Simone's husband, join us as chief overseer. In addition to this, the price of sugar, they assured me, had risen steadily since 1812. All this placed me in a position of financial independence that allowed me the time to conduct the planned field research.

THIS EXERCISE, WHICH WAS TO OCCUPY CONGNET AND ME for close to a year and a half, took us to the towns of Port of Spain, San Fernando and even to the sparsely populated, crumbling, former capital of the island, San José de Oruña. We would try to visit every person of mixed race who had signed the petition and those who hadn't, to eventually travel to the remotest regions of the island, where nature was amazingly beautiful, delightfully surprising and at times hideously raw.

We met them, the free mulattoes, in their homes, in their cane fields and on two occasions at sea. The men were sometimes taciturn, the women certainly voluble. Some were defiant, others resigned, mostly they were fatalistic. All had incidents to relate, experiences of physical cruelty, humiliation, embarrassment, and of being brought low before their wives and sons. There was anger, too, and thoughts of violence and dreams of revenge. For those who were property owners, there was the fear of losing their lands, and for others who did not have their manumission documents or those of their parents, there was the terror of being reduced to slavery and sold at public auction.

"I am beginning to believe that the governor is a threat to the whole of society," I was saying to Jean Congnet. "His mind is a mixture of concepts, dangerous and seemingly evil."

"You believe that there is evidence of a serious mental illness there?" he asked, we were guiding our mounts along the footpath called the Royal Road that had taken us away from San Fernando and would lead eventually to Siparia, where the Capuchin Order had established a mission to the Indians almost a century before.

"So it would seem, certainly from our point of view," I replied, becoming somewhat distracted, as having passed a wooden fence and a barred gate, we were entering a thick brushwood, difficult but not yet formidable.

This would be our final excursion into the interior. The journey took us southwards and through the eastern extremity of the Oropouche lagoon, where several free black families had established homesteads in a remote part of the island.

Within half an hour of leaving San Fernando we were in deep and solemn woods, with very high trees closing in upon us on all sides. I felt, as I always did when entering the high forest, awestruck by the terrific grandeur of nature—trying in vain to describe the indescribable.

Overhead, where the trees stood so tall and straight that one quailed to look aloft, the breezy forest cover was as a vast roof that admitted shafts of hot sunlight through which the forest creatures moved and flew. There were troops of monkeys chattering, and an unimaginable quantity of parrots and other exotic birds maintained a noisy cacophony. We had been told that there were ocelots, small tiger cats, and enormous boa-constrictors, some more that twenty feet in length, but were assured that they shunned the path and hid themselves in the deepest recesses of the gloomy forest. Congnet was particularly afraid of the giant constrictors, as there were stories of them falling from a height upon travellers, swiftly entangling them, choking their breath, then swallowing them whole.

Suddenly, at high noon, from everywhere came a profusion of enormous blue butterflies. They flew leisurely along with us, even as orchids, fleshy and variously coloured, sprang from mossy banks that exuded a dank and musty odour. Beautifully brilliant hummingbirds appeared, some to hover with an inquisitive eye regarding me. I could not help thinking that this must be what

30. WILD AND WONDERFUL

paradise, the imagined garden of Eden, would have looked like at the beginning of the world.

"From various people I understand that the governor is all about progress," I said, glancing over my shoulder to see how he was managing, while carefully guiding my somewhat elderly mule along the path that was criss-crossed by a web of the twisted roots lying bare upon the soil. "In private life he is all grace, charm and warmth, but from one moment to another, a perversion of the moral faculties emerges, and he becomes harsh, arrogant, domineering and capable of despicable acts. I hear from my cousin Michel that he is leaving for England soon. If I were to hazard a guess on his mental condition, I would say that here was a form of moral insanity."

There were now trees of monumental growth about us, with trunks of perhaps ten or more feet in diameter, whose buttress roots were higher than a man on horseback. Many of these were covered with a perfect mantle of mosses. Enormous vegetable cables hung down from the lofty heights, unbelievably entangled, so intricately woven that it made leaving the narrow pathway an impossibility. I had to think of the work and the cost in lives that had been undertaken by father and our uncles, who went into this forest to remove these giants. The risks they took with disease, the dangers of snake bite—even a small wound could become septic, cause blood poisoning and kill you in a month. These were heroic tasks, surely equal to the labours of Hercules.

But I had to pay attention, as Congnet was saying, "If I were a physician, I would tend to see him as an object of compassion, whose mental alienation may be helped, even if that was in a prison or what is referred to in some published papers as the Christian system of criminal jurisprudence."

"You are kind, my friend," I answered, crouching to avoid the bushes that overhung the path. "But with regard to the Cedula, reading it closely I could not help admiring it. It is a very brave document. It speaks to a humanitarian impulse that I never imagined the Spanish soul capable of."

"Yes, indeed," he replied. "Very advanced, for a society like Spain that is still anchored in the doldrums of an immovable past and imprisoned by a horrifying interpretation of religion."

"All of which can only be compared to their perpetual attempt to achieve purity of the blood," I replied, and remembering something that I read somewhere I added, "Having exported both the brain and the soul of their nation with the expulsion of the Jews and the Moors. You know, Congnet, that that was the origin of racial discrimination in the New World?"

"Is that so?"

"It is in the historic record," I answered. "However, it is difficult to ascribe to the Cedula of 1783 any other general principle than an attempt to establish equality of civil rights between free persons. The free black and coloured people received half a loaf, which was better than nothing. The new Bourbon monarchy brought to Spain the refreshing wind of the Enlightenment, expressed in the reforms that served free people like ourselves extremely well. The English here in Trinidad will never allow an elected Assembly to come into existence. It would be dominated by people considered by them to be not only foreigners, but people of a different racial composition, who would have interests peculiar to their needs."

"But Jean, they must be forced to obey the rule of law. Because according to the twenty-eighth article of the Cedula, leave is granted to both the old and the new settlers to send to the government remonstrances, which literally means to make a forceful and reproachful protest. This is why I have supported you, my friend. To achieve this, the petition that demands justice must invoke the weight of the twenty-eighth article of the Cedula."

"Bravo, my friend! But in that article, it states plainly that these remonstrances must be enacted through the means of the governor. Therein may lay the rub. Governor Woodford must grant permission for an individual to approach the English government. The other important part is that the twenty-eighth article states that for all the articles contained in that regulation to have their full force, all the laws

30. WILD AND WONDERFUL

and customs that may be contradictory to them should be dispensed with. No wonder this administration is doing all in its power to do away with the Cedula. It is far too liberal for Woodford. We must act decisively, because here in Trinidad people are being reduced to their lowest common denominator. There is no room for excellence, none for growth, little for hope and none for triumph. These poor devils, they are aware that whatever advance is made in the sphere of learning, they shall encounter neither encouragement nor favour."

"Indeed. As a consequence we become disheartened and soon lose our relish, and where there is genius, and feelings are warm and tempers ardent, they soon bid farewell to any amelioration of the head and heart." Listening to Jean, I could not help wondering if he spoke of himself, as he continued rather sadly, saying, "The inner emasculation of a people is underway, which no white person could observe or understand. A pointless way of life lies ahead for us all."

Jean and I spent seventeen days much in this manner, discussing the deplorable situation here in Trinidad while enjoying, in truth being awed by, nature. Our first leg of the journey took us to the Mission of Savanna Grande. From there, we ventured even further southward to Siparia Point, a hamlet on the south coast of Trinidad within sight of Venezuela, which lies across a strait of water marked on the map as the Columbus Channel. I had arranged, through the good offices of Jean's father, to rendezvous there with a schooner that took on produce and travellers from the estates along that remote coast, which would bring us back to San Fernando.

The campsites for the night were always selected in advance. This was done by the partly Spanish, mostly Indian guide who, along with two porters, perhaps his relatives, made up our company. It was pleasant to sit and chat with jean by the smoky fire, having eaten heartily of something wild, as in this truly magnificent jungle game was readily had.

Taking to the road on a morning, the weather warm and already humid with the rumble of thunder coming from a silent sky, we would prepare ourselves for the windy rainstorm that would overtake us by midday. Remembering one of our previous conversations it came to me that plainly, with the loss of virtuous emulation, the love of pleasure gains on young persons, and they soon yield to the habits of indolence, that parent of every vice. I said this to jean, who was riding ahead of me. Looking back, he answered over his shoulder, "Yet on many occasions, Jean-Baptiste, we did meet hope for retribution, and even the expectation of divine deliverance, and if you remember the old man who spoke of retrieving something long lost from the Chacón years. Perhaps never really had, in truth. Yet hoping against hope."

This was true. As the free coloureds told us their stories, I discerned that there was always the same sad tale, especially from the older heads. They remembered that the English had done the very same thing in Grenada: promised one thing and then changed their minds to do the opposite.

Because of intermittent showers and a steady southerly, by late afternoon we were wet through and shivering. Stopping for the day we made camp in a clearing, where previous travellers had left the remnant of a low table made up of straight boughs, bound together by vines, a circle of large stones in which a welcome fire could be built, and the skeleton of a lean-to that the porters swiftly thatched.

"We must hang our hammocks in there now and see that a fire is started," said our guide, adding, "Get a good night's rest, young masters, tomorrow we cross the Oropouche lagoon." Already the westering sun was casting long shadows and the subtle shades of evening were bringing the day quickly to a close. There was only the occasional distant screaming of birds, the weirdly harmonious notes of the cicada and, from somewhere near at hand, the now-and-then sharp, ringing clang of the carpenter bird, which sounded as if he were cutting down the trees with a silver axe.

A cooler wind passed over us as we sat close to the fire and a different sort of silence fell. There was something inspiring to it, as

30. Wild and Wonderful

the sounds that did meet the ear only served to remind us that man was far away.

Jean Congnet, remembering our conversations of the last few days, continued as if it had never been interrupted, saying, "I agree with you, there is a great wickedness taking place here in Trinidad. It will have a terrible effect on this society. It must be stopped, for the sake of the future of our children and for those born to the slaves who will be liberated eventually and will have to live under those laws, they must be reversed. Otherwise the people's collective mentality will in the future be forever shaped by low self-esteem and crippled by the phlegm of indolence and a profound lack of confidence."

"In truth, my friend, we are a country in formation, we cannot go forward like this," I answered, placing some wood on the fire and leaning back on my heels as the flames brightened. "This man, Woodford, will leave here in the next few years and more than likely take up another appointment somewhere in England's growing colonial system, and no doubt implement the very same crippling laws to deprive another population of those positive qualities inherent in all the human race. Then, having committed these crimes, upon retirement he will live out a long and no doubt prosperous life. I must stop him. I shall."

What a cruel, diabolical undertaking is afoot here, I had to think, as I sought a comfortable position in my hammock that was precariously strung inside the lean-to from two trees. If this is what is being dished out to us, who are free, what will be the fate of the black slaves when their emancipation, which is inevitable, comes to pass? Under what conditions will they, will we all, live? What we are faced with in this colony is a man whose power is supreme, but who represents an image of darkness.

It rained heavily during the night, the rain extinguishing the fire and drenching us again to our very bones. Yet, with the morning's light sparkling on every leaf and blade of grass, the day appeared renewed. The beauty of nature at her tender best brought to mind the words of Virgil, who sang of her and perhaps of love requited when he wrote: "I will be gone from here and sing my songs/In the forest wilderness where the wild beasts are." We restarted the fire and after a hearty breakfast were, with the dank smell of the lagoon in the air, on our way. By midday, we could glimpse the bright water against the bluest sky seen through the trees.

An ancient Indian was standing beneath an enormous tree. He appeared as though he was a wooden carving come to life. Quite tall, he wore western dress and from his head and over his shoulders hung a quantity of blue-black feathers. There was a boat for hire.

"What is your name?" I asked.

"I am Sarusima, son of Buchumar, Cacique of the south," he replied, tottering precariously forward and then leaning quickly backwards. It was as though his words were coming from somewhere deep inside his body, as his lips had not moved.

"We want to cross this lagoon to find our way to the Mission. What would it cost for you to take us across?"

"Four bits of Spanish silver," he replied, "and your boots."

"I shall give you the silver, my good man, but I cannot part with my footwear," I told him.

"Then it shall be eight bits of Spanish silver," came the reply from somewhere remote but near.

So agreed, we were aboard a corial that had been carved from a forest giant, with Sarusima in the bow and with our own porters in the stern, paddling towards what appeared to be a swiftly moving eddy. Around us rose the forest, which was by that time moving swiftly by. Looking into the placid, greenish water, I could see several forms, what were they I wondered.

"River otters," came a reply.

We moved quickly towards what appeared to be a passageway in the mangrove wall that lined the shore. On entering it, the world darkened as though dusk had suddenly descended. It was a gloomy

30. WILD AND WONDERFUL

way, made more so as the bird song, which we had almost ceased to hear, had fallen silent. This leafy tunnel of placid dark and slow-moving water gradually opened onto a wider waterway that was strewn with vast accumulations of lovely water lilies. These appeared like islands. On their wide, dark green leaves stalked birds with long red legs and savage beaks. There was such a quantity of life about. I noticed creatures on the grassy embankment slipping by, they appeared to be foraging. "Capybara," came again the voice of this strange man, who appeared to answer my questions even before I could frame them in my thoughts. We passed over the smooth, glassy water just as flocks of large, red birds were flying close above our heads, these must be ibis, I thought, waiting for him to say what I was thinking: "Ibis." It came as a whisper in my ear. The sun was beating down, an anvil heat that in the absolute stillness of midday felt like a red hot iron weight upon my shoulders.

"We enter here," echoed the voice in my head as the corial swung about. Silently, we passed into another passageway in the stalking mangrove. There were birds, large and scarlet, amongst the branches and other creatures too. I saw a movement in the branches. "Ocelot," said the voice that came from inside my head. "He is hunting."

In this manner, a guided tour was given without commentary, just with the naming of creatures. I saw and heard the names of many others as we moved along, at times swiftly, at other times as slow as the day, which seemed to be endless, the sky as blue and as far above as it was when we started off. There were caiman, huge, basking on the shore and the elusive manatee, a sort of sea cow, a voluptuous creature, quite ugly, with pendulum breasts, that we were told nursed her young and wailed like a woman in travail. Later on we were met by troops of large, red monkeys. They howled at us like an angry mob, and followed us from the treetops in quite an aggressive manner. Congnet fired his musket with an incredible bang that echoed and echoed again, which brought about an even more terrifying chorus from these dreadful fellows. We paddled through a field of large-leaved plants with lovely flowers that parted in our way. They stretched across the water like floating meadows, and were the hiding place for other creatures. None appeared shy, indeed they were curious at times, but mostly we were ignored even when we came quite close.

As we were about to enter another narrow passage in the mangrove, we halted. All was perfectly still. Above us the tall forest trees, with their descending vines and tendrils holding all sorts of life, were silent and apparently empty. "Macajuel," said the voice. "Where, where?" the anxious porters cried tremulously in unison. "There." I could see a disturbance in the dark, flaccid water. It appeared all about us as the canoe rocked gently. We waited in anticipation for what we imagined would be a dumping in the tepid water and a mad swim for dear life. "There."

On the left bank a huge body that seemed to be endless emerged from the stream. Upwards and onwards it gleamed, a tawny pattern of grays and blueish tans that turned to yellow. It was bigger than any living thing that I had ever seen, with a head the size of a small pony's. There were other snakes around us, beneath us, the Carib was backing the canoe away, the porters, as frightened as we, were hardly of any use. Like wheels swiftly whirling, the macajuels were revolving, their wet bodies emerged alongside and before us, as we swung about. It looked to me that a feeding frenzy of these giant reptiles was underway.

"She gone. The males are still confused," said the Carib. "We wait, they pass." It appeared that what we had witnessed was the mating of these creatures. The Carib related that up to ten or twenty of these very large snakes would be embroiled with one female amongst them. After the act was consummated, she would be on her way. And soon so were we. It took us the remainder of the day to cross the lagoon. By dusk, we were encamped in a grove of magnificent trees. The Indian, having received his money, was sitting alone at the water's edge. Silhouetted against the setting sun, he appeared for all the world like a giant bird. He was

30. WILD AND WONDERFUL

waiting, I supposed, for travellers who would be coming from the other direction.

There was tasty venison that evening for dinner. A fawn, quite small, was being skinned by the guide while the others prepared a broth of some kind.

"What in heaven's name is that?" I asked, looking into the steaming pot. A deliciously pungent aroma was rising from it.

"Cascadoo," came the reply, and with a laugh the porter said, "When you eat that, massa, you go never leave Trinidad again!"

It was a splendid repast. A feast, in fact, of tender meat and highly flavoured mud fish soup. It was the best meal of the entire journey. Later that evening, as we admired the fleeting lights of myriads of fireflies, Jean and I spoke of the future. I had been asked to go to England by Mr. Hobson to present our case to the English government, 'through the means of the governor' as stated in the twenty-eighth article, and wondered if he would be willing to accompany me.

"I would be only too glad to go with you Jean, but tell me, what do you propose we do?"

"As you know, I have been recording what we have heard. I already made a start. I wrote down what all those people whom we have interviewed had to say. I shall compile it all into a plausible, convincing argument, and we will take it, along with the petition, to London. But first, the argument must be made that our demands are just."

"It would appear that permission must first be granted by the governor for both the petition and your appeal to be taken to the English government. And to whom will you address your argument?" he asked, stretching out to make himself comfortable before the fire.

"I shall find a way to get the necessary permission. As to whom I will present the petition and what I am going to write, why, the Right Honourable Earl Bathurst, naturally. He has the responsibility for the colonies. Based on what I have come to understand of the nature of this honourable gentleman, his liberality and candour, his calm and moderate approach to all things, I believe that our case will be taken into consideration, as it will be like a claim by the mulatto population of this island to the same civil and political privileges that their white fellow subjects enjoy. I wouldn't want to personalise it."

"What do you mean, not personalise it?"

"I'll merely sign it as a Free Mulatto. It was how he, Bathurst, referred to us when we met."

Jean nodded and smiled, saying, "I like that, Jean-Baptiste."

We retired early. It had been an exhausting week and the trek ahead to the Mission of Siparia would be a long one, which we hoped to accomplish by nightfall of the following day.

We eventually made contact with the handful of planters who had journeyed from the environs of the Siparia Mission and were awaiting those who farmed in the vicinity of the one at Moruga. These outposts had been established by the Order of Friars Minor Capuchin in the latter part of the seventeenth century. The friars had not endured.

The majority of the people around were mostly of the Arawak tribe. There were a few who were mixed with perhaps Spanish and Negro strains. They lived in a humble manner in the general area of where the missions once stood. A dozen or more slaves on plantations owned by the free mulatto families mostly, although there were one or two that were in the possession of Spaniards, produced cocoa, tobacco and coffee. There was an easy traffic, we were informed, between this part of the island and the Mainland; indeed it was not difficult to share in their view that it was all one and the same place.

Siparia Point. Sarusima the Carib had told us that Christopher Columbus had sent a boat ashore somewhere along this coast, and when the natives came out in great number he fired off a cannon,

30. WILD AND WONDERFUL

and they in return unleashed a hail of poisoned arrows, causing him to sail away. Standing on this wide beach, I could just make out the Venezuelan coast across the narrow channel named for the explorer. What would have been his feelings as he sailed upon the very edge of the known world? There was about this part of the island a profound isolation, a sense of being far away from all and everything, an otherworldly sensation that only served to magnify our isolation and to increase a hardly concealed anxiety. Had the schooner that we were meant to rendezvous with come and gone? We were assured that it had not yet come.

It was during our sixth day of waiting for the schooner that early one morning, when strolling along this vast and wildly beautiful beach with Sarusima and Congnet, we witnessed a sight that was altogether horrifying but typical of the wild nature of this place.

It was the Indian who drew our attention to what appeared to be a massive piece of driftwood being brought ashore by the rushing waves. A giant, fallen somewhere in the furthest reaches of the Orinoco, had found its way to this beach. Great and gnarled, its roots, a wild mass of tangled forms bleached white, stood out against the bright blue of the sky. The trunk, perhaps more than seventy feet in length, was being washed to shore.

It was the time of morning when the people who lived in the area would come to where the Siparia river met the sea to fish, cook, gather crustaceans and glean the coconuts fallen from the trees that lined the beach. We watched from a distance as their children waded in the swift-running estuary where the salt met the fresh, no longer paying attention to the driftwood monstrosity, which by that time had drawn close to shore.

Suddenly, the Carib called our attention to what was emerging from its mass. To our horror we saw two astonishingly large crocodiles hurling themselves into the curling waves. They were plainly swimming towards the beach and obviously in the direction of the villagers. Waving and shouting we ran towards the bathers even as the giant reptiles were gaining the shore.

With an amazing swiftness the monsters were amongst the children. It was a dreadful sight. Famished by their long journey they devoured, then and there, in the bloody swirling water of the river's mouth, as many of the children that they could catch. I could hear the screams and see the uplifted elongated jaws swallowing, gulping down the young bodies, as other disjointed and decapitated parts were being devoured amidst the thrashing tails and massive bodies heaving up before our eyes. My God! We could do nothing!

Congnet wanted to fire his musket into the swirling mass of gore and turbulent sand and water, but couldn't for fear of hitting the fleeing children. We were transfixed. It was a frightful sight even as their parents, daring the terrible jaws, were rushing in, attempting to drag away the small bodies, but the creatures were too much for them. It was a most frightening thing to see, this slaughter, this devouring, this eating alive of those children.

The people were wild in their dreadful grief, their heart-wrenching frantic screams and cries of horror echoed in the silent sky. The bravest of their men attacked the creatures with cutlasses in the bloody water, and Congnet finally discharged his musket, to reload, to fire again and again. We did what we could to treat the wounds of those who were dragged alive from the swirling mass. The monsters appeared impervious to all of this, as already one was away into the bush while the other, despite being shot in the head, was still alive. It was eventually hacked to death by the villagers.

I shall never forget that frightful day. These beasts were perhaps twenty feet in length and of great girth. I have never been so terrified. The mangled bodies, the wailing of the people. What a tragedy. I could do so little for them and less for the terrible wounds suffered by the two or three survivors. I discovered that I was tearful, distracted and pained in the pit of my stomach as I stood there in the mid-morning sunlight, looking at a small white sail in the distance that was coming our way.

31. The Free Mulatto

*"What is fame? The advantage of being known by people
of whom you yourself know nothing, and for whom you care as little."*

George Gordon Lord Byron

SUNDAY MORNING IN TOWN

TRINIDAD 1821: "MASSA JEAN, MASSA JEAN, PEOPLE COME to you." It was mid-morning and I was sitting at my father's desk, having read a letter from our cousins in London that brought the sad news that uncle Edmond Thornton had passed away, when the house boy, in his own idiosyncratic fashion, staged-whispered that there were visitors at the door. "Make them comfortable, Boniface, seat them on the verandah, I shall be out shortly." I had not heard the sound of a carriage or the approach of riders. Looking up I saw that he hadn't moved away as I had expected, nor muttered his usual idiotic acquiescence.

"What is it?"

"Massa, I can't talk to those men so, they doing what they please, the tall one, he come in the drawing-room, he picking up everything, the other one he looking, it is as if they own the house, you better come, massa."

They obviously were not patients and had perhaps tethered their mounts some distance away and were indeed looking around. White people. Bold and ill-mannered. I was not at all surprised.

The paper that I was preparing for Lord Bathurst had evolved; neither an essay nor a dissertation, it had at first taken the form of an address that increasingly became a personal appeal, reminiscent of the work of Equiano the African. Although for a while it did sound like a letter of the type one comes across written by men who come out to the West Indies in support of, or in disagreement with, a position taken by a person in authority, similar to the response to Clarkson's essay on the slavery question. No, this was clearly a personal appeal to one person, whom I had actually met, whose influence was of significance.

My emotions, arising from putting into writing the testimonies of the free mulattoes, ranged from despair to disgust. I must admit to a growing anger, deeply felt, against the likes of Commandant Robert Mitchell, Attorney-General Henry Fuller, Woodford and several individuals from the white community. There were times when I had to step away from the task. I understood that I was placing myself and the family in danger, as I was being very critical of powerful and ruthless men. Closing the manuscript book and rising, I just managed to anticipate the return of Boniface and his whispered, "Massa, the people still outside waiting."

"Ah, Philip, there you are, old boy, I have brought someone. Don Antonio, may I present Dr. Jean-Baptiste Philip, late of Edinburgh University."

Paul Reinagle, having assumed this somewhat overly familiar tone, continued, "Hope we didn't wake you up or take you away from something terribly important. Don Antonio and his party are

31. THE FREE MULATTO

touring the Naparimas and we could not possibly do this without calling at Concorde. I trust your parents are well. Your brothers? In the fields I suppose. . ."

"It is a pleasure to make your Honour's acquaintance. My parents are at Philippine and yes, my brothers are at work, there is a harvest to be brought in this day," I said, bowing, and taking the proffered hand of the man who was the governor's Assessor. "Are you gentlemen on your own? Come, let us sit, over there where there is a draft, it is a warm day. Can I offer coffee, or perhaps sangaree?"

"Thank you, Doctor, most kind," boomed Reinagle. "We are not alone, Souper and the others are on their way to Lafontaine, we have detoured. And yes, please, a glass of sangaree would be refreshing."

Don Antonio Gomez was an imposing man. Perhaps over six foot, and handsome in the Spanish way, with a great shock of jet-black hair and fine features. He carried himself with an air of authority. Yet I immediately sensed an obsequiousness of the sort that is expected in well-seasoned sycophants or at times in churchmen.

"You have a most remarkable home here, Dr. Philip," he was saying. "Quite original in its contents, not to mention the grounds and the overall state of the plantation. We could not help noticing the well-ordered fields, your people healthy in appearance and at work, and the livestock—I saw foals and a fine yearling, mares and a superb stallion. A love of horses is an expression of a man's character."

"You are very kind, Señor. My father is responsible for our stud-farm. It has been his life's work," I said, knowing that my father had no particular interest in the breeding of horses. The quality of our animals, indeed the state of the place, presently, had only to do with my brothers and of course, mother.

"Don Antonio, earlier on, also practiced medicine, famously he was at Aragua, in Venezuela. Terrible epidemic. Yellow-fever, wasn't it?"

"Is that so? I have found that particular illness to be a mortal enemy in this Quarter as well, it takes a terrible toll. I must say, I always saw you, Sir, as more of a legal luminary," I said in an adulatory tone, motioning them to sit in the verandah's shade.

"It is indeed. And not just in this Quarter, it is, I am afraid, endemic. I was at the University of Caracas and fortunate to have Professor José María Vargas take an interest in me, but alas, fate took me into law, and I can assure you, Doctor, I am hardly a luminary. Presently I am more like a poor refugee in a strange land."

I was impressed. Dr. José María Vargas was a renowned surgeon, anatomist and chemist. His anatomical research, in hard to come by papers, was much sought after at Montpellier. I said so. Don Antonio appeared modest but pleased and changed the subject, saying, "I could not help noticing the remarkable objets d'art. I believe I could recognise Andean craftsmanship in some pieces. Gold. You have gold lying about in a casual manner, how remarkable!"

"My grandfather, he, ah, travelled widely, and collected things. My parents like to see them, I understand that they are from the Kingdom of Granada. And yes, they do lie about. I have heard it said that the slaves believe them to be haunted, and we have so few visitors."

"I say, Philip," interrupted Reinagle, "these are beautiful hammocks, Venezuelan, I hazard?"

"Yes, they are Venezuelan, my sisters, they, ah, enjoy that corner of the house."

"These knotted tassels in dark red, attractive, what!"

"There is a story behind those, my mother says it had to do with buried treasure." I couldn't possibly begin to explain that it was a tradition in our family to attach magenta knots to our hammocks in memory of our grandmother who buried Louis d'or, hidden in a hammock's knots, in her enslaved mother's grave.

31. THE FREE MULATTO

"I understand that you have been touring the island, Dr. Philip, visiting its distant parts," said Don Antonio.

"I have indeed, most illuminating. The island brims with potential. Ah, here is Boniface, gentlemen, please sit. The sangaree, I hope, will be to your taste, if you need sugar, we have plenty."

"Thank you. I was telling Don Antonio that your people have been here from Governor Chacón's time. Two fine estates fully cultivated, a well ordered workforce and handsome prices on the brink of rising, what!"

"We have been fortunate in that regard. May I help you, Don Antonio, to some sugar?" In fact, the price of sugar had risen in 1814 and had continued to rise, but last year we experienced a fall as sugar from Cuba, Mauritius and India started to enter the European markets in quantity.

"No, thank you, Philip. This is delicious, the citrus, exquisite, the wine, ah. . ."

"Fortunate, yes. But I see hard work and a careful dedication," said Don Antonio in a gracious manner. "Your family must be commended."

"We are fortunate. As are the French planters here in Trinidad. England's magnanimity to her former foes can only be described as more than generous. Not just here in Trinidad, but in all the islands which were formerly French, the French planters have been allowed to keep their estates and to prosper."

"While not reciprocating!" said Reinagle. "They have sent us packing in Martinique and in French Guiana! I say, Doctor, we never see you in Port of Spain, don't you ever get away?"

"Not as often as I would like. I hear work goes at a pace on the churches. His Excellency must be pleased."

"Hardly at a pace, I am afraid, the Trinity church is being rebuilt. The townsmen wouldn't have it where I would put it. Made a fuss, got up a petition and had it moved over a few hundred yards!

Spaniards, they were all Spaniards. Forgive me, Don Antonio, I don't mean to cast aspersions, what! The Catholic basilica is more promising. I say, Philip, these prints are positively sinful, what you say, Gomez?"

Don Antonio had no interest in my grandfather's collection of erotica and I turned the conversation to topics of a more general nature.

"Is that rain? What do you think, Gomez? Are we in for a shower? We must make a start, what? Thank you, Philip, for receiving us, unannounced."

Wide-brimmed straw hat in hand, Don Antonio was looking around for where he had put his riding crop.

"It was a pleasure to have met you, Doctor. It indeed looks like a mid-morning shower. Now we must join the others, wouldn't want to be left behind."

"Here you are," I said, handing him his crop. "It was an honour to have made your acquaintance, Sir."

"Oh, the honour is my own, thank you for receiving us, we shall meet again, no doubt."

Bowing respectfully, I held open the little wicker gate that led to the front steps. Our groom had by this time brought up their horses from the estate gate, where they had left them tethered. Overseeing their departure while standing between the magenta knots of my sisters' hammocks, I heard Reinagle unctuously remark, "Quite a personage, eh, for a black, rara avis in terris nigroque simillima cygno, as they say. What do you make of him? His accent, rum, what?"

"He is a rare bird in these lands, much like Juvenal's black swan. I found him hospitable, reserved and very observant. He is a cultured man. Come along, Reinagle, let's make haste."

I had come to understand that when one is paid a visit by a personage close to the governor, a sense of alarm is not unusual. I

31. THE FREE MULATTO

had heard, of course, of Don Antonio Gomez. He, like Dr. Ramón Garcia, had moved to Trinidad as the result of the civil war raging on the mainland. They were royalists, naturally, and legal men. In Don Antonio's case, I remembered being told by my half-brother Michel that when he first arrived in Trinidad in 1811, he was appointed by Governor Monroe Assessor to the Alcaldes of Port of Spain and then Judge of the Courts of the First Instance, the laws of Spain being still in force here in Trinidad some two decades after the conquest by the English.

It would appear that Don Antonio returned to Caracas after the temporary victory of the royalist forces, where he became secretary to the royalist commander General Monteverde. He came back to Trinidad two years later as an emissary on behalf of the Venezuelan government, his return coinciding with the arrival of Woodford, who was taking up the post of the colony's first civil governor after a succession of military governors.

Because of his familiarity with members of the Anderson family, Michel was able, when told about Don Antonio's visit, to expand further, saying, "The Don is close to Sir Ralph. Who is in need of support. When he became governor here in 1813, he was met with hostility, not the least coming from the Commander of the West Indian Station as well as from other high-ranking naval and military people."

"Why was that?" I asked.

"I have no idea really, Jean," he replied. "Perhaps because of his young age? Anderson thought that it was because he was a civilian. There was a revolt against the Spanish Crown taking place in Venezuela, a civil war that could have easily spilled over into Trinidad, and with such a quantity of Venezuelan refugees, from both sides, it would only have been a matter of time before their disputes would have taken root here, in Trinidad."

This might have easily happened. A surge of refugees from the Main would have outnumbered the free population, both white and

187

free coloured, here in Trinidad. And with the culture of resistance embedded from Spanish times in a part of the population that had retained its republican sentiments, along with a slave population that numbered some fifteen thousand or more, an explosive situation could have quickly developed. Woodford had need for the likes of Antonio Gomez and Ramón Garcia. At a time when the hostility of certain people could mean delay, certainly bring about confusion and perhaps even cause failure, Woodford would need the obsequious compliment. Even if it meant complying with self-serving servile flatterers, who sought favour and all sorts of advantages.

"Woodford, according to what Dr. Anderson had to say, in following the instructions of Bathurst, who is the Secretary of State for War and the Colonies, summarily dismissed the island's Council of Advice," Michel added. "This was within days of his arrival, Jean! He removed St. Hilaire Begorrat, John Black and all the other old crooks! They were leftovers from Governor Picton's time. In doing that, Woodford got himself a lot of enemies."

Woodford had indeed surrounded himself with young, educated men. Professionals like Reinagle and Lockhart, the artist Richard Bridgens, and Baron Shack, a botanist. And there was Henry Fuller, the Attorney-General, all a breed of Englishmen very different from the adventurers and criminal opportunists of the Picton era.

"Yes, I'm sure he has," I answered, adding, "I could understand that. I've heard from mother that they were responsible for many of the upheavals in Governor Chacón's last years. Begorrat, she said, was at the centre of an insurgency which could have brought Victor Hugues and his murderous cohorts here."

"Yes. But Woodford's problem is that with these people gone, he has no idea how to deal with the problems arising as a result of the confusion that they left behind, not to mention getting an understanding of the Spanish legal system that is in force in the colony. He straightaway appointed Gomez his Assessor, and Ramón Garcia, who also holds a doctorate in Spanish Law, as the Father General of Minors and Defender of the Absent, which is an

31. The Free Mulatto

important position in the Spanish legal system, apparently. Gomez has acted as Chief Judge during the absence of Justice Bigge. These are very prominent men, Jean. They would be, anywhere in the world." Then, in a more serious tone he added, "Don Antonio's coming to Concorde to meet you, Jean, I would see that as an indication of interest. I would not be surprised if it was followed by an invitation of some sort."

Which was what I was hoping for. Some weeks later, I was again at my father's desk, when I heard the sounds of a horseman drawing up his mount. I was expecting Thomas Corsbie, my brother-in-law who had in mind the purchase of Corynth estate. Boniface put his head around the door to say that the tall Spanish man's servant was outside. "He just ask me to hand you this." It was a letter, sealed, the wax still new. Breaking it, I read what was written there with a careful hand, "My dear Dr. Philip, I write to thank you for receiving us on such short notice and for extending your gracious and much appreciated hospitality. I shall be at Lafontaine with a party and would be honoured if you would accept this invitation to join us there on the morning of Sunday after next." It was signed, with sincere regards, Gomez.

Lafontaine was a modest sugarcane estate, at no great distance from Concorde. It was owned by an English family, the Fitzwilliams. In a blowing drizzle I rode my brother's sorrel briskly up the long carriageway. About me was quite an attractive setting. Flowering trees set in a park-like atmosphere. The house appeared remarkable for Trinidad, in that it was built of both wood and stone and had a gray slate roof. It appeared very much like an English manor house in miniature. Had it had a chimney I would not have been surprised.

I was met at the door by Patrick Fitzwilliam. A tall man, apparently prematurely grey, with a gentle countenance. A groom, perhaps English, had taken away my mount.

"Dr. Philip, please, do come through. Allow me to take your coat. An early start to the rainy season seems to be upon us."

Thanking him, I turned towards the entrance hall, it was handsomely arranged and looked like that of an English country house, except on a smaller scale. I recognised a bust of Shakespeare and another, unknown to me. Carpeted with a beautiful oriental, there were comfortable chairs about and a dark, polished pedestal table at its centre, also flowers, neatly arranged in China vases. Under a window that overlooked a garden, which even on such a cloudy day was a delight with flowering blooms and neat hedges, was an opened Bible on a deal table.

"Please, step this way, Doctor. Normally we would sit outside, but because of the weather we are in my study."

This too was a pleasing room. A large bookshelf filled to overflowing along one wall faced another, which was bare, except for a dark oil in a gilded frame of an austere man in wig and jabot. A vague aroma of fine tobacco and something like sandalwood was in the air. And there was a fireplace! I had to laugh out loud.

"Dr. Philip, I see that you appreciate my attempt to feel at home here in Trinidad. Don Antonio, you already know, may I present the Honourable Henry Fuller, our esteemed Attorney-General."

I was quite taken aback. Fuller, who had been for these many months my bête noire! The very mention of his name caused me a racing heart, and I had to make a conscious effort to dispose my mind of a ranting circle of vicious thoughts. And there he was before me, holding out a pale hand and smiling pleasantly. I took it and bowed respectfully, hoping that in that gesture I was able to infuse a degree of distaste or some subtle reservation. After a congenial round of pleasantries, during which we took our seats around the false fireplace, I managed to compose myself, and welcomed the cup of tea that was served by a white footman. Fuller, an elegant, well-dressed man, turned toward me, saying "Dr. Philip, I trust that your inquiries have proven to be of use."

I knew of course to what he was referring and replied: "I have spoken, Sir, to over seven hundred and eighty persons, all of whom

31. The Free Mulatto

have expressed in one way or another their fear of the governor's land policy and their disgust, in many cases their despair, about the ongoing deconstruction of what has been the established practice with regard to the laws and customs of this colony."

"You mean of course the vexing question of the position of the free blacks and people of colour presently resident here in Trinidad?"

"Sir, there is no need for this question to be a vexing one, or even raised at all. James Stephen, presently Master in Chancery, which, as I am sure you are aware, is a court of equity, has stated publicly that it is difficult to ascribe to the Cedula of 1783 any other general principle than that of establishing a perfect equality of civil rights between free persons."

"It is on the origin of those rights and privileges that we disagree, Dr. Philip," said Fuller, overtly looking me over.

"How so, Sir? These rights are founded in the Cedula of 1783 and were endorsed by a representative of the Crown here in Trinidad in 1797," I replied, meeting his gaze.

"Rights and privileges that were allowed by the Crown, extraordinary privileges which were condoned by the Crown's benevolent governors."

"I beg to differ. There has been a continuous decline of those rights and privileges from the arrival of the English in Trinidad. This decline has been contributed to by the English residents—they maintain the view that we should not have equal civil rights at all."

"Come, come, Doctor, the point of reference to be used in measuring these so-called privileges must be held against what had obtained for the free coloureds in the islands from which they came. As it is said, simile est simile."

There was of course no comparison. Trinidad's coloured community was in no way similar to those of other territories. This position, taken by the governor and Fuller, suggested that the free people of colour should consider themselves blessed, and any attempt on their part to increase ore even protect these rights was an act of ingratitude on their part.

I regarded this man, as he sat in one of the two upholstered wing chairs placed closer to the false fireplace than the one occupied by myself. I saw a confident person, who was obviously destined to be suited to something by virtue his of birth, who was taking what I was sure he would, at another time, describe as a contemptuous delight in repressing barely concealed disgust. I could not help remembering Jeannette-Rose's husband saying that he had been taught that as an officer he should cross the street if by chance he were to encounter a drunk or a madman and in so doing preserve his honour. There was nothing to prevent me from leaving. In any event *my* honour was not at risk; on the contrary, it was his own.

"There is hardly any comparison, Mr. Fuller, of the free people of colour in other places with those here in Trinidad. We are not seeking to *gain* rights. We are far more concerned to *retain* those rights that have been granted to us under the terms of the Cedula of 1783." Then, regarding him more closely, I said softly, "Sub lege veritas praevalet."

I thought I felt the eyes of the others on me and made an effort not to glance their way, but continued to regard the Attorney-General with what I hoped was a look of mild curiosity. He was saying: "It is the English colonists who have lost rights, or have less rights than their brothers in the other English-held islands from which they migrated to Trinidad, because Trinidad does not have an elected Assembly as those colonies have."

I ignored that. It was the sort of thing that the English would hazard. The very idea that the civil rights of the free coloured people here could be compared to those in other islands, like Grenada, St. Vincent or Martinique, was nonsense. For whatever reason, be it benevolence, the ideals of the Enlightenment in Spain during the reign of King Charles III, or even some personal impulse of Roume de St. Laurent, the Cedula in its fourth article clearly stated that our status shall be equally legal and granted in the same manner as those

31. THE FREE MULATTO

of Europeans. The idea that these rights had been bestowed by the English soldier governors was wrong. I said so.

"Well, my dear doctor, one could argue that neither Governor Chacón nor the English governors took it upon themselves to enforce the anti-free coloured laws that are enshrined to this day in the statute books of this colony."

"How could they have?" I wondered quizzically.

"You refer, Dr. Philip, to the final clause of the Cedula?"

"I do indeed, Sir, and also to the twelfth in the Articles of Capitulation, where it states that the free black and coloured people, who have been acknowledged as such by the laws of Spain, shall be protected in their liberty, person and property, like all other inhabitants. The Cedula makes clear that in order that all its articles should have their full force, all laws and customs which may be contrary to them were to be dispensed with."

"In my respectful view, Doctor, the Cedula only dispensed with laws contrary to the possession of land. All other laws, Spanish laws, which are still in force could apply to your people," here he paused, going on to add, "should we choose to enforce them."

"Which, of course, we would not choose to do." This was added by Don Antonio, who had not spoken before.

I was beginning to think that all this was something of a pointless exercise, when Fitzwilliam, who had also been silent throughout the exchanges, remarked, "The fourth article indeed offers civil equality after five years' residence according to the quality and talents of the settlers, and the final article dispenses with all laws contrary to the intention of the Cedula, but what in your opinion does 'quality and talent' actually mean, Doctor?"

"A turn of phrase from my days at school comes to mind, obscuris vera involvens. I would take the Spanish word *el talento* to mean a person's natural gifts. This could include their abilities, their wit, accomplishments and certainly their endowment, which has to do with what is inherited. *La calidad* indicates rank, thus defining such persons as belonging to a social class. Which would fundamentally be the same for Europeans who had achieved such a status. Surely, Mr. Fitzwilliam, those words refer to the race of the settlers as well. Thus making the free blacks and coloureds, their quality and talents being appropriate, eligible for posts in the civil service and to hold commissions in the militia. Plainly the Cedula speaks for us all here in Trinidad."

The Attorney-General was firm in his point of view, observing that truth was in no way being obscured. As far as he was concerned, there was only one article contained in the Cedula that he would support, and that was the right of the free coloureds and blacks to own land.

"Clearly, Dr. Philip, the thinking behind the Cedula did not envision the free coloureds to be equal to the white people here in Trinidad. Otherwise they would not have made that important distinction that the lands granted to the free coloureds be half of what was allotted to whites."

I had heard this argument before. Hobson's view on this was, however, that even those settlers who had received no grants of land were entitled to equal civil rights under the Cedula. I said this, not mentioning my mother having told me that she had it on very good authority that it was Roume de St. Laurent who had, without the approval of the Spanish Crown, inserted this clause into the Cedula.

"Your people say the Cedula, in its wisdom, recognised that it was because they did not have as many slaves as the whites!" said Fuller, glancing at Don Antonio, then at Fitzwilliam, as though expecting them to join in support of this remark.

I believe that the unequal distribution of land had more to do with the inequality of the numbers of people coming into Trinidad, the free coloureds being in the majority. The Spanish Crown, notwithstanding its newly found egalitarianism, would not want

31. THE FREE MULATTO

a mixed-race population to dominate a province in its American colonies. What a precedent that would set. I said so.

"My dear man, in the Cedula of 1795, called Gracias al Saar, free people of colour are allowed to buy civil equality, if they so desire. Come, Doctor, tell me why the need for this Cedula of '95, if the Cedula of 1783 had provided for civil equality at a nominal price, one that I am sure that you can afford?"

Fuller said this, rising to stand at the small marble fireplace which, though false, was elegant in its simplicity, thus revealing perhaps the values of its owner. Assuming an expression that was meant to convey, I suppose, disdain, he added, "In the end it would be at the government's disposal to decide whether you will be allowed, or not, to leave the colony for England with your petition. I must compliment you, Doctor, on your attainments, quite novel, for a person of your background."

"Come, come, dear Sir," I replied rather dismissively, "to evoke the twenty-eighth article while at the same time denying the relevance of others appears to me contradictory. As for what you call my attainments, they are hardly pertinent here. The Cedula of 1783 is specific to Trinidad, and that of 1795 is addressed to the entire Spanish empire, one that is as far flung as the Indian Ocean. They are not inconsistent. Governor Chacón, in his wisdom, and acting in the now lost spirit of impartiality, issued an 'auto de obedecimiento', which stated that the ability to buy privileges did not rule out, according to the Cedula of '83, the award of them on merit."

"I must say, well argued, Dr. Philip!" exclaimed Fitzwilliam, adding, "most entertaining. I have never met, certainly not in circumstances such as these, a person like yourself. But tell me, Doctor, why are you not actively in support of the emancipation of the slaves? Are they not of your people?"

"The freeing of those kept in bondage is inevitable. The abolition of the slave trade has paved the way for that eventuality. My concern,

Sir, is that when they indeed become free, they do not have to exist in a Trinidad created for the maintenance of bigotry."

At that I inclined my head, confident in the irony intended in the gesture, and thanking him for his hospitality, I was about to bid farewell to the company and to take my leave when Fuller said, "I say, Philip, your accent, most peculiar coming from a person such as yourself. I wonder where you picked that up."

"In the company that I was fortunate to be in as a wee lad," I replied in a broad Scottish accent, "both at the Royal High School in Edinburgh and at Craigston Castle, where I wintered the guest of the Laird. As you would have noticed, Sir, there are certain words that acquire immeasurably more power when delivered with a Scottish accent. I am thinking here of liberty, and independence. Thank you for noticing, and I hope these words would be of service to you in your deliberations, as I am sure you are aware, libertas perfundet omnia luce." All this, as mildly as I could manage.

Fitzwilliam, hardly suppressing a chuckle, saw me to the door. "Thank you for coming, Dr. Philip, most informative. Ah, the weather has cleared, appropriate perhaps to your parting remark, 'freedom will flood all things with light.' The Latin poet Lucretius, I believe. Have a safe journey home, Dr. Philip."

The weather had cleared. Around me the sugarcane fields were in arrow and every drop of rain glittered in the noonday light. My brother's sorrel, a light-footed mare, perhaps sensing my mood, broke into a brisk canter as we followed the undulating cane-breaks that would take me home.

In the months that followed, Walsh Hobson and the others involved in the petition to the English government were frequent visitors to Concorde. They saw my draft manuscript as a potent argument in support of the cause, believing as I did myself that it was a necessary addition to their overall argument, as it sought to shed light on the true feelings of the people who had put their names to the petition in the hope of justice.

31. The Free Mulatto

In the midsts of this, my father's condition worsened. A urinary obstruction was plainly the cause of a most distressing condition that brought about severe discomfort. He had been taking a decoction of Urtica dioica, stinging nettle bush, on the advice of Cécile, who assured me that this herbal remedy had been successfully employed by her in the past in treating this condition. Father had been using it as a prophylactic for several years, apparently with a degree of success. I knew of no treatment other than surgery, an orchiectomy, or removal of the testes. In some desperation I consulted a Port of Spain doctor, Joseph Driggs, an American, a respected surgeon, someone who, it was said, had somehow escaped the racist indoctrination typical to new arrivals in the colony. He came to us at Concorde and examined father who was having a relatively good day. Dr. Driggs' concern was that a prostate-rectal fistula might be in formation which would not be treatable.

Uncle Edmond's death had saddened me. I had thought of him as enduring, everlastingly beneficent. A font of generosity, a father figure that had loomed above my own father, and whom I had taken for granted. I wrote to aunt Judith and to my cousins in London and afterwards felt ashamed for the platitudes and vapid sentiments so badly expressed in my letters and in my journal. His passing deeply distressed me and was made especially acute by seeing my father thus. I hardly knew father a well man, being abroad for all those years, and with the pressing urgency to have the petition and my appeal placed in the appropriate hands in London, I was faced with a decision that I had hoped to avoid. Should I wait here in Trinidad and see father to the very end, or should I leave for England? It was mother who made that decision for me.

We were sitting outside, it was a lovely morning, and we were both very aware of the decision that needed to be taken, when I saw Jean Congnet riding up the carriageway.

"He would need to know your plans, Jean," said maman, putting away her crochet. "He is the only one, apart from yourself, who can undertake the task of carrying that petition and presenting it to the appropriate persons while making the arguments necessary to see it through. Papa's condition will not improve I'm afraid and from what Dr. Driggs has said he may linger, poor man, for some time to come."

"I know, but I can't leave here with him in that condition. I can't."

"You must, my dear, you must. For if you do not, heaven only knows what may happen here. From Michel I have heard that the governor is planning to go on leave, to England. And Jean, your papa no longer knows you or anyone else. Some days are better than others, but urination is difficult for him, painful, and at times almost impossible. He hardly sleeps, and often cries in his bed, poor man. Go, do what you must do, for all our sakes."

It was during this period of anxiety that I was again contacted by Don Antonio Gomez. On this occasion it was an invitation to visit him at his La Pastora estate in north Trinidad.

32. Absence - that Common Cure of Love

"The great art of life is sensation, to feel that we exist, even in pain."

George Gordon Lord Byron

HE DESCENDED A DOUBLE, WROUGHT-IRON STAIRWAY.

TRINIDAD 1821: LA PASTORA ESTATE. EARLY ON A SUNNY Saturday morning astride a handsome bay gelding charmingly named Falstaff, rented from a Port of Spain livery stable, I left the town to journey eastward along the Royal Road and there took a forested equestrian path that would lead past the tiny hamlet of San Juan de Aricagua, into the secluded Santa Cruz valley.

Surrounded by mountains subtly sapphire-tinted, this beautiful vale, as it opened before me, gave the impression of a world altogether different from the one in which I had lived for the past three years. I found the air cooler, more fragrant, the scenery far more varied than the sameness of the ever-rolling sugarcane fields that lend such vast distances to the view. There was a stillness here, not silent, as I crossed many a rushing brook to ride along a winding way, which

PHILIPPINE • SOULS ON FIRE

THE LOVELY SANTA CRUZ VALLEY,
TRULY A FRUIT-BASKET.

32. ABSENCE - THAT COMMON CURE OF LOVE

followed a river that led to the heart of this verdant vale, the high woods crowding ever closer.

The thick woods gradually gave way to reveal vast and neatly tended cocoa plantations which, from a distance, had the appearance of a charming forest; with the rich green of the cocoa trees and their splendid multicoloured fruit all shrouded by the exceedingly tall, flashing vermilion, flame-coloured foliage of the truly glorious bois immortelle. The coffee bushes that fringed the way with dark green leaves and jasmine blossoms exuded a subtle but exquisite perfume that refreshed the senses and delighted my imagination. The people of the hamlet La Canoe, very much like those at Aricagua, were Indian mostly, of the Nepoio people, I was told. I could see black slaves at work here and there and neat cottages, a great many vegetable gardens and a quantity of animals. All, slaves, other people, beasts of burden, the small children splashing in the river, appeared healthy.

Before my setting out, I was much amused by the surprise, approaching alarm, expressed by my brothers and others when I said that I had received an invitation to visit Don Antonio Gomez at his La Pastora estate. It was unprecedented, I was assured. André-Montrose was laughing derisively, I am sure, while Michel, though also laughing, was more supportive in suggesting that I had obviously made a good impression on Don Antonio. Susanne wondered whether the Don's wife and daughters would be present at meals, while mother merely smiled, telling me later that she believed it had to do with the petition, the interviews conducted by myself and Congnet, which had involved hundreds of people, and of course with the meeting that I had had with the Attorney-General in the presence of Don Antonio and Mr. Fitzwilliam.

"According to the newspaper Governor Woodford will soon be away, and a military man will be acting in his place. Gomez is possessed of great power. He wants to know what you intend to do, how far you both are willing to go. He wants to judge you. After all, he is the governor's assessor," this she said to me, the morning of my departure for Port of Spain. I thought that she was correct in all she said as Don Antonio would be the legal advisor to Colonel Aretas Young, the acting governor during Woodford's absence.

As for the anticipated snobberies and possibly overt demonstrations of race prejudice, I was not at all bothered. In truth, I was curious. I had suspected a certain obsequiousness, the art of the servant, about Don Antonio and believed that Woodford needed this. Was it survival that led Don Antonio to become Woodford's confidant? But what had prompted the governor to be in the very bosom of this Catholic, South American family? For if rumours presently circulating were true, Woodford was engaged to Don Antonio's daughter Soledad. Had Woodford, in his own way, much as Governor Picton had done before him, 'gone native' as it is said in England about Englishmen who adopt the mannerisms of their host in the colonies? Because in Woodford's case, he had already taken the first steps along that road by becoming as racially biased as any European long resident in these islands.

An example of the ludicrous nature of this racial bias occurred some years ago when a coloured planter, a freeman of Martinique, who either in a moment of levity experienced by a previous governor or in a more studied attempt to bait a response, was invited to dine at Government House. The scandal that ensued was as amusing as it was absurd. The Baron de Montalembert, one of the proprietors of the Coblenz estate at Sainte Anne, believing that his honour would be called into question if he were to be seated at table with a Negro, was said to have left the room at once, with an exalted sense of having been insulted. All this quickly made the usual rounds. Some days later, the Baron's response was made public. He put it about that any man who would suggest that he had sat at the same table with a Negro would be called out and face certain death at the point of his sword.

Thus, by receiving me in his home, where I would be his guest over a period of several days, Don Antonio was demonstrating not just a remarkable sense of his own independence, but an outstanding

32. ABSENCE - THAT COMMON CURE OF LOVE

confirmation of power—power to disregard the customs, norms and behaviour considered acceptable in this society.

The house and the works of the estate, as they came into view, were set in what appeared to be a well-cultivated park. It was reached by a carriageway, with a circle containing a fountain at its end, and was possessed of an elegant and original charm. It actually looked like a house. My arrival had been anticipated. There were people, his wife and family obviously, gathered in the gallery and servants waiting to take my horse and to carry away my saddle bags. Don Antonio appeared delighted as he descended a double, wrought-iron stairway to warmly take my hand and with a courtly gesture, directed me to where his wife, Doña Maria del Carmen, daughter Soledad, stepdaughter Petra, son Aziz-Philip, and Patrick Fitzwilliam were waiting. Being so graciously presented, I at once felt completely at ease as I bowed to kiss the hand of the diminutive, almost dwarf-like woman, his wife, and in turn to shake his son's and Patrick Fitzwilliam's hands.

Refreshments were served and coffee offered. There was fruit, some I had never seen before; the sugar-apple, barbadine and the mamey-apple, all presented beautifully and such a delight to sample. Doña Maria and the young women retired, offering modest curtsies to my more than generous bow. I understood. This was a rare occasion and they would speak of it as a break with tradition, an example of their father's eccentricity, and it would be passed off as noblesse oblige, the unwritten obligation of the nobility to act honourably, even generously to others. In this instance, for the purpose of fulfilling the governor's wishes. In any event, Gomez was not an aristocrat, he was a professional man, a physician turned lawyer in the service of an English governor.

There were some rare and valuable plants that the Don would show me, such as the nutmeg, which was flourishing with great vigour, the cinnamon and the clove, all introduced to the island, he told me, by Sir Ralph Woodford. Luncheon was served on a lawn beneath the sprawling branches of a samaan tree that almost touched a clear stream, with flunkies in attendance to the Don, Fitzwilliam and me.

I welcomed the opportunity to assuage their curiosity of my experiences while living abroad. It was always the Scottish accent that was the first object of curiosity.

"It came on naturally, I suppose. Although my tutor in London, an Englishman who was also a law student, did his utmost to help me lose what he called my laughable Créole pronunciations."

"How did he do this?"

"He had me read aloud from William Blackstone on the Laws of England."

This brought about much laughter, but catching Gomez's eye, I wondered if the pronouncement made famous by that learned judge William Blackstone had crossed his mind, "the public good is in nothing more essentially interested than in the protection of every individual's private rights." After telling of my education at the Royal School and my entry into the medical college in Edinburgh, curious, and wanting to know about Don Antonio, his background and relationship with Sir Ralph, I asked him about himself, and his role as the governor's assessor.

First, he told us of being born and raised on the Atlantic island of Tenerife, making it plain that his people were 'limpieza de sangre', of pure stock, white on both sides of his family, and were not in any way contaminated by the blood of the Guanche people, the island's original inhabitants. He then spoke of his schooling in Caracas, where his family had moved when he was a boy. He had had his medical education there and later his career, which he glossed over, along with the change of circumstances that led to his interest in civil law that saw his return to the University of Caracas.

He was no stranger to Trinidad, he emphasised, as he had been here in 1811 and was appointed by Governor Monroe Assessor to the Alcades of Port-of-Spain and judge of the Courts of the First Instance. His subsequent return to Caracas, I could tell, was a

32. Absence - that Common Cure of Love

topic that he preferred not to discuss. It was the ongoing civil war in Venezuela that had prompted his return to Trinidad. It would appear that on meeting the new governor, he again accepted the post of assessor. Being unfamiliar with the term, I asked about it.

"It was the disasters of Venezuela's revolutionary war that brought both myself and my friend and colleague Dr. Ramón Garcia to Trinidad in 1813. It was coincidental we arrived at the same time as Sir Ralph Woodford. Both Don Ramón and myself, having had the opportunity to be trained in law at Caracas, were approached by His Excellency to join his administration. In his wisdom, he clearly saw the need for persons with an understanding of the Laws of the Indies to reform, I should say to unravel, the Gordian knot of misunderstandings that are crippling the judicial system here in Trinidad. Dr. Garcia became the Father-General of Minors and I became the government's assessor."

Pausing to assume I suppose a more dignified demeanour and clearing his throat, he continued with senatorial gravity. "Under Spanish law, an assessor is either voluntary or necessary. The former, who is certainly not a judge, gives his legal opinion in cases referred to him occasionally by a lay magistrate. The latter is appointed by the Crown, enjoys civil and criminal jurisdiction, and holds the position of Lieut-Governor. Such an assessor, as I am presently, is responsible for judicial opinions, not the governor, who is expressly forbidden in the event of a disagreement, to name another assessor, and it is only where he may consider it fit not to agree with my advice that he is allowed to suspend the position of assessor and consult the sentence or opinion with a Superior Tribunal."

"And you have been so appointed by the sovereign as the necessary assessor?"

"I have, and acted as such."

"That being the case, it would be upon your express advice that the governor would give consent for a delegation to leave this colony for England carrying with it a petition which would be presented to the appropriate persons there?"

"Indeed."

"Is this why I am here?"

"Why yes, Dr. Philip, please proceed."

I spoke first as a medical practitioner and as a scientist, saying that I had examined the contents of the petition gathered by the committee headed by Hobson and that I had indeed interrogated well over a thousand persons who had expressed their complaints and affixed their names to the petition. I had especially noted that there was an inner process of enslavement of these people underway, an internal emasculation which no European could observe or understand. The free people of colour, I explained, finding that the society did not value them, were unable to value themselves properly; they were unable to develop their potential; thus they were becoming victims of the self-fulfilling prophecy propagated by the government and the white community.

It was obvious to me that free coloureds were treated by most Europeans in the same manner as domestic slaves. I pointed out the effect that the incremental but deliberate deprivation of civil rights was having on these people.

"We are the descendants of the French, the English, the Spanish. We have the blood of Europe in our veins. The differences of complexion cannot dissolve the ties of consanguinity."

I pointed out, speaking forcefully, that in a civilised society education and virtue, regardless of colour or race, must be rewarded with social recognition. I told them that as an educated man myself, I was shocked by the failure of the white people here, who were in authority, himself included, along with the governor and the Attorney-General, to distinguish in their public policy between the various classes among the free blacks and coloureds. I emphasised that if these positions taken by themselves were exposed to persons outside this colony, they would be found to be unjust, in truth uncivilised. I said that persons like myself, university-educated, well-bred and wealthy, should be among the social and political

32. Absence - that Common Cure of Love

leaders of the colony. That plainly not all the coloureds were fit for this—nor all whites, for that matter.

"It is not our fault that we are closely related to the white families here, or anywhere." I said this because white people prefer to forget this fact. "We should not be punished for that."

Obviously the white people here were also victims of these stupid colonial customs and habits, which had an adverse affect on everyone in the society.

I said to them that I was sure that the governor, though I hardly imagined him being prejudiced *before* his arrival, had become a victim of the all-pervading racism of the society, and that he, Gomez, by claiming to be of pure blood, could attest to this colonial malady. I then reiterated that if these conditions were known in London with the present notions of civil rights held by certain members of Parliament, certainly condemnation and even prosecution might be in the offing. It was my intention to lift this veil of secrecy that was obscuring the truth, exposing a corrupt and degenerate mind that was dishonouring the post of governor in one of His Majesty's colonies.

Without pausing, I went on to say that it was plain that the very terms of reference that had brought the free people of colour to Trinidad were being eroded. I repeated that according to the Cedula of Population, their rights should be equally legal and granted in the same manner as to Europeans. The present administration was plainly in breach of the law.

The planned, indeed organised deprivation of positive human qualities was alarming, I said, and I saw it as criminal. This begged the question—I think here I shouted—what of the enslaved? In the next five or ten years, they would be emancipated, some twenty-five thousand black people would be added to the existing fourteen thousand free blacks and people of mixed race. All would become free subjects of this colony. "The governor does his duty in enforcing the laws of the colony for the protection of the slaves, but on the subject of slavery and colonial prejudices of caste, Sir Ralph is by no means in advance of his times."

There is something wonderfully contradictory in human nature, some peculiarities of conduct difficult to be accounted for, when one applies it to common principles. Realising that I had their attention, I added: "The actions of Sir Ralph Woodford's government, of which you both are a part, have been more oppressive and galling than those of any preceding governor, when it comes to the free black and coloured people here in Trinidad. The governor sets himself up as the patron of the slave population, but his philanthropy is all hypocritical and sanctimonious talk. His expressions of benevolence are just an echo of the language of those truly charitable and Christian men in England who endeavour to break the chains of slavery. Their praises will eventually be sung by myriads of Africans yet unborn. I wonder what sort of society will come into existence in Trinidad? Is it not harebrained to have a Protector of Slaves who is himself an owner of slaves? It is an absurdity to pretend to build a society on the rule of law, when the law is being harnessed to deprive free subjects of their legal rights. All being contrary to what in a civilised country would be considered natural justice."

I then expressed my confidence in the system of justice in Great Britain and formally asked the Assessor for permission to lead a delegation, comprising myself and Jean Congnet, taking with us a petition which would be presented to the Secretary of State for War and the Colonies.

For a brief while we sat in silence, the shifting wind lifting the branches above us. At a distance, a dog barked, and birdsong commenced. A party of women and children were coming along the sloping lawn towards us. Don Antonio rose, bowed in a formal manner, and said, "Dr. Philip, I shall give careful consideration to everything that you have said here today in the presence of the Honourable Patrick Fitzwilliam, member of the Illustrious Cabildo of this colony, after which I will give my advice to His Excellency before he and I depart for England."

32. Absence - that Common Cure of Love

Stepping onto the lawn, I could see his manner change. He was now a husband and father who with open arms was stooping to receive an embrace from a little girl who whispered something in his ear.

That Gomez would be departing for England in company with Woodford had come as a surprise to me. I said nothing and continued to admire the beauty of the pastoral nature of the surroundings.

That evening we all dined together with cordiality and good cheer. Afterwards we were entertained by a performance executed by his son, daughter, neighbouring friends and I supposed a quantity of family retainers, incorporating a bit of everything typically Spanish: music, dance, singing, prose and poetry, called a Zarzuela.

The following morning, as the family attended a church service in a small wooden chapel on the grounds of the estate, I strolled out to enjoy the Don's experimental orangery. It was a charming novelty, made especially so as I could hear the mass beautifully sung in Latin by a Spanish priest. Over an acre was planted with the product of a cross between the pomelo and the mandarin. I enjoyed the brightness of the green leaves between which large golden fruit shone in the sunlight. The air, alive with all sorts of insects, was fragrant and the atmosphere peaceful.

I wondered at the Don's relationship with Sir Ralph. They appeared to be opposites in both manner and personality. Compared to Don Antonio, whose way of conducting his affairs was marked by gentle modesty, the governor had from early on surrounded his person and residence with a type of splendour never seen before in the colony.

Mind you, I never had the pleasure or discomfort of being in the governor's presence, but he was certainly spoken about. Don Antonio had the night before commended him on the improvements that he had made to the town, the building of the two churches, the market house and the gardens being planted at Sainte Anne.

He spoke of him as dignified and graceful in manner, although admitting that his appearance during hours of business, his look of haughtiness and his abrupt manner, could be off-putting, but he said, "All would vanish once his domestic life resumed." Others here, the newspaper editor Edward Joseph for example, are said to have described him as a caliph rather than an English governor. Some spoke of him as a person who saw himself more as a Spanish viceroy armed with the most absolute authority, and not at all as a representative of a constitutional British sovereign.

I later breakfasted, déjeuner à la fourchette or I should say in Spanish desayuno fuerte, with the family. I so enjoyed the company of the gentle Soledad, who had on that very morning received from Henry Nelson Coleridge, a recent visitor to La Pastora, a charming letter from which she read with much blushing but obvious delight: "Soledad! thou wilt never read the book that I am presently writing; few of those who will can ever know thee, and I shall never see thee again on this side of the grave. Therefore I write thy name whilst I yet remember thy face and hear thy voice, thou sweet and ingenious girl!" Sir Ralph, preparing for his departure to England, had presented her with a pair of superbly crafted silver cruet dishes that were engraved with the Woodford escutcheon. It was an engagement gift on display for all to see.

Coleridge was the nephew of the poet Samuel Taylor Coleridge, who was seen in some circles as the progenitor of Romantic thought and writing in England. That Coleridge had been here standing on this very spot, seeing what I was seeing, moved by the charm of this girl with whom I had breakfasted, was sufficient to fire my imagination as I spent the remainder of the day touring the estate's extensive and absolutely delightful fruit orchards, reading from his little book of poems. I couldn't help thinking that in this tropical setting, Coleridge's work lost the tendentious, even tumid quality that I previously found unsettling in his work.

It was exciting to experience the icy waters of the deep mountain pools. The cool breezes that rushed amongst the towering bamboo

32. Absence - that Common Cure of Love

arches spoke of nature at her best, and of course I enjoyed the company. It was the first time since leaving Europe that I had experienced such congeniality. I was not surprised when Fitzwilliam agreed with me that the British here were vulgar, selfish, and full of ridiculous pretensions, without qualifications of any sort to justify it. That there was an utter want of principle amongst all classes, and that great peculation was known to be going on in many of the official departments, "but no one likes to interfere." Gomez was circumspect when I inquired the reason for Woodford's departure, saying simply that he had not gone home on leave for some nine years. He preferred to speak about the adjoining estates and the cocoa crop and his hope for a continuation of good prices.

I could not help wondering if Woodford, knowing about the petition for our social equality, and about other such movements in the region, was going to London to cover himself for the abuses he had committed in Trinidad. For surely the rising stench of hubris would have reached London's nostrils by now.

For luncheon we enjoyed amongst other delights a mountain cabbage, which is held here in great esteem. It was a pity to see such a towering cabbage palm destroyed. I was to understand that this was a compliment paid to guests who were held in esteem by their hosts.

That night, after dinner, we were once more entertained, this time by a most accomplished amateur of music playing the piano-forte and singing in a masterful manner. I later learned that he was a French Viscount, but was now a shopkeeper who had dropped his title.

Rising with the dawn and sharing coffee with Gomez and Doña Maria, I was reassured by the Don's friendly and supportive manner. Thanking them both sincerely for their more than kind welcome—not mentioning of course the most unusual nature, the hospitable entertainment of me, of all people—I set out to take again the winding way that led up and over the steep hills and through a narrow define known as the Saddle, down into an equally wonderful and spacious valley called Maraval.

The idea that both Gomez and Woodford would be in England long before Congnet's and my arrival became a troubling thought as I took the descending bridlepath through the coffee bushes that grew from the river's banks into the steeply rising hills. How different from the people of the Santa Cruz valley, whose lingua franca appeared to be entirely Spanish, were those of Maraval. There are many French people here in this valley. Even before I saw them I heard their voices singing in Patois. It was a party of women, several of whom, apparently white, were washing clothes at the river's bank. To them I waved, admiring the natural charms of the feminine form when more or less covered by linen when it is wet.

Don Antonio had said the night before, in a voice that suggested that it was something of a tragedy, that Maraval estate had been taken over by Jean de Boissière. When asked why, he replied, "He has no interest in agriculture, he acts as a money lender! Came to me the other day, said that he needed to make an official declaration. He said that he wished to take an oath under the notarial act in order to swear that while he was not renouncing his prerogative as a noble to the use of the particle 'de', he was presently acting as a merchant, so he would not be employing it in his business dealings, becoming in future, John Boissière. Now that the wars in Europe are over, many of the ci-devant nobles must make a living here. You met one the other night, a very fine musician. Boissière comes from a family of Huguenots. His father, it is said, is a republican and a member of the former revolutionary government in France. God only knows how he got here. I have found no record of his arrival. But there he is now, with an aunt, two younger brothers and a wife, much older than he, that he does not take into society! There's a story there, I'll wager."

I knew of de Boissière. He was an acquaintance of my father's. He had been a slave importer as well as a money lender. In that capacity, he had foreclosed on a mortgage and came into possession of the Champs Élysées plantation, which comprised most of the lower Maraval valley. Maman told me that it had originally been

32. Absence – that Common Cure of Love

granted to the Marquise de Charras, formerly of the de Gannes family of Grenada. "She was Philippe Roume de St. Laurent's mother, it was their country seat. Losing that estate to such a person as Boissière is a blow to the prestige of all the French Créoles here in Trinidad." Her son made possible the Cedula for the population of this island. When some of the French islands fell to the English, French aristocrats in the service of the Crown came to Trinidad. The ordinary French people went to Louisiana. That estate, owned by Roume's mother, became a symbol of their status here in Spanish Trinidad. Then the English came and everything changed.

"There is no money in the de Gannes family any more, they have lost everything in Grenada," said maman. "It was said that your friend, the governor, wanted to buy Champs Élysées for a government house, but de Boissière wouldn't budge, so he bought Paradise estate in the Sainte Anne's valley from Madame Peschier on behalf of the government." I knew of this, as Lockhart was converting Paradise estate's former cane fields into a pasture for the benefit of the town.

On approaching that expanse, I was attracted by a large crowd that was gesticulating, gazing and pointing in the air. I saw against the brilliance of the late afternoon sky a multi-coloured hot-air balloon of at least twenty-four feet in diameter. It was sailing with the prevailing breeze above and across the town in a south-westerly direction. In the distance, over the tops of the houses and past the newly erected steeple of the recently built Trinity Church, I could see clearly the uppermost yards of a barquentine at anchor. Would she be taking Don Antonio and the governor across the Atlantic Ocean to England?

Dreading the idea of having to overnight at our cottage in the town or of another voyage aboard the *Woodford* on the morrow, I walked to the waterfront in the hope of finding alternative transport that day. I was fortunate to meet Thomas Corsbie, and we both found accommodation aboard the schooner *Jacques' Wake,* captained by Joseph Ventour's son Henri. He was my nephew, my sister

Marie Louise Lazarine being the young skipper's mother. We were happy to be in the company of such a youthful and jolly crew. With a light easterly filling her canvas throughout the journey, we sat with our backs against the main and enjoyed old rum mixed with coconut water and a long, dry-season sunset. We made San Fernando wharf in just over three hours.

As the months went by, I was saddened to see my father in such a condition and became increasingly frustrated by not being able to be of help, so limited was medicine for such a condition. Mother, resigned to the inevitable, reached within herself for the strength to maintain a brave front for the unavoidable change, not only our father's death, but also with regard to the running of the estate. It was in the first instance a question of labour.

To maintain a viable labour force, it was becoming necessary to consider purchasing estates that were bankrupt to obtain their workers, and beyond that, the price of sugar had fallen so low that the estate was becoming unprofitable and no longer viable to maintain. For now, we could refinance ourselves without borrowing, but for how long? It was during this time that Thomas Corsbie, my sister Simone's husband, became my mother's support in the day-to-day management of both the household and the estate, this because of my brother Belizaire's failing health. Corsbie had by this time become the proprietor of the Corynth estate which was no great distance away from Concorde.

33. Long Ago and Far Away

"All who joy would win must share it. Happiness was born a twin."

George Gordon Lord Byron

CONCORDE ESTATE 1823: TO SUBSTANTIATE MY FINDINGS I made every attempt to avail myself of as much information as I could find in the public records of the colony, and set about rewriting the manuscript for the third time. Even then I would return to one or more of the informants so as to refine my thinking and express their feelings more clearly. It was on one such outing some months later when news was brought that a government messenger was waiting for me at home. Permission had been granted to Congnet and I by the acting governor Colonel Young to leave the colony with the petition. This was welcome news indeed!

Woodford's return appeared to coincide with the publication of the Order in Council of 1822, an obnoxious directive that would affect the free black and coloured people in a most deleterious manner.

The Order that stated that sentences were to be handed down for petty thefts, minor breaches of the peace, contravention of the police laws and regulations and all similar misdemeanours, by the Chief of Police or by his assistants, and that they would have the power to adjudge the prisoner on a verbal and summary hearing. A jail term not exceeding two months with or without hard labour, or work in chains in cleaning the streets or other public work, could be handed down on a summary hearing. Cases involving free blacks and people of colour brought before the courts would be heard and if convicted, the accused was to be committed to the gaol. The magistrates might order corporal punishment not exceeding forty stripes in number, solitary confinement or hard labour, with or without chains, for a period not exceeding three months. This law was plainly harsh, punitive and meant to terrorise the free black and coloured population.

The alarm and indignation they expressed on the publication of that Order generated street protests over several days, on a scale not seen since the days of the Chacón administration, objecting to the clauses. As a columnist in a local paper wrote of the governor's return: "The whole town was in motion, drums beating, horses galloping, the whites giggling, whilst the face of every coloured man, woman, and child bore the unequivocal expression of discontent, sorrow and fear." In protest to the Order the coloured militia, The Royals, did not turn out for the reception parade to welcome the return of Sir Ralph. This immediately generated rumours that a rebellion was being planned, and there were calls for the coloured militia to be disarmed.

Some days later I received a correspondence from Government House requesting a meeting with the governor, this I attended in company with Walsh Hobson, Jean Congnet and Désir Fabien. The meeting took place at what was being called the new Government House. It was, until recently, the main house on Paradise estate.

33. Long Ago and Far Away

Wooden and appearing somewhat jerrybuilt, it overlooked an expanse that had been the estate's cane field, now converted into a pasture.

We were greeted by the governor with much cordiality in the main reception room. Present were Don Antonio, Henry Fuller and Colonel Young. It was like being received by an acquaintance, one that had not been seen for some time. It would appear that the governor was receiving us in an informal style. We had expected otherwise, as Sir Ralph was well known to behave in a haughty and disdainful manner towards most people during the hours of business, resorting to a more amiable manner in his domestic life. After a round of pleasantries, during which we were shown some of the improvements being made to the old mansion, we were invited to be seated. Sir Ralph then addressed me in what I took to be a candid manner, saying, "Dr. Philip, I would like to express to you and to your people my regret that the Order in Council should have been so misunderstood. It was intended actually to better your position rather than to impair it."

To which I responded with equal candour, saying, "With respect, your Excellency, the clauses in the Order in Council that refer to 'free people' could mean only us. White people in the Caribbean are never referred to as 'free'."

"Is that so, Doctor?" He seemed at a loss, or was pretending to be.

"Indeed, your Excellency. These new laws place people like ourselves on the same footing socially and politically as those of a similar background in the English islands, Barbados and Jamaica for example, and could not possibly apply to us here in Trinidad, not as far as the Articles of Capitulation are concerned, where it states that 'the free coloured people, who have been acknowledged as such by the laws of Spain, shall be protected in their liberty, persons and property, like other inhabitants.' Plainly, these laws leave us in a worse position than we were in previously."

I saw before me a person who, with great dignity, much restraint and calming measures, was attempting to deal with a situation that he would prefer not to escalate. Without waiting for me to go further, he went on to add that in his opinion the free coloured community should have acted with restraint and should have waited to see how far and in what manner the new laws affected them injuriously before expressing any discontent with them.

Plainly Sir Ralph was alarmed, as he went on to say somewhat unctuously, "As I am sure you are aware all matters, even those of a most vexing nature, could be attended to with calm and mutual understanding for the benefit of all. And I would add that you and your people are quite at liberty to make any representation upon this matter which you may deem advisable."

The words barely out of his mouth, both he and I realised that unwittingly, and in the presence of witnesses, Woodford had just fulfilled the stipulations of article 28 and given us permission to take our petition to London! With this, I assured him that we would be approaching the pertinent authority in London, and thanking him for receiving us, I rose to take my leave, the others who had come with me following suit. This action plainly caught the governor by surprise, accustomed as he was to being in command of all occasions, nevertheless he rose and with hands behind his back, thanked us for coming. We took our leave of Government House with racing hearts and a sense that we had been, if not victorious, certainly satisfied that we had faced a fearsome authority and survived. Together with Young's written permission, we were now amply equipped to legally make our representation.

The governor's attempt to cajole us into some form of acceptance had failed. Plainly this Order had been generated by the governor with the connivance of the Colonial Office during his stay in London, for the purpose of further suppressing the free blacks and people of colour in Trinidad.

The following day I placed a notice into the *Gazette* stating that during my absence Dr. Andrew Welch would fulfill my duties as

33. LONG AGO AND FAR AWAY

physician. Seeing that most of my patients were free coloureds and French Créoles from the south of the isle, I thought I would express my sense of gratitude for having been honoured by their confidence, encouragement and liberality. The notice was published on 20th March, 1823, just a few weeks before Jean Congnet and I were to depart for London.

In the midst of preparing for our departure aunt Judith arrived from Gran' Anse. I had not seen her since my childhood. Maman had kept her informed of papa's worsening condition and was happy to welcome her as they had not had an occasion to meet in some five years.

Aunt Judith, plainly the matriarch of the family, commanded respect without lifting an eyebrow. There was about her a reassuring sense of ease even as she told maman, after staying with papa for most of the morning following her arrival, that it had been her experience that calm people quietly dying were a great deal easier to deal with than angry people fighting for their lives. Although father was in pain and did not recognise her, she saw in him, her brother, much that she had always loved ever since they were children.

Aunt Judith's concern with the state of Trinidad appeared to me to be as if seen from an immeasurable distance. She seemed a visitor from a calmer world. It was, however, interesting to see her interact with Susanne and Cécile. Plainly they had shared a great many experiences and there was much to report about the estates in Grenada and on Carriaou and the investment made here at Philippine. The sugar price had fallen to a depressing low while the planters' lobby engaged in a vigorous campaign that saw Parliament inundated with petitions to perpetuate slavery and maintain their preferential treatment. Yet there was nothing to stop the East Indian traders from importing sugar from India. Patently they were prepared to move heaven and earth to break the West Indian producers' monopoly.

Aunt Judith had received news from her son in London that a quite vigorous boycott of West Indian products had been launched.

All this, together with the government's order of a general registration of slaves and fresh rules for their treatment, brought new and more alarming thoughts to mind. Then there were the enslaved themselves. Because of the hurried movement of slaves to both Trinidad and Grenada from a variety of islands, there were now some who could read the newspapers. They saw these measures, which were plainly in their favour, and the news of the boycott as a prelude to their emancipation, and were already becoming almost impossible to control. To me, plainly an era was coming to a close.

My own time spent with aunt Judith was largely to report on the meeting that I had had with Woodford, and on what I had discovered with regard to the condition of the free people of colour in Trinidad. To this she listened closely, at times interrupting to compare the situation here in Trinidad to the circumstances that had led up to the Fédon rebellion in Grenada. I was gratified when she said that she agreed with me that the time of estate slavery was coming to a close and that it was important that the soon to be liberated should not, at least in Trinidad, be freed into the environment that the governor and his cohorts were creating.

That she was proud of me, of my attainments and especially of my present undertaking, was very evident.

I felt enormously pleased. There were letters to be written to Louis-Edmund, her son, and to her daughters Anne-Rachael and Magdelaine-Judith.

Saying goodbye to mother, it was all that I could do not to succumb to the anguish that was plain in her stern eyes. We dined that night, aunt Judith, mother, André-Montrose, Simone and Thomas Corsbie, in virtual silence, except for commonplace remarks about the estate. No one wanted to discuss what the future would hold and what would be the outcome of my journey.

While I was not particularly distressed nor dismayed when I took the decision to leave for London at a time when my father was at death's door, I was, as I wrote that night in my journal, more

33. LONG AGO AND FAR AWAY

touched by the thought that in the same manner I had not known my father in his maturity, I might not see mother again as she was that night: wise, gentle and very much in command of affairs, as there was no telling how long my stay in England would be. I knew that Congnet felt much the same about his aged parents, but the task at hand demanded that action be taken. Parting from Susanne brought another bewildering emotional upheaval, for on arriving at Philippine some weeks before our departure I discovered that my visit had been anticipated in a manner that came as a surprise.

She was waiting at the door. Her manner, different from previous occasions, was calm and affectionate; she would have me stay the night. It was a fond and passionate farewell. She said gravely, while looking at me with a strange, even somewhat alarming expression, "I have taken you into my body because I want to have your child, even if you do not live to see him become a man. Quiet," she put a finger to my lips. "Beware," she murmured in Patois, then, continuing in French, said, "Beware of what comes from that woman's mouth." She said this several times as if recalling something seen. Then, rising from the bed, she turned to leave the room. For a moment I saw her stark beauty framed by the open window, etched against the rising sun. She looked back at me, her expression was of a person distressed. It crossed my mind to rise and follow her into the vestiaire where her bath had already been prepared, to ask who was the woman whose words I should not accept, but didn't.

THAT LAST MORNING AT CONCORDE. My father's uncomprehending look as I kissed him goodbye, with mother there and Michel Maxwell Philip looking kindly at us all. Susanne and our parting, her beauty for a fleeting moment like a wild thing inside her in which she appeared to walk. Her personality so original, at times inharmonious, a blending of the enigmatic darkness of her character, so powerful and uncommon, and the lightness with which she treated me and our erotic encounters. Her attractiveness, "all that's best of dark and bright", so extraordinary, so immeasurably impressive that it seemed to surround her like an aura or a cloud, a kind of consonance, as perfect as it was rare. I was already yearning for her.

The very same ship that I had seen at anchor upon leaving Don Antonio that Sunday morning almost two years ago would sail with Jean and myself for London. The *Nimrod* was a four-masted barquentine that had sailed the China trade between the Puget Sound and Shanghai for several years, and had been recently purchased by Gregor Turnbull, a burley Scot from Roxburghshire. He welcomed us, expressing his delight in making the acquaintance of, in his own words, 'the most peculiar-looking Scot' he had ever met.

Before noon, the pilot came on board, and with a steady south-easterly we worked our way towards the mouth of the dragon. By dusk, Tobago was already falling astern and barely seen beneath a mantle of storm clouds, and with a favourable wind our course was set to take us first to Barbados, and thence to cross the dark-heaving, boundless, seemingly sublime Atlantic Ocean.

That night, as I stood at the ship's rail, Byron's *The Dark Blue Sea* came to me, and to the startled delight of Congnet and those who stood beside us, I theatrically called out: *Roll on, thou deep and dark blue ocean—roll!*

An early riser, I was on the weather deck before dawn in anticipation of seeing whales and to enjoy the cloudless clime and remnant stars. Standing in the pouring wind, listening to the sea as it rushed past, hearing the wind humming in the rigging and the thud and groan of the *Nimrod's* timbers was a delight—but one that came with much reflection.

All around there were passengers who were for "home", as they said, and others who were being posted elsewhere. Not a few were planters, with several from Barbados. From the start I was aware of them. I could discern that they could not bear the thought of Congnet and I sharing with them the intimacy of an ocean voyage.

33. LONG AGO AND FAR AWAY

We avoided their company as best we could, but on the sixth week out a sudden windstorm arose. In the swiftly shifting wind the *Nimrod,* hitherto so steady on her course, began to plunge from side to side. Unable to seek shelter below, Congnet and I, clutching her ties, crouched behind the weather deck hatch covering.

There was great commotion. Sailors were climbing aloft to attempt the hazardous task of reefing the sails as the wind came on stronger, charging the water at a high speed, creating huge waves through which we crashed, sending icy water along the pitching deck. An awful darkness was growing as low, rolling, gray clouds thickened and distant lightning, quite startlingly, appeared to crack the sky apart. As this was taking place, I saw that consternation had overwhelmed a group of passengers who were taking shelter behind another hatch covering.

A wheeled perambulator, obviously with a child within, was being blown along the slanting deck. It had escaped the hold of the woman who was now screaming soundlessly into the storm, having fallen heavily on the deck as a the result of chasing after it. No sooner had I seen this, Congnet was running across the plunging deck, and grabbing the child from the contraption, which was instantly flung over the side, he went crawling on his knees, holding the baby to his chest, towards the terrified woman who was being supported by her husband. Bracing myself for a sudden fall, I first staggered and then crawled across the deck towards her. She was in pain, having injured her hip and very likely dislocated her shoulder.

Seeing that Congnet had handed the baby to her frightened relatives who were holding on to the ropes that secured the covering, I held her close and we both crawled across the pitching deck, being soaked along the way by the waves that were crashing over the sides. Congnet by this time was being embraced by a man, the child's father no doubt.

As it sometimes happens with sudden storms at sea, the whirlwind that had overtaken us was by then moving away, whipping the water astern. In the sudden sunlight, we were all quite bewildered and drenched. The child's mother needed to be attended to, this was done below deck rather quickly by myself and the ship's doctor, an elderly man with much experience in shipboard accidents.

The captain, along with Mr. Turnbull, came up along with other members of the ship's company. The child's mother thanked us for saving her baby and planted a kiss upon Congnet's lips, held him close, and taking his face between her hands, kissed him again and again, the child's father and others looking on, some with embarrassed laughter, others—including Jean—with frank surprise upon their faces. The couple, he an American, she a Barbadian, could not thank us enough and insisted that we should take a reward. This, of course, we declined. Several seamen and a few passengers had been injured during the storm, and I assisted the ship's doctor to set a number of fractures, while bringing comfort to those who, recovering from their hysteria, had been convinced that their end was near.

For the remainder of the voyage, the event naturally altered the relationship between Congnet, myself, and the other passengers.

33. Long Ago and Far Away

We were from then on "hail fellow well met" and spoken of—in a manner that ensured our overhearing—as examples of "a different sort of black". I took it as it came, remembering the treatment that I had received from people with whom I had crossed the Atlantic four years ago, people whom I had helped when they became seriously ill or distressed at sea, who, on their arrival in Trinidad, had laughed at the gross mistreatment that I received from the immigration officials in Port of Spain. Yet the sun was shining to light our way, and a favourable wind was bringing a fine drizzle, even as one of the planters could be heard sniggering, as another echoed Cowper's ironic lines:

> *I own I am shock'd at the purchase of slaves,*
> *And fear those who buy them and sell them are knaves;*
> *What I hear of their hardships, their tortures, and groans;*
> *Is almost enough to draw pity from stones.*
> *I pity them greatly, but I must be mum,*
> *For how could we do without sugar and rum?*
> *Especially sugar, so needful we see?*
> *What? give up our desserts, our coffee, and tea!*

34. THE OPEN DOOR

"T'is pleasant, sure, to see one's name in print.
A book's a book, although there's nothing in't."

George Gordon Lord Byron

THE COLONNADE AT BURLINGTON HOUSE

1823: LONDON IN SUMMER WAS AS I REMEMBERED IT. Warmer than one could tolerate, noisier than ever and overly crowded with bustling people, carts and coaches, drays and hearses, the hubbub of its sooty business rising above the ever-present grime. We made our way through the mud and filth in a hired carriage to Great Coram Street, where we were received by a surprised Anne-Rachael, my aunt Judith's eldest daughter who nevertheless welcomed us and showed us to rooms where we were made comfortable. Anne-Rachael, still unmarried, had assumed the role of head of our family in England after the death of uncle Edmond at Whittington Hall.

The house was still in mourning and the sadness and grief for the passing of their father was very touching for me, especially so as I had left my own father on his deathbed. That evening we all remembered the kindness and generosity of uncle Edmond, recalling

34. THE OPEN DOOR

what he had done for us all. Patently we would not be where we were if it had not been for him.

Anne-Rachael's youngest brother Philip was away at school and Louis-Edmund, some years younger than she, had joined the firm of Campbell, Baillie and Harper, all former business associates of uncle Edmond. Louis-Edmund was seeing a lot of a young lady, Elizabeth Charlotte Western, and I was surprised and pleased to learn that in spite of the obvious differences between uncle Edmond's two families, a very cordial, in truth loving and loyal relationship, existed between his children with aunt Judith and those with his wife Jane. Uncle Edmond had managed to continue a plaçage relationship with aunt Judith in England, very much in the same manner as my father had done in Trinidad with Cécile.

However, it was Vincent Wanostrocht whom I was most anxious to meet. I was haunted by the thought that he might have died, as I counted on him to help me to make contact with Lord Bathurst on a less formal basis, in whose hands I wanted to place 'A Free Mulatto', the study that Congnet and myself had conducted based on the names on the petition. Together with accompanying documents—these were voluminous—I felt the need to discuss with Vincent the nature of my appeal, so that a clear understanding of its content and purpose could be explained. After all, Bathurst himself had asked me for a report on understanding the nature of my academic work.

Congnet and I first found our way to the cottage at Camberwell Green, where Vincent and I last spoke, only to learn from a neighbour that the family had moved away. To where? The man had no idea. After several inquiries, we discovered that Vincent was now living in the county town of Norwich in East Anglia. Congnet and I travelled there by Royal Mail coach some weeks later. It was a long, one hundred mile journey that took us east from London, then northward to this rural county.

The journey was first made horrendous by the rain that flooded the abominable roads, and then dangerous, in truth frightening, when at dusk we were pounced upon by a company of horsemen, posing as highwaymen, from the shadowed interior of a copse of trees. One would have thought that this sort of attack was a thing of the past! The postilion rider, who was guiding the team through the difficult terrain, was shot and wounded. The coachman, with great shouts and wielding his whip, with the poor postilion clinging to the harness, just managed to outrun the bandits, the guard firing a huge brass blunderbuss loaded with iron nails at the foremost of the villains. With a great clang and crash we were across a bridge, just managing to make the safety of the next staging post. The postilion rider, hardly more than a boy, died in my arms that night. He had been shot through the descending thoracic aorta; the ball, entering his chest, had lodged itself in his ribcage. Jean and I felt quite outraged about the incident! One would have thought this type of attack, in civilised England, would more suit a previous century.

Two days on and still quite shaken we entered Norwich, an ancient place overwhelmed by its very large cathedral. The man at the coaching inn, after recovering from our appearance, he had never before seen Negroes, was able to tell us that there was a newly arrived family living at Stump Cross farm, on the edge of the city where two roads met. We found them there, Vincent, his wife Mary and their four children. They were staying at a cottage on a farm owned by his uncle Nicholas. It was a lovely setting that overlooked a vast heathland. He had moved there because of his failing health, believing that the prevailing wind rising from the sea would alleviate his consumptive condition. It was tragic to see him so terribly wasted, although well cared for by his Mary, who was herself hardly more than skin and bones. She had a bad cough and an inflamed throat which I examined but was unable to recommend anything except gargling with salt water. Congnet and I were accommodated in the large barn, as there was no room for us in their cottage. This we shared with several horses and at night with the cattle.

The morning following our arrival we sat in a sunlit garden where I related to Vincent in some detail the condition of the free

34. THE OPEN DOOR

blacks and people of colour in Trinidad as I found it. I told him that my approach in writing the appeal to Bathurst was from a scientific perspective. That as an alienist, I had listened carefully to the complaints of the free people and to what was being imposed on them by the governor, while paying attention to their sense of wellbeing, their mental health so to speak. I then described to him what appeared to me to be not just grave infractions of the law, but a crime being perpetrated against the very humanity of these people. That mental and financial damage was being done to a free people by a representative of the Crown who ironically was the colony's first civil governor.

"That an educated man, a person placed in a position of absolute authority, could be setting about so vile an undertaking as to belittle the majority of the free people in a British colony has come to me as a shock, Vincent. To deprive them of the simplest privileges! To threaten their legal right to own and bequeath property is to render their lives meaningless. The interviews that Congnet and I conducted revealed evidence of specific incidents of cruelty and actual harm. What clearly emerges is the hopelessness, fear and overall depression that we have found right across coloured society, but especially amongst the young. It is all very alarming. And Woodford was just here, in England, no doubt to defend his monstrous position."

Vincent nodded, and appeared to want to add something to what I had been telling him, but I could see that he was either lost for words or perhaps afraid that he might have a coughing fit. Continuing I told him:

"In Trinidad, there is a people in formation. Trinidad is not like the other, older colonies, Vincent, where a society had been created over generations, where black and white, slave and free, the mixed race, a product of history, all existed over generations in the miasma of plantation slavery. In Trinidad every individual, every family, has only just arrived. People with all sorts of experiences, views, opinions, political allegiances, who have come from all over the Caribbean. We people of colour, who are in the majority of the free people there, wherever we came from, we are the ones who represent the most cohesive unit. We are, or should be, the *cornerstone* of the society. That is why I must meet with His Lordship, to impress on him that this destruction of sense and sensibility must end."

"Do you not concern yourself with those who are enslaved?"

"No, Vincent, I do not. Emancipation of the slaves is inevitable. I am concerned with the future of *everyone* in Trinidad. If these injustices against the free people are not addressed now, they will certainly go into the future and affect the freshly emancipated, even more so than those who have been free for generations."

"And what would be the result if these issues are not addressed?"

"An armed uprising will surely take place, much like in Grenada in '95, and only ruin would follow. The habit, or I should say the culture of resistance, is already embedded in the population. But I can see that you are not yourself, old friend, you must now rest. I have to find your uncle Nicholas so that he could help me to meet Lord Bathurst. I did promise to give him a report, remember? Here it is, in manuscript, all three hundred pages with supporting appendices."

I had with me the manuscript that I had entitled *A Free Mulatto - An Address to the Right Honourable Earl Bathurst*. I showed a few pages to him, but there was no question of him perusing them. He had neither the interest nor the strength.

"I'm afraid uncle Nicholas is dead, Jean," he said sadly. "The person who might help you to arrange a congenial meeting with his Lordship is Lady Charlotte Cavendish Bentinck. She was for many years uncle Nicholas' friend and patron. He had tutored her brothers in French and dedicated a work of his, 'Petite encyclopédie des jeunes gens,' to her. She recently married Captain Charles Fulke Greville. A very wealthy man they say, invested in the East India Company. They are well known to Lord Bathurst. Greville was the Naval Officer for Demerara and Essequibo, and is presently Registrar and Clerk of Council for Tobago, I believe."

34. THE OPEN DOOR

Vincent, overcome by a fit of coughing, could not go on, and holding to his mouth a handkerchief, appeared for lack of breath on the point of fainting. I glimpsed blood and mucus on the handkerchief. The coughing attack had tired him, and with some help he retired to his bed. Later that evening, as we sat close to the fire in the small room, I could see that he was attempting to carry on his work which, he said, was a revision of his uncle's editions of Marmontel and other French classics. I could tell that the surprise of our visit and the excitements of our conversations had worn him out.

"His Lordship is pressing for colonial reform." He spoke so softly that I had to lean forward to hear him. "He sees existing conditions as cruel and a waste of human life. He also knows that it has a corrupting influence in the politics here. He has given his support to Clarkson and Wilberforce. He will be interested in what you have to say concerning the blacks when they are eventually freed. You will need to have what you have brought with you printed and bound, Jean, with several copies made." Plainly his chest when breathing was painful, and very much so when coughing. This, I knew, would make him exceedingly weak to the point of losing consciousness. Yet rallying, he went on, "It would make for easier reading, you know. I would recommend S. Gosnell, Printer, Little Queen Street, London. I will pen a letter to his Lordship reminding him of our meeting, recommending you to him. He is a just man, humane, I am sure that he will listen to what you have to say."

We stayed with them for another day. His eldest son, Nicholas, assuming the role of host, was kind and thoughtful. I recorded in my journal how troubled I was to see Vincent in what was obviously the advanced stage of his illness, and remembering the work by Dr. Benjamin Marten who had conjectured that consumption was caused by microbes that were spread by people living in close proximity to each other, I became more than a little concerned. It was a deadly disease and, according to Marten, contagious. I must say I was relieved to leave poor Vincent and his Mary and take the long and miserable road back to London, after promising that I would follow all his advice.

Some weeks later the freshly printed petition, and the voluminous list of several thousand names along with the relevant documents and testimonials, were taken by ourselves to the office of the Chief Clerk in the office of the Secretary of State for War and the Colonies. It was in an unprepossessing room in the basement of Whitehall, dingy and cold, that this indescribably important body of work, which carried the hopes and ambitions of a generation, was left by Congnet and myself. I had deliberately placed it in the hands of an austere, disturbingly dignified man, whom we mistakenly believed to be the Chief Clerk himself, only learning later that he was the Chief Clerk's Under Secretary's assistant!

Where would it go? Into whose hands would it fall? What would become of it? We had not an idea. Leaving Whitehall that evening and walking into the silence of its vast courtyard, Congnet and I both experienced a sense of anticlimax difficult to express even to ourselves. I became increasingly anxious that my written appeal would not find its way to Lord Bathurst himself. But a lucky turn was to come our way that very evening.

Returning to Great Coram Street, I made the acquaintance of Henry Amendroz, a person of French Huguenot descent who was Chief Clerk to the First Lord of the Admiralty, Sir John Jervis. Amendroz was engaged to marry Magdelaine-Judith, Anne-Rachael's younger sister. He was an amusing man who enjoyed relating anecdotes overheard at the Admiralty that highlighted the calm tenacity of the English, whom he admired excessively.

That evening at dinner he regaled us with stories of his superior's intrepidity, saying that it was on the quarter-deck of *H.M.S. Victory* that Admiral Jervis at the very start of the Battle of Cape St. Vincent displayed "the true equilibrium of his race". It would appear that Jervis' post-captain, one Robert Calder, had commenced the counting of enemy ships rounding the cape. Assuming a role and imitating the singsong upper-class voice of Calder and the taciturn

34. THE OPEN DOOR

stoic tone of the Admiral, Amendroz drawled the conversation between Admiral Jervis and his post-captain:

"There are eight sail of the line, Sir John."

"Very well, Sir."

"There are twenty sail of the line, Sir John."

"Very well, Sir."

"There are twenty-five sail of the line, Sir John."

"Very well, Sir."

"There are twenty-seven sail of the line, Sir John."

"Enough, Sir, no more of that; the die is cast, and if there are fifty sail, I shall go through them."

"And with this," Amendroz exclaimed, "Jervis hoisted the signal: 'Take suitable stations for mutual support and engage the enemy as coming up in succession.'" Here he paused apparently for effect, continuing, "this was when Jervis discovered that he was outnumbered by nearly two-to-one."

Later that evening, the ladies having withdrawn to the parlour, I asked Amendroz if he was acquainted with Captain Charles Greville. He said that he was, and after learning that I had already met Lord Bathurst, then listening closely to my reason for wanting the meeting with Lady Charlotte, he said that he would be pleased to introduce us to the captain. He added, I suppose not clearly understanding the nature of our cause, that Bathurst had moved a motion in the House of Lords in May of this very year to the effect that it was expedient to adopt effectual and decisive measures for ameliorating the condition of the slave population in His Majesty's colonies.

As we drew up in the Thorntons' brougham, I had to think of the poor drenched coachman, as the Admiralty Office, facing Whitehall, was barely visible through the pouring rain. The United Kingdom Hydrographic Office, as it was also known, was a vast and imposing building. It was responsible for the command of the Royal Navy throughout the world. It was where Amendroz worked and where Congnet and I were to meet with Captain Charles Greville.

Greville was plainly a man who had been to sea. He was perhaps a few years older than I, ruddy-faced, apparently affable and sophisticated. He rose to greet us as we entered what appeared to be a vast circular map room, where he had been engaged in conversation with another man who immediately left through a hidden door.

"Doctor Philip," he exclaimed, taking my hand. "My colleague Amendroz has explained the purpose for your making our acquaintance. Very noble, most admirable, your quest. My experience with colonial governors tells me that your fellow—what's his name, Amendroz? Ah, don't tell me, you said Woodford, that's it, Woodford—the office has gone to his head."

"Thank you, Sir," I replied, going on to present Congnet and to explain that we had just recently submitted the petition together with its relevant appurtenances to the office of the Secretary of State for War and the Colonies.

"But, having met the honourable gentleman on a previous occasion, my situation would be enhanced if I could speak to him in-camera, so to speak!"

"I understand from Amendroz here that you were tutored by Vincent Wanostrocht?"

"It was to my benefit. He introduced me to literature and the classics, and because of his own interest—he was attending an Inn of Court at the time—I was made aware of the effectiveness of the rule of law in the British legal system."

"Yes, quite, if you can pay for it."

I thought it best to be silent, and after a moment asked when it might be possible to meet Earl Bathurst.

"I must say, Philip, you are the first civilised black man I have met. Are there many like you where you come from?"

34. The Open Door

I assured him that there were others like myself and Congnet, but did not venture further.

"Bathurst will be at Burlington House. He will be visiting Lady Charlotte on the morrow. You know it, in Mayfair! It's where we are, when in town. Come at six. Now I must leave you."

Burlington House was the most imposing mansion on Piccadilly, save perhaps Devonshire House just along the way. I had with me one of the printed and bound copies of *A Free Mulatto*. I was relieved to find that Congnet and I had been expected. We were escorted by a tottering lackey in green, gold and powder to the colonnade, a distinguishing feature of this magnificent residence. Consisting of more than twenty exceedingly tall marble columns curving gracefully to receive the early evening's sun, it overlooked the inner courtyard.

From a distance I could hear a woman's echoing laughter and the sounds of children at play. Lord Bathurst was as I remembered him, a handsome man now in his fifties. He was apparently pleased to see me as he came towards me with an expression of happy surprise, saying, "Doctor Philip, we meet again, after all these years."

I was presented to Lady Charlotte Cavendish Bentinck, who, to my utter surprise, held out her pale hand, which I took in mine and bowing, raised to my lips.

"There you are, Charlotte, didn't I tell you Dr. Philip would possess the art of kissing hands! He was well brought up and has appropriated to himself all of the more pleasing pretensions to gentility!"

Lady Charlotte with a lively eye looked me over from head to foot, withdrew her hand, and said, "And handsome too, Harry, for a darkie. Doctor, do tell, what of Vincent Wanostrocht? He shared the nursery floor with you, Harry, when his uncle Nicholas taught us Italian and French."

"I am sorry to say, my Lady, that he does not do well."

"I received a letter from him just yesterday," said Lord Bathurst, "reminding me of when last we met. He recommends you highly. In it he tells of a report that you have prepared, based on your findings as a medical man, and that you wished to have a word about it before handing it over to me."

"I do indeed."

"Philip here is a medical doctor who has specialised in maladies of the mind. A new field of medicine. Remind us—what took you into that area of research?"

"I suppose it came about as the result of wondering at my own very active imagination, and from reading what came to hand on the subject of the human mind. Then, shortly before a final decision was made on the topic of my dissertation, the school of medicine was visited by Dr. Johann Spurzheim of the University of Vienna. He delivered a lecture on his craniological and phrenological theories. His view was that the brain is the organ of the mind and that human behaviour can be usefully understood in neurological rather than philosophical or religious terms."

"How fascinating, Doctor," sighed Lady Charlotte. "The very idea sets my heart to racing."

"Come, Philip, let us take a turn. I am sure that her Ladyship will excuse us."

Bowing discreetly to her, who in turn curtsied with a charming glance that I noticed contained no irony, we stepped away.

"The colonnade is pleasant at this time of day, and you can speak of your concerns, but before, I must tell you that I have met with Sir Ralph Woodford and Don Antonio Gomez, his Assessor, and listened with care to what they have had to relate concerning the situation in Trinidad. Now, tell me, what is the state of mental health in *your* Trinidad?"

"I am sorry to say, Sir, that it deteriorates daily. Our principal grievance lies in that subjection, that degradation of the mind, by

34. THE OPEN DOOR

which our class is condemned to lose all idea of dignity, and by comparison is depressed to an abject and grovelling condition. This mental slavery has become the prime cause of the accusation with which we are taunted. It creates circumstances that may lead over time to social unrest, particularly as a result of the recently published Order in Council."

"Yes, we are aware that there are problems arising out of the condition of the free mulattoes in Trinidad. Contrary to what is being put about, the British government did not have the opportunity to actively protect your people in Trinidad against these supposedly unfriendly regulations. These locally made ordinances, regulations and what have you, were not sent to us first, but were simply implemented by the military men who were there from the start. They created them for reasons of security. But I understand that Trinidad is in a special category."

"We are. As you may already know, we do not seek *new* rights, we wish only to retain those we already have, and to plead for the unfair laws that were passed over the years, and particularly in more recent times, to be repealed and annulled. I understand from Vincent that the British government, at vast expense, has undertaken to fight the international slave trade."

"We have indeed, under the Mitigation and Gradual Abolition of Slavery policy, which was inaugurated at the start of this year. We have paid large sums to several countries as an incentive to abolish this trade. In addition, we have dispatched the navy to enforce this imperative, and we are pleased to see that the United States have passed their own Act prohibiting importation of slaves."

"It is gratifying that you believe it expedient to adopt effectual and decisive measures to end the Atlantic slave trade and to work towards ameliorating the condition of the slave population in His Majesty's colonies, in such a manner as may prepare it for participation in those civil rights and privileges which are enjoyed by other classes of His Majesty's subjects. However, in Trinidad, because the civil rights for the mulatto class are being diminished by the actions of Governor Woodford, I fear that by the time the enslaved are liberated, the situation would be such that what you intend could be beyond your reach."

"How so, Doctor?"

I told him that in addition to what I had discovered when looking into Sir Ralph's improprieties and impositions on the free coloured people, I had found that there was a dangerous current of defiance embedded in the very history of this small underpopulated place, and that the soon-to-be-liberated would be entering an environment in which a culture of revolt had long taken root. This culture had originated in Grenada, I said, as well as in other islands during the French revolution, and had been brought to Trinidad. It existed in my own family, where two of my uncles had been executed by the British because of their involvement in the Grenada rebellion of 1795, a republican-minded rebellion, I told him, which had been resorted to largely because in the minds of the free coloured people in Grenada, the British had reneged on their commitment to maintain a certain status quo. After the rebellions in Grenada and in other islands had been crushed, a quantity of republican-minded refugees fled to Trinidad. I explained further that they were both coloured and white, and that they had resisted the Spanish government at every turn, seeking to create an atmosphere of upheaval so as to allow Victor Hugues and the republican forces under his control to seize Trinidad. This French element, in a Spanish colony, with slaves armed, rose in their hundreds to face a British ship's company brought ashore by its irate commander, and action that resulted in war being declared between Britain and Spain. After the British conquest of Trinidad this French element, vengefully believing that the Spanish Governor Chacón had handed over Trinidad to the English to prevent a French republican takeover, went so far as to influence the French government later, during the Bonaparte era. Pressure was brought to bear on a compliant administration in Spain to overturn the verdict of a court-martial that had exonerated the Spanish governor. "Vice Admiral Chacón was subsequently

34. The Open Door

sentenced to perpetual banishment in Portugal where he died, old and wretched."

Another example of this clique's mischievous intention to undermine authority, to support radical causes and to keep alive the spirit of resistance within Trinidad's society, I said to him, may be seen in the serious charges brought against Sir Ralph by them and laid in Parliament some years ago through their agent Marryat. It had to do with the governor's handling of the refugees from the war in Venezuela. "It would appear," I went on to relate, "that hundreds, perhaps thousands of poor people, chiefly women and children, died when forced by Woodford to return to Venezuela, where they were killed out of hand by the Spanish royalists. The plight of these people, regarded by the governor as republicans fleeing Spain's royalist forces, was seized upon by this radical element to discredit the governor."

I said that in my opinion, the governor had little or no choice in the matter. A war of extermination was raging on the Main. Both sides had liberated their slaves. "Governor Woodford governed a slave colony within a day's sail of a terrible war, and he could not have allowed the indiscriminate reception of persons from Venezuela, as this would have proven to be very dangerous."

I explained that with the conquest of the island by the British in 1797, this tendency towards agitation and mischief had deepened, because many saw themselves as French, even if they were in fact of mixed race. They perceived the British as an occupying force. They feared that the British would once again default on their commitments, in this case, to what they had agreed in the Articles of Capitulation, viz accepting the terms of the Spanish Cedula which had brought the French to Trinidad in the first place. This had now been made worse by the Order in Council of 1822, which was plainly punitive, and would generate even greater resistance against the Crown. All this would certainly find its way into the minds of those newly liberated once slavery was abolished, and could conceivably, possibly inevitably, lead to social unrest and violence on a scale comparable to Saint-Domingue.

Woodford's locally contrived ordinances and regulations, I said, interfered with the former grants of land by the Crown of Spain during 1783 and after. Owing to the rude state of society, the want of sufficient records and surveys, people found it difficult to prove their titles, let alone papers that confirmed their freedom. "That being the case, my Lord, especially with the aforementioned Order in Council, there will be resistance going forward. It has been implanted in this colonial society. It is where conflicts begin, it is embedded in the dichotomy of the skin and as such, it must be carefully addressed."

Then, remembering Percy Shelley who had recently died, I spoke of hope seen beaming through the mists of fear, in this instance of Woodford's strictures. I told him that I was a supporter of the policy of amelioration and believed in the need for social reform, emphasising that all we had ever asked for was that whatever distinctions might exist in society, there should be no distinction before the law. Injustices were being perpetrated by a representative of the Crown at a time when at the very seat of government, in the Palace of Westminster, men like himself, Buxton and Wilberforce were striving for humanity and justice to be demonstrated in the affairs of the colonies. I declared, quoting Lord Byron and no doubt straying from the point, "It is not one man nor a million, but the spirit of liberty that must be preserved," going on to add that the waves which dash upon the shore are, one by one, broken, but the ocean conquers nevertheless. Then, adding altogether over-dramatically, "It overwhelmed even the Armada, it wears out the rock. In like manner, whatever the struggle of individuals, the great cause will gather strength."

In my pause for breath, Lord Bathurst inquired how many free mulattoes there were in Trinidad, and I answered him some fifteen thousand, as opposed to the whites who numbered less than four thousand, and that we were increasing in number and wealth, in knowledge and respectability.

"Half the property of the colony is in our hands," I said, "and we are advancing rapidly in all the arts of civil life."

34. THE OPEN DOOR

"Your complaint against Sir Ralph, together with the remonstrances contained in the petition and the public response to the recent Order in Council, has taken both myself and Mr. Stephen, our lead legal advisor, by surprise," he said. "A Judicial Commission, with significantly widened terms of reference, has been dispatched to investigate the conditions of the free mulattoes on your island, among other issues, I rather suspect you missed their arrival. Their report will illuminate, inform and guide us. I must thank you for what you have related. It is an unknown history and one that must be given close attention when it comes to making decisions about Trinidad."

Indeed, I had no notion of this Judicial Commission, as we had departed Trinidad before its arrival. I said so. Lord Bathurst inclined his head, leading me to think that there was a great deal I did not know.

"From your sentiments, I see that you have inculcated the ideas of our Romantic writers into your thinking," he said evenly, perhaps reflectively. "You are something of a paradox, Dr. Philip, in that you are obviously a Romantic on the one hand, and on the other a man of science. You have identified yourself with those you see as being marginalised, yet you view yourself as separate from them, an outsider, even perhaps an heroic one, which is interesting in itself when coupled with your training. You have reacted to the obvious social injustice, in truth the political injustice that you have found on returning to your island, as a doctor trained to a particular discipline."

"Truly, my Lord, I do see myself as an individual, even as an outsider. I cannot help but approach this situation in Trinidad in a scientific manner because it relates to lives—the souls and minds of a free people—the manner in which the society is organised. I have written a study on what I have found and would like very much to present it to you."

I said this, taking from my coat pocket the book, printed and bound, which I had collected that morning.

"Why, thank you, a handsome work, I see that you have availed yourself of Vincent's printer, most thoughtful. Inflammatory, I'll wager. I see that you have signed it as 'A Free Mulatto'. In speaking to you, Byron comes to mind. He is presently in Genoa. Was living there with Countess Guiccioli, and I have heard, the Blessingtons. He may have accepted overtures for his support from representatives of the movement for Greek independence from the Ottoman Empire."

"Has he taken up the Greek cause?"

"I have heard that the Countess has returned to her husband. That, I am sure, will precipitate Byron's decision to go and fight on the Greek side in their war for independence."

"The Romantic writers appear to be changing the way that people see themselves and the world."

"Voltaire, as I am sure you know, thought that almost nothing great has ever been done in the world except by the genius and firmness of a single man combating the prejudices of the multitude. You seek to liberate your people in much the same manner that Byron would liberate the Greeks! You push at an open door, my good man. I will read what you have written on behalf of your people, remembering *The Prisoner of Chillon*, where Byron himself wrote of liberty as the eternal spirit of the chain-less mind. Your petition and its accompanying appurtenances that were delivered to the Chief Clerk's office are already with James Stephen, into whose hands the Judicial Commissioner's report on Trinidad will also be placed."

"Thank you, my Lord, you are most kind."

Our footsteps were echoing on the flagstones as we left the colonnade. Twilight had fallen and shadows were crowding close. There was nothing more to be said and we parted with a firm handshake.

34. THE OPEN DOOR

I RETURNED TO GREAT CORAM STREET WITH MIXED EMOTIONS. My meeting with Lord Bathurst had been a turning point, clearly. After a long, arduous and at times exciting buildup, it had come to such a quiet ending, even a candid exchange of ideas. I wrote in my journal that I did not know if to laugh or to cry. Jean Congnet was first amused, then excited. He kept repeating, "What luck, Jean!" I suppose it was. It had only to do with a somewhat marvellous pattern of coincidence, starting with Vincent being my tutor. Who would have guessed that Vincent was connected to the Bathurst family by virtue of his uncle Nicholas being their French tutor?

"And how connected they continued to be" said Congnet, adding, "Imagine, Vincent's uncle, of all people, enjoying the patronage of Lady Charlotte, who was also taught by him,"

"He ran a school for many years. He would have influenced many. Vincent certainly shaped my future. What a remarkable family."

"What a remarkable time."

"Had it not been for uncle Edmund, nothing of the sort would have ever happened to me."

"How so, actually?"

"I was sent to him as a boy. My parents had no idea what it meant to have a formal education, a classical education, gaining a profession by attending a university. Neither did yours."

"I was apprenticed to a writing clerk when I was thirteen. In Manchester. The firm that acted as our agent there, Athelstan and Davidson. Did I tell you that?"

"No, what was that like?"

"I learned to read and write. That opened my eyes. Over time, I came to understand how our money was made. I would have remained in England. Left to me, I would not have returned to Trinidad, but I had to be ready to take over from father. You've seen the type of man he is. Everything all mapped out."

"For my part," I told him, "it was uncle Edmund who engaged Vincent to tutor me, who placed me with Dr. Gilchrist in Edinburgh and with the Urquharts at Craigston Castle in the Highlands. I would like to visit uncle Edmund's son Butler at Whittington Hall. Come with me, you will enjoy it."

Butler Thornton was a year younger than I, which made him twenty-nine. He was the new lord of the manor. We had never met but, because of the principles of mutuality in which the family was reared, he was pleased to receive us. Having recently returned from Good Hope, their sugar plantation in Demerara, there was about him, in his appearance and manner, the look of a man of affairs. His bronzed face still bore the tawny hue of the traveller in the tropics.

Whittington Hall was much changed; there were no parrots in cages in the morning room and neither were there black servants about. But, there was still an innumerable quantity of stuffed creatures under glass, a very fine collection of tropical butterflies, quantities of dusty coral and several enormous conch shells, used as door stops, which I was sure came from Carriacou. Butler was a man of business. His firm Bruce, Thornton & Company in London acted as agent on behalf of several estates in Demerara, Barbados and other British territories in the West Indies.

He introduced us to the gentry who lived in the vicinity of Kirkby Lonsdale, a quaint market town, situated on the edge of the Yorkshire Dales. We were quite a novelty, and were presented as men of great substance, the owners of slaves and sugar plantations in the West Indies. It was a restful time and Congnet and I enjoyed walking out, taking part in shoots, and boating on the river Lune. We were fascinated to see a great house, Underley Hall, under construction. We parted, Butler and I, with mutual feelings of being well met, especially after Louis-Edmund and young Philip, my cousins, his half-brothers, joined us for a short stay. It was for me a most pleasing time. These men were my family and I had so much in common with them. It was, however, time to return to

34. THE OPEN DOOR

London where Louis-Edmund, soon to be engaged to the lovely Elizabeth Charlotte Western, had business to attend.

Some weeks later, we were returning to Great Coram Street from Hatchards bookshop on Piccadilly, where I had purchased Walter Scott's latest novels *The Betrothed* and *The Talisman,* a stranger, appearing quite distracted, stopped me on the street to give the alarming news that a collapse in sugar prices had occurred. Because of our appearance, dark men, dressed in the height of fashion, he may have been a planter and assumed that we were as well.

"Surely, this means ruin for the industry," siad Congnet glumly. "And for us."

Louis-Edmund was waiting for us at the door. Letters had arrived from Trinidad. The one addressed to him was from Frédéric, it contained the news of my father's death and the wish that I be informed so that I could return as soon as possible. The other one was from Susanne, addressed to me. It too spoke of the death of my father, but also told of a stroke or seizure suffered by mother in the weeks following his funeral, and it also urged my return to Trinidad. The third was to be sent on to Susannah and Guillaume Robin in France. We said very fond farewells to Henry Amendroz, Louis-Edmund, Magdalaine, Anne-Rachael and young Philip who had been away at school in Tunbridge Wells. By the following week, we were at St. Katharine Docks to take ship for the West Indies.

35. The Baton Is Passed

"A change came o'er the spirit of my dream."

George Gordon Lord Byron

TRINIDAD 1825: I WAS NOT AT ALL PREPARED FOR THE CHANGES that had taken place during my sojourn abroad. On the surface, all appeared to be the same, except for a quiet that permeated the household at Concorde. A silence that said mother was resting and should not be disturbed. A stillness that suggested an alteration in the order of things and that no one had assumed control. Neither André-Montrose, nor Frédéric who was at Philippine, nor Belizaire who also was ill, appeared to have the energy to man the breach left by the seeming collapse of mother's will to continue after the passing of our father. It was my brother in law Thomas Corsbie who gave the impression of being the master in charge of affairs. And even he on my appearance was only too eager to hand over the reins.

My first care was for mother. I found her resting in her room. Not in bed where I had expected, but in a planter's chair, close to an opened window in her bedroom, her legs elevated along the long attachments to the armrests that allowed the occupant to recline in comfort. She had not suffered a stroke. She had simply collapsed as the result of the mental and physical strain that followed father's death and the onrush of overwhelming circumstances that had followed. Her immediate concern was for Belizaire.

"He is so thin, Jean," she said after we had settled ourselves. "It is as though Belizaire will follow your father. I noticed that he hardly eats anything anymore and he has neither strength nor energy. Cécile is treating him, but I know, she doesn't have to say, that

35. The Baton Is Passed

there is nothing that she can do for him. Then I became so beside myself when I realised that his complexion had changed. And then papa! Even though I had been expecting your father's passing, and I had become accustomed to his condition, I had no idea that I would be so upset. Jean, I cannot tell you how much I miss him. And poor Cécile, she too is heartbroken. We find comfort in saying the rosary, praying that he is at rest, in peace, in God's heaven."

She made a helpless gesture with her hands that tore at my heart and seemed at a loss for words as she closed her eyes, smiling sadly.

Looking at her, the drawn features, her eyes sunken and shadowed, I could see how the passage of time had taken its toll. Yet, plainly this was not the end for her. She was simply worn out and afraid. I took her thin hand in mine and brought it to my lips, she smiled, her eyes still closed, and taking a deep breath said, "Jean, I am so glad that you have come back home at last. Go, see to Belizaire, he is very sick and I don't know how to help him, go."

Belizaire lay abed in an adjoining room. Plainly very ill, he attempted to rise as I entered. It was all that I could do to restrain him. He appeared emaciated, his complexion an awful yellow. Jaundice, I thought as I examined the sclera, his white of eye, it was yellow. The chamber pot, as yet not taken away, contained the dark urine that I had hoped not to see.

"How do you feel?" I asked, lifting his shirt and passing my hands over his stomach. He shook his head. "Bad, Jean. I itch all over, my back aches, my belly is so painful, I can't eat. I'm shitting myself. This is terrible. I know I am dying."

Feeling him, feeling for his organs, I became aware of a malformation in the region of his liver. Even to pass my hand gently over the area made him wince with pain. A case of acute pancreatitis, perhaps, had overtaken him, I wondered, then, looking more closely at what else was contained in the chamber pot, I could not help but feel that very likely something far more deadly was at play. There was nothing that I could do for him other than administer laudanum.

It was a very sad homecoming. Later that evening Susanne came. I had anticipated her arrival and was standing in the carriageway waiting. As the sunlight faded I heard the sound of hoof-beats in the distance and there she was, drawing up her stallion in a cloud of golden dust. She too seemed changed. In my mind, while away, she had become more beautiful, even ethereal and in a way not of this world. She looked older now, harder, and I could see that she knew what I was thinking.

"I'm not as I was, eh!"

"Oh Susanne, please, don't say anything. I am so glad that you came, come, let me hold you." And she was in my arms. Her hot cheek, wet with tears, was against my own. I had no tears to mingle with hers.

There was much to tell. I listened. We could be all facing ruin, she said. She was au courant with the financial collapse that had overwhelmed the British economic system. The European wars, the tightening of bank lending which made it almost impossible for planters or even merchants to raise capital. She spoke without a pause of the economics of slavery, the effects of the Amelioration Order. The collapse of sugar prices. The difficulties presently being experienced with labour, the growing recalcitrance of the slaves. The increasing cost of their upkeep. The state of the colony, her state of mind, my state of mind. I told her what I thought of Belizaire's illness. She said that she knew that he was going to die very soon. She had seen it, plainly. We spoke of mother.

"Your mother is not sick. She is tired. Uncle Jean's never-ending illness had taken a lot out of her. As for Belizaire, she is already in mourning for him. You cannot imagine how a mother feels to see her child die. That too will pass. You are here now. All will be better." Then, taking my face between her hands, she looked closely at me, into my eyes, and said, "Oh Jean, don't go. Stay with us for as long as you can. We need you here now. The others are useful, but you are the only one who can see us through these changes."

35. The Baton Is Passed

Then, as though caught in a moment of confusion, so uncharacteristic, she said, "I lost the child I was carrying for you, Jean. Cécile said it was God's will. Your mother didn't say anything, but I knew she thought that it was God's punishment. I was ill for some time after. I could not keep the reason why a secret. I needed their help. Now everyone knows about us."

She wondered if that bothered me. I told her no. What else could I have said? It was late when we supped and even later when I took her to bed. There was no passion in our reuniting that night. We were both relieved to have found each other after being apart for two years, but the thought that she had carried a child, my child, I found hard to dismiss. My child! She was going to have our baby. A boy, a girl. I would have been a father, had she not lost it. What a tragedy. Something of me had died. Or, had not been born. It went round in my head for several days and it still does.

"Yea the first morning of creation wrote what the last dawn of reckoning shall read." The words of Omar Khayyam, the Persian poet, which I had come across in a German translation, came to my mind as Susanne and I rode out the following morning. Concorde estate had brought in its sugar crop. The raddled fields were in disarray, burnt in parts, hacked and trampled, giving off a rich, earthy aroma.

"Concorde is short of hands, Jean, you must see to that." She had, with the morning light, already become a different person. Even the stallion could sense it. I fell into the role. "What should I do?"

"Buy the Aurore estate. The La Chapelle people can't maintain it. There are ten or twelve slaves there. Buy it for those. You have to act before someone else does."

The idea of buying an estate for its chattel slaves made me quail inwardly, to say the least. I personally had never owned a slave. But I knew that she was right.

"Where is Aurore?"

"In Laventille. Close to your father's old estate. Apart from the slaves, it has livestock and there are some buildings on it. Perhaps even a few coppers. We need coppers. It's about three and a half carreaux. You can easily resell it. Michel says there is valuable limestone, an abandoned quarry. You have to act, Jean. Oh for God's sake, you look half asleep."

In the weeks and months that followed my life changed. I continued to see patients and practice medicine, but increasingly I found myself in the role of estate manager, helping my brothers, conferring with mother and Cécile and riding out with Susanne to oversee the work of preparing the fields for replanting on both estates. I was learning "estate work", as it was called. When I could get away, I would ride out to Cupar Grange to pass the time of day with my half-brother, Michel Maxwell, with whom I became closer. His wife Catherine had given him another boy, they have christened him Samuel to honour a Mr. Pinto, a Jewish person who was friendly with Catherine's mother. He seems to be a bright boy and Michel is quite right in thinking of sending him to be educated abroad.

While in Port of Spain—I was there to finalise the purchase of Aurore—I was informed by someone whom I hardly knew that a coloured priest had arrived here. It was all the news. Several people had seen him, it would appear, when he assisted at a High Mass in the newly consecrated Catholic church. A coloured priest. The very idea came as something of a shock to me. I could hardly imagine what that would mean for black people, slave or free coloured, here or anywhere, for that matter. And the white people, what would they be making of that? It was on returning to San Fernando on the *Jacques' Wake* that I heard some more about him. Henri, my nephew an the ship's captain, had all the news and was eager to impart it. Fr. Francis de Ridder was apparently from the British colony of Demerara. He was not a black man but a mulatto. He apparently had been in Trinidad for some time, arriving some months before my return in mid-1825.

35. The Baton Is Passed

"They didn't know what to do with him when he arrived. Nobody had ever seen a coloured priest before. Well, bacchanal!" Henri said, laughing. "Black people, slaves, all kind of people, even white people, started to follow him in the road, to see what he doing, which part he going, who he talking to. Uncle Jean, Trinidad is a really crazy place, oui."

Well, I could attest to that.

"So they had him hiding in the Presbytery in George Street. They now letting him go out again, but he have to have another priest with him. And to say mass too, he have to have a priest there with him. People don't believe that a coloured man could change wine and bread into the body and blood of Christ. Nobody ever hear that!"

"This is a place where change does not go down easily."

"Well, people like us, I suppose are pleased. People are saying that it is because of you, Uncle Jean, and Mr. Congnet that the Church is acting even before the government. That things are changing."

The Judicial Commission had come and gone—three legal experts sent out from England to several West Indian colonies to look into the situation of the free coloureds. They came to Trinidad in 1823 and left in 1824, making a recommendation to the Colonial Office that legal disabilities suffered by the free people of colour should be removed, and in 1826, some of the most glaring discriminatory regulations against us were revoked. Governor Woodford didn't like that much, I suppose—he was as he had been before, some said worse.

My brother Belizaire breathed his last on the 30th of December 1825. It came to me, as I closed shut his eyes, that I had hardly known him. His funeral service, held the morning following his death, was to be conducted at Concorde, followed by his interment next to father in the estate burial ground. Belizaire had been laid out in the drawing-room in a coffin built that very morning. Maman, my sisters, their husbands, the domestics and others had been saying the rosary for what seemed hours and I was waiting for the priest to start the service. I was standing in the verandah awaiting a priest from the Mission when I saw coming up the carriageway what appeared to be a procession.

It was the priest Father de Ridder, obviously, in a black cassock, hooded, and bearing a golden monstrance held high, followed by another priest, also in black, who carried a tall crucifix that flashed in the sunlight. They were accompanied by acolytes and mourners and a great many of the estate's slaves, all enveloped in clouds of what must be incense. My word, we were hardly prepared for this.

Father de Ridder appeared to me to be the one in charge. After being greeted by my brother André-Montrose, who introduced him to maman and the others, I had stepped away to observe all this from the obscurity of the Venezuelan hammocks with the magenta knots. De Ridder proceeded to hear confessions in the privacy of my consulting room and then to say mass, after commandeering the use of the dining room table, there to give them all communion. The other priest, a Spaniard apparently, and the two acolytes, both "pass-for-whites", were in attendance. I came away very impressed. I had never before seen a Catholic Mass and funeral service. De Ridder had even encouraged André-Montrose to give a eulogy, a panegyric of sorts praising Belizaire. So effective was it that there was not a dry eye in the room. I never expected André-Montrose having that sort of oratorical talent!

It was after another service at the burial ground that I had the opportunity to meet Father de Ridder. His informality was refreshing. He spoke very good French and his handshake was firm as he kept my gaze, saying, "I have heard only good things about you, Dr. Philip."

He looked like a man in his middle twenties. Brown-complexioned, with high cheekbones, perhaps a mixture of an Amerindian strain somewhere in his African-Dutch ancestry? We spoke of this and that, pleasantries, his voice kind as he inquired after mother and

35. THE BATON IS PASSED

became genuinely sad when he commiserated with me on our brother's death. Plainly this was his professional manner, as people, family members and others were so obviously arranging themselves to hear what we were saying. He was a novelty, perhaps even a sign of things to come. We parted pleasantly with the unspoken understanding that we would meet again.

That evening, as I spoke with Hobson, Fabien and the others, I found that they appeared optimistic, enfranchised as the result of the Judicial Commissioners' visit. They had been interviewed by the Englishmen. Taken seriously and, most importantly, respected. What they had to say was written down in their presence. That in itself was perceived as an astonishing achievement! Further, a group of white planters were making a case against Woodford. His laws were apparently having a deleterious effect on them as well. Pamphlets had appeared, crudely printed but explicit. Woodford was being demonised! He was being compared to other English governors who were said to have possessed a "genuine spirit of manly British feelings." I could not imagine what that could possibly mean.

"People are comparing you with Woodford, Jean," Hobson was saying. "They see you as their champion. Nowhere has an English governor been so openly maligned. He is characterised as a monster!"

"And you, a saint," said Susanne, laughing dismissively, when the following day I was reporting to her on the evening spent with Hobson and the others. Michel, who had joined us at Philippine, said he had heard it said by Ramón Garcia that Woodford and his circle were extremely anxious to learn what action would follow the judicial inquiry, in as much as the British government had asked the governor to send copies of all the laws discriminating against the free coloureds on to the Colonial Office in London.

"And has he forwarded them to London?"

"I have no idea, Jean, that was just something that I overheard. But I will tell you this, white people, ordinary white people, feel that they are fighting a losing battle to maintain their power and keep their status. Some even believe that their lives are in danger!"

I was not entirely surprised. The planters who were close to their slaves knew that the blacks were aware that people had come from England to talk to the free coloured people about what was going on in the colony.

"Mr. Garcia says that the white people, those around old Begorrat, are putting it about that we are agitating the slaves. They say that we are undermining the government!"

Again I was not surprised. Most of the whites now were new. Glasgow's merchants and traders were rapidly expanding their trade with the cane estates. Setting up stores in the town. Overseers and writing clerks, tradesmen of all sorts, were coming out. Even women travelling on their own. Upon arrival, having found their own level in the society, they would be soon indoctrinated with the manners and customs of the place.

"They say," Michel continued, "that we have been treated too well. That we have been indulged. That legal rights for slaves and equal rights for us are going to derange the balance that has existed since the conquest, and that an uprising of the slaves will surely follow."

"Is there any truth to that? Are the slaves being agitated?"

"No, but they know that things are changing. Those who can read tell the others what is in the newspapers, but they don't understand what they read and they talk a lot of rubbish."

"It's not a matter of if they understand or don't understand," said Susanne, "it's the talk. Because the talk is what gets into their heads."

She was right, of course. The difference between the slaves of today and those of long ago was the access to information and the relative freedom to discuss things among themselves. In times past, if a slave was suspected of anything, anything at all, the severest of

35. The Baton Is Passed

punishments would be brought to bear and that would put an end to that straight away. Now things were different. I said so.

"Well, Jean, not everyone is falling in line," said Susanne with a shrug. "Fabien is still riding out with his whip and flogging black women for insubordination right there in the field."

I rather suspected that she did the same as well.

"Yes, well, he knows that it is the women who instigate the stupid men, but, Jean, when are we going to hear what the final verdict is going to be, I mean, we can't just go on like this?" asked Michel.

I said that I had no idea, but that I imagined it would be soon. Plainly, there was a great deal taking place. It was just beyond our point of view and we would have to have patience and wait.

Maman, much improved, was awaiting my arrival at Concorde that evening. There was a matter to be discussed. It would appear that I was possessed of a female slave. I had no idea.

"Rosebelle was bought from Mrs. Angeron in your name just after you left for England. It was André-Montrose who made that decision. We needed someone to help with your father and she came recommended as a person with experience with people who, well, were dying. She is a Créole from Grenada and was of great comfort to both Cécile and me. I would like her to have her freedom. There are some papers to sign. Jean, you should meet her, she is a very good person."

I said that I would, but I didn't meet her. However, I went into Port of Spain on this occasion to make the necessary arrangements for her manumission and also to have our title deeds re-registered, this had become an urgent necessity. The deed for the Laventille estate could not be found among the family papers. Perhaps it never existed. We had, however, paid land taxes on that property for many years. The Spanish records would have to be searched.

The town had grown in proportion with the advancements made financially and socially. Some said that it was now six times the size of the old Spanish capital. Mother's house on Nelson Street—which was called Rue d'Eglise by the town's inhabitants, I suppose because of its proximity to the Catholic church—had been renovated and I stayed there. The town fairly teemed with people. Just about every nationality and skin colour could be found in it. It all appeared so natural to them. But to me it was an amazing sight to see a black man in Muslim garb standing next to a Chinaman dressed in black silk pajamas with a long plaited queue, being interrupted in their attempt to purchase something from a peddler, who was himself a Spanish peon, by a French gentleman who still had the airs of someone in a powdered wig and Breton lace collar.

The town had become even more dominated by the French-speaking free coloureds than it was when Congnet and I did our first interviews there. They appeared to own the majority of the small properties in the town, mostly ramshackle dwellings, as the more substantial houses were few. Those were owned by the influential people, the administrators, magistrates and the merchants.

It was in the Port of Spain that race prejudice and various forms of discrimination were more obviously demonstrated and naturally most resented. I couldn't bring myself to venture outside after nine because I refused to carry a lantern. I thought that it was too degrading. The undercurrent of resentment was palpable. It was increasingly noticeable that the young free black and coloured people were, I was told by our domestics, drawn to Francis de Ridder. The politics of Port of Spain, as I knew well, were from Spanish times a bubbling cauldron that boiled over from time to time. All it required was a leader, and they were making de Ridder their leader.

One afternoon, I was on my way back to Rue d'Eglise when I recognised de Ridder on the street. I suppose it was merely out of curiosity that I invited him to join me for a cup of tea. This led to a conversation that lasted late into the evening.

"I grew up in my father's house. My mother, who carried the single name Suzanne, was a slave on the estate. She may not have been of pure African descent. I hardly remember her."

35. The Baton Is Passed

He said this, I could see, without remorse. "Is it because you have entered the priesthood that you have come to terms with your origins?" I asked, appreciating his calm, even detached, way of expressing himself.

"Oh yes. Through the sacrament of Holy Orders one's life is forever altered. Through this sacrament, a man enters a world where people are made one with the unity of the Father, the Son and the Holy Spirit."

"Holy, that has always struck me as a strange word. What does it mean to you? Is it to be saintly or God like?" I found that it was easy to speak to de Ridder about such things. I would never have broached such topics with the men who were ministers or elders of the Church of Scotland whom I had met while at school. "I must tell you I have little or no interest in religion from a spiritual point of view, although as a scientist, a student, if you like, of the human mind, I recognise its emotional necessity," I hastened to add.

"The word holy means set apart for a sacred purpose."

"And do you believe that you have been set apart for some special purpose here in Trinidad, where obviously great injustice is being dished out to people like ourselves?"

"Of course not. In Romans thirteen it is said: 'Let every person be subject to the governing authorities. For there is no authority except from God, and those that exist have been instituted by God.'"

"I must say that is not at all the case here in Trinidad. But before we become distracted by politics, tell me about yourself. Where did you go to become a priest? What made you think of that life? I mean, coming from a background such as ours, which is hard at the best of times, to be priest must be awfully difficult."

"I was born on a sugar estate on the east bank of the Demerara river. Plantation Wendelmoet. My father was a part of a Dutch consortium that developed cotton and sugar plantations. My mother was a slave. He took me away from her when I was very little. I grew up in his house. If you knew him, you wouldn't think that being a planter was, as the English say, his cup of tea."

"Why do you say that?"

"Well, he was frail, often ill and a bookish sort of person, as I remember him. We were very far away from any sort of European company. A solitary man, even as a boy I somehow recognised that. It was a vast estate, worked by more than three hundred slaves. I don't think that there is anything like that here."

"No, there is nothing here on that scale, but please, go on."

"Demerara is a huge colony. I realised that when I arrived here in Trinidad, which is so small in comparison. Father taught me to read and write. I suppose he wanted me to have a profession. Then one day a woman, a white woman, arrived. This may sound strange, Dr. Philip, but I had never seen a white woman before. At first, after they were married, it was very good. Everything got better. But after my brother was born, my father changed. I suppose that I did as well. It was on a visit to Starbroek that I realised I was to be sent away. I must have been fourteen."

As he told of the ocean voyage, the strangeness of everything and his time with his father's people in the Dutch city of Limburg, I had to remember my own experiences. Plainly, his father cared for him and had instilled a sense of confidence, because as he spoke I could not detect regret, disappointment or skepticism.

From there he was sent to a seminary, the Irish College in Douai, in northern France. "I have always thought of the Netherlands as Protestant, Calvinist actually, so, how was it they sent you to a Catholic seminary?"

"The de Ridder family is Catholic. They have lived in Limburg for generations. Limburg is in the Catholic part of the country. I suppose that they had in mind to be simply rid of me."

"Schooling at an Irish Catholic seminary in France, my word, that must have cost a pretty penny."

35. The Baton Is Passed

"I suppose. I have no real relationship to money. It was for me a wonderful experience. The seminary had been closed during the revolution but was returned to the Irish priests in 1802. I arrived there in 1814. I had very little French, but learned quickly. The Irish priests spoke and taught in English, of course, and in Latin. I studied logic and philosophy. Rhetoric I enjoyed, and theology. It was a remarkable environment, the Irish College. Very different from other Catholic seminaries in the Netherlands at the time, I was told."

"How so?"

"Well, in the Dutch Catholic seminaries, Warmond for example, a theology was practiced that was radically opposed to Enlightenment thought. So too the English College at Douai."

"I see, that would have made you different, as a priest, being taught at the Irish Catholic seminary."

"I believe it did so. The essential Catholic doctrine was inculcated as well as an implicit acceptance of complete freedom of the church from state control, the equality of all men before the law and the primacy of love over church regulations. But I didn't choose Trinidad, Dr. Philip. That decision was made for me in London when Archbishop Poynter was appointed Vicar Apostolic. He, too, had had his training as a priest in Douai. In his case at the English College which, like the Dutch seminaries, was very political! Ours, the Irish, was more typical. It was when Poynter appointed Monsignor Buckley Vicar Apostolic for these islands that the challenge was taken up to oppose the British government with regard to foreign priests serving in their colonies."

"And because you were a free coloured, perhaps the only one in the priesthood, and a foreigner, you were selected."

"Very likely, Dr. Philip. I see it as God's will that equality and justice before the law must be achieved, yes, through love. As our Lord Jesus himself said, 'A new commandment I give to you, that you love one another: just as I have loved you, you also are to love one another.'"

God's will or not, I could hear as he spoke that he had already started to absorb the undercurrents that crisscrossed this divided society. It was a very pleasant encounter, one of many that I was to have with Fr. de Ridder. As time went by, whenever his name was mentioned by the coloured people, I noticed that it was always complimentary. His excellent French was remarked upon by the French people here. He was admired by the young coloured women for his good looks and manly manner and according to Michel, even some of the white French people of the town saw him first as a priest, and only secondly as a mulatto.

"He is seen by them as pious and also as very learned."

"That's a leap! I don't believe that at all." Susanne was lying sprawled across the great bed at Philippine. It was an extremely hot day and we had retreated to the most shaded side of the house where the master bedroom received the cooler easterlies. "They only say that so as to appear liberal, broad minded and impartial when it comes to their faith. But in their hearts they are just the same as ever. He will soon find that out."

And he did. It was close to a year later that I had occasion to dine with Fr. de Ridder. He had taken over a small house built by Reinagle during the construction of the Catholic church on its grounds. We had enjoyed an excellent meal prepared by a young, free coloured Martiniquais man in his service.

"There is a profound duplicity here when it comes to faith and morals. On the one hand the white people, the Catholics, attend Mass, pray the rosary or the stations of the cross, wear scapulars and religious medals, take communion regularly, but never come to me for confession."

Well, what did he expect? I said so. "You think that a white woman would confess her sins to you? Really, Francis, you have been here for over year. Don't you see the sort of place that this is?"

"Oh yes, I first noticed that only free black and coloured men were, how you say? Alguaciles, policemen. And that musical instruments could not be played by coloured people in the grog

35. The Baton Is Passed

shops or even in public places, and there is this carrying of a lighted lamp if one went out of doors at night. I was at first puzzled. Then I realised the deep state of degradation that the free people of colour live with. The horrifying contempt that is endured by them."

"By us," I corrected. I had noticed that he still saw himself as a white priest and had not yet recognised that out here, he was a coloured man who had in some mysterious manner become a priest. A curiosity, but coloured. I had learned that by experience.

"White women adjudicate over a host of social mores, Francis. The men are fine with you, the educated ones. They welcome the opportunity to speak of worldly things, even religious matters of a personal nature, man to man, even dine with you with no white women present. But if a white woman appears, everything changes."

He nodded, adding, "I have been asked to excuse myself by fellow priests who I would not have thought capable of such a thing."

I nodded and said nothing. He was obviously gaining an understanding of the realities of Trinidad and the role his church played in the order of things. Although there was not as yet any criticism of his superiors, I could detect his disappointment. This was when he told me that to his consternation he realised that Bishop Buckley did nothing when Woodford in his role of Vice-Patron of the Catholic Church forced two coloured men to perform public penance in the church because they had not removed their hats when a Spanish priest was passing on the street with the Blessed Sacrament.

"There were others on the street when Fr. Alfonso came by, including myself. Other men, white men, were there. Yet, when he heard of the incident, Woodford immediately issued an order that these young fellows be identified, apprehended, brought before him and summarily sentenced."

As he spoke, I noticed that he had no respect for Woodford and thought of him as someone who had usurped an ecclesiastical jurisdiction. "Privately, I have come to think that he is our enemy, the enemy of all Catholics. Outwardly he enjoys the role, the regalia, the ceremony, the actual solemnity may thrill him, but inwardly, that is a different matter."

That he was confused by the social currents that pulled and tugged between the rich and the poor, the free and the enslaved, the Catholics and the Protestants, was natural. That he was increasingly compromised by his church's role in the degrading of the free black and coloured people, was obvious. He said that he prayed for God's guidance and admitted that his greatest misfortune was the lack of someone from within the church to guide him. I found that quite touching. I commiserated, telling him that in my own experience there was no one who could be of use and that he had to find it in himself. It was, however, when he spoke of telling his feelings to other priests that I cautioned him to be discreet.

"Race shapes and reshapes everything in this colony, Francis. They may be your fellow priests, but you are a coloured man. Their loyalties will be to their fellows, not to you."

Over time, his feelings and opinions found their way to his superiors and together with his growing popularity among the free coloured people of the town, he was perceived as a danger and he was sent away to one of the most distant parishes on the island, Cumana in Toco. It was a place that Congnet and I had visited. It was in the extreme north-east of the island. There were perhaps two or three hundred free coloured people living there, a few dozen slaves, some tribal people and any number of villains hiding from the authorities. I was sorry to see him go. He was good company. I had enjoyed our time together. But he had become too popular. Evidence of this was at the last mass he said. Hundreds of townspeople attended, I was told. The majority were coloured, but there were a great many white people as well. Those were the poor of the town. He had spoken in the past of the equality of all men before God and before the laws of the land, and of God's love for all His children. In this sermon he emphasised the need for the

35. The Baton Is Passed

church to be free from the government's control. There were many young men who wanted him to remain in Port of Spain. Michel said that he had a following, a large following of men and women. I was not surprised. De Ridder was sincere, he spoke plainly and was not afraid of authority. The townsmen had found a leader. Even in his absence he had a following.

PHILIPPINE • SOULS ON FIRE

"You had to wait until it was night to hide your true intentions. eh?" said she in the Patois that I was only just beginning to understand.

36. A Soul on Fire

"They never fail who die in a great cause."

George Gordon Lord Byron

1829: NOTES FOUND BY ME, MICHEL MAXWELL PHILIP, in a journal kept by my brother Dr. Jean-Baptiste Philip:

It was becoming increasingly obvious to me and I am sure to others that I was not well. A cough that I believe had been caused as a result of the smoke from the burning cane fields had become chronic. Swollen spots on the right side of my neck had also appeared. Night sweats and a general malaise have overtaken me and I have lost weight.

Susanne, with whom I have been intimate, has also been taken ill.

My brother St. Luce has returned from Edinburgh qualified as a doctor and a surgeon. As my condition worsened, both he and I agreed that in both our cases it was a case of Scrofula, indicated by a chronic swelling and inflammation of the neck. Through his contacts at the Medical School, he has attempted to get hold of a copy of "An Essay on the Nature and Cure of the King's Evil, Deduced from Observation and Practice", written by John Morley, but without success.

Fr. Francis de Ridder has been of great comfort to both Susanne and I. Fr. Francis is not my confessor. I, however, have found in him a true friend, a person with whom I could speak of the things that have touched me over the years.

My cousin and dear friend Susanne has passed away.

After discussions with mother and my brothers, we have decided to ask Guillaume Robin to return to Trinidad to help with the administration of Philippine, Concorde and Champ Fleurs estates.

> "*Sorrow is knowledge, those that know the most must mourn the deepest, the tree of knowledge is not the tree of life.*"

Dr. Jean Baptiste died on the 16th of June 1829 at Philippine estate and was buried in Paradise Cemetery, San Fernando, Trinidad. He had returned from England a sick man. His illness was diagnosed by both himself and St. Luce, who is also a physician, as cervical tuberculosis or scrofula. They were treating him first with sarsaparilla, then with cinnabar ointment. When it became worse, they tried an incision to evacuate the soft content. St. Luce hoped that these treatments would have cleansed his body and balanced the humours, thus curing the disease. Jean-Baptiste's close friend and confidant, the mulatto priest Fr. Francis de Ridder, offered a mass, the entire family attended. Everybody prayed to Almighty God for him to live. He had so much to look forward to. He was just thirty-three years old when he died.

We have kept his journals and all his books. We treasure them because they were his. I sometimes smell them and find deep in their hearts the faint aroma of distant places and read his journals to hear his voice. The works of Byron are the most worn, particularly his *Childe Harold's Pilgrimage,* and of course, *The Corsair*, which would have reminded him of our grandfather, Papa Honoré, who, as that poet mused:

> *His death yet dubious, deeds too widely known;*
> *He left a Corsair's name to other times,*
> *Linked with one virtue, and a thousand crimes.*

Papa Honoré, from what I have heard tell of him, would have been pleased to be thought of as being virtuous and chivalrous like Conrad, the pirate chieftain in *The Corsair*. A single virtue? I have wondered what that might have been. As for a thousand crimes, there are so many stories told about that man, I wouldn't be surprised at all.

Jean-Baptiste challenged Governor Woodford's local laws. He was passionate about this cause and went out and made a study of

36. A Soul on Fire

it, which he called "A Free Mulatto" and took to England along with a petition, which was upheld by the government. He was passionate about the situation of us, the free coloured people in Trinidad. We were in imminent danger to lose the land that our parents had been granted to create plantations, and of our civil rights that had been enshrined in the terms of the Cedula for Population, which were no different than those for the whites. But now, you could even be re-enslaved if "your free paper bun!"

The Order in Council, for which Jean-Baptiste and others had worked so hard to fight Woodford, was finally issued by the Privy Council of England on the 13th of March, 1829.

Sir Ralph Woodford, the island's former governor, died on the 17th of May last year. It is a coincidence that these two men, my half-brother Jean-Baptiste and the governor, who were adversaries, should have departed this life as comparatively young men almost within a year of each other, Woodford having attained the age of forty-four.

Jean-Baptiste was too ill to notice that the Order in Council was not proclaimed in Trinidad with the usual pomp reserved for such things. The new governor, Major General Sir Lewis Grant, did not read the proclamation from the window of Government House. There was no official ceremony. Equality before the law for free black and coloured folk arrived like a whisper. It was our relatives in England who understood the momentous nature of such an event and sent us a copy of *The London Gazette*. I have of course have committed the report to memory: 'His Majesty therefore is pleased to order that every law, ordinance, or proclamation in force, within the said island whereby His Majesty's subjects of African birth or descent, being of free condition, are subject to any disability, civil or military to which His Majesty's subjects of European birth or descent are not subject, shall be forever repealed and annulled'.

I paid attention the other day when I overheard Anderson say that nowhere in the western world were free blacks and people of mixed race regarded as equal to white people when it came to justice. Don

Ramón Garcia replied, in his important tone of voice, that the duty of the judiciary was to act fairly to all under the law, but admitted that it was not always the case, going on to add that the government did not want that Order to be perceived as a major achievement, an advancement in the lives of the more than sixteen thousand free people of colour here in Trinidad. I suppose that was why it was merely inserted in one of the newspapers without a comment on the morning of its proclamation. That, I suppose, would have served the interest of the four thousand four hundred and some whites who live here in Trinidad.

Jean-Baptiste was such a unique man, a doctor of both the body and the mind. He was passionate about us, his family and our cause. His friends abroad, as Fr. de Ridder said in his oration, described him as 'a Soul on Fire!' I knew him as a man inspired. In a profound way, his endeavour and ultimate success is going to influence our lives here in Trinidad and define our destinies. It will surely shape the future of those tens of thousands who shall soon be emancipated. We are now all to be protected by the law.

BOOK THIRD

THE REPRESENTATIVE MAN 1829–1870

IN THE SPRING A YOUNG MAN'S FANCY
LIGHTLY TURNS TO THOUGHTS OF LOVE.
THEN HER CHEEK WAS PALE AND THINNER
THAN SHOULD BE FOR ONE SO YOUNG,
AND HER EYES ON ALL MY MOTIONS WITH
A MUTE OBSERVANCE HUNG.

Alfred, Lord Tennyson

THE SOLICITOR-GENERALSHIP.—We have much pleasure in announcing that the Hon. M. MAXWELL PHILIP has been confirmed in the Office of Solicitor-General. Mr. PHILIP has filled the acting appointment on two or three occasions and for lengthened periods, and his confirmation is but a just recompense for past services. As a son of the soil, Mr. PHILIP's appointment has given general satisfaction, but by a large section of the community it will be regarded with feelings of pride and rejoicing as another triumph over a narrow-minded policy which was wont to create and maintain invidious distinctions of birth and race. Mr. MAXWELL PHILIP is a representative man, and as such, his appointment is the more notable.

37. MICHEL MAXWELL PHILIP
NOMEN EST OMEN

Tis strange,- but true; for truth is always strange;
Stranger than fiction: if it could be told.

George Gordon Lord Byron

TRINIDAD 1829: CUPAR GRANGE ESTATE, SOUTH NAPARIMA. The night air is replete with the reassuring aromas of woodsmoke, warm molasses and cow dung—this last because Dr. James Anderson, the owner of this plantation, following the Barbadian adage "the planter who makes the most dung, makes the most sugar", furnished the estate with a herd of horned cattle. Dr. Anderson, a retired regimental surgeon, commenced the development of Cupar Grange in 1812, replacing the old ground provision gardens with the new Bourbon sugarcane variety with remarkable success.

Anderson came to me when he needed to set up his medical practice in Port of Spain, because with his sons Alexandre and Henry abroad in England, where Henry was being prepared to study law, he required the estate's earnings in addition to what he made as a physician to maintain himself and his family in town as well as both boys who would be over there for at least another five or six years. I have been the manager at Cupar Grange for the Anderson family for the last five years.

His decision to have me as his manager here at Cupar Grange came about largely because of the recently published amelioration regulations for the protection of the slaves. Under that law, heavy financial penalties for inflicting cruel and unusual punishments on slaves are to be imposed on their owners. This brought about a reluctance to hire a manager who would rely on severity, or in many instances brute force, in managing labour on large estates. These fools, they simply overwork their blacks until they die of exhaustion.

These steps taken by the government, I suppose, were inevitable. Sheer greed, desperation in the face of financial collapse, but more often than not the cruel side of human nature, have brought about tortures and acts of savagery that belong to a previous time. The people in England who want to bring about the end of slavery have seized upon the lurid accounts of the torture of slaves in Trinidad that have appeared in the London newspapers. It has served to reignite the anti-slavery movement in the English Parliament.

Anderson has brought me into the company of an eminent Venezuelan family headed by Ramón Garcia, a Doctor of Law, who holds the office of Father General of Minors and Defender of the Absent. Garcia's son George is also a barrister. Through them I have met Etienne Duruty and other white men. I am a source of information as to what is taking place in the wider society, a sounding board, perhaps, to gauge what would be the reaction to Governor Woodford's machinations, and I suppose an opportunity for them to believe themselves liberal when it comes to dealing with coloured people such as me. I enjoy their company, the intelligent conversation on lofty topics, and when I take them on hunting expeditions into the high woods or to shoot water fowl in the Oropouche Lagoon, for a while, we are all simply men together. However, our situation here at Cupar Grange, I fear, may soon change, as there are rumours making the rounds that this estate may be sold to a Mr. Burton Williams of the Bahamas.

This evening I have sought to escape the inescapable anxieties of childbirth by sitting beneath a venerable samaan tree to listen, as the French Créoles here in Trinidad say, to our sugar growing. My wife Catherine, God willing, will soon give birth to our third child—born five months and almost to the day after my half-brother Jean-Baptiste Philip passed away at Philippine. Our first, a boy, we named Honoré for grandfather. Our second we christened Samuel, named for Samuel Pinto, a close friend of Catherine's mother.

37. MICHEL MAXWELL PHILIP: NOMEN EST OMEN

Samuel showed promise at a young age. I have arranged for him to attend a school run by a Mr. Young in San Fernando, where he will be taught English and other subjects. He learns quickly and is eager to be taught. On Mr. Young's recommendation, he being a devout Catholic like is my wife, we have in mind to send him to a Catholic seminary in Scotland, St. Mary's College, Blairs. Mr. Young has assured me that not every boy who enters a seminary, even at a young age, becomes a priest, but training at such a school, in addition to an education in Latin, would make him eligible for a university education.

The house here at Cupar Grange, which Anderson has kindly allowed us to use, is very well appointed. Catherine loves it, the flower garden, the home farm, and the dairy. She loves animals, especially the very young, and was quite shaken the other day when one of the domestics came running to say that a boa constrictor had swallowed all the eggs laid by her favourite hen, but was relieved when told that the snake was shot in the head and killed and when cut open, all eleven eggs were found perfect and replaced in the nest and the hen returned to it. They all hatched and are the pride and joy of both the hen and Catherine.

Catherine is fragile. At twenty-five, she still looks sixteen, which she was when I asked her to marry me. My being some years older was one of the reasons, really excuses, raised by her mother against us marrying. The true reason was that I was too dark-skinned. I understood. In these colonies race, shade and hair texture trump every attainment, every virtue, even wealth! There were also notions of class. Catherine's mother, Catherine Wickins, is what is called here a well-born *quadroon*. Much like our late relative Marie-Madelaine-Vigi, she is the product of generations of women of colour who have cohabited with wealthy white men, becoming fairer-complexioned with each generation, and who see themselves as socially superior to people like myself and second only to the aristocratic French people who came here a long time ago.

Catherine's father, Louis-Christopher Lefer, was one of three brothers and a sister who arrived in Trinidad from France soon after the English conquest, and because of making the acquaintance of the illustrious Garcias and business dealings with the eminent O'Connors, they have elevated themselves well beyond their quite ordinary Parisian middle class origins, this according to Dr. Anderson.

Catherine's mother lived with Lefer openly in Port of Spain, even after he married Louise Bernard. That sort of thing, in those days, generated little comment. It was in some circles acceptable, I suppose because Trinidad was still a wild place on the frontier of the New World. Catherine was their only child. Lefer was for some years in the mercantile business and departed Trinidad for France with his wife and daughter Olympe with sufficient money to live a good life. On leaving, he left a modest living and a little blue and pink chattel house on upper Queen Street in Port of Spain for them. This was where Catherine was carefully raised by her mother and her spinster aunts with the expectation of her marrying a white man. Their dreams may well have come true, if I had not stepped into the picture, as she is a lovely woman, a perfect *mètif,* if there was ever was one, with her lively auburn eyes, a complexion that is clearer than a lot of white people's and dark brown curls falling almost to her waist.

Reversals over there, in France, forced her father to return to Trinidad. His brothers, themselves struggling in their businesses, were not in a position to assist him financially. I, with father's encouragement, was only too pleased to advance him something to help with the restarting of his business. After that there was no objection from him to Catherine and I getting married. They are very boring company, the Lefers. They are obsessed with making connections to wealthy or titled people here in Trinidad and the only topic they have is cocoa, coffee and salt-fish, as the first two are very cheap and the latter dreadfully dear. It becomes tiresome to be in their company for any length of time.

It was in 1820 that my brother Frédéric, our mother Cécile Maxwell and I were manumitted by our father, Jean-Baptiste-Louis

37. MICHEL MAXWELL PHILIP: NOMEN EST OMEN

Philip. This word, "manumitted", I was told, comes from the Latin, "send forth from the hand". I found that sounded Biblical, the sort of thing that Moses or Abraham may have uttered in conferring a blessing, and I have taken it as such. The decision to formally give us our freedom came about because father had decided that the time had come to make his will. His health was failing and his mind was no longer as sharp as it once was. Also there was my decision to marry Catherine.

Neither my brother Frédéric nor I, nor even our mother had ever raised the subject of our being enslaved, actually owned by the Philip family, nor was it ever a topic of conversation. As a result, Frédéric and I had some decisions to make as to what we were going to be called officially. Frédéric, being older, had no problem in remaining Frédéric Maxwell, but for me, the Philip name was possessed of a certain prestige, which made us quite distinct from the other free people of colour. I wanted this distinction, so I became Michel Maxwell Philip, with our father's blessing.

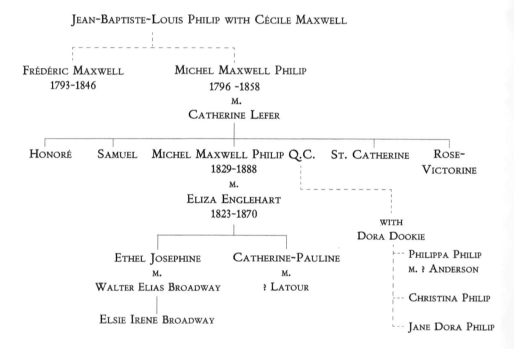

38. Meeting the Free Mulatto

*"Self-reverence, self-knowledge, self-control;
these three alone lead life to sovereign power."*

Alfred, Lord Tennyson

Cyril Lionel Robert James 1901–1989

C.L.R. James, Port-of-Spain, Trinidad, 1929. "Mr. James, you are here *again*!" We had had a brief conversation the day before. Mendes, in search of a provocative topic, had asked me to write a story for the second issue of his new magazine, *Trinidad*. "Something historical, original you know, even controversial."

I would have much preferred to write on e first time that a side from the West Indies had been allowed to take part in a Test match against England. Previously, Test matches had been restricted to all-white teams from England, Australia and South Africa. But Mendes had insisted.

In those days, I was engaged in writing Captain Arthur Cipriani's biography. We had agreed that this was not meant to be an account of his personal life but an arresting description in which the true social and political situation in the West Indies would be highlighted, especially as it affected the ordinary people—"the barefoot man" as the Captain would say.

Before starting that day's interview, we had discussed what Mendes had in mind, and a Mrs. Ethel Broadway was suggested by Cipriani as a useful source for the *Trinidad* piece. He said that she was the daughter of a legendary barrister of the previous century and was regarded as something of an authority on the history and folk traditions of the colony.

"Thank you, Mrs. Broadway, for receiving me, again," I said as ingratiatingly as I could manage to the tall, thin, gray-haired woman whose look of frowning disapproval had apparently become a permanent feature on what had once been a much simpler face. I had not met many white women socially, but I understood that habit and custom demanded something of the sort. Feeling increasingly uncomfortable, I continued, "As I mentioned yesterday, why do the people here think that they are so special, so different, as they are fond of saying, from people from the other islands in the British West Indies?"

"I have no time for that today," she declared. Handing me a small, almost square, hard-covered book bound in brown cloth, and pointing to a bentwood rocker in the sunlit verandah, she said, "So, Mendes told you that he was looking for something different, something original, eh, historic: I can give him that. Well then, read! You people always want to get everything the easy way. And look here, don't take that book away with you. When you're leaving, put it on the table in the billiard room."

I took neither umbrage nor special notice of her manner of speaking or her remarks, understanding full well that it was directed not merely at my station—a common black person, but a schoolteacher of all things. I chose instead to be amused and pleased that I should be here at all, sitting in her verandah, breathing the cool damp atmosphere of her freshly watered maidenhair ferns. I had arrived, or so it would appear.

38. Meeting the Free Mulatto

The house, a large cottage actually, was perched on a rise called Cotton Hill on the outskirts of Dr. de Boissière's village. It overlooked the Botanic Gardens Experimental Station and was within sight of the St. James Barracks. It was called Loyola, named by her late father, Michel Maxwell Philip, for Saint Ignatius of Loyola, a 16th century Spanish theologian and founder of the Society of Jesus.

The dark brown, cloth-bound volume had been typed, copied in secret, I was to later learn, from an original kept under lock and key in the Colonial Secretary's office in the Red House in Port-of-Spain ever since its introduction as supporting evidence to petitions which were presented to the British government in 1823. Its title page read:

> "*An Address to the Right Hon. Earl Bathurst,*
> *His Majesty's Principal Secretary of State for the Colonies*
> *relative to the claims, which the coloured population of Trinidad*
> *has to the same civil and political privileges*
> *with their white fellow-subjects.*"

The author, choosing anonymity, had signed himself *A Free Mulatto*. As I perused the elegant prose, couched in the elaborate language of an educated person of the time, which described all manner of crimes, I was more than a little amazed to realise that what I was reading was an exposé of historic events that had taken place here, in Trinidad, some one hundred years ago. Explicit, it detailed the depredations and actual offenses, deliberate insults and violations, indeed the studied endeavour perpetrated by the governor of the day, Sir Ralph Woodford, to systematically reduce, and to actually deny, the lawful privileges and rights of a large and distinguished portion of the colony's free population, the free blacks and people of colour, in the period before the emancipation of the slaves. I was not surprised the book had been locked away. It named names and was, because of the nature of Crown Colony rule, even for me a deeply disturbing work.

"You're still *here*, Mr. James?"

"Yes, I'm sorry, I hadn't realised the time . . . I am surprised that a work of such a scientific nature would have been produced here, in those days."

"Well, *I'm* not surprised that *you* are surprised, Mr. James."

"And this book! No wonder it is kept under lock and key. What were the consequences? What happened as the result of its publication?"

"Why, the Trinidad that *you* live in today, Mr. James."

"Who was he, this free mulatto?" I asked, intrigued. "What was he? What possessed him to undertake this?"

"His name was Jean-Baptiste Philip. A relative of my late father, from a previous generation. He was a medical doctor from Naparima, an educated man, well travelled. A man who felt strongly about how things were in those days."

"What were the issues?"

"The issue was one of civil rights. It began with a Spanish document remembered as the Cedula of Population of 1783. Ever heard of it?"

"No, not really." This wasn't true—I had of course read about the celebrated Cedula, but I didn't want her to think of me as one of those "over-educated Negroes who think that they know everything."

Her manner of dismissive intolerance was suddenly replaced by a more earnest expression. With eyes widened she said, "I believe, Mr. James, that your true initiation into Trinidad's history is about to commence. Read, go to the public library, see Mr. Comma, he may help you."

I knew that writing a piece on a subject such as this would be exactly what Mendes and the editorial committee of the *Trinidad* magazine would want to accept. It was what the magazine was all about, the exposing of colonial bigotry and the systemic racism that have characterised this colony for what appeared to be centuries. I was also aware that an article such as this would be seen as sensational, designed to evoke memories of the past, and in Trinidad the past, for black people and for most of the whites, could only mean one thing: slavery—a topic that was not discussed. I understood that

38. Meeting the Free Mulatto

the subject of the article singled out an individual who through his efforts brought about social change, which would be sufficient to ensure its censure. Nonetheless I felt compelled to undertake it, because as everyone knew, in a great many ways things had not actually changed.

She was right, to tackle this properly I really needed a great deal more background information. Something more substantial, more pithy than the typical historical references. I asked to see Mr. Comma at the Public Library who, after listening patiently to me, suggested that I pay attention to both volumes of *History of Trinidad* by Lionel Mordaunt Fraser.

"It's a pity that you don't read French, Mr. James. From what you've explained, it would benefit you to also read Pierre Gustave Borde's historical account of these islands. Pity." He regarded me through his thick lenses while sitting back in a large wooden chair that creaked complainingly on its iron springs while slowly shaking his large, bald, very black head from side to side with an expression of compassion that hinted at some sort of hidden shame.

"Mr. James, you are a young person with a literary pretension, idealistic, but at the moment misguided. I will allow you access to our special collection. Miss Blizzard, senior, will be of help. I am sure that you would be pleased to hear that we have added your novella *La Divina Pastora* to our collection."

I was pleased to hear that, and said so. I did have some French, contrary to Mr. Comma's assumption. Mr. Pilgrim, the sixth form master at Queen's Royal College, had taught me the language. Schoolboy French, as they say. Apart from that, I had grown up in Tunapuna. The sound of Créole Patois had been in my ear from the time I was born. We did not speak it at home, because both mother and father—he was a schoolteacher—were Barbadians. I had in fact read Borde's *History*, as well as *The History of Trinidad* by E.L. Joseph, so I was not unfamiliar with the Cedula of Population. I had found much that was worthwhile about the free black and coloured people in both those books and came away with the feeling that the Cedula may be seen as this island's first constitution as it gave in extraordinary detail the legal conditions under which the island was settled.

It was on reading Fraser that afternoon that I saw that I discovered that he identified the author of *Free Mulatto* as Dr. J.B. Philip. Fraser described him as "a respectable person of colour" who was invited to attend a meeting held at Government House on Belmont Hill to discuss what appeared to be a popular response to "an obnoxious" Order in Council that had caused an uproar in the town. Fraser reduces the significance of the meeting by saying that Philip desired to convey the impression that Woodford, alarmed at the attitude of the people, had attempted to "cajole him with fair words." Fraser goes on to add that a large sum of money was raised so as to meet the expenses of a delegation who embarked for the United Kingdom to lay their grievances before the King's Ministers.

Leaving the Public Library, after meeting the formidable Miss Blizzard and making the necessary arrangements to have access to the library's newspaper archives, I walked across Woodford Square to St. Vincent Street in the hope of meeting up with Mendes or Thomasos or any of the others who gathered at the Black Lion to have a drink or two. There was nobody there whom I cared to pass time with, so I took the Belmont tram that would carry me home to Juanita, as I knew she would be thinking that I was coming home late again.

An article entitled "An Oration" that I found in one of the very old newspapers at the Public Library—obviously written by someone who knew J.B. Philip well, a close friend, a priest perhaps, he was a Catholic, in any event a person sufficiently familiar with his reminiscences to understand the significance of his undertaking here in Trinidad as well as the importance of the one person whom he met over there, in Europe—recognised Philip as a "soul on fire" and a "child of the sun."

I, in turn, wrote about J.B. Philip in a laudatory tone. I posed the question "What is the role of genius in history, or, of man versus the state?" I extolled the effort of this remarkable man of colour, this uncommon man from the Naparimas who had chosen anonymity, describing himself simply as 'a Free Mulatto', who, against almost insurmountable odds, brought the immovable colonial administration of the day to heel, causing the debilitating and obviously racist local laws to be revoked, while effectively removing all legal disabilities against the free blacks and people of colour who had come to Trinidad under the aegis of the Cedula of 1783.

I then noticed that he died in June 1829, and that I had read the Oration, obviously a eulogy, one hundred years later almost to the day! What a coincidence! Made especially so when I recalled that Michel Maxwell, Mrs. Broadway's father, was born six months after J.B.'s death, on the 12th of October 1829.

I portrayed the Free Mulatto as a man who incarnated the spiritual yearnings of a people who, in the words of the one who had memorialised him, was messianic in character. It was my first attempt to analyse history and politics through a biography—the template that I was planning to employ in the work that I was doing with Captain Cipriani as well. Plainly, this man from the Naparimas had suffered, hoped and toiled for us, his people, a people that he would never know.

The editor was impressed. But the article never ran, because after the first issue of *Trinidad,* there was not going to be another due to a lack of advertising support. The writing of the story stayed with me. There had never been a monument raised in Philip's memory or any sort of memorial. Only once—I was informed by Farrell, a colleague at Q.R.C.—a torchlight procession to his grave took place in San Fernando, where he was praised, not for what he did in upholding the laws of the land in a manner that would guarantee a better future for his unique class and for those who would be eventually emancipated, but as a hero of all underprivileged people. Which, according to Farrell, was not at all the case. Patently the work of obfuscation and confusion had long commenced, the purpose being to forget the *heroic* elements of our past, and to accept this pallid colonial present.

Some weeks later, I again called on Ethel Broadway at Loyola. I had left a copy of the unpublished article with her housekeeper, asking her to please hand it to her mistress. I wanted to know what she thought of it, and was curious to learn more about this interesting episode in the colony's history, and perhaps get a better understanding of the Philip family.

"Mr. James, the Madame say she coming. She say you must wait in the gallery, she coming just now."

The maid, whose name was Mavaline Shemuerl, was a small, brisk, dark-skinned woman. She was obviously accustomed to itinerant appearances at the back gate. Like many women of her occupation, she was au courant, fully informed on the running of the house, and knew the difference between sanitary inspectors, schoolteachers and those whom she should usher into the living room, or the few who, knowing their way around the house, could be left in the hallway to find her Madame by the sound of her voice as it sang out their names with the melodious rising inflection of the French Créoles.

Mavaline was standing to one side of the walkway that led to the front steps. These were wet, wide and made of white marble, and rose gently towards the great doors that I imagined were only opened on state occasions, weddings and funerals.

"Wipe your foot," she said, glaring up at me while pointing at a doormat.

The verandah unfolded to the right and to the left. I ventured to the right. Mavaline stood firm. I was not to be seated with my back to the billiard room door, Madame would be more comfortable if I were placed on one of the bentwood chairs behind the maidenhair ferns at the end of the gallery near to the steps that led down to the lawn. These ferns grew thick in their baskets and shaded that side of the verandah from the afternoon sun and I suspected blocked certain visitors from being seen from the street.

"What you want to know that for?"

I had asked Mrs. Broadway to tell me more about her father's people. She immediately became guarded and plainly suspicious. I

38. Meeting the Free Mulatto

appreciated that she would see my interest as scurrilous. Yet she did let me read that book supposedly written by his relative, J.B. Philip, who was obviously a coloured man—which would have made her a person of colour as well, a topic that could not possibly be raised.

"I was thinking, did you get a chance to read the article that I left with the maid?" I said, while studying this actually white-looking person. Unmistakably, there was about her the authoritative air typical of Head Mistresses or even Matrons in the nursing service. I was dying for a cigarette, but couldn't risk the distraction, suspecting that either I would be told no and be frowned at, or, if allowed, Mavaline would then have to be summoned by ringing an alarm which was operated by a button attached to a cord that was hidden in the folds of the cushions of her chair. Then an ashtray would be brought, together with a small occasional table. This would have implied refreshments, which was of course out of the question.

"What did you think of what I wrote?"

"I read it. You have a lot to learn. The Philip family was the most distinguished of all. Their homes, at Cupar Grange and Philippine, were centres of culture, propriety was the norm, Mr. James. Everyone came to them, the governors, even visiting royalty."

I mentioned that the article would not be printed.

"Well, I'm not surprised, Mr. James. It was entirely about *your* brilliance, no wonder it was not accepted."

I nodded. "Yes, I suppose so. But who were they? How did they manage that, being . . .not white, not European, not English. Did they. . .?"

"They were who they *were*, Mr. James. And yes. You did do a passable job in getting across the issues and a fairly good one at analysing the social outcome of his work but nothing of the family, their significance."

"Oh thank you. Was it because they were wealthy?"

"Yes, there was money. But breeding, upbringing, the values inculcated from the cradle, yes, the cradle. And from the hands that rocked them."

"The hands that rocked them?"

"Yes. There were many hands. And many cradles."

Pleased that she was up to form, I asked again about her father's people. She must have been anticipating this, and despite being suspicious of my intentions, had clearly decided to encourage me in the pursuit of what I was calling my research, because on being invited to the billiard room, where, I must tell you, there was no evidence of that game whatsoever, I saw that there were several documents, books and papers tidily arranged on a large table at its centre.

"These may interest you, Mr. James. A few of my father's many certificates. His letters of appointment to various posts, some speeches that he gave while mayor, and other addresses to various causes. Here, an old appointment book of his. This lithographic print of his likeness was made in England. Here are some of his contributions to debates in the Legislative Council, and a few other things written in his hand. This is the manuscript of a book he wrote and published while in England, he was preparing for the Bar. Unfortunately, the last printed copy that he owned was lent to a Masonic brother; it was never returned, of course. You may want to read it, as it gives an insight of sorts into his imagination, and the fancies of the Philips as a family, on the whole. Here, Lord Byron's epic, *The Corsair*, it was a favourite of his. This is a first edition. Very valuable. Don't take away anything. Leave everything as you have found it. Mavaline will see to that. I have to go into town."

The manuscript was a stack of thick paper that had lived an unruly life. The elegant handwriting was so real and personal that I brought it to my nose and smelled it. My excited imagination anticipated the flavour of the adventurous voyages made by this man, Maxwell Philip, a man who I would later come to understand had emerged, large in stature, perceived as outstanding because of his grasp of the law and his dramatic courtroom appearances. I read out loud,

38. Meeting the Free Mulatto

MICHEL MAXWELL PHILIP Q.C. 1829 - 1888

Emmanuel Appadocca;
or,
Blighted Life.

This was handwritten in a large slanted script across the quarto size sheet of the title page. Beneath this was carefully, rather elaborately inscribed,

A Tale of the Boucaneers.
By Maxwell Philip.
London 1853

The lithographic print certainly conveyed the impression of a handsome European-appearing man of imposing stature dressed in the robes of a barrister, wig and all.

PHILIPPINE • THE REPRESENTATIVE MAN

THE FOLLOWING DAY I returned to the old house across the street from the Catholic cathedral. It was where Captain Cipriani met his constituents privately, where as president of the Trinidad Workingmen's Association he received just about anyone who sought his assistance, and where the Association's newspaper, *The Labour Leader,* which was edited by Howard-Bishop, was looked over by him before being sent to the printers. He was, in those days, mayor of Port-of-Spain, and his business office—he was a general commission agent and auctioneer—was at 40 St. Vincent Street.

I entered through the wicket, the main gate being bolted shut just as the late afternoon's brilliance was pouring into the quiet of the deserted backyard, and took the wooden stair to find Cipriani sitting at a roll-top desk in the antiquated room where we had met previously. The Captain rose as I entered. "Please, come in, Nello, have a seat. Coffee?"

A well-cut, fawn-coloured suit now replaced the khaki drill worn during his hours of business.

"I'm having dinner with some old friends later this evening," he said, smiling, "different strokes for different folks."

For his own reasons, he had decided to allow me access to his sanctum sanctorum, which overlooked the quiet end of Marine Square. We had already gone over the state of society in Trinidad, having examined each sector—the colonial Englishmen, the white Créoles, the coloured people, the black masses, "the proletariat" as he called them, in considerable detail. To me, being of Barbadian parents, an Anglican, and having grown up in the village of Tunapuna, which was several miles east of Port-of-Spain, this was all mostly news.

We were about to examine the period after the Great War, when I was just a young lad. He spoke up in defense of the men under his command who were the recipients of the usual racial prejudices meted out to black people anywhere in the world, when the subject of my visit to Mrs. Broadway was brought up. I told him of my surprise in reading what J.B. Philip had written about in his address to Lord

38. Meeting the Free Mulatto

Bathurst, and about my meeting with Mrs. Broadway and of my encounters with her maid and with Mr. Comma. He was amused by the way I described my experiences with "shade prejudice" and the social snobbery that was common among both Negroes and people of mixed backgrounds. Cipriani, as a French Créole, had his own stories to tell of class prejudice among the white people.

He eventually returned the conversation to the Philip family. "You know, Nello, it is because of J.B. Philip and those who were around him that we are here today."

I thought that was interesting, as Ethel Broadway had said something similar. "What do you mean?" I asked.

"Well, lemme tell you. You were an exhibition winner, so you could go to Queen's Royal College without your parents paying a cent, and from what you say, you're thinking of leaving your teaching job at Q.R.C. and taking up a post at the Government Teacher Training College. Man, you can thank J.B. Philip, the Free Mulatto, for that. Look how everybody can now rise to a higher social and economic position. The opportunities, limited as they are for the ordinary man, all came about as a result of J.B.'s work. He and his circle of friends successfully challenged the government of the day, and even though it was for their own benefit, within a few short years, emancipation saw tens of thousands gaining their freedom and they too benefitted from the work done by Philip and those who followed, literally walking in his footsteps. They cleared a path for us all to follow."

"What do you mean? Who is 'us'?"

"Well, everybody. The proletariat. The barefoot man. Philip and his comrades planted the seed of a nationalistic sentiment. It was a struggle! They came out of a class of people who saw themselves as founding fathers. Notwithstanding their differences in colour and in class, and their francophone identity, they considered themselves to be the true Trinidadians, patriotic to the Crown, but with a very nationalistic tendency. They described themselves as the Créole

Party. This sense of nationalism was also expressed in the work of John Jacob Thomas."

"Yes," I interjected, "I have read his work. He was the island's most important intellectual at the time, the first linguist of African descent to produce a grammar of a Créole language, and of course, *Froudacity*."

"Yes exactly. Have you come across Borde's *History of Trinidad*? It was the first history of this island written by a Trinidad-born historian."

"I read that as well, at school, in French actually."

"In French! You well good for youself!" chuckled Cipriani. "I remember my father saying that you could find in Borde a list of all the first white people to come to Trinidad, and the first set of free blacks and coloured people to reach here following the Cedula of Population. Borde put them in the book, and to me, he was making the point that we are a unique people here in Trinidad—all these French and Patois-speakers, Catholic, in an island that soon was conquered by the British. The root of our sense of nationalism begins first and foremost with these first people to come here under the Cedula. They resisted British imperialism in its worst form. It is from them that today we draw our inspiration. Out of their struggle emerged our political consciousness. You see me here—even I am part of the same movement, which is committed to reforming crown colony rule and must ultimately lead to home rule. Trinidad has had a long tradition of resistance to colonial repression."

"I remember that Borde wrote that it is not by erasing history that we arrive at unity. But he wrote in French, didn't that upset or even alienate a lot of people at the time?"

"No, when that book was published, educated people, both coloured and white here in Trinidad, read, spoke and wrote French. Many still do. You know that."

"I always find that there is no contemporary history, no recorded history of our recent past, and significant events are readily forgotten."

38. Meeting the Free Mulatto

"Yes, all we have is English history. It is difficult to find a record of local events. You have to go and dig it out of the old newspapers."

"Father was friendly with a man called Mr. Sylvester-Williams, he said that they spoke about the total absence of local history. They were both originally from Barbados, they came to Trinidad together with Alphonso Nurse, who, like my father, was also a teacher. He taught in San Fernando. We spoke about him just the other night at the Maverick debating club meeting."

"Still with the Mavericks? Yes man, that's good. That's why you have such a command of language. You can argue logically, and persuade others that your point of view is correct. That will serve you well in the future, Nello. You'll make a good trade unionist!"

"The Mavericks is great. We read what we can put our hands on and then discuss it avidly. There is always a lively debate. It's what I really enjoy."

"Sylvester-Williams was a founding member of the Trinidad Elementary Teachers' Union."

"You know, father mentioned that."

"Because you care about what social justice means, lemme tell you this. The labour movement is all about that, otherwise you wouldn't be here, speaking to me. Labour is about creating a more stable society through equality and equity, and as such it is a civilising force. Ordinary people, when they study the history of labour, they find that it mirrors their own experiences. Sylvester-Williams also founded the African Association when he went to England."

"What's that about?"

"It's about promoting and protecting the interests of the working man in the colonies. They circulate accurate information on various subjects that affect their rights and privileges as subjects of the British Empire. Issues that I rather suspect will occupy you, as time goes by, if you keep up your interest in J.B. Philip and me!"

"But tell me Captain, what has become of them, the Philip family? Why is their story, so obscure? Mrs. Broadway spoke to me a bit about her father, Maxwell Philip. She allowed me to see some of his papers. I was able to read a few of his contributions to debates in the Legislative Council. I actually held the manuscript of a book he wrote. He was an outstanding man, obviously. What has happened to them all, his people?"

He smiled, I thought sadly, and spread wide his arms as if describing something beyond words. "They were prominent, possibly they still are in some circles in England and in Europe. Those here in Trinidad, and there are several, have fallen into poverty and I suppose have only half-baked memories." He shrugged.

Taking a sip from the delicate demitasse, I inquired about Maxwell Philip.

"He was extraordinary. The most accomplished local man of his generation. Certainly from his background." The Captain paused to place a cigarette into a slim black holder and lit my own and his with a small gold lighter. "A distinguished Queen's Counsel, Solicitor General, sometimes Attorney General, which meant that he had a seat on the official side of the Legislative Council. Mayor of Port-of-Spain, the first man of colour to achieve this, amongst other distinctions."

"And?"

"And because of what he was, he may have been the most lost of his people."

"Why you say that?"

He glanced at me in turning towards the open window. As if recalling a thing long forgotten, with a note in his voice of a person engaged in sentimental reverie, he said: "Nello boy, you want to write about me, I must tell you, I stand on the shoulders of those who have gone before. Men like Henry Alcazar, Mzumbo Lazare, Leopold Tronchin, Philip Rostant and many others. Maxwell Philip was among the best of them. He unfortunately, as some of the others did as well, fell between two stools."

"How so?"

38. Meeting the Free Mulatto

"Well, as you know here in this colony, no matter how educated, how polished a local man is, there is a ceiling beyond which he cannot rise. Maxwell knew this, yet he dared the establishment. He forced them to respect and honour his credentials, his command of the English language and his knowledge of the law. His very presence demanded this."

"But why do you see him as lost, the most lost of his people?"

"The English played him, I think, in the way that they play all colonials. They brought him into their fold. They gave him the post of Solicitor General. That earned him a seat on the official side of the Legislative Council. They dangled the higher post, that of Attorney General, before him. He never held it as a permanent position."

"Why not?" I asked, carefully putting the tiny cup and saucer on the desk.

"I don't know. Perhaps because he was too politically popular. The Attorney General has to represent the Crown in court and be the legal adviser to the governor. He has to act as the guardian of the public interest in a quasi-judicial capacity. As far as the Colonial Office was concerned, Maxwell was hopelessly compromised because of his own popularity, and also because of his antecedents like J.B. And there were other matters, I seem to remember, that shone an unfortunate light on him."

"Was it simply because he was a coloured man?"

"No, not really. The British, to serve their own interest, were elevating men of colour to official positions in several of their colonies. In Barbados, for example, a coloured man, Conrad Reeves, became Chief Justice in the 1880s. As your father might have told you, Barbados is a very segregated place, so it cannot have been primarily a matter of colour. Although even now people say it was."

"Was it because they did not trust him? Did they see him as both running with the hare while hunting with the hounds?"

"As you know, Nello, the governor in a crown colony such as ours has, depending on his interest and his personality, the power to shape the administrative policy. Maxwell may have had governors who supported him and those who did not. Why don't you do a study on Maxwell Philip? Look into his life. Read the newspapers of the day. There would be the trials that he appeared in, people whom he defended. Cases that he won or lost. Official stuff. And later his obituaries, eulogies, that sort of thing. Talk to people who remember him, if you can find any. Use that political consciousness of yours. So when you write about Philip, put him in the political and social landscape of his time, in much the same way as you are attempting with what you and I are doing presently, and see how it turns out. I do believe that your future as a writer lies along this route, couching your social conscience in political biographies. Much better reading than the barrack-room dramas that you and your literary colleagues are presently engaged in!"

I didn't respond to that remark. But I knew what he meant. I, however, believed that what I and what he called 'my literary colleagues' were about was much the same thing as what he and his comrades in the Labour Movement were striving towards: bringing to the public what ordinary people, his 'barefoot man', were experiencing at the hands of the powers that be. *Minty Alley* is the name of the story that I am presently working on. In a way it is my own story, although I did not grow up in a barrack yard. I, like my cast of characters, am engaged in the conflicts of class and ethnicity. While those with wealth and the right pigmentation squabble pointlessly amongst themselves, people like me are only thinking of leaving this place.

ETHEL BROADWAY, WHEN NEXT WE MET, WAS EVASIVE, but in her way helpful. In describing her father, she was often lost for words. However, she was able to tell me that he was born on October 12, 1829 on a sugar estate in the south called Cupar Grange, a plantation that she said was owned by the Philip family, and then something of his education at a Jesuit-run school in Scotland that she said was a sort of seminary.

38. Meeting the Free Mulatto

From one of the obituaries I had gleaned a hint of his connection to some of the leading legal luminaries of the day, the Garcias and the Andersons. This caused me to ask her if she knew what were the circumstances that led the late Dr. de Boissière to allow her father to build Loyola on the outskirts of his estate. I had not yet discovered the relationship between the de Boissière, the Gomez, the Anderson and the Garcia families. Her response was characteristic.

"You are altogether too *fast*, Mr. James. That is not your concern." Glancing at her small gold wrist-watch, she added, "Well, you have to go now. My husband will soon be home. Good evening, Mr. James."

That brought the conversation to an end. She gathered together the papers and photographs that she had taken from a chest of drawers in the billiard room and without a backward glance left me alone with the maid who scowled a black look as she shut the doors behind me.

The following morning, I returned to the Public Library to peruse the newspapers of the late nineteenth century and to examine the obituaries written in his memory, and the at times sensational reports of the trials in which Maxwell Philip was involved. I had by this time read Maxwell's *Emmanuel Appadocca, or, Blighted Life: A Tale of the Boucaneers*. I found it a rollicking tale, not as well written as *Treasure Island*, but offering as a hero a different interpretation of the black man, in this case, a free mulatto. It says that in his youth Emmanuel was rejected by his father and by society, and he became, in his imagination, a man of loneliness and mystery, who perceived himself a "villain", a freebooter, a Corsair. It tells of his revengeful wars against humanity and how he is empowered, not only by the wind that filled the sails of the black ship but by the man he was, actually. The "high-spirited and sensitive" pirate Emmanuel Appadocca who sets out to revenge himself against the cruel white world.

I came away with the impression that Maxwell, in writing this book in his youth, long before he became a legend, was moving within the contours of inherited memories. I had to gain an understanding of why he carried the burden of other people's expectations and why he was so enigmatic, apparently even to his friends, what sort of life that he had lived. To find as little as a silhouette or even a shadow of his in passing would require my returning to, and in a sense transposing myself into his time and to the places once inhabited by him. I understood what the Captain meant when he spoke of the prohibitions of the Catholic Church, but Maxwell's *Emmanuel Appadocca* spoke to me, as a black person. In this colony, we are the walking, talking debris of the past. The factory has shut down, but the workers are all still here.

In merely glancing at his addresses to the Legislative Council I could already hear his voice. I wanted to visit the south of the island where the Philip family first planted their roots. I would have to see what he saw, perhaps even glimpse him, standing on the borderline of fact and fiction. But fact is not the only kind of truth. I understood that. I would search out what was his own utopia and dystopia avoiding, as they say, viewing the events of the past with the eyes of my own time. But first, I had to find the right voice to convincingly imagine him, and that I undertook to do.

CONCORDE ESTATE HOUSE, SOUTH NAPARIMA, TRINIDAD, B.W.I.

39. Memory, Love and Eternity

"Theirs not to reason why, theirs but to do and die."

Alfred, Lord Tennyson

Hotel Naparima, King's Wharf, San Fernando, Trinidad 1837.

C.L.R. James, Port-of-Spain, Trinidad, 1929. I imagined him kicking at stones as he walked to Mr. Young's school, repeating:

> *"The boy stood on the burning deck,*
> *Whence all but he had fled;*
> *The flame that lit the battle's wreck,*
> *Shone round him o'er the dead.*
>
> *Yet beautiful and bright he stood,*
> *As born to rule the storm;*
> *A creature of heroic blood,*
> *A proud, though childlike form."*

Because he had been told of a certain Demosthenes overcoming a speech impediment by placing pebbles in his mouth while declaiming over the roar of the sea, he put it about that he had done the same. In truth, there was no speech impediment, perhaps a slight lisp that lent a certain charm to what he had to say, but he did repeat those verses

Influential Families in the Career of Michael Maxwell Philip Q.C.

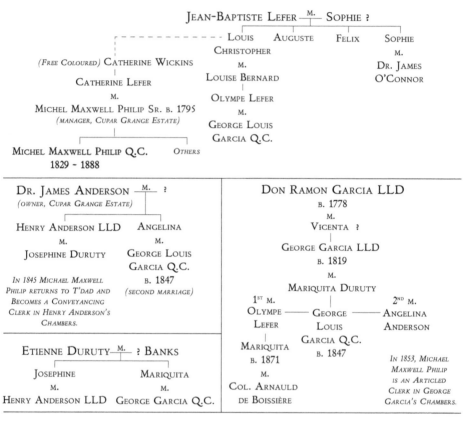

39. Memory, Love and Eternity

from "Casabianca" every day as he made his way from the tavern at King's Wharf, which was both his home and the place of business of his parents, to number five King Street, where Mr. Randolph Alan Young would be waiting, rod in hand, to instruct him and an assortment of others on the uprightness of austerity, the goodness of loyalty, the nobility of honour, and the virtues of service—along with reading, writing, arithmetic and an enduring appreciation of British culture.

Mr. Young's fondest method of inculcating an appreciation of British culture in his students, while at the same time teaching history, was to include in the school's curriculum the heroic poetry of the century. These trumpeted the military triumphs that had changed the course of history, creating nations, dominions, colonies and dependencies. As such, there was a lot of Byron, Wolfe, Tennyson and, for that particular term, the works of Felicia Dorothea Hemans.

Mr. Young would call up a boy who, having prepared himself, would stand beside him at his desk and repeat word for word to the class the poem that he had memorised. After which Mr. Young would place the poem in its correct historical context. Beginning with the Biblical, they heard of "The Destruction of Sennacherib" which took place in 701 BC: *The Assyrian came down like the wolf on the fold, And his cohorts were gleaming in purple and gold; And the sheen of their spears was like stars on the sea, When the blue wave rolls nightly on deep Galilee,* as told by Byron. In much the same manner, "The Burial of Sir John Moore" by Charles Wolfe was used to teach them of the Peninsular Wars, when on 16th January 1809, a French corps under Marshal Soult attacked a British army, resulting in Moore's death, who was buried, apparently in the dead of night, *the sods with our bayonets turning: By the struggling moonbeam's misty light and the lantern dimly burning.*

This year, it was his turn, and he had been given Hemans' "Casabianca". It told of an incident that occurred in 1798 during the Battle of the Nile between British and French fleets, and described that aboard the French flagship *L'Orient* Giocante, the young son of the ship's commander Luc-Julien-Joseph Casabianca, remained at his post and perished when the fire reached the ship's magazine and *L'Orient* was destroyed by a great explosion. Mr. Young told them that it was a true story of a boy, a young sailor, who was obedient enough to wait for his father's orders, not knowing that his father was no longer alive.

> *The flames rolled on — he would not go,*
> *Without his father's word;*
> *That father, faint in death below,*
> *His voice no longer heard.*
> *He called aloud — 'Say, father, say*
> *If yet my task is done?'*
> *He knew not that the chieftain lay*
> *Unconscious of his son.*
> *'Speak, father!' once again he cried,*
> *'If I may yet be gone!'*
> *— And but the booming shots replied,*
> *And fast the flames rolled on.*

And fast the flames rolled on. That a boy who stood in the doorway of life would prefer to die because his father had placed him at that post, to Maxwell appeared stupid. For a variety of reasons he found it difficult to memorise the remainder of the poem. This troubled him because he knew that it had entirely to do with his own father, his relationship with his father, or their relationship with each other.

He had overheard it said that his father, also called Michel Maxwell Philip, had not been able to "find himself" or "find it in himself to progress" after he "lost" Cupar Grange estate. The circumstances surrounding this "loss" occurred when a man named Burton Williams, who in 1821 had brought into Trinidad some four hundred and fifty slaves from the Bahamas, acquired first the Williamsville and Picton estates and in 1829 Cupar Grange, which belonged to the Andersons and was managed by his father. It was the year that he, Maxwell, was born.

39. Memory, Love and Eternity

Old Dr. Anderson and his son Henry, who had recently returned from England having passed the Bar, were more than sympathetic towards his parents; they were grateful. It had been a gentleman's agreement or understanding that his father would manage Cupar Grange, profitably, and in so doing allow Henry Anderson to be educated at Tonbridge School, and later be maintained in London where he had been admitted to the Inner Temple. In return, Maxwell's brother Samuel would eventually receive an education in Scotland at a Jesuit seminary that also catered for boys being prepared to enter a university, in Samuel's case the medical school at the University of Edinburgh.

Compelled to vacate Cupar Grange shortly after Maxwell's birth, the family moved to Philippine estate, where his father assumed the position of assistant to his brother Frédéric who, still unmarried, managed the estate. It was a difficult time for them. Catherine, Maxwell's mother, had grown accustomed to being in charge of her own household at Cupar Grange, and must have found it difficult to adjust to the new environment. Not that widowed Marie Renée—who had moved to Philippine from Concorde after the return of her recently married son St. Luce, who had completed his medical studies in Scotland—had made it difficult for her. In truth, Marie Renée welcomed her company and enjoyed having the children, a pleasure that she shared with Cécile, who was actually their grandmother.

Maxwell's brother Samuel was among the earliest pupils of Mr. Alan Young's school. Samuel proved to be worthy of the assistance promised by the Andersons, and having attained the age of fourteen, was sent to Great Coram Street in London, where Judith's eldest daughter Anne-Rachael was the mistress, and in the following spring he was introduced into the care of the Jesuit fathers at St. Mary's, Blairs in Scotland.

For Maxwell, as he was called to distinguish him from his father who was always referred to by his full name, Michel Maxwell Philip, Samuel's departure was of little account. Perhaps he may have been relieved because Samuel, being some seven years older, had always exercised his superior disposition by treating him with a studied disdain, augmented at times by casual cruelties.

Samuel's behaviour towards his little brother had not gone unnoticed. One day, when Samuel had emptied a bottle of black ink on baby Maxwell's head, Cécile said, "You see that! He is jealous of him because of his complexion," a remark that elicited much laughter but contained more than a modicum of truth. Maxwell had taken after his mother Catherine as far as his complexion was concerned, and after his father with his height and bearing. Not only was he as fair-skinned as his mother but he also possessed her eyes, which were large, luminous and of a golden amber, a trait shared with several members of the Lefer family.

Although Michel Maxwell Philip was no longer at Cupar Grange, his close association with the Anderson family continued, in fact it deepened when Henry Anderson invested in a cotton plantation of some one hundred and fifty-four acres on Carriacou belonging to the heirs of William Todd, and Michel went to manage that plantation. It was felt by everyone that because of an outbreak of yellow fever on Carriacou Maxwell, who was barely a toddler, should remain in Trinidad in the care of his uncle St. Luce and aunt Claire at Concorde estate.

St. Luce Philip, physician and surgeon, returned to Trinidad in the final months of his brother Jean-Baptiste's illness. He too had attended the Royal School in Edinburgh in preparation for his matriculation to the medical school at the University of Edinburgh where, like his brother, he was apprenticed to the venerable Dr. John Gilchrist. It was during those formative years that he had the good fortune to meet Claire Carmichael, a relative of Dr. Gilchrist. The two formed at first an easy-going friendship which found a common ground in their mutual interest in medicine. Over time they both experienced the very clear sign that their friendship had turned into love. Before leaving Edinburgh for home, St. Luce proposed that they should marry. Claire accepted his proposal but cautioned that her family would not readily accept him, not only because of his colour,

39. Memory, Love and Eternity

but also because he was an "outlander" and she was a relative, albeit a very distant one, of their clan's Chief of the Name. This did not especially disconcert him. He too had wintered at Craigston Castle and in so doing, much like his brother Jean-Baptiste some years before, gained an understanding of Scottish traditions, the customs of the clans and the way of life that had endured in spite of the political union with England more than a century before.

St. Luce immediately suggested that he should meet her parents who were presently at Carmichael House in South Lanarkshire where the clan's Chief, the actual head of her family, who to his surprise turned out to be a most formidable woman, was presiding over various family matters. It was an awkward meeting where they were laughed at—at first in the good-natured manner that he knew and recognised as typical of the Scottish temperament, but one that became belligerent, even threatening, when he insisted that Claire had the right to choose her own future.

Tempers were not cooled even when it was explained to him that Claire was a member of what was called a "derbfine," a group of cousins who were all at least the great-grandchildren of former Chiefs of the Name, and as such had certain responsibilities peculiar to their station, especially with regard to the inheritance of land. Therefore, the idea that she should marry a foreigner and a "blackamoor", as he was called, was simply outrageous, and possibly injurious to the family's financial interest. It was with a feeling of dismay that he left Claire at Carmichael House for Edinburgh, even though she had whispered her family's motto in his ear as he entered the stagecoach that would carry him away, "toujours prêt à être courageux". It was like a kiss, he took it to be a promise—it meant, always ready to be brave.

CONCORDE ESTATE, SOUTH NAPARIMAS, 1840: Maxwell was taken by surprise when one afternoon, upon stepping from the carriage that had been sent to San Fernando to meet him at Mr. Young's school, he saw both his parents among the crowd of people sitting in the verandah at Concorde. They were back from Carriacou!

He was hugged close by his mother who kissed him repeatedly, covering his face with her tears, and after shaking hands rather solemnly with his father, he was hugged even tighter. He had seen them last a little over two years ago, when he was nine. He now had a baby brother who was strangely named St. Catherine and a sister called Rose-Victorine. He noticed straight away how dark-skinned they were.

His mother took his sweaty hand and guided him to a recamier, and sitting close, put her arm around his bony shoulders. Listening closely as they spoke, he gathered that aunt Judith, who lived on Carriacou, was a ubiquitous figure. She was seemingly a point of reference to any number of important things and her name, whenever it was mentioned, always conveyed authority and decisiveness. He understood from their conversation that his parents were returning to Trinidad for good. They had been in Carriacou for almost ten years, and everything had changed. For one, his father no longer worked for the Andersons in Carriacou, and when they spoke of the slaves having been emancipated, his mother kept repeating, "Free as birds! Free as birds!" His father had brought the Andersons' investment in the cotton plantation on Carriacou to a high level of profitability with minimal detriment to the former slaves, who represented presently a respectable surplus of permanent labour. This was so because although fully emancipated in 1838, the entire complement of sixty-eight men, women and children had elected to stay on at the Anderson estate. His father knew how to treat them well.

Decisions were being taken. Some, it would appear, had already been made. It would seem that his father had also been of immeasurable help to aunt Judith in this regard as well. "Four hundred acres under the plow at Gran'Anse, St. Luce," his father said. "Aunt Judith received over six thousand pounds sterling in compensation for the two hundred and seventy-six slaves on the estates. Most of them stayed on. Some of the older ones, a few, a mere handful, elected to go to St. George's. I don't know what will become of them."

39. Memory, Love and Eternity

THE FOLLOWING DAY, he accompanied his father and St. Luce to Port-of-Spain. There, in a beautiful building that overlooked a tree-lined square, painted white inside and out, he was presented to Don Ramón Garcia, a ferocious-appearing old gentleman who glared menacingly at him. There also was his son, George Garcia, an equally ferocious version of the father, and his wife Mariquita, a startlingly beautiful, very white-skinned, dark-haired woman who seemed to be enveloped in a warm and very personal fragrance whose every movement was accompanied by the tinkling jingle of golden jewellery. There was much laughter and rapid conversation. Everyone spoke Spanish mixed in with French, and English words thrown about apparently for emphasis or derision. His father looked well placed among them all; his uncle St. Luce, a respected member of the colony's Legislative Council, was granted, it appeared to him, a distinctive albeit subtle courtesy. Jet-black servants in dusty dark green velvet hovered, their bare feet oiled. One had a silver tray pressed to his chest, he noticed, and trembled a little all over every time the old gentleman glanced his way. He saw that this servant's hair was dusted white with what? Flour?

Then a tall, handsome, white man walked in. It was Henry Anderson. He was accompanied by his wife Josephine, an even more flamboyant version of her sister Mariquita. Then their father, Etienne Duruty, arrived, lean and pinch-faced. His voice, thin and high, rose above the others'. The party moved with noisy chatter into the atrium. There a fountain blew a misty drizzle. He saw the sunlight create a dancing rainbow through the fine spray. His father, Mr. Anderson, St. Luce, Mr. Duruty and George Garcia were talking together. The women, hovering, had joined in. His father was nodding, smiling and glancing at St. Luce who was also nodding.

Suddenly, he realised that he had become the object of attention as he stood, wordless, betwixt these talkative, so animated people. One of the women, Josephine—although he could not by then tell them apart—was saying something in French while the other, Mariquita, was holding his chin and tilting up his face into the sunlight. "He could pass! Look at him, Josephine! His eyes! Michel, you have made a white child!" said Mariquita.

Everyone laughed. So did he. He struck a pose, one foot forward, a casual hand on his hip.

"My dear!" said Josephine, also speaking in French. "Look, doesn't he take after his mama, he looks just like a Lefer!"

"Just like his grandfather Louis-Christopher, before he got fat," announced Mariquita. "He will be a quite the lothario when he grows up."

"Yes, yes, he can pass, abroad, not here, not here," the old man was saying, waving a dismissive hand. "As a half breed, he is not too bad to look at."

Everyone laughed. Maxwell had no idea what he had passed, but felt pleased, and when asked what he thought of everything he replied remembering something or other while employing the rhetorical style encouraged by Mr. Young in his pupils, and declared, "This long exercise, father, inures the mind; and what we once disliked we pleasing find." And saying this, he smiled at the two ladies as brilliantly as he could manage and made a courtly bow in the direction of the old gentleman, who to his surprise, and apparently to the others', laughed out loud and clapped his hands.

"He is a fine boy, Michel," Henry Anderson was saying to his father, "a credit to your people."

St. Luce was smiling and the ladies were chirping like parakeets, and everyone appeared pleased with him and with his father. Actually, much more than he could have imagined had already taken place.

RETURNING TO SAN FERNANDO UNDER SAIL, the conversation was all about aunt Judith. His father was saying, "I saw her the day before I left. I had gone over to Gran'Anse early, I wanted to catch the foreman before he took the gang out. I saw her, she was walking

39. Memory, Love and Eternity

through the long grass coming from the promontory that overlooks the bay. I waved. She hadn't seen me. I looked at her. From the distance she seemed so youthful, upright, walking strong. The sun came out just as a little drizzle passed over her, a spectrum of colour flashed about her before the wind took it away. It was for her. A rainbow's end. I had to laugh. I waved again, she waved back. We met and spoke together that afternoon in the lookout. The availability of currency to pay the emancipated was becoming a problem. There was a shortage of specie on the island. I told her that I was going back to Trinidad. She said yes, it was a good idea for the children. She asked about Samuel. I told her that he was doing well over there. She wanted to know about you, Maxwell. I said that we had plans for you to go to the same school in Scotland that your brother is attending. I left her there in the lookout."

Some days later Maxwell overheard that his father had decided to take over a dilapidated building on King's Wharf. St. Luce said that it was one of the family's earliest investments. One of the several parcels of land owned by them came down to the San Fernando waterfront. That particular allotment, said St. Luce, was first used as an embarcadero, and in those early years it was from there that their sugar was shipped, going on to add that in those days it was hardly more than a large shed, with a collection of shacks adjacent to a long, unsafe jetty that sagged into the tepid water, adding that there were still some mooring buoys there to which crab traps were attached.

Maxwell's father joined in saying that as the town grew and something resembling a wharf took shape, the family's investment in its development took the form of making their slaves available for the work of creating the wharf's facilities, such as they were, and that one of his uncles, André-Montrose, saw to the construction of a building that stood above the water on tall pylons. It offered in those days overnight rooms to travellers in their comings and goings. St. Luce thought that at the time no one believed that it was an hotel, because it possessed no amenities, there was no service and there were but one or two iron beds, probably without mattresses, and some mildewed hammocks. The rooms had no doors, he told Maxwell, so there was no privacy and more often than not there was no one there to receive guests, and as such there was no income to speak of. His father then said that he was going to change all of that.

Some days later Maxwell accompanied his parents to see the old place. It was being refitted. Doors were being hung. Beds manufactured. And chairs and tables too. All on site. There were painters everywhere. He was shown the family's quarters. Rooms that overlooked a newly built abattoir. His father told him that it was to be their new home. It was all being arranged quite quickly.

There was no doubt that Maxwell hated leaving Concorde estate. He had grown accustomed to the certainty, the regulated life at Concorde. Most of all he appreciated St. Luce, his uncle, whose medical practice brought to the estate a variety of interesting people, mostly his friends, who were always grateful and who treated Maxwell with respect, some believing him to be the doctor's son. He had grown up at Concorde astonishing them with his ability to read, which had come to him at an early age. A love for learning manifested itself as soon as he was able to understand the meaning of the books placed in his hands, first at school by Mr. Young, and later on by discovering those at Concorde.

The house, large and freshly rebuilt, held the family's amazing collection of heirlooms. There was a small but substantial library. This contained among others books those that had once belonged to his great-grandfather Papa Honoré. Among these were the writings of a French cleric of a previous century, he wrote about adventuring with the pirates as well as the setting up of plantations, the building of windmills and the creation of aqueducts. Maxwell absolutely loved to listen to St. Luce's telling of the brigand wars, of his great-grandfather who had sailed the seven seas with the French corsairs, and of relatives who lived "away", some in England and others who owned a magnificent castle in France.

There was as well a number of volumes of poetry by Lord Byron, a great many quite worn. Byron's *The Corsair*, a long tale in verse,

39. Memory, Love and Eternity

was especially exciting to read. It spoke of deeds of daring, desire and danger. A complete collection of the plays of William Shakespeare, illustrated, which Maxwell perused with an avidity and assiduity really surprising in a youth of his age, and there was the astonishing assemblage of mezzotinted pornographic prints. He was warned by St. Luce that they were not for him to see, so he took a particularly close look. Books written in French by Jean-Jacques Rousseau and Voltaire stood next to those on travel, biography, the popular novels of the day and textbooks on medicine, also well worn. One other that was kept apart, which he discovered in his final year in Trinidad, was written by a Free Mulatto, his uncle, Dr. Jean-Baptiste Philip.

He had also grown attached to Claire, a Scottish noblewoman as he understood. He was hardly three years old when she had arrived and was not at all aware of the sensation caused by her coming, but because of the manner in which it was retold, it became a part of his remembered experience. Claire had, against her father's expressed objection, taken her family's maxim literally, "Always ready to be brave", and with the connivance of Dr. Gilchrist, she chose to deliberately ignore all other advice and sailed incognito from Port Glasgow to Port-of-Spain, where she was met by a more than jubilant St. Luce. It was a highly unusual affair, their marriage. There had been just one such in all the short history of the Church of England's presence in Trinidad, and the ceremony was conducted in virtual secrecy in the Trinity Church in Port-of-Spain by the Reverend George Cummings with Désir Fabien and Simone Corsbie as witnesses.

The days had dwindled down to just the few that would remain as memories spent at Concorde. Maxwell, having enjoyed the better part of the morning riding out beside St. Luce on his inspection of the estate, saw a procession of fine carriages approaching the entrance of the estate yard. Standing at his bedroom window, he heard welcoming shouts of greetings, answered by boisterous hellos. Visitors were arriving! He had heard them speak of a man called Antonio Gomez, always in laudatory terms, as a Spanish gentleman of high degree who was much liked by the family.

"The Don", as Antonio was referred to by St. Luce, was visiting them at Concorde. Together with his wife, or as he was to later overhear, his second wife, an English lady. They were touring the plantations in the Naparimas. It was long-established custom during the dry season, after the trash was hauled from the fields, that the estates would receive visitors. Marie-Renée, who had been supervising the preparation of the day's callaloo in the outside kitchen, had already greeted them. St. Luce was shaking hands with the tall, gray-haired man, and Claire was being embraced by a large woman in a huge hat, who had with her what appeared to be a very little man carrying her parasol.

Coming downstairs, he was presented to the visitors. Would they be staying overnight? No, it appeared not, but they would be lunching. Magically, it would seem, everything was in process, tables were laid out with white table cloths on the green lawn beneath the widest-spreading samaan tree, a red and white marquee had been erected and all the domestics were turned out in their best. The visiting party may have been seven or eight or more people, but Maxwell only had eyes for the Don and his impressive lady.

Marie-Renée, silver-haired and becoming a little frail but still strong of voice, was regaling them all with stories of long ago. The visitors were familiar with the family's affairs. They laughed and spoke of Gran'Anse and the cotton estates on Petite Martinique, of aunt Judith and uncle Jean-Baptiste. His parents arrived just as luncheon was served. A tour of the two plantations was being discussed. He was allowed to join them. Claire, his mother and the English lady were to ride in the first carriage, others were to follow and the gentlemen were on horseback. They saw Concorde and Philippine and then rode on to Corynth where the Corsbies received them for tea. It was a long and very exciting day.

That evening, Claire read to him as she or St. Luce had done ever since he was a small boy. His favourite was Byron's *The Corsair*. As the long dry-season twilight crept over the sleepy garden wall, he closed his eyes and imagined his great-grandfather Honoré as its

39. MEMORY, LOVE AND ETERNITY

hero, a singular man, a man of adventure and of mystery. He would be such a man.

Now all this, he realised, as he made his way to school some weeks later, had come to an end with his removal to Hotel Naparima.

HE DID NOT FLINCH WHEN HE WAS CALLED UP TO STAND BESIDE Mr. Young's desk to recite *Casabianca*. In his mind he had come to terms with his father.

> *There came a burst of thunder sound –*
> *The boy – oh! where was he?*
> *Ask of the winds that far around*
> *With fragments strewed the sea!*
> *With mast, and helm, and pennon fair,*
> *That well had borne their part,*
> *But the noblest thing which perished there,*
> *Was that young faithful heart.*

The following year, at the funeral of his aunt Marie-Lazarine who had married Joseph Ventour, he learned that he was to be sent away to Scotland, where he would follow his brother Samuel at St. Mary's College, Blairs, close by the river Dee.

40. Present, Past and Purpose

*"Made weak by time and fate, but strong in will
To strive, to seek, to find, and not to yield."*
Alfred, Lord Tennyson

THE CHANCEL, ST. MARY'S, BLAIRS.

SCOTLAND 1841: MAXWELL WAS FORTUNATE that his brother Samuel had preceded him at St. Mary's College, Blairs, a Jesuit minor seminary in Aberdeenshire that also accommodated boarders, boys being prepared for entry into institutions of higher learning. Samuel was the first coloured student to be admitted, the first to be prepared there for the Medical College at the University of Edinburgh, and the first boy from the school to swim the Dee Mile. This was a treacherous downstream swim of a mile and a quarter that took the swimmer around the crook of the river Dee, to finish at the town's old suspension bridge. As such, much was expected of him.

Maxwell rose to these expectations by excelling firstly in the liberal arts: grammar, rhetoric and dialectic, then, music, arithmetic,

40. PRESENT, PAST AND PURPOSE

geometry and history. Latin, Greek and an appreciation of the classical thinkers were believed to be paramount in the disciplining of young minds, but his prowess on the school's playing fields, which was seen as just as important, earned him the notice of his teachers and the respect of his peers. Early on, he had instinctively grasped the nuance of all this. He was being trained to enter the legal profession, where memory and the command of language were of the utmost importance, and where social status would be ascertained by the user's choice of words—thus mantelpieces were to be "chimney pieces", note paper "writing paper", and mirrors "looking glasses".

There was as well the mastery of dramatic monologue. In this he excelled, as the school was already well known for its theatrical performances, especially the plays of Shakespeare. Then there was the ethos of the school itself. The Society of Jesus, the Jesuits, founded in the sixteenth century by St. Ignatius of Loyola, inculcated the notion of magis—a Latin term meaning "more". It suggested the spirit of generous excellence—the striving for the greater good. This meant that one did things for the greater public good and benefit, because that was what actually mattered in life. Ad Majorem Dei Gloriam, all for the greater glory of God, was the Jesuit motto.

Debate was encouraged to explore this idea. Some of his colleagues suggested that magis meant the striving for excellence, others believed that magis meant generosity. The elderly sacristan, who adjudicated, thought that both were good words, although they expressed different ideas. A younger student thought that it expressed a more universal good. Going on to add that discerning choices based on what would make the widest positive impression on people, which was itself a criterion that St. Ignatius Loyola identified with, was characteristic of the Society's way of proceeding. This caused, Maxwell noticed, the sacristan to hide a smile within the wrinkles of his kindly face. Someone suggested magnanimity, while another said greater efficiency.

Maxwell thought of saying summum bonum, as described by the Roman philosopher Cicero, but said nothing. The sacristan suggested that multiple definitions were all a benefit, because although the definitions offered were not synonymous, neither did they appear irreconcilable, and therefore, all should be allowed to illuminate the vigorous character of the ideal.

And on another occasion, quoting Robert Browning, Father Sharpe, the school principal and also Maxwell's Spanish teacher, said to him, "Mide el talento de tu inteligencia a partir del final de tu sombra". They were walking on the banks of the Dee at sundown.

"I should measure my mind's height by the shadow it casts, Reverend Sir?"

"It is the sign of a great mind to dislike greatness, Maxwell, and to prefer things in measure to things in excess."

He was often to forget that sage advice, but the debate on magis was to stay with him through the years.

C.L.R. JAMES, PORT-OF-SPAIN, TRINIDAD 1929. During Maxwell's time away at school, well over twenty thousand slaves in Trinidad found themselves experiencing a new reality, one that was disingenuously called "freedom". A letter, faded by time and almost ruined by its handling, which was handed to me, interestingly without comment, by Mrs. Broadway, described a scene that made me think of the Exodus. It was written by Michel Maxwell Philip to his son Maxwell, who was at school in Scotland. In the letter, his father remembers seeing—it was in September 1838, some time after emancipation—a long procession of the freed slaves, representing perhaps the population of several estates, passing through San Fernando in the pouring rain. On their way to where? He did not say. But I imagined them, old and young, some sick, many seemingly well, all weary, men, women and children dressed in rags, their tattered garments stained by their wretchedness. Michel Maxwell Philip wrote that for some reason, as they passed along, he kept looking at their feet, deformed by labour, mud-splashed, bent out of shape, their crooked and deformed toes leaving grotesque muddy prints, to be instantly washed away by the pouring rain. After their passing, it was as though they had never come that way at all, he

40. PRESENT, PAST AND PURPOSE

wrote, going where? The letter then went on to say that some of "their people" had stayed on at Philippine and at Concorde. Others, he did not say how many, went to Corynth, where Thomas Corsbie welcomed them. The planters, perpetually pessimistic, had apparently anticipated some sort of an uprising, which never came to pass, but a mischievous agency had been at work putting word about that they might be sent back to the estates and as such the planters were anticipating trouble.

It made me think that for months, perhaps even years, this population of some twenty-three thousand must have reshuffled itself. For the first time in their lives, people were free to move about. Those from the south heading for the north, while of those who had been domestics in Port-of-Spain—they were in the majority—setting themselves up in trades. Many, with nowhere to go, or no idea what freedom actually meant, stayed on with their former masters, even as some were taking to the hills that surrounded the town. No longer was there to be a legal difference between the free coloureds and the formerly enslaved. They were now equal before the law.

"She is letting you see the family documents and read letters! You've become fast friends, Nello, like you really reach for true!"

We had met, as was usual, in his rooms to work on his biography and the Captain was pulling my leg. I ignored that remark. I was curious about a speech that he had delivered on the May Day celebration of the Workingmen's Association in the grandstand of the Queen's Park Savannah some weeks earlier. On that occasion, speaking as President of the party, he revealed to a very large gathering of workers that the following morning at ten o'clock he would again be entering the premises of the Trinidad Electric Company on Park Street to request a take over of the company.

"I was addressing them as a labour leader and a member for Port-of-Spain. I was not there in my capacity as mayor—I wanted that clearly understood by my good friends of the press—and statements made by me were not made with the permission or on behalf of the municipality of Port-of-Spain."

Cipriani was warming on one of his favourite topics, representative government, going on to describe his meeting with Mr. J. H. Thomas, one of the leaders of the British Labour Party. That particular meeting had taken place in 1926. Paying close attention, I employed the Pitman technique of note-taking, as I had to not only quickly grasp the substance of the speech but also understand it in the context of his meeting with the British labour leader.

It was after six when, having exhausted the subject, we took a break to stand in the gallery that overlooked Marine Square to smoke a cigarette. A late afternoon shower had left a sheen on the street below that was being highlighted by the new streetlights. From the nearby railway station came the hiss and clang of an engine and the final whistle of the last train to arrive for this evening.

"Yes, she is allowing me to have a look at some correspondence," I said to the Captain, remembering his jibe. "I have in fact gained Ethel Broadway's confidence to some small degree. You see, in spite of her brittle surface, I cannot help but feel that she wants her father's story to be told afresh."

Several newspapers in the Public Library carried obituaries for Maxwell Philip, written in 1888, extolling him. These offered clues of his stay in Scotland at St. Mary's, and suggested that he must have interrupted his studies to return to Trinidad sometime in his teens and later in his early twenties. I also noticed in one of the old newspapers that a Dr. de Boissière had moved a motion in the Legislative Council for a pension to be paid to Mrs. Broadway and her sister Catherine. A Mr. Tronchin appears to have known him best. There was a lecture given by Tronchin at Greyfriars Hall in Port-of-Spain, where Maxwell was described as "The Great West Indian Orator." This lecture appeared in full in *The New Era*, a popular newspaper of the day. I asked about Tronchin at the Public Library and learned that he was prominent Afro-French Créole intellectual of the 1880s, principal of the Trinidad Model School and the author of a novel, entitled *The Phantom Nun of Mount Moriah*. They were no longer in possession of a copy—what a pity!

40. Present, Past and Purpose

"Well, my boy, that means you are winning her trust! What else has she shared with you?"

"I wouldn't go so far as to say that we have become fast friends. She still keeps me at a distance, but she obviously wants me to tell her father's story, and that is why from time to time letters mysteriously appear. All so furtively. Sometimes between the pages of his prayer book that I have already looked at. I would notice that there is an envelope sticking out between the pages and find a letter. One or two were written by his father and some others by Maxwell himself.

One day she showed me a lithographic print of a handsome man who wore a form of judicial garb. I asked if that was a relative of theirs. She said no, it was Antonio Gomez, a former judge and a high official from the days of Governor Woodford, adding that his wife Amelia was the widow of Robert Smith who was previously a Chief Justice of Grenada. She said that they were once frequent visitors to Concorde estate, which then belonged to or was managed by the Philips. She said all this assuming the haughty air that she employs whenever she speaks of people whom she thinks of as important, going on to say that her father told her that Antonio Gomez and his wife would receive his aunt Claire and uncle St. Luce at their townhouse in Port-of-Spain. She had a letter written on pale lilac paper, she showed me where it said thank you, it appeared to be from Gomez's wife Amelia. They had taken tea at St. Luce's town residence and were planning a visit to de Boissière's terraced garden in company with a Lady Chichester. She made a point of saying that de Boissière's garden was on the very estate, Champs-Élysées, where Loyola is located. Then, assuming an even more pompous attitude, she said, 'Sir Charles Chichester was appointed acting governor here, in Trinidad!' Adding, 'they were very close to us, you know, the de Boissières.' Apparently her father's family's connections to the de Boissières went back for generations."

"Lemme see," answered Cipriani reflectively. "I think what she is getting at is that both Gomez's wife and Lady Chichester accepted her uncle St. Luce and his wife as part of white society. That could

317

be because St. Luce's wife Claire was considered a lady. Meaning that she was of the same social standing in England as the Gomez's."

"Is that so! Is that how it works? She was the daughter of a Scottish clan chieftain."

"Of course. White women of high social rank, not white men, have always set the social standard in these islands. If St. Luce had married a common white woman, they would not have been invited anywhere, or visited. As a Scottish noblewoman, she must have been seen by them as coming from the same class as they."

"Mrs. Broadway said that they were all related—the de Boissières, the Gomez, Garcia and the Anderson families—and that they were 'her father's people' from long ago. I didn't say anything at the time, but I did remember that only the day before I read in one of the old newspapers that there were people here at the time who saw the Philips quite differently. In fact they saw it fit to reproach them publicly. This was in an editorial in the *Trinidad Sentinel* in 1858. I copied it down. It was addressed to St. Luce Philip. Can I read it to you?"

"Yes of course, go ahead."

"'Tu quoque Brute.' It is no surprise to hear black and coloured people reproaching each other of being a Negro or a mulatto, and attribute one another's faults to the colour of their skins; it is no wonder to see a descendant of Africa of a fair complexion committing the cowardly act of abjuring his origin in broad daylight, and trying to manufacture himself into a white man to avoid the stigma, and to obtain favours; so strong is the belief that the model of perfection is a white face.' What do you think of that?"

"The perennial problem of coloured people. They live in the no man's land between the black and the white. During slavery days, they were free men and their European ancestry was preferred over their slave ancestry. But with emancipation, their distinctive position disappeared. If they sided with the blacks, they were reminded by the white people that they, too, once owned slaves, and if they identified with the whites, who privately laughed at them behind their backs, they were attacked by the blacks. The Philips, because of their wealth and their other attainments, had become socially white. They were not alone, there were others like them. Trinidad is not as rigidly segregated as say Barbados, you know. St. Luce may have been resented by some blacks, especially those who owned newspapers because he supported what the local press perceived as British colonial interest.

"So in speaking about her family's connection to important white people, she is letting me understand that in spite of their colour they, the Philips, were well connected?"

"And so they were," said the Captain, nodding.

"It must have been no small social achievement, whether you were black or white, to be in the company of people like the Chichesters."

"The Philips lived a life that reflected in many ways the attitudes of the white Créoles. But there were people, especially those who controlled the press that spoke for black people, who resented that. St. Luce Philip may have looked like one of their own, so they were shocked and felt betrayed when he appeared to be leaving his family's true moorings, so to speak, and crossed over to the other side."

"Tell me, who did Ethel marry? Who is Mr. Broadway? He is never there when we meet."

"Mr. Broadway, Walter I believe is his first name, is an Englishman. A botanist, attached to the Botanic Gardens here in Port-of-Spain. They may have met when Ethel went for walks, Loyola being next door to the Botanic Gardens."

"Yes, that's possible. But what gave the Philip family such prestige? At the end of the day, they were not white people. Rich, yes, but there are rich people today, not white, who are not in the governor's company, or the acting governor's company."

"Mmh, I think it was because of J.B. Philip, who was, back then, still actively remembered as the first champion in the cause of political liberty in this colony. Certainly in legal circles for having the punitive and racist laws that Governor Woodford enacted, removed. I have heard it said that these laws would have proved detrimental not only to the free coloured people of the day, but, had they stayed on the books, would have been a danger to civil society because of how they would have affected the soon-to-be emancipated. The British did not want that known. And there are a lot of people even today, both here in Trinidad and in the Colonial Office in London, who do not want that to be known. His book remains kept under lock and key."

"Why is that?"

"Because it is important to some people that ordinary black people—the grandchildren, the great-grandchildren of the slaves, you included—should be kept in the dark about what was done by J.B. Philip for them. For all sorts of reasons some people want his efforts to be seen to be only about the free coloureds. Then there was your 'Tu quoque Brute', Dr. St. Luce Philip. He was, in Lord Harris' day, the first coloured man to be appointed as an unofficial to the Legislative Council. Probably some sort of gesture meant to placate him or others, but it was very significant, as it demonstrated J.B. Philip's success, the Free Mulatto's success in the redemption of not only his people but all black people. Then there was of course their wealth. And, in St. Luce's case, he had married a white woman from a social class sufficiently high to impress both Lady Chichester and Gomez's wife. When they travelled to Europe, for education or for pleasure they were probably received by their relatives over there and by the society that they moved in. The English people, the officials here, would have known about that. It is their business to know about things like that. It was not only Maxwell's education and training as a barrister that gave him eminence. No, it was from what he came. The class of people to which he was connected, not just here, but in England. The English are racists, no doubt about that Nello, and they are also snobs. Maxwell, I am sure, knew well how to snub them. I think that he saw himself as an aristocrat. As better than most of them who came out here to lord it over us. The people must have loved him for that. Everybody knew who he was. What he came from. And they expected a lot from him."

"Did I tell you, I discovered that Maxwell was born in 1829, the very same year that J.B. Philip, The Free Mulatto, died?"

"Is that so?"

"Yes, I wondered if the writers of his obituaries, obviously his devoted followers, knowing this, saw him as the heir to something almost spiritual."

"I'm sure they did, and look at you, one hundred years later writing about them, you may come to see yourself as a successor to the Free Mulatto's cause. One coincidence following another. Here, I have something here that may be of use to you." Cipriani took from his coat pocket a small blue book. I could just make out in the fading light the title, it read: *Observations on the present condition of the island of Trinidad and the actual state of the experiment of Negro emancipation*, written by a William Burnley, and published in 1842.

"In there you will find the testimony of St. Luce Philip, then proprietor of Concorde estate, and another given by a Frédéric Maxwell, manager of Philippine estate. Most informative. Gives one an idea of what management thought of the worker in those formative years after emancipation. You can take it with you to have a look, careful with it, there are not many of them still around."

"I can't imagine that when it comes to labour much has changed," I answered, and thanking him, promised to return it on our next meeting, which would be on Monday of the following week.

Frédéric Maxwell's name had caught my eye. I had seen a notice in the *Port-of-Spain Gazette* stating that he had died in 1846. Michel Maxwell Philip had given notice that by order of the Chief Justice, he was seeking Letters of Administration with respect of the personal estate of Frédéric Maxwell, his brother. Two brothers, but only one carried the Philip name. Interesting, but certainly not unusual.

When next I met with Ethel Broadway I asked about the family's relationship with the Garcias, I was curious to know who they were. She naturally took offence and said, "This is what I can't stand with you people, you're always on the lookout for scandal!"

Plainly, for reasons best known to herself, she was not inclined to divulge any information about that particular family or another, the Andersons, both of whom I had seen mentioned in Maxwell's obituaries. On a previous occasion I had asked her about the information that appeared in the obituaries. Had she been their source? She said yes, she had been. In any event, I wanted to read what St. Luce Philip and Frédéric Maxwell had to say, to actually hear their voices, as they discussed the "experiment of Negro emancipation". Most fascinating, the term experiment.

1842: St. Luce Philip, Concorde Estate, "There you are! I thought that you would be going on to Philippine. Did Frédéric come back with you?" Claire had been gathering anthuriums in the estate's greenhouse and was surprised to see St. Luce standing at its door.

"No, he went on alone to Philippine. We left Port-of-Spain immediately after he gave evidence. But I will be going to back to town day after tomorrow as I want to hear what Martin Sorzano has to say. Remember him? The surveyor?"

"Yes, of course. So how did it go? Was Mr. Burnley on his best behaviour? And what did you have to say with regard to the experiment of Negro emancipation? I can't get over the term experiment, as if you can have a trial run on freedom. Only the English can come up with such notions."

St. Luce smiled. Claire's Scottish accent always became stronger when she spoke about the English.

"It went well enough, Burnley was in the chair and Union Hall Estate house is airy. What's today? 23rd or the 24th? I seem to have lost track of the days this week."

40. Present, Past and Purpose

"Today is the 22nd, my dear, the 22nd of March 1842."

"Thank you. Well, he wanted to know for how long was I a resident in Trinidad, I told him that I was born in the colony, but educated in Europe, where I had passed some fourteen years. Then he asked my profession, and how I employed myself in the colony? I said that I am a doctor of medicine but that I practice only among my friends, and chiefly employ myself as a sugar planter, being part proprietor, with my family, of three sugar estates. He asked if I was acquainted with the state of affairs in the colony, social and agricultural? I told him I was, generally, but in all matters of agricultural detail, he should hear what our manager, Frédéric Maxwell, who was originally a slave, long liberated by our family, had to say, as he would give the committee better information than myself on both the present social and certainly the agricultural state of affairs."

"You told them that Frédéric was once a slave! Why?"

"Those people have all sorts of clichéd ideas about slavery. I wanted them to know that a man's a man. Burnley then wanted to know whether the expenses attending the cultivation of a sugar estate are greater now than before emancipation. Well of course they are! He knows that! Most of his questions were about the economics of sugar production, all obvious, all well known, certainly to him. Then Frédéric was called in, and examined. He was asked what was his occupation and employment. In his usual manner he told them that he was manager of the Philippine estate, in South Naparima, a position that he has held for the last seven years. Going on to say that at five years of age, he was brought by our father from Grenada, and that he worked first at Concorde estate, which belongs to the family, until he was liberated."

"They have no idea that he is your half-brother?"

"No, of course not, no one knows that. It was never made much of in the family in the first place. It was not important. We were not unique in that regard. John de Boissière has sent both the sons he

323

had with a slave woman, I think I've heard that her name is Zuzule, to France to be apprenticed to a firm of shippers. They went there to learn about business, how it works. And there are others. That is not important."

"Not important? As I have come to understand in this colony the stigma of slavery is a dark shadow that follows all mixed-race people. The further removed, the better their status. I'm curious to know that if the de Boissières or the Garcias knew that Michel Maxwell was Frédéric's brother and their mother once your family's chattel, they would treat him the way that they do."

"I don't think they would care. Michel has made a lot of money for them. And beyond that, they have an understanding of sorts."

"What sort of understanding?"

"Well, Michel Maxwell helped his wife Catherine's father, old man Lefer, restart his business when he returned to Trinidad. With father's money of course. Michel Maxwell also saw Dr. Anderson through a very difficult time when both his sons were away at school in England. He made Cupar Grange profitable. That earned a lot of money for Dr. Anderson. All this helped later on, when both Henry and Alexander, Anderson's sons, attended the Inns of Court. They had to be maintained in London. In turn, the Andersons offered to help Michel with his eldest boy, Samuel, who wanted to study medicine in Edinburgh. And they did. And Samuels's little brother, Maxwell? He charmed them all the other day when we were in town. The Lefers are connected to the Garcias through marriage and also by virtue of having grown up in their company. Being white-looking and pretty helps Catherine. She takes after her father's family, the Lefers. It makes it easy for them to accept her. Catherine knows her place, she is timid, as you can see, and very charming."

"Now, tell me about Frédéric's testimony. What did he tell them?"

"He told then what he thought. When asked if he believed the former slaves to be much improved since their liberation, he answered them, I thought without a trace of irony, yes, they were very pleased with their condition. He then went on to add that he found them, the former slaves to be lazy and unwilling to work consistently because they are paid too much. I thought that William Burnley was on the point of applauding as Frédéric added that if they were paid less they would work more. He also said that the Americans, the former soldiers, who were once slaves themselves, worked harder and were more dependable."

"You have said so yourself."

"Indeed. The former slaves enjoy idleness, living off their more industrious friends and of course, the canes on the estate. As you know, we have at times stopped paying their wages, but then they simply leave the estate and go to another. We cannot afford to lose time taking them before a magistrate, so we let them go."

"Did they ask if they, the former slaves I mean, were saving some of their wages? I know that some do."

"Oh yes, Frédéric told them that he was acquainted with a few women who did. A hard-working woman or man can easily save six or seven dollars a week. A woman whom he knows is saving to buy a parcel of land. She is an African, his goddaughter apparently, and he is holding above one hundred dollars for her."

"They trust him with their savings. That's amazing."

"I would trust Frédéric with my life. He is a very sound fellow. When asked if more Africans should be allowed into the colony, and if he would hire them, he answered yes, three hundred would suit him fine. Going on to say that presently he needed hands to weed and to haul trash from the ratoons. Our present stock of canes would yield one-third more sugar if properly cultivated, he said, going on to add that he would put in more cane-pieces, as our engine was quite powerful, enough for a much larger crop."

"Is he going to be the only black man to give evidence before this committee, St. Luce?"

"Oh yes, there is no other like Frédéric. As he spoke I could see the surprise on the faces of the Englishmen, those recently arrived in the colony, they could never have imagined that a man as dark-complexioned as he, a former slave, could speak in such an authoritative and well-informed manner, and address them all as an equal. Especially when he spoke of the immigrants from the other British colonies. He dismissed these, saying that left to him, he preferred to have the locals, even though they were bone lazy and very undependable. But undoubtedly his choice for labour are the Americans."

"The disbanded soldiers."

"Yes, former slaves who opted for or were pressed into the English army during the American War of 1812. They fought for the British against the newly formed United States. They were established here as a community in the southern quarter in a number of villages around 1816. They came with their families. About five hundred and seventy men, and about two hundred women and children. To strike a balance, more black women were subsequently brought in. Some of these women had been freed from other places, such as captured French slave ships. Six companies were eventually settled in separate villages under the command of a corporal or a sergeant, who maintained a military style of discipline. They are Baptist."

"And surrounded by French-speaking Catholics. How are they making out."

"Apparently very well. I haven't heard of them converting. Would you?"

"Convert to Catholicism? I would prefer to be burnt at the stake!"

"Come here, let me convert you."

"No you don't! No! not in the greenhouse!"

"Why not? Isn't this where young things are planted?"

"Oh, let me be. And here comes the new gardener. . . ."

41. Conveyancing Clerk

"I am a part of all that I have met."

Alfred, Lord Tennyson

THE GARCIA RESIDENCE IN PORT-OF-SPAIN

C.L.R. JAMES, PORT-OF-SPAIN, TRINIDAD 1929. As previously arranged we met, the Captain and I, in his rooms overlooking the Catholic cathedral. That evening, I especially wanted to hear what he had to say about the controversial divorce bill that had been introduced in the Legislative Council some three years ago. It was a modern piece of legislation that sought to allow divorce under conditions similar to those in the United Kingdom. It was supported by Cipriani, being in essence the position taken by the Trinidad Workingmen's Association. Even though he threw his considerable weight behind it, it was subsequently withdrawn by the Trinidad government because of the intense and highly organised opposition mounted by both the Catholic church that represented the majority of the population and the influential French Créole community.

I thought that being both a Catholic and a French Créole, the Captain might feel uncomfortable if I were to broach the topic head on, so I approached it by mentioning that I had come across some information in the newspapers of the 1850s concerning Maxwell Philip's entrée into local politics. It would appear that Maxwell, some years after his return to the colony, became involved in an abortive constitutional reform movement that sought to ameliorate the Marriage Ordinance of 1863.

I went on to say that when I last met with Ethel Broadway I mentioned this, and she told me that her father was a staunch Catholic, adding with obvious pride that she was the godchild of no less a person than a previous bishop!

"Really! Did she say which one?" asked the Captain, passing me one of those uncomfortably delicate demitasses that contained the strong unsweetened coffee that he enjoyed. Taking the tiny saucer between thumb and forefinger I was relieved that I hadn't trembled as I placed it on his desk.

"Oh, thank you. Yes, it was the one with the impossible to pronounce Italian name, what's it again?"

"Spaccapietra. Vincenzo Spaccapietra," he answered, taking a careful sip. "He was the first non-British subject to head the Catholic church here in Trinidad. I remember my uncle Leon Cipriani saying that Maxwell had been prominent among those who welcomed the new bishop."

"Maxwell must have become very popular, then and there," I said.

"I dare say," he replied, settling himself. "And I am sure there were powerful families in the Catholic community who would have been in support of him for that."

"Who were they?"

"The Rostants and the de Verteuils, to name a few, and of course the Garcias. Over several generations, the Garcias were able to walk that delicate line between maintaining the popularity and trust of the common people, who were almost entirely Catholic, and the confidence that the Colonial Office placed in them in so far as their judicial appointments were concerned. The Garcias held positions, from father to son, such as Solicitor General and Attorney General, as well as acting as Chief Justice. You know in those days, Nello, the politics was sharply divided between the Catholics in the colony and the ever-

41. Conveyancing Clerk

encroaching English led by a man named Charles Warner. One of Warner's many causes was to anglicise the population. The Garcias, as Catholics, were the counter-weight to Warner and the English party. As Attorney General, Warner wielded great influence for decades in this colony. When old Mr. Ganteaume went bankrupt—I seem to think that could have been in the 1840s or 50s, he was my uncle Leon's father-in-law—he resigned from the Legislative Council. Ganteaume was the only Catholic on the council, the only one who spoke for the tens of thousands of people, black and white alike, who were Catholic. George Garcia was nominated in his place. The Garcias, along with some others, were at the heart of what you could call the Catholic party."

"I saw in an old newspaper that Garcia was also involved in community affairs. He signed a protest against testamentary laws before the Legislative Council. I got the impression that this was the start of an anti-Catholic campaign. And in another paper, I think it was in the *Public Opinion*, one of Maxwell's obituaries stated that the first time Maxwell returned home from school in Scotland, he must have been just 17 or 18, he went to Henry Anderson's office. Anderson was a solicitor. And some years later, according to another obituary, to George Garcia's chambers before going off on his own. What do you make of that?"

"Really, I had no idea, very interesting. Ramón Garcia, Raymond as he became when he anglicised his name, was a part of Woodford's judicial administration. He lived to a great age. Died in his nineties. Ramón Garcia's son George was the one who took Ganteaume's seat in the Legislative Committee. He was very successful as a barrister, married a Duruty. He became Solicitor General, a Puisne Judge and acted as Chief Justice of the colony on many occasions over a great many years. His son, George Lewis Garcia, married a Lefer, and after she passed away he wed an Anderson. George Lewis also became Attorney General."

"I always find it amazing that you have such a memory for the machinations of people so long ago dead. Who they married, who their children were and their children's children, three, four generations. Black people don't have that."

"Not all white people do either. It has to do with perceptions of class, and I suppose the maintenance of one's identity. I know that you are thinking that it's a lot of rubbish, and it probably is, today, but let's not stray, we have a lot to do this evening. What I am about to tell you could be of use to you. The Garcias are very interesting as a local family of Venezuelan origin. And I think you're going to like this, Nello, there is mystery, quite romantic, about them."

"Is that so? What is it, a black ancestor, a touch of the proverbial tar brush hidden somewhere in their remote slave-owning past?"

"No, nothing of that sort. Who Ramón Garcia's parents were and where he was born is the mystery. It was believed, in fact accepted by society here, that he was the natural son of a Spanish princess, an Infanta as they are referred to over there, and her confessor. According to their family tradition, to avoid a scandal, young Ramón was sent away from Spain to Caracas in the care of a priest, in his own ship, which carried a fortune in gold. It is said that he took the name of the priest who accompanied him."

"Really, that all sounds very far fetched. But I understand white Créoles, present company excepted of course, like to decorate their past with all sorts of stories of nobility, when in truth they come from very ordinary backgrounds."

"That may be the case with some, but I must tell you that we, the Ciprianis, are connected to the Bonaparte family."

"Do your constituents know this, not to mention your comrades in the Association?"

"No, of course not," the Captain laughed. "I have no interest in that particular sort of self-aggrandisement. But it meant a lot to them, the Garcias. They displayed the arms of Spain on gold watches, silver, china, all sorts of things. When Ramón's grandson, George Lewis Garcia, was appointed Attorney General by the Colonial Office, he revised the laws of Trinidad. These legal tomes were

41. Conveyancing Clerk

produced by the Government Printer with the Spanish royal coat of arms and his name on the title page. Extremely unusual for a government publication of that sort. Those volumes can be seen at the Court House."

"But Captain, we must make a start, look, it's six o'clock already, the church bells are ringing."

"They are ringing for the Angelus, Nello. That's another mystery. Where were we, oh yes, the controversial divorce bill, you were anxious to know how its failure made me feel."

Apart from that topic I wanted to hear about his early life. What shaped his convictions and points of view, and especially something more of his activities during the Great War and how those led to his taking a position which would eventually lead to him becoming involved in the labour movement.

THE ISLE OF ARRAN, SCOTLAND, 1845: MAXWELL PHILIP received the news of his father's inability to continue paying for his education and upkeep at St. Mary's with dismay. He was ordered home. The coming term would be his last at the school. He sat the final examinations and as far as he knew, he did well. The coming year was meant to be a victory lap. He had achieved several distinctions. Senior prefect the previous term, he was seen as a role model for students who increasingly came from various parts of the world. Deputy head boy to be appointed, he was expected to lead fellow prefects in their duties. He had already represented the school at sporting events held in Aberdeen, and had made one or two public speeches at local farming and agricultural shows where he was mistakingly taken by the locals to be an expert in tropical agriculture. But all this was now moot. He had to pack his trunk and leave the school.

The journey by stage coach from Aberdeen to Glasgow was a nightmare. The terrible October weather. The icy wind, the lowering sky, the people taciturn, he believed to be more so because he thought that they somehow knew that he had very little money. This was why he was sailing from Greenock aboard the schooner *Chasseur,* a Baltimore Clipper that was bound for Barbados. Stepping aboard he could smell the cargo. Going below to find his bunk he felt ill. It was too close, too low, the other passengers too near.

Maxwell at sixteen had achieved six feet and some. His complexion was fair, his manner gentle, his look that of a worried boy. Within hours of departing Greenock, the *Chasseur* was overtaken in the Firth of Clyde by the winter's first storm, forcing her to enter Lamlash Bay, a sheltered cove on the east coast of the isle of Arran.

He found himself the guest of Captain Woodward, the Chasseur's master who had introduced himself as a Yankee. They were put up in a farmhouse where they would wait out the storm. This allowed him to gather his thoughts. Before leaving Aberdeen, he had given a promissory note to the bursar, covering the remainder of the sum required to pay for his attendance at the school up to his departure. He was now worried that it would not be met. Could that mean that he might be deprived of the school's certificate?

He would need to write a letter to the school's principal. To do this he must find paper, ink and a pen. Captain Woodward was pleased to oblige. Sitting in the ghostly light of midday, the wind outside howling across a deserted landscape mhe wrote:

To: Reverend John Sharpe
St. Mary's College, Aberdeen.
Lamlash Bay, October 29th, 1845

Rev'd and Dear Sir,

I was very sorry that fortune proved so hostile as to deny me the happiness of taking your leave. I trust however that an epistle may serve dearly as another.

I was sorry also that I did not get a certificate from you. You know, Dear Sir, the use of a good certificate. Without this I must make my way through the world with very great difficulty.

41. CONVEYANCING CLERK

I shall thank you therefore, Dear Sir, if you are so kind as to transmit it at once in a letter. My address is M.M. Philip, Naparima Hotel, San Fernando, Trinidad. I shall thank you to give me a certificate merely of probity and what I have learned, that is to say if you can do it in conscience.

I, along with four other passengers, left Greenock on Saturday last and have been compelled by unfavourable winds to put into Lamlash Bay, so herein are we to lay. Please do remember me to all the worthy professors.

I remain, Rev'd Sir, your most humble servant.
Michel Maxwell Philip.

The farm was a ghastly place. The food, that because of Captain Woodward's generosity he did not have to pay for, was tasteless, the rooms were icy by day, and at night the very small fire did not help at all, the water in the dented wash basin turned into ice by morning. The outhouse, because of the wind, was a torture chamber.

After an indeterminable period, during which he became convinced that he had somehow lost, misplaced, several days. The weather cleared and the *Chasseur* hauled her anchor and set her sails to leave the Firth of Clyde for the Atlantic Ocean, where they were met by a series of rainstorms. The early winter sun ominously illuminated the dark rushing water and dramatised the towering thunderheads in whose billowing bosoms lightning flashed by day and by night.

Obstructed by wild and unpredictable headwinds and an angry sea as they sailed into the tropics, they were forced to bypass Barbados and enter the Gulf of Paria through the Columbus Channel with the sea running high, the winds contrary, the rocky outcrops drawing nearer. The risk of floundering became increasingly real as night fell.

Maxwell being the only passenger bound for Trinidad, Captain Woodward dropped the *Chasseur's* anchor within sight of the Naparima Hotel. By late morning he was being brought ashore. His mother, together with his brother and sister, in some mysterious manner, had anticipated his return, and was standing on the windy waterfront. It was a miserable homecoming. His father had suffered a stroke that left him partially paralysed along the right side of his body and unable to speak. Maxwell, taken to him by his mother, could hardly recognise the dark, wizened face that grimaced as inarticulate sounds reached for words. He could only imagine what his father uttered as he admired the tall, handsome youth who stood at his bedside. Maxwell felt to flee. It was all so unbelievably alien.

Hotel Naparima, in a sad state, was now home to several Venezuelan families, all of whom had little or no money. They were escapees from the irreconcilable conflicts down the Main, with no hope of returning to their native land. It was also infested by swarms of enormous flies, the nearby abattoir their obvious source.

His mother, as those first days of his return went by, was doing her best to encourage the Venezuelans to find alternative accommodations. He realised that they could become permanent, albeit non-paying guests. She was very glad that he could speak to them in a language that they understood. He was firm. A few of the men responded to the authority in his voice and moved with their wives and children. In the privacy of his thoughts he was very touched by his mother's show of competence. He felt for her and she, realising this, became increasingly cheerful and did all she could to make him feel comfortable. She was in control of the domestics, fewer now, but clearly devoted to her. He said that he would be leaving for Concorde. His mother did not encourage this. No, she said, don't go, stay here, please, we need you here now. He sensed that something had changed. His worried thoughts were still focused on St. Mary's. His debt. The note at hand. He asked her for money. There was very little. She showed him what was in hand. Several crumpled dollar bills, he had no idea of their worth, and a collection of English sovereigns and half crowns, a quantity of shillings and some small change, mostly copper pennies and some others of indeterminable origin and value that she kept in the space under a drawer in her dressing table.

He left early the following morning, the sun not yet up, for Concorde, riding on the back of a cart drawn by a pair of horned Zebu bulls, driven by a turbaned man wrapped in white cotton

41. Conveyancing Clerk

whose English he was able to understand if he listened very closely. The driver was among the very first Indian indentured immigrants to enter the colony and had been assigned to St. Luce Philip of Concorde estate.

Concorde was much as he remembered it. The heat of the day rose from the rolling fields of sugarcane in arrow as far as the eye could see. The house, the great trees dripping Spanish moss from their massive boughs crowding close. Horses, their coats shining in the midday sun. Workers, mostly black, but here and there he could make out the slighter forms of Indian men and there, a veiled woman. And here was aunt Claire. He was embraced. Uncle St. Luce was with his father's brother Frédéric Maxwell, who was bedridden at Philippine.

There was so much to relate. An addition to the family. St. Luce and aunt Claire had had a son, he was christened Louis. There had been a falling out between them all. Over what? She was guarded. Over money? Yes. Hotel Naparima, somehow ill-fated from the start, had drained away his father's savings. St. Luce was generous, but times were changing. Had changed. The family in Trinidad could no longer draw upon the proceeds of investments made in London so many years ago. That era had ended. Great-aunt Judith Philip, with characteristic thoroughness, had parcelled out what money was due to her nephew St. Luce and his sisters. Nothing had come to his father. There were quarrels. Bitter words were spoken. Not by Frédéric Maxwell. No. Not at all. By his father? Yes.

St. Luce arrived at sunset. Maxwell, well met, was put at ease. His note of hand would be honoured, the school paid, the certificate secured. He retired for the night in the room that he had known as a boy and enjoyed a night of complete rest, the first, it felt, since he had left Scotland.

Some days later, wearing the clothes of his uncle St. Luce as his own were being laundered, he sat in the wide verandah at a small table, pen in hand, and wrote:

> To: Reverend John Sharpe
> St. Mary's Collage Aberdeen.
> Trinidad, December 17th 1845.
>
> Reverend and Dear Sir,
> I am conscious that my note of hand had become due long before this missive.
>
> My Dear Sir, I gave the note of hand on the supposition that we would have had a very short passage, but contrary to my expectations, after dallying a long time in Greenock, we have had an infernal, excuse the expression, long passage.
>
> Therefore, Dear Sir, I am all together incapable of remitting to you the sums owed in my note by this present packet that sails shortly, for I have barely time to write this letter. But, by the next packet, you may confidently expect your money.
>
> Let not this implicate my work and argue anything in disparagement of my probity, as you yourself know, I have not had time as they say, to look about me. I give my compliments to all the professors.
>
> Your humble servant,
> Michel Maxwell Philip. (jnr.)

Maxwell was inexpressibly relieved when he received from his mother's hands the school's certificate that had obviously been dispatched even before his last correspondence had arrived in Scotland. Reverend Sharpe plainly had never lost confidence in his probity.

The Naparima Hotel was a frightening liability. It had to be sold. The time for all of that had passed. He agreed and was much relieved, the idea of having to live there, the squalour, the daily chaos, the smells, the flies, the embarrassment of seeing his mother, who looked like a white woman, cooking in their bedroom, he hadn't known what to do with himself when he saw her doing that. There had been nowhere for him to be in Hotel Naparima. It was closed down, the property sold off and the proceeds made available to his mother. There was a house, not far from the San Fernando waterfront. Built by André-Montrose more than fifty years ago on

41. CONVEYANCING CLERK

one of the allotments owned by the family, it was small, rustic. St. Luce would make it comfortable for his parents.

He was to be outfitted. The great double armoire at Concorde contained a variety of dress, formal and sporting, winter coats and hats, some carnivalesque, others still possessing the patina of when last they had been worn by Jean-Baptiste or by St. Luce during their student days abroad.

It was some months later, and after he had celebrated his seventeenth birthday with his parents in their new home, that he was presented by St. Luce to Henry Anderson in his offices in Port-of-Spain, in the vicinity of the new Government buildings on St. Vincent Street.

He immediately felt comfortable. The atmosphere in Anderson's office was convivial, club-like and manly. They spoke of their mutual interest. Cricket, tennis, and of boating excursions on the river, in his case the Dee, in Anderson's at Dorchester on Thames, of friends, tutors and headmasters, all the while engaging in rituals of self deference. Patently they held the same values and could even laugh at the same inanities.

He was shown a desk close to the entrance, given a hard, uncomfortable chair and was introduced to Jesus Alcala, an elderly conveyancing clerk. He was to assist Alcala in all matters concerning the preparation of transfers of legal title, of real property from one person to another, the granting of encumbrances, such as mortgages and charges upon real or personal property for the satisfaction of debts or duty, ordinarily arising from Spanish Law which was still to some considerable extent extant in Trinidad in those days. He thought at the time that it was because of his knowledge of that language that he had been placed with Alcala, who was a Spanish speaker. Maybe his gaining an appreciation for the Laws of the Indies would enhance his future career?

The small chattel house built by Marie-Renée, St. Luce's mother, on Henry Street in Port-of-Spain in the previous century that had been shuttered for some years. Now he had it aired, cleaned, repaired, repainted and eccentrically furnished. Maxwell was provided with a servant, the youngest son of Boniface, who had once been houseboy at Concorde, a washer and a cook. In the stable was a mature gelding named Captain. A stable boy, elderly, would be both gardener and groom. It was his first household.

He was received by Josephine Anderson, Henry Anderson's wife, at their residence on Clarence Street, where he was presented to George Garcia and his wife Mariquita, a sister of Josephine. They all remembered him, and the lively Mariquita exclaimed: "Look, Josephine, he did turn out quite the lothario, just as I predicted!" Everyone laughed.

He knew very well that he was being observed as he was served at dinner by the careful servants. He was acquainted with this ritual. Even though it had more to do with polite conversation and genteel gestures, he still enjoyed the meal. Placed around the dinner table in the candlelight, they did not seem or act like strangers to each other. Formally turned out that evening, in white tie and tails, he appeared elegant. He was very tall, well over six feet, handsome in a manly manner. Importantly, he looked and behaved like a confident white man, except for his hair, which was black cropped short and like a Negro's hair, which did not matter because his features were entirely European.

There had been about him, ever since he was boy, a natural hauteur which they especially admired. They knew that along with his name it would appeal to the Créoles. It was that quality, together with his much remarked upon intelligence, that had attracted both the Garcias and the Andersons in the first place. Maxwell so obviously had what was required to be a successful lawyer as well as the possibility of becoming an attractive public figure. And they did not yet know the profundity of his memory or truly experienced his theatrical flair. Would he like to be articled at George's chambers? Yes, he would be honoured to have such an illustrious preceptor.

His uncle Frédéric Maxwell died at Philippine in March of 1846. His father, partially recovered from the stroke but unable to speak,

41. Conveyancing Clerk

himself, his mother and his siblings all arrived at Concorde to be greeted by St. Luce, Claire and their son Louis. They travelled together by coach to Philippine where the remainder of the family was assembled in the drawing-room. Planters both coloured and white from North and South Naparima and their wives arrived to extend their condolences. White people from Port-of-Spain who were visiting the southern estates came, some he recognised. Everyone's demeanour was respectful. The coffin, large and imposing, appeared to Maxwell to occupy the entire room where every picture was turned to the wall and the great gilded mirror was draped in black. The previously enslaved assembled in such a large quantity that it became alarming to some. The funeral service was conducted by a youthful Spanish priest from the Mission who was assisted, he noticed, by barefoot half-Carib boys. It would appear that Frédéric, without the family's knowledge, had become quite devout in his old age.

The Ventours, Romains and Corsbies crowded close to inspect him. He was not fazed by the attention and assumed the appropriate role. He realised that he was being treated with degrees of respect by both the young and the old. His uncle St. Luce, who stood at his side, was honoured, it seemed to Maxwell, as the inheritor of the admiration once bestowed on his elder brother, Jean-Baptiste. St. Luce had burnished that lustre with his own attainments, not the least of which was upon his appointment to the Legislative Council in 1838, when he moved that the apprenticed condition of the emancipated slaves be ended.

It was for Maxwell the first public intimation of the unique distinction held by his family. He could feel himself altered in some subtle manner as his hand was taken and his eyes looked into, searchingly, appreciatively, as if confirming an accolade that had been passed on as a precious thing from one generation to the next. He sensed that a great many eyes were fixed on him as the cortège arranged itself to proceed to the small graveyard adjacent to the great house.

From all around arose the sound of drumming and the chant of female voices. Former slaves on the estate were performing their own sacred rites for Frédéric Maxwell, whom they had come to know, trust, and hold in high regard. Maxwell was touched by this, thrilled actually, not just by the rolling drums but by the original, in truth archaic sound of their voices. This brought tears to his eyes. There was something terribly real unfolding here, something altogether foreign yet not alien taking place, as Frédéric's coffin was lowered into the grave. Once again he sensed their eyes on him. He held himself erect as he took his father's arm, already holding his mother's, as the drums reverberated across the rolling hills of cane. He knew that something old, very old, had ended and was passing away even as the red sun slid behind the hills of gold and a little drizzle fell upon them all.

Maxwell attended to the letters of administration for his uncle's estate, carrying the documents to the Registrar General's office himself. It may have been entirely in his imagination, but he believed that he was treated with respect, even deference by the white clerks, mostly local men, in the Government building. He assumed a formality, a studied dignity that was perceived as being beyond his years.

The family was still wearing mourning for Frédéric when they received the very distressing news that Maxwell's older brother Samuel had died in Edinburgh. That Samuel had sickened and died alone, so far away from home, was plainly more than his parents could bear. He worried that his mother would become ill and that his father would suffer another stroke.

"There are these," his mother told him, unwrapping with hands that shook a little what looked like an embroidered table cloth. "They were given to your father by your grandmother, Cécile. She received them from your grandfather. I believe that they are of great value." Saying this she drew away the last fold of cloth to reveal several silver dining plates. "It is all your father has left of his inheritance. They were meant for Samuel. They are now yours, don't sell them, even if you are hard pressed to do so."

His brother Samuel's passing was not the last death in the family that year as word came from Grenada that his great-aunt Judith had

41. CONVEYANCING CLERK

died in her sleep at Gran' Anse. He sailed for Grenada with St. Luce aboard an aged schooner, the *Crispin Wayne*. Sitting uncomfortably on a wooden box, his back against the main and holding on to a bundle of wet stays, as the *Crispin Wayne*'s plunging bow sent saltwater to splash across his face, it was impossible for him to believe, to truly accept, that this very old, toothless black woman, with untidily knotted gray hair, dressed in a costume obviously of the previous century, who could hardly speak English, wore a man's leather belt around her waist on which was affixed an iron ring that held a quantity of keys, and who treated him with an unnerving familiarity, could possibly be his grandmother.

There were matters to be dealt with of a legal nature in St. George's. He was surprised at the amount of properties in London that were owned or leased by his great aunt Judith. Then there were the houses and vacant lots thereabout in the town, and the seemingly abandoned lands on its outskirts. The estates on Carriacou, those on the island of Petite Martinique, the tenants, workers, all former slaves, not to mention the hangers-on, creditors, historic dependents on the family's largesse and the many persons who claimed to be relatives, descendants of people that he had never heard of, all to be dealt with.

Arriving at Gran' Anse estate he realised that his grandmother was the source of all sorts of useful information. He came to understand that she was the manager of these estates for many years. She knew where every boundary stone was located, where everything was kept, and had in her possession the keys that unlocked every door, drawer, cabinet and safe. She knew everything about the lands owned by the family and treated with the tenants as if she had never moved away, even recognising the grandchildren of those who were long dead.

Her memory of people was accurate, her manner was kind but often dismissive, even harsh, when dealing with people that she considered knaves. One morning, he had only just taken coffee, she took him by the arm and led him to the rear of the old house. Just off the pantry was a small dingy room. "I lived here from the time I was a girl," she said. She boasted, while looking up into his startled face with a grimace that he could not endure, "I was the only slave girl to ever live in Gran' Anse great house!" A slave! She was a slave? This strange woman who was his grandmother was once a slave. This must be a secret. A scandalous secret that he surely did not want to get back to Trinidad.

St. Luce was straightforward when Maxwell, sufficiently composed, was able to broach the subject, and tried to disabuse him of that notion. That his grandmother, Cécile, his father and his uncle Frédéric were all born in slavery was not a secret, he was told. Neither was it a scandal. Of course there would be people who knew this.

"My father, your grandfather, much like many men in those days, had two families. One here on Carriacou and another in Trinidad. Cécile grew up in the bosom of our family, she is remembered as the one who took care of your great-grandmother, Jeanette in her old age. She was like a sister to them all, and later when everyone moved away, to England, to France and to Trinidad, following the revolt that destroyed the future of Grenada, she was left in charge here, in Gran'Anse, for several, several years. It is of no consequence whatsoever that your grandmother was once a slave who was owned by the family, none whatsoever."

There were no words for the many things that he wanted to ask about.

"All this must appear strange to you," said St. Luce, "because you were away at school ever since you were a boy and you have no idea of life in the colonies neither in those days nor even now."

St. Luce gave him an amused smile, saying, "There is nothing to be ashamed of or even to be embarrassed about. My father, your grandfather, took his sons with Cécile, your own father and Frédéric, into the heart of our family where they were they were brought up by my mother alongside all of us. Cécile came to us at Philippine after she left Gran'Anse. Look here boy, we are who we are. All of

41. Conveyancing Clerk

that can bother other people, but it means nothing to us, nothing, absolutely nothing!"

Maxwell felt that he could never be the same, that something about his sense of self had been permanently rearranged.

He saw that St. Luce followed Cécile's lead, listened closely to what she had to say and took her advice when it came to appointing persons who would be in charge until everything could be settled with Judith's children who were all living in England.

He wrote letters to Judith's children dictated by St. Luce, sitting on an antique chair whose upholstery, his grandmother assured him, was stuffed with the hair of slaves long dead. They were in a small, square, lamp-lit room that overlooked the estate yard and the great bay below. It was called the lookout.

He stepped out onto a narrow gallery, the east wind blowing about him. The sky, no longer golden, was now tinged to deep maroon on the far horizon.

It was altogether a very peculiar sojourn for him, especially at night when he was drifting off to sleep, which came with an almost physical sensation of falling backwards. He had a dull headache over several days and a sort of nauseousness. He kept this to himself. Often left alone in the old house, he almost always had that eerie feeling that he had been here before.

One particular morning, which seemed to him to possess an unnerving stillness, he found himself in a shuttered room that he had entered without knowing why. There was nothing there but an unsafe chair near the rusted frame of a wide, vacant, iron bed. Was this where his father was conceived? On that iron bed? A dark mirror was hanging on an unpainted partition. He saw himself strangely in it, not unrecognisable but somehow differently. Suddenly, rolling thunder was vibrating the floor under his feet. Then a quiet, it contained what? He left hurriedly and felt ashamed for being almost overcome with fright. But it was on a windy promontory that overlooked the bay where he was actually overwhelmed by a feeling of je ne sais quoi, that certain quality that cannot be described or named so easily. He could not believe that he was seeing all that expanse of sea and sky for the first time. He was unable to move away. It must be the isolation of the place, he thought. The vast distance. A horizon that appeared to go round and around. He felt that he should offer a prayer. He said an Our Father out loud and resisted feeling ridiculous. It was difficult to move away. He felt that he should stay and wait. But they were to sail for Petite Martinique at noon. He saw St. Luce, he was waving from the house. He felt relieved and ran through the long grass past a withered clump of bushes. He did not know that they were dead cotton trees, nor did he notice the pigeons circling above, quite white against the gray thunderclouds.

Petite Martinique now hovered in the distance. It seemed to him a smudgy bruise of memory. Of what? That they could own an island appealed to him, even as the wind rushing through the rigging took the thought away. About and all around the swelling sea, bright green, with an ever moving lacy trim quite white upon every wave, rushed by. It was all so isolated, so distant from everything and everyone he knew. It was like travelling on a far-flung wheel that was taking him towards an horizon that must be on the very perimeter of the world. A frontier where heaven was brought down to earth. Madame Pierre, the place was called. A hill that rose above a smiling turquoise bay which was so named because one of his great uncles had bequeathed it to his wife before leaving to fight for political liberty in France. His name was Pierre-Jean Philip, he too was a revolutionary. There were others. He came from a revolutionary family. They were at a place called North Point. A cotton estate owned by his cousins. They were all black people, the only thing that distinguished them from their former slaves was their dress and manner. They, the women were all dressed in white cotton and resembled each other to a remarkable degree. They seemed to be versions of the same woman, someone called Jeanne-Rose.

He would hear about the revolutionaries. St. Luce spoke of one called Joachim and another named for his great grandfather,

41. CONVEYANCING CLERK

Honoré. They had been executed in Market Square in Bay Town, Grenada. Hanged by the neck until they were dead. In the flickering candlelight, St. Luce related that people like them, free people, had been betrayed by the British in Grenada. His uncles had plotted and formed a fighting force that took to the mountains of Grenada in 1795, they had freed the slaves and unfolded the French Republican banner. There, they kept the English army at bay for more than a year. A terrible war was waged for freedom, it had been fought and then lost. The uncles were the unknown heroes of a past that the British had buried in the dust of history. He wanted to know more. St. Luce spoke of his brother Jean-Baptiste, who had carried that fight to the British Government and had won freedom for people like themselves in Trinidad. Yes, he came from a long line of men who fought for freedom in these colonies. This was why they were who they were, and not like other people. He, St. Luce, Jean-Baptiste, the uncles Joachim and Honoré, they were representative men. The forefront of a vanguard that was leading the way for the masses to follow. He must never forget that. The weight of that burden was the duty that every Philip, man or woman, bore.

They sailed for Trinidad with a following wind that fairly lifted the *Crispin Wayne* to ride the waves. It was, taken altogether, an experience that he would describe over and over and each time the memory would return, vivid, as vivid as the words that he had memorised from one of the battered books of poetry found in the bookshelves at Concorde:

> *"They say that Hope is happiness—*
> *but genuine Love must prize the past;*
> *And mem'ry wakes the thoughts that bless*
> *They rose first—they set the last.*
> *And all that mem'ry loves the most*
> *was once our only hope to be:*
> *And all that hope adored and lost*
> *hath melted into memory.*
> *Alas! It is delusion all—*

the future cheats us from afar:
Nor can we be what we recall,
nor dare we think on what we are."

THEY SEEMED TO BE VERSIONS OF THE SAME WOMAN.
SOMEONE CALLED JEANNE-ROSE.

42. Articled Clerk

"Knowledge comes, but wisdom lingers."

Alfred, Lord Tennyson

C.L.R. JAMES PORT-OF-SPAIN, TRINIDAD 1929. I NOTICED IN ONE OF his obituaries that Maxwell's education at the Inns of Court was supported by "his friends". What friends, I thought, could young Maxwell Philip actually have had who would be in a position to advance him sufficient funds to maintain him in London while he attended law school? It would appear that he did return to Trinidad when he was about sixteen in 1845 and according to the obituary in the newspaper, *Public Opinion,* he worked in Henry Anderson's chambers. In *The New Era* obituary it said that "he read law in the chambers of George Garcia". That would have been in 1853. Surely it must have been the partners of those firms who had seen something in him, maybe his future potential, to afford him financial aid sufficiently generous to see him through some three or four years in London.

I thought I would revisit Loyola in the hope of finding out more about his time in England from Ethel Broadway.

It was a rainy afternoon in August when I stepped off the St. Clair tram to make my way to the outskirts of Dr. de Boissière's village and to Loyola cottage. Cotton Hill, so called because of the mighty grove of silk cotton trees that dominated the surroundings, was windy, wet and slippery, and I was not well prepared for the weather.

"Put it in the corner Mr. James, over there, don't drip everywhere. Here, hand it to me! Give it to me! Wait here. Madame not expecting you." Mavaline Shemuerl, perhaps roused from her afternoon siesta, exuded impatience as she snatched my umbrella, twirled it, sending droplets in all directions, to deposit it in the furthest corner of the gallery.

"Wait over there."

It was not a long wait because it would appear that Ethel Broadway was expecting me.

"Mr. James, come. You look like a wet fowl, better take off that wet jacket. Yes, take it off, hang it on the back of that chair. Look, I have found a few things that might interest you."

Handing me a large envelope, she pointed to one of the chairs at the table in the middle of the billiard room, declaring in a commanding voice, "You sit down there," and, turning in the direction of an open doorway, shouted, "Mavaline! you can bring in the tea now."

Apparently we were to take tea. The envelope, covered with blue and red stamps that showed the profile of Queen Victoria in silhouette, contained a quantity of what looked like official papers. At a glance I could see what appeared to be a bundle of legal documents tied with red ribbon and some other folded papers. To be sitting with my damp collar and tie and in shirtsleeves, having tea with Ethel Broadway served by a disapproving Mavaline, was in itself extraordinary. Moreso were the documents that I carefully laid out on the table. One was a marriage certificate, two others were covered with cryptic signs and strange symbols, the third appeared to be another certificate, issued by the Middle Temple apparently. There was as well a carefully written letter. Reading it quickly, it stated that in late 1853 Maxwell submitted a petition to the Parliament of the Inn—I would later learn from Cipriani that was its senior governing body—requesting to be called to the Bar early, having kept his required twelve terms but not attending certain required lectures, but needing to return to Trinidad due to ill-health and other matters.

From what I could make out the Parliament discussed it on 25th November 1853 and deferred it to the Council of Legal Education, which I supposed was a central body that oversaw legal education across the Inns of Court. There were as well several notes from a doctor confirming his ill-health.

"So he returned to Trinidad before completing his final exams? I don't understand?"

"Of course you don't. How could you? He was ill. A bronchial infection. He had to seek a warmer climate. Look, there, that's what it says. They understood that. The other thing was his father was dying. Was dead before he stepped off the ship that brought him home."

"What did he do?"

"Do? He did what he had to do, Mr. James. Look after his affairs of course. I believe that he entered the chambers of Mr. George Garcia before returning to England. Look, his articles of clerkship signed by Garcia himself. He would have needed that to continue his studies."

Looking over his handwritten certificate I saw that it was headlined Middle Temple and simply stated that he had resided at Great Coram Street, Bloomsbury, London, that he was the son of Michel Maxwell Philip of Trinidad and that he was called to the Bar on the 17th of November 1854. I somehow imagined something more grand.

"Leave it alone, Mavaline! Mr. James isn't finished."

Ethel Broadway had poured the tea and, assuming that I took sugar, placed one teaspoon of it in the steaming cup and I, taken up with the documents, hadn't touched it yet.

"Thank you Mrs. Broadway, it's delicious. Red Rose tea?"

"Of course not. Darjeeling. We only have Darjeeling. Have a Graham cracker, Mr. James. There's guava jam. Help yourself. And for God's sake, Mavaline, will you stop hovering. This is my father and mother's marriage certificate. See where it says that he was a Barrister. They were married in 1854."

I could see that they were married in London at St. Brides Anglican church in 1854. That would mean that he was married in an Anglican church to an Anglican woman. The other document that I looked at was the one with the cryptic signs and strange symbols. I somehow knew that it had to do with Freemasonry.

"Yes, he was a Freemason. He received this from the Royal Prince of Wales Lodge. See their seal, there, there. Many influential men were. Are. You would not know anything about that, Mr. James."

I didn't, actually. What I had heard was that Freemasonry was banned by the Roman Catholic church here in Trinidad. "How come he was a Freemason and apparently at the same time did so much for the Catholic church here? I saw in the newspapers that he was very involved with the Catholic church and had the support of the Archbishop."

I could not of course mention that I thought that as a Catholic his marriage to an Anglican in an Anglican church may not have been recognised by the Catholic church—after all, she had boasted of being the then Archbishop's godchild.

"My father, Mr. James, as *you* will discover, was a man of many parts. Horses for courses, Mr. James. Ever heard of that saying?"

I smiled deceitfully as I applied a lot of guava jam to a Graham cracker. Of course I had heard the expression, it meant simply the practice of choosing the best person for a particular job, or the best means to achieve a specific end. She then spoke rather dismissively of several people, mentioning names like Needham and Warner. I had heard of Charles Warner. I gathered that they would have been his adversaries. She then spoke admiringly of a previous governor of the colony, Sir Arthur Gordon, a frequent visitor to Loyola and a man who was greatly admired by her father.

"They dined together on plates of solid silver. These were but a part of my father's inheritance."

"He must have been very versatile," I murmured, just before taking the cracker, guava jam and all, into my mouth.

"There is no room for sarcasm here, Mr. James," she snapped, looking around for Mavaline who instantly removed my half empty cup and saucer.

Unmoved I ventured, "And he named this house Loyola for a Catholic saint, how strange."

"You are entirely too sly, Mr. James, too sly for your own good."

"Oh, I'm sorry. I'm really just trying to understand. He was a Catholic but married an Anglican lady in an Anglican church in England, came back to Trinidad, joined the Freemasons and became a supporter of the Catholic church here in Trinidad. Did you ever hear that discussed? I mean I am an Anglican, my parents are. If that sort of thing happened in our family we would be talking about that a lot."

"I'm sure you would be, Mr. James. But in *our* family there was no room for such banality. My father read aloud from the works of the classical scholars every morning and in so doing kept his knowledge fresh. We spoke French and Spanish here. I see the rain has let up, Mavaline will show you the way out."

"Has it? The other thing I wanted to ask you was who gave the information that went into his obituaries? I read in one of them that he was helped by his friends to remain at law school over there. Who were they, his friends I mean?"

"I spoke to the men who came from the newspapers, Mr. Broadway and I. We dealt with them. Why?"

"Well there are some contradictions. . ."

"Mr. James, there were people here who believed in him, young as he was at the time. They were his friends. Look here, it's time for you to go."

"What a pity. You mentioned Governor Gordon, I wanted you to tell me something about their relationship. They were friends, I take it?"

"Yes, they were close, very close. There was a bond of trust, the sort of thing that gentlemen share."

She was saying this while gathering the contents of the envelope.

"May I take those with me?" I asked, pointing to the bundle tied with a red ribbon.

"Certainly *not*, Mr. James."

"Pity you didn't get her to tell you who paid for his education in England. I would have been interested in that," exclaimed Captain Cipriani, fanning himself with his khaki corkhat. The suit, also made from khaki—he was famous for that—was drenched with perspiration. He had returned from addressing a delegation of workers who had come all the way from La Brea in the hope of being included in the Workingmen's Association and I, early for our appointment, had caught him at the gate.

"I couldn't, but it appears to me that Maxwell had the support of the people for whom he worked while he was in Trinidad. His obituaries all seem to agree that when he first came back home from school in 1845 he was in Henry Anderson's chambers for about four years, and when he returned from the Inns of Court in 1853 he was in George Garcia's for at least a year before returning to England. His obituary in *Public Opinion* claims that he was a pupil of Garcia's, who was Solicitor General at the time. They must have seen in him the making of a lawyer, don't you think?"

"Oh yes. Come, Nello, lewwe go upstairs, it's hot like hell and I am dying of thirst."

In the cool shadowed shade of his office we both enjoyed a refreshing glass of iced water from a tall thermos flask. Resuming his thought while loosening his tie the Captain said, "Solicitor General, eh? That's a powerful man in this place. He has the ear of the governor and the colonial secretary, and between them they decide what goes to trial, depending on the case. You would see him representing the government in the courtroom. He is the second only to the Attorney General. But what we were talking about just now was as a novice, Maxwell would have started off as a conveyancing

42. ARTICLED CLERK

clerk with Anderson. Learning, for example, how to transfer legal title of real property from one person to another, the granting of encumbrances such as mortgages, that sort of thing. How long did you say he stayed with Garcia?"

"For a year or so I think. I saw in one paper that he spoke Spanish fluently."

"Spanish would have been very useful in those days. Only a year with Garcia, that's short. Anyway, then you say he returned to England. I have heard from friends that upkeep at the Inns of Court is very expensive."

"I saw in one of the Inns of Court documents that Mrs. Broadway showed me that he attended the Middle Temple and lived at a London address, I can't bring it to mind now."

"If he had a place to live that would have saved him a lot of money. There's an old adage that goes, 'The Inner Temple rich, Middle Temple poor, Lincoln's Inn for law, and Gray's Inn for a whore.'"

"Really, Gray's Inn for a whore?"

"Gray's Inn is for the whore because Gray's Inn Park was a notorious haunt of prostitutes! There are all sorts of stories of how law students financed themselves. They would write for the papers, or be a barman. They have one here today, enormously popular, who was a ships chandler in London."

"Ah! That makes sense. Maxwell would have written his popular novel about pirates to make money. The publisher would have given him an advance. His book may have sold well."

"And always remember, Nello, Maxwell was a Philip. A relative of theirs, Dr. St. Luce Philip, was in the Leg Co. as a nominated member. I know that because he was the first man of colour to sit with the governor in that chamber. Another family member, J. B. Philip, was a famous man, well known for what he had done for the coloured people, but also for the ordinary folks in the black community. They were well respected, the Philips, and importantly they were seen as a family that came from the common people and had done well, and had always represented them and their concerns."

"I understand that. But what about the Garcias? They look to me like men who were very close to the governors here in Trinidad and to the Colonial Office in London. Why would they want to accept a coloured fellow, who represented the common people, as their protégé?"

"You know, Nello, the answer to that could be that no matter whether we come from the old French and Spanish families or from the free coloured people of long ago, we are all born Créoles. We may work as the servants of the Crown, but we hold on to an ideal that we belong here and that this place, this Trinidad, belongs to us. Not to the British. It is an old thing, this belief. A very old story in these islands. One could even argue that the proletarian movement had its origins in Haiti, with the slave uprising over there. At the end of the day, the slaves were working people. I have felt myself that here in Trinidad the movement ultimately springs from what Maxwell's relative J.B. Philip achieved when he was able to force the powers that be in London to alter the laws in Trinidad in favour of the free people of colour."

"With that he set in motion the growth of a political consciousness that we see today expressed in a vibrant labour movement? On several levels of the society?"

"Not only that, but in the manner how ordinary people express themselves, their individualism, their creative urge to satirise authority. In Maxwell's day people were looking for a leader, the Garcias, the de Boissières. A man called Philip Rostant, and others like him, saw in Maxwell the potential, the possibility, that here was someone who, with the working people behind him, could wrest from the almighty British Crown what was wanted here in Trinidad, political liberty. Home rule. An elected Assembly that truly represented the will of the people. Reform in the truest sense of the word. A reformation of the society that would remove that glass ceiling under which we live here."

42. ARTICLED CLERK

"You think Maxwell knew that? You think that he was aware that ordinary people, working people, were looking at him as some kind of champion? Or was Maxwell a cat's paw, an instrument for the purposes of older and cleverer men, so to speak?"

"Both might be true. There was a need then, as now, for representation. People like the Garcias by that time were high up in public office, old Dr. de Boissière was a nominated member of the Council, and others like Mills and Rostant who owned newspapers that spoke for the common people, they wanted a leader. Philip Rostant expressed the hostility of the French Créoles against the English in his editorials. Créoles like Garcia and de Boissière defended the practice of drumming, the bamboola, when outlawing it was being considered. Take Rostant—he developed a kind of anti-colonialism which aligned all the respectable colonists, white, coloured and black, against both British officialdom and the expatriate firms that exploited locals. Just as they do today. Lemme tell you, I don't think Rostant's own family liked him much for that! As the old Patois saying goes: Behind dog's back, it's 'dog', but before dog, it's 'mister dog'."

"Yes, someone called Samuel Carter, who I suppose was editor of *The New Era,* remarked—I noted it, look—'A Crown Colony is despotism tempered by the press. In Trinidad, more than in any of the other colonies, has the existence of the independent press been an absolute necessity; in none has it done more good.'"

"There you go. The governor of the day then was Lord Harris, he understood the subversive nature of the Créoles. He changed the school system in favour of a more English one and proposed Indian indentureship, all to obstruct this striving for political liberty. Maxwell would have inherited those leadership credentials from his forebears. And he looked right. He was a big man, tall, handsome, he had a presence, he was educated, he had achieved what every mother here wanted for her son. A profession and respectability. In the eyes of the man in the street the Philips were seen as wealthy, respectable people. He was seen as a man who could represent them, as his relative J.B. Philip had done."

"I saw in one of the old newspapers, I started from the 1850s, that Maxwell took an active part in the political agitations of the day. He was only twenty-one but he contributed to the local press on important questions. One person wrote, I have it here, I noted it, he was a correspondent for the *Telegraph*—I gathered that it was a newspaper that supported black and coloured interests — he wrote that no amount of wealth or education enabled a man in Trinidad to enjoy social prestige, if he lacked 'the correct tinge'."

"I would think that Maxwell would have been a strong supporter of those sentiments," said the Captain, "in much the same way that both you and I are. Planters of wealth, merit, and character were 'tabooed' if they were without the 'colonial passport'—whiteness, which was more potent than education, habits, principles, behaviour, wealth, talent, or even genius itself."

"I am sure that he was. He appears to have been a reporter of *The Trinidadian* newspaper and apparently was a promoter of the Trinidad Literary Association, taking a very active role in the debates. I suppose that was when he was first recognised as an orator. That would have gone down well. And then he left for England again."

The Captain laughed softly, offering me a cigarette.

"Thank you. Mrs. Broadway showed me some sort of certificate that he received from the Freemasons. He was a Lodge-man at the same time that he was à la porte de l'église, as it is said here. How could that have been? I thought the Catholic Church frowned on Masons."

"No idea. I didn't know he was a Freemason. But I'm not surprised. A great many legal men are, even magistrates and judges, it is very influential. But I have no interest in that sort of thing."

"Nor me either. The other thing is she showed me his marriage certificate. He was married in London in an Anglican church, St Brides, I looked it up in the Encyclopedia Britannica, to an Anglican woman. The Roman Catholic church would not have recognised such a marriage, what do you think?"

"Only if he had the consent from the diocesan bishop and obtained a dispensation in writing for the marriage. How very strange, he would have had to be a Roman Catholic to be accepted at St. Mary's, a Jesuit seminary and school for boys you said. Very strange."

"Very. She said something about horses for courses. I suppose that means all things to all men."

"Ah, Corinthians, 'I have become all things to all people, that I might by all means save some.' I suppose that notion may be applied to him. You are discovering that Maxwell Philip was a man of many contradictions. Interesting."

"She spoke about his career as a barrister. It would seem that although he was very successful he had setbacks. Some people in official circles didn't like him. I noted their names. Then she told me about his close friendship with Sir Arthur Gordon, who was a governor here."

"That explains the post he held as Solicitor General and other appointments. Gordon is remembered to this day. The Town Council named Gordon Street for him, and when the old Tranquility estate was taken over, one of the avenues was called Stanmore, because Gordon had been made Baron Stanmore. That was thirty-odd years ago. Long before all those handsome houses were built. In those days all there was still pasture."

"I would like to learn more about Gordon's tenure here. How should I go about that?"

"Read the newspapers of the day. There are of course official documents. But, for what you have in mind to write, I think you should try not to make it heavy going. But I can see that you are quite taken by it."

"Well yes. I find Maxwell to be a very fascinating personage. On the one hand he plays the role of a man of the people, who appears to be the inheritor of a mandate, and on the other, he is a part of officialdom. Contradictions yes, but very fascinating. And there is his book, *Emmanuel Appadocca, or, Blighted Life*. To what extent was it autobiographical? To me, *Appadocca* retells the story of every mulatto man, free or not—a tragic figure, who, neither fish nor fowl, could not fit in anywhere, a victim of history, but with a difference. In his preface, Maxwell admits the indignation he felt by reading the reports of the brutal treatment meted out by American slave owners to their illegitimate mulatto children. But instead of being the typical downtrodden half-breed, the author projects his hero differently; he portrays Appadocca as a man who seeks revenge with a vengeance. He politicises the black man."

"May I make a suggestion?"

"Yes, by all means."

"I think that just like how you explored the life of J. B. Philip against the political background of his times in that piece that Mendes didn't publish, and as you are attempting to do with me, you should do the same with Maxwell Philip. Don't just write an article for a magazine, do something with more depth, show what the political currents of those times were like. See if you can find what drove and shaped his ambitions. Sé lè van ka vanté, moun ka wè lapo poul!" The Captain laughed.

"What does that mean?"

"When the wind is blowing we can see the skin of a fowl! By the way, I have never heard it said that his birth was a subject of speculation, or that he was illegitimate, the son of an overseer and a slave or a female member of the Philip family. If that were true, people like my own family would know about it. Also, for him to enter a Jesuit-run school in Scotland, that you tell me was also a seminary, he must have been born of married parents. Their marriage certificate and his baptismal certificate, which would show that they and he were Catholic, would have had to be presented for him to go to that school. Illegitimacy is seen by the church as an irregularity. It can bar a person from receiving any of the sacraments. It is the baptismal certificate that is the passport of the Catholic Church."

"Is that so. I had no idea. In one of the obituaries, in *The New Era* I think it was, it mentions his aged parents living in San Fernando. So maybe what he wrote could not possibly be an autobiography."

Cipriani paused thoughtfully and after a moment added, "Nello, for a man like him there would be all sorts of reports in newspapers. Some were put about by people who did not mean him any good. His family was scattered on both sides of the Atlantic, and those here in Trinidad may not have been in a position to refute those derogatory notions. He also had enemies in very high places. But come, lewwe get started, I want to tell you about the speech I delivered at the British Guiana and West Indian labour conference. It was held in the Guiana Public Buildings in Georgetown, Demerara in January 1926. That may interest you Nello, as the point I was making was a question of labour, pure and simple, and that they should import neither class nor colour into it. Get your pencil and notebook ready."

43. In Pursuit of a Competency

"We are like the herb which flourisheth most when trampled upon."

Alfred, Lord Tennyson

MIDDLE TEMPLE HALL

C.L.R. JAMES PORT-OF-SPAIN, TRINIDAD 1929. "MY MOTHER'S people, Mr. James, were originally from Leipzig. A city in the German state of Saxony. *Bildung*, Mr. James, is a German word, it stands for education, truth and virtue. Education, truth and virtue, Mr. James, were the watchwords of my family."

She was standing at the birdbath in the middle of her garden, idly taking apart a bright red hibiscus flower.

"My mother's great-grandfather was a famous man. A portrait painter by profession. He painted King George the Third. Several times. He was a miniaturist, a perfectionist. He was sought out by royalty. He worked in their presence. The family removed to England because of the wars. My mother's father was a plasterer, a master of

43. IN PURSUIT OF A COMPETENCY

Italian gesso work. The creator of classical mouldings on the ceilings of important buildings in London. We were a well-off family. My mother's brother John would enter business in the City and do well."

The red petals were floating, spinning about in the gentle late afternoon sunlight, they could have been magenta galleons in miniature or large drops of blood.

I wanted to ask how did her parents meet, but was wary of broaching the subject because I knew that she knew, as a person who was born and grew up here, that would mean telling me how a mixed race man from the West Indies could meet and then marry an English woman, a white woman in London. What would her family have made of that?

The moment of silent contemplation that appeared to pervade the atmosphere was broken by the raucous calls of her pet parrot. It seemed to be screaming "your mother ass! your mother ass!"

"What is he saying?"

"He is repeating the words 'muchas gracias'. Mr. James, it's time for you to go. You have sucked me dry. Like an orange. I have nothing more to add. Come."

It had been nevertheless a useful visit. From what she told me earlier, it would appear that her father had passed his Bar exams in 1854, married her mother in that very same year and also saw his novel published. Quite an achievement. All of that must have been very impressive to anyone paying attention to Maxwell Philip at the time. I couldn't help thinking who they might have been and what they would have thought.

LONDON 1850: THE HONOURABLE SOCIETY OF THE MIDDLE TEMPLE: Upon entering the sunlit precincts of Elm Court, Maxwell was immediately attracted to the badge of the Middle Temple. From his catechism class at St. Mary's he recognised the Agnus Dei, the Lamb of God, with a flag bearing Saint George's cross. It was a designation of Jesus Christ in Christian liturgical usage. "Behold the Lamb of God, who takes away the sins of the world!" John the Baptist, he recalled, had shouted out those words when he saw Jesus coming towards him. Here it was, against a background consisting of the same white cross against a red field. The cross and the lamb with the flag, he was informed by the Master of the Temple, who came upon him gazing at the escutcheon that hung above the Inn's main door, were symbols of the Knights Templar.

Having read Sir Walter Scott's *Ivanhoe*, Maxwell was even more moved when he visited the round Temple Church and saw the slumbering stone knights, recumbent on its flagged floor. There was, however, no time for such ruminations, as it was said in his hearing by one of the seniors "given health, time, industry, and perseverance, everyone of ordinary abilities may reasonably rely on securing a competency."

In pursuit of a competency. He had already been attached to a conveyancer and an equity draftsman while at Anderson's office, and later as an articled clerk in the chambers of George Garcia, who was at the time Solicitor General. It was now time to apply himself to the task at hand.

At Great Coram Street he was received by his cousins Philip, Anne-Rachael and Judith Thornton. Their brother Louis Edmond had passed away some years before, and their sister Magdelaine, who had married the late Henry Amedroz, was living at the family's Bond Street house. Philip Thornton, Louis Edmond's son, some fifteen years Maxwell's senior, was for all intent and purpose a gentleman of leisure. He welcomed Maxwell, introducing him to his circle of friends in the city, several of whom were engaged in various businesses ranging from stock brokerage to shipping insurance. Philip found Maxwell, young as he was, good company and offered to accommodate him at Great Coram Street if he so wished. Maxwell was pleased to accept this kindness and spent time there when not eating the required suppers at the Middle Temple Inn.

43. IN PURSUIT OF A COMPETENCY

Philip, a portly figure, dark-complexioned, perhaps once handsome, with European features, was a fount of information when it came to members of the family living in England as well as those in France. Maxwell was particularly interested in these, who Philip laughingly described as "our foreign cousins."

"Who are they?" Maxwell asked.

"They are baronial, dear boy! They live in a grand château surrounded by vineyards. Didn't your people tell you about your aunt Susannah and her mercurial climb up the social ladder?"

Yes, he had heard of aunt Susannah. He knew that she had married a Frenchman, uncle Guillaume and that they had a daughter who had married a nobleman. Stories of aunt Susannah and her family were always related in a jocular manner ,where she was portrayed as an amazing person who somehow was able to demonstrate the more determined, ambitious and daring characteristics of the family. As for her daughter, Jeanette-Rose, she was always spoken of as a great beauty, who in more ways than one was a perfect reflection of her mother.

Maxwell read, studied, memorised and attended every course. He wrote and submitted, spoke up and argued, defended and more often than not conceded at the mock courts set up for what was called Mooting. Time, and it was always short, went quickly by that first year.

The company of young, hopeful gentlemen, whose aspirations and dinners he shared at the Middle Temple Inn, was as inspiring as it was exhausting. The students of the Inn maintained a medieval tradition of a period of condoned riotous disorder leading up to Candlemas, presided over by a Prince of Love. To his amazed delight, he was elected to take this ancient role. William Shakespeare's *Twelfth Night* was staged in the Hall, with Maxwell in the role of Sebastian.

London during this period was already the world's largest city and the capital of an expanding British Empire. Its population then numbered in the millions. It had grown to become two-thirds larger than Paris, as he was informed by John Apple Englehart, a friend and sometime business associate of Philip Thornton.

They were to visit The Great Exhibition. It was an international trade exhibition mounted in Hyde Park. Seen from a distance, the enormous glass building that housed the event reflected the late spring sky, a faultless dome across which a vast swoop of swallows appeared to return again and again, making intricate patterns and dizzying reflections of themselves in the mirror-like surface of the gigantic building.

"Perhaps they think that the glass is a great pond and they are swooping to drink," laughed John Englehart.

"They are early, I think we could be in for a hot summer," added Philip. "I seem to remember their early appearance some years ago. That summer was truly splendid. But it is always summer in the West Indies, isn't it, Maxwell?"

"Indeed, cousin, but when it rains it pours for six months of the year."

"And the great storms, hurricanes, I hear they are called, they sweep away everything in their path. How do your people manage, Maxwell?" asked Englehart.

"Ah, my friend, we live in the fortunate isles, there are no hurricanes in Trinidad, we are barlovento, to windward. Our island is below the wind."

"And that was why we were so prosperous," said Philip. "Our crops did not perish when the wild winds came. Tell us about Trinidad, Maxwell, we always thought of it as a very special place, the place to which the family removed from Grenada so as to remake our fortunes in a grand plantation called the Philippine."

And he did. Drawing from an imagination that was not exactly his own, he regaled them as they walked across Hyde Park's shady lawns with stories that he had overheard in St. Luce's and aunt Marie Renée's conversations when a boy, as they spoke of the 'long time

43. In Pursuit of a Competency

days'. Their pioneering on the farthest edge of a frontier that stretched, in his imagination, all the way to Venezuela. The Grenadines, a chain of small islands scattered on a luminous turquoise sea, where the family's fortune was built with the production of sea island cotton. The great houses at Concorde and at Philippine, and the adventurous men who had built them. He could have enlarged the telling if he wished to include the voyages of a great-grandfather as a person whom he could picture in a variety of ways. Best of all, he could have told them of that man's pirate past. That would have caught their interest, as the tall tales of the buccaneers were becoming very popular both in America and here in England. These bore evocative titles like *Jack Junk* or *Tar for all Weathers*, published in twenty-two parts in the local press. He had enjoyed them all. But he didn't, because they were being joined by a party of lovely girls.

"Ah! here come my sisters Sarah and Emma, and where is Eliza? There she is, hiding behind a posy. Come, meet our new friend, a cousin of Philip's, he hails from the British West Indies!"

It was an absolutely splendid afternoon. Carriages were drawing up, elegant ladies were being handed out of them. There were great lords and foreign princes arriving. Officers of the Brigade of Guards in brilliant red tunics and bearskins were strutting about, and the pipes and drums of a Highland regiment filled the air. He saw that Eliza was at the centre of a happy frivolity and was the source of much laughter. She, however displayed an understated elegance, a casual refinement that suggested maturity. He could not take his eyes away from her.

The great Crystal Palace, an enormous glasshouse built in an iron frame of unimaginable proportions, fairly shone as shafts of sunlight illuminated the spectacular exhibits that had arrived from every country in the world. Great trees formed the backdrop to huge red velvet marquees in which were displayed the achievements of science. Fountains sparkled in the sunlight, the noise of the gathering crowd, the calls of the exhibitors, the shrieks of children, the laughter of beautiful women, a medley of aromas, the excitement of seeing fantastic things and brilliant ideas, so thrilling, so new, so of the future.

There were tiger skin rugs and elephant tusks, Russian samovars and a giant telescope near a tiny microscope, a locomotive engine and a fine porcelain display, electric telegraphs, air pumps and barometres as well as musical, horological and surgical instruments. A marvel, before unknown, called the daguerreotype. The likeness of a person anchored in glass. Unbelievable. A gigantic statue of Queen Victoria made from zinc. They visited the tent in which the Koh-i-Noor, meaning the "Mountain of Light", the world's largest known diamond, was displayed.

The produce of Britain's colonies, from mountains of cocoa pods to bales of bright white cotton, were prominently featured. For Maxwell, the most surprising exhibit was the actual mechanised process of cotton fabric production, from its spinning to the finished cloth. This was demonstrated by a steam-driven cotton mill. It was a vast and very noisy contraption of innumerable moving parts that revealed the weaving process, producing reams of bright white cotton cloth. That his great-grandfather had been a planter of sea island cotton, and was at the forefront of that industry in those early times, thrilled him. The thought that it was the mills of Manchester that turned their bales of cotton into miles and miles of fabric, spinning gold like Rumpelstiltskin that flowed into their pockets, he would have loved to reveal but didn't, until Philip casually remarked that he, Maxwell, was an heir of a fabulous entrepreneur, a Frenchman by the name of Honoré Philip, who not only owned vast cotton plantations in the West Indies, but was also the sole proprietor of an enchanted island called Petite Martinique. All eyes turned towards him, but he only noticed Eliza's, which he saw were blue. He smiled into them, even as the others thought that he was being unassuming and unpretentious.

At the Schweppes exhibit, as they enjoyed the renowned carbonated mineral water that was becoming very popular, Eliza, turning towards him, in a quiet voice asked about those mysterious islands. That they were picturesque he assured her, and that they were considered of enormous value by the Crown was evident. Holding her charming gaze, he said that they were by far and away the most comfortable and charming place in the world to call home. Her engaged expression turned into a delighted smile when he said this.

Nearby was the American exhibit. It featured a grain reaper, a display of India rubber goods, and Samuel Colt's formidable revolving charge pistols. Among the various firearms, sewing machines, locks, clocks, ploughs and pianofortes were several books. His eyes fell on *The Quadroons* by Lydia Maria Child, *Uncle Tom's Cabin; or, Life Among the Lowly* by Harriet Beecher Stowe, and *Clotel; or, The President's Daughter* by William Wells Brown. Picking up the latter he quickly read the foreword. It spoke of a tragic octoroon, a light-skinned woman raised in her father's household as though she were white, until his bankruptcy and subsequent death placed her in a reduced and menial position to be eventually sold as a slave at auction.

"Abolitionist writing, dear boy. It serves the interest of some politicians. Very popular I hear, over there," remarked Philip, taking his arm. "Come away, Maxwell, a crowd is gathering. We must not become a centre of attraction." The others in the meanwhile had wandered off. Maxwell, however, because of being recently made shockingly conscious of his origins while at Gran'Anse estate, made a mental note to visit the Foyles bookstore on Chancery Lane.

Queen Victoria and her family were to arrive at any moment. The people in the upstairs gallery were peering over the cast iron rails, the trumpeters of the Irish Guards were sounding a thrilling call, his heart was racing. Eliza was at his side and had placed her gloved hand on his arm for a moment perhaps longer than propriety necessitated. Looking at him, she smiled in an open and friendly manner.

It was a very happy day, made more so when, in parting, to his delight he was invited to tea the following day by Emma Englehart, the elder of Eliza's sisters. The invitation included his cousin Philip and was intended as a reciprocal gesture for having enjoyed a lovely occasion together.

There was so much about Eliza that attracted him. She was quite tall with a mass of brown curls that contained as if secretly strands of the purest gold, very lovely blue eyes and a smile that to him held a promise of words that he wished he could hear. When he bent his head to listen to what she was saying to her sister Emma, for a brief moment he could smell her breath. It carried a whiff of something so unfamiliar, so personal, yet strangely exciting that he could feel his heart leap. That it had come from such a happy smile! Again their eyes met. It was as though they had instantly shared a secret.

Did she know? She must have known. He knew. He had no idea what he knew, but he knew how he felt. Thinking about it as he lay in bed in Great Coram Street, his eyes peering into the half-light of the darkened bedroom, he could hear his heart thump as he strained to remember her elegant profile and the sound of her voice. By morning it had all faded, overwhelmed by the memory of a dream of swallows making fleeting patterns against a cloudscape that was perhaps a vast curtain, the backdrop of a stage set on which the performers had frozen with half-completed gestures and unspoken words.

The Engleharts' townhouse, a substantial villa in grounds which displayed some very old trees, was situated on Chapel Street, Pentonville, near an ancient chapel in one of London's newer suburbs. They were received at the door by a supercilious butler and shown into the parlour, where the family members had arranged themselves to receive them. The ladies appeared to Maxwell to fairly overflow in flawless lace. Elegant furniture and delicate objects made from fine porcelain were displayed on intricate crochet. There were lifelike portraits executed in maroon and black crayon on pale lilac, lotus-patterned partitions, depicting lovely women with languid eyes and almost exposed bosoms. Placed on occasional tables with elaborately turned legs were quantities of exquisite miniatures of handsome people caught in gilded elliptical frames. A fireplace

43. In Pursuit of a Competency

displayed classical Greek motifs made of pale blue marble. The misty smell of moonlight or something of the sort, even like cool, clear, rainwater filled the air. He could taste its freshness. Everything was so clean and looked so new.

Mr. Englehart, a small man with a delicate hand and a little gold-rimmed pince-nez perched on the very tip of a superior nose, examined him and smiled professionally. Mrs. Englehart, plump, quiet, obviously self-effacing, smiled genuinely, appreciatively, as he bent over her overly large be-ringed fingers. John Englehart recounted yesterday's thrills even as his sister Sarah corrected his memory of events. There was much laughter. Tea was brought in, Sterling silver and almost transparent bright white China, sponge cake covered with granulated sugar, savory sandwiches, salted biscuits and sweet treats, candied fruit and a variety of jams.

Philip spoke earnestly of the usefulness of trade exhibitions to Mr. Englehart, who answered with humming noises, while Emma asked Maxwell quietly about himself. He could see that she was the one who would always be in the lead. He told her of some of his experiences at the Inns of Court, the arduousness of study, the usefulness of having Latin and the pleasure of having Philip Thornton's generosity. She nodded gently and was seemingly pleased in a polite but distant manner.

Eliza sat at her mother's side, her smile hovering on the brink of laughter, her voice, when she spoke, so clear and crisp, much like the voice of a person who had learned to speak English correctly. She seemed to him to possess beauty of a classical nature. The type that captures one's imagination even when it is displayed in cold white marble. Every time he glanced at her she was just then looking away, having glanced at him.

Maxwell, confident, spoke up, he knew that he possessed a fine speaking voice and employed it as he described the Indian exhibit, recounting the luminescence of the gems, the singular lighting that must have come from carbide lamps, the magnificence of the great diamond and the enduring triumph of British enterprise, generosity and daring, that was this great Empire's gift to the world. They may have applauded had it been a different occasion. Their delighted eyes were taking him in, he realised, even as Mr. Englehart allowed a smile to almost escape his primly pursed lips.

Then it was time for them to make their farewells. They parted, the young people did, like friends well met and Maxwell felt her hand linger in his for a moment longer than it might have otherwise.

"He is a very wealthy man, Englehart, owns a swathe of London properties, some in the very heart of the city, not to mention his substantial interest in Antigua. He has a country house down in Dorset somewhere, not far from Corfe Castle. Good shooting I hear. Never quite lost his German accent. Why do you ask?" They were sitting at the fire in Great Coram Street and Philip was being generous with his brandy.

"Just wondered," answered Maxwell, "just wondered."

"Just wondered, eh? You have an eye on Eliza, I saw that, I did. And she has an eye on you. Her parents saw that too. They are all unmarried and of a certain age. Too low in the social order in the eyes of some, too well off to be handed over to a mere tradesman or artisan, as far as her father is concerned. Have a care, my boy, for hearts will break—yet brokenly, live on."

Then came news from home. Money had become a problem. He was aware that his tuition was being paid for by St. Luce and to some unknown degree by Henry Anderson. St. Luce's letter plainly stated that he should expect a shortfall of at least two hundred pounds. It intimated that he could augment that by either seeking a form of employment or by approaching his cousins. He knew that he could not possibly seek any sort of employment while at the Inns of Court, nor could he bring himself to approach Philip Thornton. It was very worrying. It brought back bleak memories of that final year at St. Mary's.

It was on a wet and foggy evening, while briskly walking along Old Bond Street, he was to dine with his cousin Magdelaine, that

43. In Pursuit of a Competency

for some unknown reason he stopped in front of a shop window. It was a bookshop. Displayed in the brassy lamplight of its show-window were several books. Looking closely he read their titles. *The Pirate* by Walter Scott and another, *A General History of the Pyrates* by Captain Charles Johnson. At the centre of the arrangement was a huge cutlass, brightly burnished, laid across a black flag with a skull and crossed bones clumsily painted in white, and a larger book bound in Morocco leather and blocked with gold leaf. Its title read, *Black Beard the Pirate*. It was on impulse that he pushed open the bookshop's door. A bell tinkled in his ear.

"Yes, may I help the young gentleman?" A voice, kindly, enquiringly, just a trifle subservient, seemed to come from somewhere near. He turned with a start and there was an elderly white-haired man with gold-rimmed spectacles dressed in an old-fashioned black frock coat. The old man was vaguely smiling up at him.

He bought both *Black Beard the Pirate* and *The Pirate*. "They are very popular," he was assured by the elderly bookseller. He read them avidly over the next few days and was encouraged when he discovered that Black Beard had actually raided Port-of-Spain, taking away tens of thousands of Spanish gold pieces. Because he had experienced sailing among the pale blue islands of the Grenadines, and because he had listened closely to aunt Claire when she read *The Corsair* to him, which told of the trials of Byron's privateer captain Conrad, an idea for a story began to take shape in his mind. Clearly, Conrad in his youth had been rejected by society. This was why in his later years, Conrad believed that he had to fight against all humanity, thus becoming eventually a man of loneliness and mystery.

That he was a descendant of a French corsair made it all decidedly easier. He knew the family's stories, in a real way he knew that they belonged to him. He would set his story in the Caribbean and would draw from another emotive and increasingly popular genre, one that had aroused, to a high pitch, his indignant excitement, that of the tragic mulatto. These often told of a radical young man who refuses to accept inferiority as his burden. This was especially meaningful particularly in the wake of revelations that so recently had detailed his own mixed-race origins. His father and uncle could have been turned out into the fields to labour at the lashe's sting.

Postponing his studies, knowing that he would miss certain important lectures, he made himself comfortable in the library at Great Coram Street and set about writing a story that told how a black woman, a virgin, dishonoured by a cruel white slave master, produced a son, and thinking of the Gospel of Matthew he called his hero Emmanuel, a high-spirited and sensitive boy who was abandoned by his father. The last name for the lad? He would name him after Admiral Ruiz de Apodaca, the Spanish admiral who burned his squadron to their gunwales in the Gulf of Paria. Thus emerged in the space of two or three months *Emmanuel Appadocca or A Blighted Life: A Tale of the Boucaneers*.

"You've lifted this directly from Byron's *The Corsair* and decorated it with your own fancy," laughed Philip, the manuscript's pages scattered on the drawing-room floor at Great Coram Street. "Your preface is original, the rest, brazenly plagiarised, elaborately over-written, but amusing, perhaps. It could even become popular. Take it to a publisher, a friend of mine, Charles Skeet in Fleet Street. He may even give you an advance."

He did and received ten pounds, and three or four weeks later an additional ten. This would help to see him through the winter months. He was sitting close to a window in his bedroom in Great Coram Street, Blackstone's *The Commentaries on the Laws of England* open on his lap, when he felt the need to close his eyes and put his head back. A headache was coming on.

He must have slept for a while.

There was a letter in a silver tray on the small table next to him. The maid must have brought it in while he slept. His head was a throbbing pain. He opened it. It was from Henry Anderson and stated simply that he should make arrangements to return to Trinidad at once, as there would be no more advances. The letter contained a

43. In Pursuit of a Competency

note from his mother, it said that his father was very ill and was not expected to last the year. He saw where her tears had splashed across her childlike handwriting and smudged the ink. He put his head back and fell asleep again.

"Maxwell, wake up, dear boy. My word, you are burning with fever. I must get a doctor, come, let me help you to bed. You must lie down."

44. Barrister at Large

*"If I had a flower for every time I thought of you
I could walk through my garden forever."*

Alfred, Lord Tennyson

The Mavericks. C.L.R. James is second on the left, middle row.

C.L.R. James, Port-of-Spain, Trinidad, 1929. "The time had come when the inhabitants of this colony should have a voice in the government by electing the unofficial members of the Legislative Council."

"Captain, you are getting ahead of yourself here. Let's try not to confuse things."

"What do you mean confuse things? That's what I told them."

"Yes, but did that come before or after what you told me last week that you said you told them?"

44. BARRISTER AT LARGE

"What does it matter, Nello? The important point that I was making then, and I'm telling you now that I still hold the view, is that vested capital interests have this colony by the balls. I told them that we had been informed, we knew it all, that the resolution was moved by the Vice-President of the Chamber of Commess, I beg your pardon, Nello, I meant Commerce, Mr. George F. Huggins, and that it was ably supported by Mr. Samuel Duncan Harding, the Czar of the tramways, and in turn by Mr. John Phillips, of Anchor Cigarette fame. In their great effort to denounce representative government, Harding had the temerity to criticise and ridicule the Constitution of the United States of America. Can you imagine? And strange to say, that was the sentiment that seemed to have pervaded the entire body of the Chamber on that day and, it would appear, ever since. Look here, why don't you just copy the whole damn speech?"

It was proving to be one of those difficult days. In August 1921 the Captain had moved a resolution that a memorial be forwarded to the Secretary of State for the Colonies that effect be given to another resolution, previously passed at a public meeting that had been held at the Princes Building with regard to the issue of representative government. He had some of his notes but was relying on his prodigious memory.

"Yes, all right, I'll do that," I told him, adding, "Why don't you give me both speeches and I will build them into that chapter, and we could review the entire thing next week?"

"All right. Not a bad idea. I have Howard-Bishop arriving at any moment to go over the *Labour Leader's* editorial. So, what about you, what are you going to do? Are you seeing Ethel Broadway this week?"

"Yes, I'm really hoping to get some more information. There must be a story there, him marrying an English woman and bringing her back here."

"Very good, au revoir, see you next week. Tuesday at 4.30?"

375

"Yes, that will be fine. My last class finishes at 3.45. Thank you, Captain. Until next week then."

"Right right, Nello, if you see Howard-Bishop tell him to come up at once."

There was no sign of Howard-Bishop and I was in a hurry to get home, it was going on seven and I couldn't remember where I had parked my bicycle.

ETHEL BROADWAY HAD SHOWN ME A FOLDER with documents some weeks ago that seemed to explain what appeared to be Maxwell's hurried departure from England in 1853. Among these were a doctor's certificate and correspondence that he had received from the authorities at the Inns of Court, giving him permission to return to Trinidad. His stay in Trinidad would not have been long. He was called to the Bar the following year, 1854. It was the same year that he got married, this coincided with his novel being published. He then, according to *The New Era* obituary, which did not mention either his marriage or his novel's publication, 'lingered in Europe and there by travel and observation, gained the knowledge and wide experience of men and things which were useful to him in afterlife'. The obituary went on to speak of him enjoying 'the Bohemianism of literary life in the capital cities of Europe'. All of this would have cost money and could hardly have been achieved in less than a year.

It was a sunny Saturday morning in the season that is called by the Créoles petite careme. I took Cotton Hill Lane to make my way to Loyola cottage. Not having set a date for our meeting, I was chancing it.

And there was Ethel, on her knees before a beautiful hibiscus bush in full bloom that overhung the bird bath. It was where we had last parted. She wore a wide straw hat and was garbed in what could be taken for a man's trousers and shirt. "I see you. I see you. Good morning Mr. James. Step that way, come this way."

"Good morning Mrs. Broadway, what beautiful flowers."

"Good morning Mr. James. Yes, aren't they. My husband cultivates them. Everything he turns his hand to thrives. Elsie, Elsie! where is that child?"

A young woman, a paler, even thinner version of Mrs. Broadway, appeared.

"Take these, and the things that you were working with, to the shed. This is my daughter Elsie. This is Mr. James. He is here to find out whatever he can about us." This was said quite loudly, then turning to me, "Come Mr. James, let's sit on that iron bench over there. Elsie, Elsie! tell Mavaline to bring the lemonade now. With ice! Now, Mr. James, what have *you* brought?"

I hadn't brought anything, it was just her way of speaking.

"You have a beautiful garden. Such a lot of lovely flowers."

"Yes. You've already said that. I see you have your notebook and pencil at the ready."

"Yes, well, I saw in one of your late father's obituaries that having passed the Bar he travelled in Europe. Would that have been after he and your mother were married?"

"They travelled extensively on the continent, a grand tour. Visited our relatives over there. *You* look surprised, Mr. James."

I wasn't at all surprised. Captain Cipriani did tell me that they were connected to people in France. She was being brusque, so I fitted in, "Your father had relations in France? That's interesting. Did you ever meet them?"

"No, I never met them but *we* corresponded. Jeannette-Rose, her mother was a Philip, is the present Baroness Folch de Cardon de Sandrans. The château at Dracy Le Fort is their home. My father and mother spent their honeymoon there. In their castle."

"How were they related to your father?"

"Mr. James, must you always be on the lookout for scandal? The Baroness was my father's aunt's daughter, she married a French nobleman of high degree. They never lost touch with us. Mavaline! put it on the iron table. And then go. Yes, go, Mr. James is harmless. They named their eldest daughter Philippine in our memory. *We* are very close."

She then spoke of her husband. He was an Englishman who had worked his way from England to Trinidad, where he became one of the more important botanical collectors. It would appear that he came here from The Royal Gardens at Kew where he had been a gardener. He was well recommended, it would appear, and was armed with excellent qualifications, much experience and it would seem boundless enthusiasm.

"Mr. Broadway arrived in Trinidad on the 28th of June, 1888. My father died two days later. We met at my father's funeral. Mr. Broadway had accompanied Mr. Hart, a colleague at the Royal Botanic Garden, to my father's funeral." I noticed that she always rolled the R when she said the word Royal.

"Why?" I muttered, thinking why would he go to a funeral of a person whom he did not know.

"He wanted to become acquainted with people. He was a stranger here and a funeral is as good a place as any to meet people, don't *you* think so, Mr. James?"

I had to agree.

"We were married on the 1st of January, 1890."

Speaking of her husband's attainments, the morning breathing a cool breeze that hinted of Christmas, seemed to ease the tension that had been previously so ever-present in her manner of speaking.

"He was born in Exbury, a village in the area of the New Forest. He came here as an assistant to the Superintendent of the Royal Botanic Garden. A colleague, Mr. Caracciolo, introduced the navel orange and the grapefruit to Trinidad. That grapefruit tree that you see over there was one of the first ever planted in this colony. We spent some years in Grenada. Mr. Broadway was appointed curator of their Botanic Garden."

She threw her head back a little and closed her eyes, the wind lifting the gray curls of her close cut hair.

"Ethel, the postman has arrived! He is waiting. There is something that you have to sign for. I presume you *must be* Mr. James."

I hadn't noticed, but a dark-skinned and leaner version of Mrs. Broadway was now standing before us.

"Oh, Catherine, couldn't you have dealt with him? Bother, bother. Mr. James, you should go now."

"Aren't you going to introduce us, Ethel? Mr. James, *you* have been our favourite topic for months. Never mind, I am her sister Catherine, one of the niggers in the woodpile."

"Mr. James, this is my obnoxious sister, Catherine Latour."

"How do you do?"

"I do very well, Mr. James. How do *you* do? Never mind. I must leave you, farewell."

So saying, they both departed and I was left alone in the garden. Turning to leave I saw a coolie man, quite old, obviously the gardener, he was laughing, giggling actually. Feeling suddenly exasperated I left Loyola Cottage to take a windy walk around the Queen's Park Savannah. I had in mind a visit to the Royal Victoria Institute, where an Amerindian burial site, along with the latest findings from the Pitch Lake, were on display.

TRINIDAD 1853: MAXWELL'S VOYAGE HOME REMAINED A HORRENDOUS memory of enduring headaches, body pain, seasickness and most of all loneliness. He had sailed from the Port of London in the haze of a fever, a terrifying headache and wracking pains all over his body that altogether made him indescribably weak. Before departing, he had just enough strength to go to the Middle Temple to make his plea, seeking permission to return to Trinidad. Aboard ship he had been isolated, kept in a tiny, airless, cell-like cabin, except for when he was taken up on deck by the ship's doctor. For more than eight weeks he had endured this. Upon his arrival in Trinidad, in spite of his apparent recovery, the ship's captain had handed him over to the port's officials. He was then placed in quarantine on a small island within sight of Port-of-Spain that housed scores of Asiatics, until he was rescued by a Dr. Saturnin, a friend of his uncle's. Still weak and afflicted with occasional bouts of fever he was treated by both St. Luce and his grandmother. His recovery was ultimately attributed to his mother's prayers. It was an awful time all around. His father had died. So had aunt Marie-Renée.

Maxwell felt relieved when invited by Henry Anderson and his wife Josephine to their Clarence Street home in Port-of-Spain. The evening commenced with an easy conviviality. They had all met before. Henry and Josephine Anderson were as lively and welcoming as he remembered. They were joined by George Garcia and his wife Mariquita for supper. He saw that Garcia had become portly; it suited him. He conveyed several layers of a subtle dignity that by all appearances could not be reproached.

He was asked about his mother, Catherine. How was she faring? Was she alone, now that his father was no longer with her. He assured them that she was settled, not alone, and in passably good health. He then told them of his progress at the Middle Temple, describing the communication between himself, the Parliament of the Inn, the Council of Legal Education and the circumstances, in fact the conditions that had allowed for his return to Trinidad. Speaking candidly he explained to his hosts that his family's fortunes had changed dramatically. His uncle St. Luce and his aunt Claire were thinking of selling the estates and moving to England. No decision had yet been taken in that regard, but it was being considered. He could not ask them or the present company for continued financial help and was considering simply giving it all up. He was assured that having come this far there was no question of his giving up, as there were people who had an interest in him, who believed that a person like him would be of great use to the cause of political liberty in the colony. He did not need to be persuaded to go back to England and resume his studies and accepted the offer of a pupillage on his return to Trinidad. He was grateful and said so. This appeared to put the company at ease and the evening ended pleasantly with fond farewells and good wishes.

LONDON, FEBRUARY 1854: "MY DEAR BOY, HAD I KNOWN OF YOUR financial difficulties I would have been more than happy to be of help. Why didn't you say?"

Maxwell had returned to London after a stay in Trinidad of just a few months. To have described his financial situation to Philip Thornton, upon reading Henry Anderson's letter that took him back to Trinidad, would have been too embarrassing. He said so, adding, "Thank you, Philip. You are very kind, but I could not have imposed. As it is, you have been more than generous."

"But we are family, dear boy, a family. We help each other. As it is I have news, Skeet of Fleet Street has sent you this."

"What is that?"

"It's a note to be drawn on his account at C. Hoare & Co. for £30! Your book, my boy. It's for your book! I told you, Skeet's a good fellow."

That was indeed a very welcome surprise. His return to the Middle Temple was another matter. Conditions had to be met. His successful completion of the Bar courses that he had missed and the qualifying sessions needed to be dealt with.

He was possessed of fresh energy. This was apparent to others and he attracted a different crowd at the Inns of Court, young men with money, not a few who were connected to the titled, even to members of Parliament. He bought new clothes and saw himself outfitted, wigged and gowned, in the appropriate dress to be called to the Bar in November of that year. He was fascinated, believing that he was in step with history, having published a book on piracy, when he was told that the 'cupboard', actually a table at which the newly called barristers stood to enter their names in the Inn's books, was reputedly made from the hatch-cover of Sir Francis Drakes' ship, the *Golden Hind*, and the lantern that hung at the entrance to the Middle Temple Hall allegedly came from the ship's poop deck. Another note for the sale of his book arrived, to be drawn at C. Hoare & Co., this one for £34.

He wished that he could meet Eliza Englehart again. Seeing her, now that there was some money in his pocket and his prospects of being called were becoming increasingly realistic, would have made the world a more perfect place.

"They have gone to the country, dear boy. A place in Dorset close to Corfe Castle. You would enjoy a walking tour. Ha-ha, collect butterflies. Visit historic places. You may run into her, ha, ha. Go to the Waterloo Bridge station, take a train from there and make your way south!"

Then, regarding him closely and in a serious tone Philip said, "Maxwell, Eliza will be an heiress, and from what I understand of your circumstances there is nothing coming to you. One could say that they, her people, are among the newly wealthy. John, her brother, will not be a craftsman like his father. He is hoping for connections that would take him into the City, which with the growth of industry has become something of a reflection of the new society. I will help him as much as I can. He has money to invest. My father Edmund Thornton has left me in good stead. Not just in terms of wealth, but the goodwill that he earned, which in turn has come to me. No one pays attention to my complexion when I enter The Exchange. I've come to buy or to sell. John is depending on me for a leg up, and he will get it. As for you, well, you will be a barrister with the courtesy title of Esquire. Hereabouts, that title garners respect. It indicates a man of a certain social rank. If your suit should be successful, it would transform Eliza into a lady. The first in her family. Making you a desirable catch for the Engleharts!"

Sitting back in his armchair, Philip smiled, Maxwell thought with a wry expression that caught the glow of the dying fire, and said, "And you look like a white man, Maxwell. The Engleharts were German the day before yesterday. They have no idea about people like us."

NO ONE IN CORFE CASTLE VILLAGE had heard of the Engleharts. He was directed to venture further south to Swanage, a seaside town, where at the Town Hall he might find someone who could tell him if there were any Engleharts about. He set out, it was on an early spring morning, on a rented palfrey and was still in sight of the village when he noticed that there were several people making their way up the hillside that led to the ruined castle that overlooked the area. On impulse or perhaps in desperate hope he turned his mount towards the track that led to the castle. Urging the animal onward, he never saw the low branch that struck him on the face and did not remember falling. He awoke to a crowd of curious but very helpful faces. His cheek was bruised and there was a large lump forming on his forehead. Even in this state he had only thoughts for Eliza Englehart. No, there was no one there by that name, but he should lie still until the doctor, who lived close by, could have a look at him. He had received a hard blow and had experienced a nasty fall that had caused him to roll down the hillside. He certainly had a pain, very sharp on his side that with every breath became worse. A bruised or broken rib, he was informed by the young doctor. He would need to be still for a while.

His room at the Greyhound Inn in Corfe Castle village was comfortable enough. The doctor, his name was David Earl, wrapped him tightly to help splint and immobilise his ribcage. He brought him books, he was a Dickens enthusiast, but was concerned because Maxwell's shallow breathing could put him at risk of developing pneumonia. He should get up and move about as soon as possible. It was an awful time.

"Eliza Englehart, why yes, I have met her," said Dr. Earl, peering into his opened mouth. "The Engleharts took over a charming farm. They renovated the farmhouse quite nicely and are presently in residence."

It was an agonising wait of three or four weeks but there was no other way. Sitting near a small fire, propped with pillows in a wing-chair close to a window in his room at the Greyhound, he was reading from Blackstone's *The Commentaries on the Laws of England,* when on hearing a carriage in the courtyard below he looked down and there were Eliza and her sisters. They were being ushered towards the entrance by Dr. Earl, and to his surprise Mrs. and Mr. Englehart were also alighting.

It was the most marvellous thing that could possibly have happened. He was not actually speechless. It was only afterwards, when he tried to recall every moment of the brief visit, all that came to mind was his babbling of the most meaningless euphemisms. It was a mere diversion, their visit, he understood that. It was to alleviate the monotony of country life that is especially experienced by people new to it. And there was no plainly stated invitation to visit them at Lowlands, the name that their farm was known by since the days of Edward the Martyr, neither was there an invitation to call on them in London.

His dismay was alleviated the very next day. On Dr. Earl's advice, he was walking in the onn's courtyard when, to his delight, he glimpsed Eliza and Emma Englehart strolling along Corfe Castle's single street. It was easy to encounter them, as everything began and ended in the village square. They were happily met. The cloudy morning turned into a bowl of light. There was so much to recall. It had been a lovely day spent at the Crystal Palace Exhibition. He told them of his writing, making it sound like something that he had shaken out of his sleeve, as a magician might. They were thrilled. An author and a barrister too. He was modest. A barrister at large he was to be, and as for being a writer, well, he was just an amateur. It had been a diversion. That his book, *Emmanuel Appadocca or A Blighted Life: A Tale of the Boucaneers,* so elaborately titled, had sold so well, was merely due to fashion, a passing popularity, reminiscent of a bygone time. They would be returning to London by month's end. So would he. He promised, at their insistence, to call on them at Chapel Street. He did, and was received by the family in a manner that put him at ease. He would see more of Eliza.

To his delight this was accommodated by her brother John, who intimated that they would be at Twining on the Strand the following afternoon. It was a pleasure to be with her, John appeared to be in a hurry to get away. In the pleasantly aromatic atmosphere of this jolly, crowded, very busy establishment, where ladies were allowed to browse the variety teas offered, a novelty in itself, for prior to this, ladies had to send a servant on their behalf to make selections, they revelled in a conviviality that encouraged familiarity.

Eliza was as amusing as he was talkative. He told her of his relatives in Trinidad and of the sugar plantations owned by his family. That his uncle, a medical doctor, was a member of the colony's Legislature and that his aunt Claire, a Scottish noblewoman, hailed from the Highlands. She spoke of her father, hinting at his social aspirations, in a manner that made him laugh out loud. He told her of the books he had read recently. Did she know that Jane Austen was once a customer of Twining, and may have sat where they were today? How did he know this? He shrugged, as if to say, he knew such things, never mentioning that Philip had told him that and that he had never actually read any of Austen's books. They were so well met. It was as though they had known each other for a very long time.

Over the following weeks he became a frequent visitor to the Englehart's residence on Chapel Street. He found her father an interesting man. He was knowledgeable, in an understated but entertaining manner, on the architecture of the City and spoke of the work of Sir Christopher Wren as though he had known the architect personally. He recommended that Maxwell visit Pembroke Chapel and the Sheldonian Theatre, outstanding examples of Wren's work, assuming that he had already marvelled at St Paul's Cathedral, on Ludgate Hill. He explained, humbly, that he had been called, some years ago, by the Provost of Emmanuel College Chapel at

Cambridge to assist in the restoration of some of the gesso work, designed by Wren himself, which had been damaged by moisture.

"My dear boy, you mean to propose marriage to the fair Eliza! Have you obtained permission from her father? I'll bet he'll be chuffed. Ha, ha! His daughter married to a gentleman—that will make her a lady! The first in that family!"

Philip Thornton was again joking about his marriage to Eliza. He didn't mind or care. He was in love with Eliza and she with him. There was still much for him to do. His work at the Middle Temple had suffered. He was told in no uncertain terms that he had to do better. He did. And there were the necessary papers to be obtained to show that he had no criminal record. The bureaucracy was horrendous. Only to be alleviated with the help of Philip. These were accepted by the Middle Temple.

His conversation with her father, where he formally asked permission for Eliza's hand in marriage, was brief. They were that day making their way across Green Park towards Marlborough House where Mr. Englehart had done some plasterwork as a young man. He was keen to point out to Maxwell yet another example of Wren's genius and in his way was pleased to welcome him into his family, saying that a handsome mitgift was in the offering. A mitgift? It was a German word. Her marriage portion. He would not be disappointed. He wasn't.

The following evening, in the Engleharts' drawing-room, with his cousin Paul present, their engagement was announced to the Englehart family and a jolly circle of their friends.

It was a surprise when he discovered that she was almost six years older than he. They were at the London Registry office. He pretended that he hadn't heard her answer. He was twenty-five and she was thirty-one. There was so much to do. He would be called to the Bar on the 17th of November and they were to be married on the 21st at St Bride's church. Mr. Englehart, who witnessed their marriage and gave the bride away, could not have been more pleased, because St Bride's church in Fleet Street was yet another architectural marvel designed by Sir Christopher Wren. "This is the second tallest of all Wren's churches," he whispered as he placed his daughter's hand in Maxwell's. Her sisters Sarah and Emma were her bridesmaids. St Bride's full peal of twelve bells were rung in celebration. They honeymooned at the Engleharts' farm, Lowlands in Dorset. The winter weather in the south was comforting and there were several surprises, one being the absolute novelty of coming downstairs one evening and seeing a tree, an evergreen of some specie, alight with small wax candles, colourful sugar ornaments and ginger Christmas cookies. It was a German Christmas tree, he was informed, by a delighted Eliza.

It was the most remarkable time of his life. He realised this, actually, consciously. The intimacy. He had never know this, neither had she. It was as though they were at the beginning of the world, he an Adam and she an Eve. It may have had to with the isolation, they were snowed under for days on end.

The servants, all German, came and went unnoticed. Eliza, rising early, would supervise the baking and the preparation of breakfast. A variety of hot and hearty Brot and Brötchen would appear, decorated with butter, sweet jams, honey, and always thinly sliced meats, cheese and delicious Leberwurst. This was a German breakfast! As German as the Christmas tree and sauerkraut, he was assured, not to mention the real German pretzels and Black Forest cake and the variety of hams, sausages, cheeses, and pickles. She was amazing. Everyday he was amazed.

He loved to see her take charge of the kitchen, lay out the dining table, the silver shining, reflecting their happy laughter, the fine crystal, which she would tap her finger against to hear the true ring of Bohemian craftsmanship. There were letters of congratulations from family members in England and an invitation from his relatives in France. Would they like to come over in the spring. It was a beautiful time of the year. They would, and in March 1855 they sailed from Dover to cross the channel to France, the home of his forebears.

45. Colonial Life

Fresh from brawling courts; And dusty purlieus of the law.

Alfred, Lord Tennyson

"They're changing guard at Buckingham Palace"

C.L.R. James, Port-of-Spain, Trinidad, 1929. "This was when her sister Catherine, Mrs. Latour, appeared. She introduced herself, then declared, 'I'm one of the niggers in the woodpile'. That was shocking. I never heard that expression before. Have you?"

"It's an American turn of phrase," said the Captain, chuckling. "It means a thing of substantial importance is being withheld, hidden away, implying something unsavoury or embarrassing."

"My word! Was she referring to herself, because of her complexion you think? She is obviously coloured. Whereas Ethel absolutely looks like a white person."

"She might have. Or maybe it was some other thing. Come to think of it, it may be both."

"What do you mean?"

45. COLONIAL LIFE

"I seem to remember some ten or twelve years ago, there was a case—I don't remember by whom it was brought—against the estate of Maxwell Philip. It caused a sensation in certain quarters among the people who still believed in him as somebody whose memory should be revered, even venerated. After all, he was a Philip. They felt he would serve their cause, which was of course to keep the resistance against colonial rule alive. As opposed to certain elites, porto l'eglise, if you know what I mean."

"What did the case involve?"

"Well, if memory serves, it had to do with an Indian family claiming to be his daughters. Why don't you look it up in the newspapers? It's not long ago."

That sounded interesting.

"As for her, the sister, in mixed-race families, who through marriage with Europeans acquire lighter complexions, it sometimes happens that over the generations one or more of the siblings can be darker than the others. Haven't you heard of the throwback? Surely you must have?"

"I have. People say these things all the time. What do you make of it?"

"Well, it shows, I suppose, a division in the family. One is darker, the other lighter. In a society such as ours, as you must know, Nello, skin shade and hair texture indicate acceptance and opportunity—or lack thereof. It was easy for the fair-complexioned sister to get a foreigner. It would be much harder for the darker one to find a husband of her kind, brown-skinned, educated, upper class, in their class—which is what she apparently did, as she married one of the Latours. And remember who their father was. She could not have married an ordinary black man and hardly likely a white man, even a foreigner."

I, of course, understood. I had been to school with boys from different backgrounds, some black, some white, many of indeterminable racial mixtures. The Captain and I had discussed the 'coloured people' some months ago as one of the many segments in our society, but to hear something like that expressed, between sisters, in front of me, a stranger, well, it was a shock. And she did not appear to have spoken only about herself. Were there others? The Indian family? And there was the coolie gardener, who laughed—I'm sure at me looking stupid after they had left. I said so.

"There is a story about that gardener. I'll relate that another time. Now lemme tell you, Nello, this is what we are all about in this movement. When I spoke in British Guiana three years ago, we had just received here in Trinidad Frederick Roberts, a member of the Labour Party and of the International Socialist Trade Union Congress. I emphasised that what we were preaching was a labour question pure and simple, and that they should not import class or colour into it. I think that in these colonies, notions of class and colour interferes with material progress, human development, family relationships and everything else. What we aim for is to make the worker, all workers, socially and economically secure. Unfortunately where we are today here, in Trinidad, this colonial administration is not inclined to be politically, legally, or administratively inclusive or even fair."

"I don't suppose it is in their interest to be fair, Captain. After all, a segmented society is easier to control."

I said that while thinking that having read *Free Mulatto,* I had gained an understanding of the struggle undertaken by that family. So to hear her say such a thing about herself was fascinating. I said so, adding, "Aren't you shocked by her remark?"

"Whose?"

"Catherine Latour's."

"Oh her. No, not really."

"Yet, the work of J.B. Philip did define a class of people who were protected by the law, and looking at the population figures in Frazer's *History* they, in Woodford's period, numbered somewhere in the vicinity of above ten thousand, while the whites were less than three thousand and the slaves around twenty thousand."

45. COLONIAL LIFE

"They were the start of this colony's middle class. It was from a handful of the educated and those with money to educate their children that a small but growing intelligentsia took root. And look at what it is today!"

I knew what he meant. That somehow in the privacy of one's mind one could be free. For me it had always been books. Education was the key. But it was a key that could only open part of the way. The more that one read and learned about the world, the more that one's imagination was fired, you realised how limited your scope was here in this colony. At best you could become a solicitor, a schoolmaster, hold a junior position in the Civil Service or even become a policeman and after thirty years in the Force become a Station Sergeant. It was a frustrating thought that I tried my best to avoid. A trap that only the pursuit of knowledge and chancing it abroad could assuage.

"You are fortunate, comrade, you have a brain, an imagination and most importantly, a highly developed critical faculty."

I wanted to hear his thoughts about Indian indentureship now that it had come to an end, and how it was reshaping the labour market, bearing in mind that the Indians were now about a third of the population. But he wasn't interested. It's strange, but I have the impression that to most people the coolies are not here permanently, it is felt that they could all return to India at any time. But they are here, all over the countryside. They fill up the hospital and you see them on the streets in a terrible condition with all sorts of diseases. But there is no competition really between the black labouring class and the coolies, although they are prepared to work for nearly nothing. But he wanted to tell me about his efforts to achieve legislative reforms that would have actually benefitted the masses as an elected member of the colonial Legislative Council from 1925.

It was growing dark as we finished for the day. As was our custom, we stepped out on to the gallery to enjoy a cigarette. I asked about the coolie gardener who had laughed at me.

"Oh yes, there is a story about him that I heard from my father. It is said that he came to Loyola as a small boy and Maxwell, typical of his class at the time, always referred to him as 'you coolie dog'. Well, one day Mrs. Philip was entertaining the Colonial Secretary's wife and some other ladies to tea, when the gardener appeared in the drawing-room—in rags and smelling of compost, he must have come directly from the garden—and declared, 'Hey monkey! When hag come tell'im dag gan home!'"

"Is that true?" I asked, laughing.

"I have no idea. But you'll hear a lot of stories about Maxwell as you go along. Well my friend, that's all for today. We'll meet next Tuesday as usual. Good night."

"Good night, Captain, see you on Tuesday next."

As I got my bicycle out from under the shed it came to me that there was much to learn about Créole Trinidad, it was a very complex society.

I WAS FASCINATED TO READ IN THE NEWSPAPERS OF THE DAY that Maxwell had returned to Trinidad in the wake of possibly the worst tragedy that the colony had ever experienced: the cholera epidemic of 1854. What an emotionally charged time that must have been. In Tronchin's lecture I saw where he claimed that the ravages of a cholera epidemic had 'disappeared' by that year, 1855, and the inhabitants of Port-of-Spain had 'emerged from the stupor and dread that had long paralysed their energies' and that they were 'delighted with the intelligence that Maxwell Philip had arrived in the colony with the intention of practicing in the courts of law'. He was suggesting that Maxwell's return had contributed, in some mysterious way, to the lifting of the horror, grief and fear that must have overwhelmed the entire population for almost a year.

I had no idea that such a calamity had befallen Trinidad what, just some seventy-five years ago. That was an example of what

45. COLONIAL LIFE

I was beginning to understand, to be an organised forgetfulness. Because our history was not taught in the schools, our past, recent even, vanished over the horizon of memory with every generation that passed away.

I saw in *Guppy's Yearbook* of 1855 that the population of Port-of-Spain was about eighteen thousand five hundred. In those days, much as it is now, the town's population was mostly Catholic and largely black and coloured. I was quite moved when I saw in the newspapers of the day that in a nine-week period, two thousand one hundred and twelve persons had died of cholera, a great many of them from the poorer parts of the town. That was more than ten per cent of the population of Port-of-Spain! Weekly interments at Lapeyrouse cemetery were startling.

The number of deaths ranged from as low as forty to fifty a day at the start of the epidemic to average between three hundred and sixty to close to five hundred per day at its height. That's a horrific death toll for such a small place. Just about everyone would have had deaths in their family. The newspapers claimed that those who lived in the countryside fared a lot better.

The newspapers also spoke of tar being burnt in barrels on street corners, filling the air with its own vile odour. It was believed that the acrid smell would somehow kill the disease. Sitting in the Public Library's reading room, in my mind's eye I could see and hear the clip-clop of mules hauling carts filled with rigid corpses through the smoke-filled streets at dusk as they joined the hearses, decorated with wilting wreaths, drawn by black-plumed horses, draped in black net.

The other thing that shocked me was that there had been so many suicides. People having lost their loved ones, their children, their spouses, took their own lives. There were no figures given for the suicides. The entire colony was gripped by the fear of death. Grief-stricken, virtually everyone was in mourning.

Tronchin claimed that Maxwell and Eliza landed on the very spot that J.B. Philip did on his return to Trinidad 'holding in his hand the famous dispatch of Lord Bathurst to Sir Ralph Woodford, with reference to the civil rights of the coloured people.' If that was true, it would mean that his ship would have put in at San Fernando. He goes on to add that they were greeted by what the author claimed to be 'friends of liberty'. That suggested that Maxwell would have been received at either Concorde or at Philippine estate by his uncle St. Luce and his circle.

This then were the circumstances and importantly the emotional, even political mood, which Tronchin wanted his audience to believe dominated the place upon Maxwell's return to Trinidad.

Within months of his return Maxwell apparently gave his support to the Catholic church. We had discussed that, the Captain and I, some months ago when Mrs. Broadway had boasted of being Bishop Spaccapietra's goddaughter. It would seem that when he returned a barrister, Maxwell made himself very popular by his support for the Catholic church and the bishop himself, by making a case that Spaccapietra receive his salary from the government. It had been withheld on the grounds that he was not an Englishman! In one of the obituaries the writer actually claims that Spaccapietra gave it all away to charity upon receiving it.

Maxwell would not have stayed in the south of the island for long, as it was agreed by the obituary writers that he went into practice almost immediately. In every report mention is made of his growing popularity, his appearance, his stature, his manly good looks, the sound of his voice, his command of language, and his dramatic appearances in the courts. He must have indeed seemed messianic to a great many people. I could well understand that, especially having made a study of Captain Cipriani and his relationship with "the barefoot man".

People were, just as they are now, on the lookout for a saviour, a champion who would represent them. Plainly Maxwell, no doubt with the help and guidance of those who were promoting him, was positioning himself as a representative of "the people". The other thing I saw was that by the following year, 1856, he was appointed

45. COLONIAL LIFE

to the position of Acting Inspector of Schools, filling in for one Alexander Anderson. Was he a part of the Anderson family that had supported Maxwell? Very likely he was. And the Department of Education giving him an acting appointment and he so recently come home. That would have taken some influencing, or, knowing how this colony operates, it could have been a decision taken so as to start the process of making him one of their own. Maxwell was nevertheless plainly positioning himself as a populist politician and was no doubt enjoying it even as the colonial authorities were already planning a future for him.

Ethel Broadway did say that it was she and her husband who spoke to the newspapers following the death of her father. I could just imagine those conversations. This was why some wrote that Maxwell went on a grand tour of Europe in the style of the wealthy French Créoles of the cocoa boom days, while another thought that he followed the Bohemian lifestyle in his European travels, a sort of vagrant gypsy life. It was Ethel, however, who said to me that he went to France to visit his cousin who lived in a castle surrounded by acres of vineyards.

The then resident Baroness Folch de Cardon de Sandrans at the château at Dracy Le Fort in the 1850s was Jeannette-Rose, daughter of Susannah Philip and Guillaume Robin de Livet. This I found in a large and impressive tome, which was kept under lock and key in the public library. Mr. Comma had the key and there was the *Dictionnaire de la Noblesse de la France*, 2nd ed. 18v. Paris: Bachelin-Deflorenne, 1850–73.

"This was gifted to the library by the Honourable Dr. Louis Antoine Aimé de Verteuil," uttered Mr. Comma in the most unctuous of tones imaginable. "He was mayor of Port-of-Spain, an admirable man, admirable, the perfect gentleman."

"Yes, I'm sure he was. It says here that Jeannette-Rose was born in Trinidad and that she married Paul-François Folch de Cardon de Sandrans, a baron, and her children were Paul-William-Philip, Elizabeth-Marie-Louise-Philippine and Susanne-Judith-Rose."

"Yes, they were all named for our family. My father dined only off silver plates, Mr. James. We are proud of our origins, wouldn't you be? But I suppose not. This sort of heritage must mean little to you, your people being Barbadian."

I couldn't bring an appropriate answer to mind, so I hastily made some notes, thanked Mr. Comma for his help and left the library by the Pembroke Street door to find my bicycle where I had parked it. I was late for class and my students, who were mostly in their twenties and former pupil teachers themselves, would be making the most of it, the cat being away.

The following morning being Saturday I decided to visit Loyola. Ethel's daughter Elsie received me at the garden gate.

"Mother is not at home, Mr. James, but she has left some correspondence for you to have a look at."

I could sense the vigilant presence of the maid Mavaline hovering in the vacant spaces of empty doorways that led to nowhere as we entered the billiard room.

"These are some letters from our cousin Jeannette-Rose to my grandfather."

Elsie was fair-skinned, with soft flimsy brownish hair, green eyes, slim, and quite tall. Her small facial features, not unattractive, were entirely European. Seeing her there standing in the sunlight, indicating with a pointed finger the little bundle of letters that was arranged on what appeared to be a leather-bound portfolio, she appeared elegant. I had to think of the portrait of her grandfather Maxwell. There was a resemblance, it was mostly in her manner, the arrogant tilt of her head perhaps, which I imagined Maxwell must have exhibited as well.

"Thank you, Miss Broadway."

"Would you like some tea, a glass of water, a jug of wine, a book of verse? Do forgive me, Mr. James, I have been reading the *Rubáiyát* of Omar Khayyám, do you know it?"

"No, I don't think so." What I really wanted was some coffee.

45. COLONIAL LIFE

"Some tea then. Mavaline! We'll have tea in here, now!"

The letters were in French and written in mauve ink in an elegant hand. Each had a small embossed crest at the top of the page. The first was an invitation to visit in response to a letter presumably written by Maxwell and was signed with an elaborate monogram J.

"'J' stands for Jeannette-Rose. They visited them in France, you know. My grandfather told us about it. It was during the rise of Napoleon III. Ever heard of him, Mr. James? Ah, Mavaline, just put everything down there. Yes, there, and go."

I had read some French history and was aware of Napoleon III. To me he was a very clever politician, who achieved a great deal for his country but lost a war against Germany, and in so doing brought closure to one of the great myths of the French revolution: the citizen emperor. But she was saying: "This was a period, one could say that it was the foreshadowing of the belle époque. The emperor reshaped the face of Paris. My grandfather was there, here, look at these, Mr. James."

She showed me what appeared to be a quantity of engraved postcards, all from Paris, pictures of imposing buildings vividly retouched in primary colours. Their captions read, The Gare de Lyon and Gare du Nord, these were apparently railway stations, The Avenue de l'Opéra and some others. I was more interested in the letters.

"You read French, Mr. James? How interesting."

The letters were short and spoke of family matters, the birth of grandchildren, that sort of thing. I noticed that several of their names contained the name Philip. She must have seen me paying attention to this, because she said as she poured a cup of tea for me, "Yes, Mr. James, the Philip name has been handed down through the years in that family, although my cousins have never been here. The Cardon de Sandrans named two of their children after our family in Trinidad, their eldest, the future heir, Paul-William-Philip, and the second child, a girl, Elizabeth-Marie-Louise-Philippine for our estate in the Naparimas."

"Why was that?" I asked, taking the cup and saucer from her.

"It was our money that bought their château. My father told us that. He told us a lot of things about them. They are apparently very grand, you wouldn't think that they had a touch of the tar brush. But then so do many other European royals, don't you know, Mr. James."

"Really, I had no idea."

"You are very handsome for a darkie, Mr. James. Has anyone ever told you that before?"

I had no idea what to say to that.

"And then there are these," she said, opening the portfolio. "Have you ever seen anything like this?"

It was an astonishing assemblage of very old, mezzotinted pornographic prints, quite explicit. I think I must have jumped from the chair as it fell back to the floor with a thud. I had never seen such a thing.

"Are you shocked, Mr. James? Come, we are adults, we can look at these, enjoy them all without a trace of sin in our hearts, look, *look*."

There was no chance of that. I had to leave right away. My heart was pounding. I looked at her standing in the sunlight that was coming through the open doors, her face was shining, her eyes were wild and she was breathing with her mouth open. She mad like hell! was the thought that consumed my racing mind.

"Your mudder just reach back, Elsie, you better put back everything. Mr. James, finish drinking your tea, the madam outside, she say to tell you. Come, Elsie, is time for you to go upstairs now, come, the Angelus will ring just now, come." All this from Mavaline, who spoke with a resigned exasperation in a voice that did not lack authority.

As I turned to go, Elsie was carefully rearranging the letters, having put the prints back into the folio. I stepped out of there and

45. Colonial Life

there was Mrs. Broadway sitting with the parrot perched on the back of the iron bench close to the blooming hibiscus that Mr. Broadway had planted so long ago.

"Mr. James, you are here *again*. Has Elsie been showing you the letters that my father received from the baroness? They were quite close, you know. My parents visited them over there several times. Bring up that iron chair, it's not wet. So you wanted to know about our family in France. Father said that we financed them, but that was how the family was in those days. We helped each other. What's the matter with you, Mr. James? Has Elsie frightened you? Don't mind that. She's just highly strung. Her godfather was Archbishop English, he succeeded his grace Archbishop Spaccapietra, my godfather. Archbishop English founded the *Star of the West* newspaper, you know, and sought to draw souls together in the fold of the One Shepherd. Elsie is very devoted to the sacred heart of Mary, very devoted. Will you sit down, Mr. James, instead of towering over me."

46. The Prodigal's Way

"A lie that is half-truth is the darkest of all lies."

Alfred, Lord Tennyson

LOYOLA COTTAGE, MARAVAL.

TRINIDAD 1857: MAXWELL WAS ALL TOO WELL AWARE THAT he was possessed of a shocking quality: an extreme sharpness of the mind which could realise beyond the extraordinary. He knew, too, that his command of the English language was as subtle and harmonious as if it were French. He could, at will, invoke a Shakespearean purity, evocative and moving. In this colony, the street orator, the chantwell or even the inspired lay preacher could conjure with a "lavway" or an impassioned discourse an emotive response from the people. The use of words, circumlocutory or even invented, could lionise and embolden the champion stick-fighter or the most timid altar boy, and move the listeners to cheers or to riot. It was all part of that make-believe so necessary to exist in this colony's borrowed reality. He knew, too, that he was not alone. Crowding close about him were the shades of ancestors, many real, others mythical. He was moving in a drama that had its origins in resistance and revolution, and he was expected to assume a leading role in that drama, one that must transcend the legendary and bring about a new reality.

46. THE PRODIGAL'S WAY

That here were men who had seen in him those possibilities, who held the strings that made him move and shake like a Punch and Judy show, was not lost on him. In his own way he was pleased, because it made it easier for him to play the role that he loved best: the performer who relished the hurrays coming from the gallery. The cultivation of this persona, partly real, always moving with the currency of the present, was most enjoyable. Every morning he would strike a pose in front of the mirror to admire his reflection. First the jabot, bright white, starched and ironed, the wig in place, then the black gown thrown about his shoulders like an unscrupulous Lothario, declaring to the delight of Eliza, "I wonder who will pay the piper today?"

IT WAS EARLY AFTERNOON when the black butler in glistening white silently opened the door to the old mansion. Maxwell was expected. Left alone, he admired the room's furnishings, which were few but apparently excellent examples of French craftsmanship. On the walls hung several paintings of eighteenth century gentlemen in jabots and wigs. He admired the crystal chandelier that descended from the carved ceiling, it matched the lovely candelabras on the walls. There was about the place a sense of refinement as in a thing withdrawn and kept away from the vulgar.

Just then the sunlight penetrating the room threw the shadow of a woman upon the far wall. Sharp, for the briefest of moments, it revealed a lovely profile cast in silhouette. Turning, there was no one to be seen. All was quiet except for the birdsong and the retreating rustle of many petticoats.

Maxwell had been informed that Dr. Jean Valleton de Boissière was a veteran who had held the rank of Surgeon-Major in the British army. He had recently returned from both the Crimean war and the Indian mutiny and carried himself with an effortless affrontiveness, even when addressing the president of the Legislative Council who happened to be the governor of the colony. Maxwell had been summoned by Dr. de Boissière to Champs Élysées estate because George Garcia, presently Solicitor General, a man whom the doctor held in esteem, had suggested that a cottage on the outskirts of the property be made available to him. But first he would be met and inspected.

Invited to walk in the estate's famous terraced garden, Maxwell assumed the role of the interested but woefully uninformed. The doctor spoke of the Paraphalaenopsis, the Bartholina and the very rare Masdevallia. He pointed out the exceptional Disa and the even rarer Oeceoclades which, he informed Maxwell, had been discovered by the English botanist John Lindley in the Orinoco delta and brought to the estate in 1820. And there was the family Heliconiaceae, of which he was obviously proud, particularly the Heliconia bihai, known locally as the Balisier. Maxwell was experimenting with variations of appreciative murmuring noises, all while being distracted by glimpses of a woman on the terrace above.

Dr. de Boissière was saying that he had never met his uncle, Dr. St. Luce Philip, but had learned of a brother, Dr. Jean-Baptiste Philip. He thought it fascinating that St. Luce and his lady wife had visited Champs Élysées while he was abroad, and had been entertained by his father. He said that he understood that Maxwell was the scion of the most notable coloured family in the island, if not the British West Indies, and that Maxwell's people had been known to and held in consequence by the late Don Antonio Gomez. Most extraordinary even for those barbaric times.

That the Surgeon-Major was a plain man who went straight to the point was made apparent when he informed Maxwell that as a born Créole of this island, he would want to see the more educated element of the coloured population become engaged in the work of bringing about home rule. Garcia and himself, together with others, saw themselves as the Créole party engaged in accomplishing this. Maxwell, who was thought of as exceptional, could be the representative man who would express the will of the common

46. THE PRODIGAL'S WAY

people. Maxwell knew well that he could not possibly impress this supercilious Surgeon-Major nor, apparently, did he need to.

That he was being given the opportunity to live on the outskirts of Champs Élysées estate, in a cottage that was rumoured to have been built by Dr. de Boissière's father, infamously remembered as "Henri the Devil", for his mulatress Rosalie Rose of Champs Élysées, he found amusing. Maxwell couldn't wait to tell Eliza about the visit. The cottage would have to be rebuilt, but the view was enchanting. That they would want his skill as a lawyer and the prestige of his name to further their own ends, he had no problem with, because he who pays the piper calls the tune.

C.L.R. JAMES, PORT-OF-SPAIN, TRINIDAD, 1929. "Lemme tell you this, Nello, people today take their situation for granted. They have no idea, actually they do not have the information that would give them an understanding of what it has taken for them to feel so Trinidadian. Which they do at carnival time or when there is cricket at the Oval and we are up against the MCC and we fouti."

We were setting out to motor down to Point Fortin and the Captain was at the wheel of his A-Model Ford. He was to address oil workers on issues ranging from the abysmally low wages they received, the horrifying living conditions that they endured, as compared to the lifestyle enjoyed by their employers, on to the developments in the labour movement in England. This talk would include the nature of capitalistic entrenchment in the British society and how all of that compared to our situation here in Trinidad. In his way he had been preparing this speech since the day before yesterday. His way was to repeat, as if in rehearsal, the salient points that he wanted to make. He never committed anything to writing, it all came to him spontaneously from memory. As a born Créole he was an excellent raconteur.

I was always more interested when he spoke of the nationalistic ideals that were becoming a topic shared by so many people I knew.

I understood it as a form of consciousness, quite distinct from the loyalty that was felt towards the British Crown, to England and to the Empire to which we belonged. It tended to glorify Trinidad above all and to place an emphasis on the promotion of our culture and particular interests as opposed to those of the colonial power. I was thinking of how the calypsonians exalted us as Iere, the Land of the Hummingbird, Trinidad, the home of the famous pitch lake and even Angostura bitters!

We had touched on this inherent patriotism before, because I had been thinking about Maxwell and the role that he had assumed on returning to Trinidad. I wanted Cipriani to tell me more about the origins of this need to express patriotic ideals, because plainly from looking at the newspaper accounts of Maxwell's life, he appeared to have been very much involved in all this. The other thing was I had not as yet had a chance to tell him about my encounter with Elsie, Mrs. Broadway's daughter. That conversation would require a different moment, as it could not possibly be shouted above the noise of the motor and the rushing wind, which was making it difficult to have a conversation.

"I saw that Maxwell wrote for a paper called *Free Press* and for another, *The Trinidadian*. Do you know anything about these newspapers?" I asked, turning towards him.

"No, not really," he shouted. "I think the *Free Press* was probably a weekly paper. I found a copy among my father's things. It existed in the 1850s. I think it represented the interest of a few dozen educated, coloured people."

"Maxwell almost certainly did write for a similar paper, *The Trinidadian*," I answered, holding on to my hat. "But you are right, it can't be more that a couple dozen. I saw in *Guppy's Yearbook* that the population of Trinidad was over 170,000 in the 1880s. But these weekly newspapers had a circulation of only about 100 or 200 copies, so they definitely were writing for a small group of people."

"*The Trinidadian* I know of," he said, maneuvering his way past piles of gravel and stones to be employed in road repairs. "It was

46. THE PRODIGAL'S WAY

owned by a Dessources, published around the same period, and it addressed similar issues."

I nodded, thinking, Maxwell must have been liberal-minded then. Maybe he was supporting some sort of constitutional reform that would promote the interest of ordinary people.

"When Maxwell came back in 1851 he involved himself with politically-minded men," I said while trying to adjust the vent window so as reduce the amount of wind that was coming in. "I saw in the old newspapers that he associated with what seems to me like a group of reformers and would-be politicians. Men like Thomas Hinde, who had been elected to the Town Council in 1841, and Henry Jobity, who spoke publicly in favour of representative government. Another, William Herbert, owned two newspapers. Were these all coloured men?"

"I am not aware of them, but yes, those are all coloured families," he shouted, overtaking a column of plodding cane carts. "But I'm not surprised, as I told you before, this colony has always had a movement, a resistance to crown colony rule."

"I read in one his obituaries of his tension with Charles Warner on the one hand and of his friendship with Governor Gordon on the other. Ethel Broadway said that her father and Gordon were very close."

"The Warners? Ah! Lemme tell you this. The Warners were the watchdogs of British interest, not just in Trinidad but in the entire West Indies. Charles Warner was Attorney General here for years. Governors came and went, but Warner dictated the Colonial Office's social and economic policies. Then he fell from power, forced to resign by Governor Gordon. If I remember, it had to do with a trust fund that he presided over. Two minors. They lost everything. Governor Gordon, now he was liberal in outlook."

"What was that?"

"I said, Gordon must have been a liberal! He came here in 1866. He opened up crown lands to the poor. Five acre lots! He made them available at a reasonable price. This meant a great deal to ordinary people. Twenty years later, when cocoa boomed in the 1880s, the small cocoa planter benefitted, and that was one of the things that allowed for a black middle class to take root. Gordon was very tolerant of the Catholics and the French Créoles."

"I can imagine what would have been the thinking in government circles when Maxwell called for a celebration to mark the emancipation of the slaves."

"What?"

"I said I wonder what would have been the thinking in government circles when it was learned that Maxwell was calling for a celebration to mark the emancipation of the slaves!"

"Government would have started to pay closer attention to him from the moment he associated himself with Hinde and Jobity. They would have seen him as highly political." He held on to his hat as gusts of hot wind swirled through the car, steering with one hand. "And look at the people who supported him, men like Garcia and de Boissière. They did not always toe the official line. They supported black people when it came to things that were embedded in the culture, like communal drumming and dancing the bamboola. They saw in him the making of a representative man."

"A representative man? What's that?"

"You could think of it as someone chosen or even appointed to act or speak for ordinary people, the barefoot man."

"I saw that Maxwell became mayor of Port-of-Spain in 1867. The first coloured man to hold that post. I thought it interesting when I read that he condemned the stickfighters for chanting an invocation where they sang that 'The Devil is a Negro, but God is a white man' so as to make themselves invincible when under an attack by an opponent who was intent on cracking their skulls."

"Did he? I'm not surprised. That sort of thinking is still around, it is what we are up against. But Nello, this shouting is making me hoarse. I need to keep my voice for the meeting!"

46. THE PRODIGAL'S WAY

We drove on in silence along the Southern Main Road. Around us, as far as the eye could see, were acres upon acres of undulating sugarcane fields—a vast capitalistic enterprise, he said it was. It occurred to me, as we travelled through this intensely cultivated part of the island, that there has never been any communal problem, no form of antagonism between the Créole population and the coolies who I could see in the surrounding fields. I suppose this is so because the latter are concentrated in this, the sugar-growing part of the island as well as in other agricultural districts, and we only see them in town poor and more often than not, quite ill. In the distance I could make out the Naparima Hill. We would be spending the night in San Fernando at a boarding house close to the waterfront, before making the final leg to Point Fortin in the morning.

Doing this work with the Captain has definitely made me politically conscious and more aware, socially. The knowledge that there are people starving here, who have no work and who live in terror of the bailiff, has caused me to listen even more carefully when he speaks about things like political freedom and the purpose of the Labour movement, and to examine notions like the social ownership of the means of production. What a thought. I find that I have changed in my outlook since leaving Q.R.C. in my thinking actually, and certainly in my growing understanding of this society and the true purpose of its rulers.

Through the many prisms of the Captain's life experiences I believe that what we are doing here is extraordinarily useful, as it will bring before all who may be interested the true political situation in the West Indies today. A fresh understanding. The change may have had an earlier beginning. Getting to know people like Ralph de Boissière, Albert Gomes and Alfred Mendes was eye-opening. They are all anti-colonialist, some people call them left-wingers. They want to encourage local writers, through the publication of their magazine, *Trinidad*, to examine our own several societal groupings, and to leave behind the British template with its preconceptions about differences in class and colour. Now, increasingly, I wish to see myself as a writer engaged in not only the fictionalised examination of the working class, as I am presently attempting in my story *Minty Alley*, but also in the effort to analyse history and politics through working on the Captain's biography.

Before joining the Mendes group I occupied my time as a teacher, studying, reading and writing, and of course with sport. A keen club cricketer I am, and something of an athlete. I did set the Trinidad high-jump record. Five feet nine inches. But it was on reading *Free Mulatto* and now this Maxwell Philip project, which I first thought of as a mere diversion, that I have gained an understanding of how this society started off and how it has evolved in spite of the oppressive nature of colonial rule. Naturally loquacious, I have also begun to express my myself with the words and the ideas that I have been hearing as expressed by the Captain and my new friends. They are all more or less involved in the Labour movement, they are modern men, I suppose they see me as a bright black man and as a person who may have something to offer as an endorser of, even a contributor to, their ideals. My wife Juanita has noticed these changes. She said to me the other day, "Like you only have white friends these days!" This was after Hugh Stollmeyer, a white Trinidadian, an artist and a friend of Mendes, also a white man, had dropped me home.

Our night at the New Naparima Hotel was not unpleasant. It did take the Captain's quiet authority to override the unspoken whites-only policy, and there were some hostile stares and angry mutterings. I saw one couple leave as we entered the little dining room, but they may have been leaving anyway. We paid no attention, ate our dinner and retired early.

Point Fortin is a ramshackle accumulation of a few old houses, grotty parlours that sell almost nothing, a huge Chinese shop that sells everything, a gas station and an oil refinery. Nearby was the white employees' encampment. High fenced and barbed wired, there was a black guard at the gate and a police post, empty, not far away. All around were huge oil tanks painted silver, extraordinarily

46. The Prodigal's Way

tall oil derricks and a great many pumpjacks, bowing and rising in a disharmony that was a bit distracting. Then there was the smell, strong and distinct.

The meeting was held on a cricket field. I was surprised at the turnout; there must have been over a hundred people there, and as if to me, the crowd grew larger as various speakers took the loudspeaker and by the time the Captain spoke, this was after sundown, I saw that several cars had arrived. There were the police as well, of course. An inspector, a young Englishman, presented himself to the Captain, they spoke. He appeared respectful, after all the Captain is the member for Port-of-Spain as well as mayor. But tonight he is the Labour leader who the oil workers wanted to listen to.

We were accommodated in the Chinese shop. The proprietor apparently was well known to the Captain and had a bedroom at the back ready for us.

We set off the following morning after a quick, early breakfast. After leaving the part of the Southern Main Road that passed close to the pitch lake—that I really wanted to see, but he ignored that—we took what seemed a demented tour through innumerable rutted country roads, past level crossings, sugar factories and estate barracks surrounded by endless fields of steaming hot sugarcane. We had left the oil-belt behind to eventually find ourselves driving up overgrown wheel tracks that led to an old estate house. The Captain said: "Nello, I have a surprise for you. Philippine estate," he said, pulling up the hand brake. "I thought you should see it. Here, take a photograph." He handed me his Brownie camera.

It was an experience! First, it was the silence after the noise of the motor, and the sound of the tearing wind. I left the Captain in the motorcar and after taking a few snaps walked up the weedy driveway towards the large, wooden, upstairs house. Even from a distance I could see where windows had fallen off, the paint peeling and the overall dereliction that spoke of a long abandonment. It had once been painted in cream and trimmed with maroon. The emptiness seemed to echo in my ear.

I took the short flight of steps that led to a wide and vacant verandah. I had no idea what to expect as I pushed at a tall door that opened without a sound. A large square room was before me. There was an odour of vacancy into which the afternoon sunlight flowed as easily as a gentle breeze. The dusty floor was stained with bat droppings and the pale blue partitions showed darker rectangles where once pictures had hung. An intricately carved mahogany sideboard, huge and battered, stood against a wall. I caught a glimpse of myself in one of its small mirrors. I looked hot, sweaty and dishevelled. Two old chairs sat facing each other as if in quiet consultation.

All was silent except for the innocuous birdsong that came along with the inoffensive afternoon sunlight. There was a sense of outside and inside. Ahead of me was a wide staircase with a dark, carved newel post and balusters to match, rising. I hesitated. Was I afraid? No. There was nothing to fear. At the top of the stair, a long shadowed corridor of many doors. It appeared an endless procession of doorways. I passed between a dusty velvet drape at its end and there was an enormous bed with an elaborately carved headboard and four magnificently turned bedposts in the middle of an empty and darkened room. The bed had been stripped down. There were neither mattresses, nor bed-boards or testers. It looked liked like the skeletal remains of a monstrous creature. What did I expect? Yet in its vacancy, in its very dereliction, there was an atmosphere, a mood. What had happened here? Where had all that history gone?

I had a sense of anticlimax as I walked towards the motorcar. But what did I expect? The Captain was asleep. I stood around gazing at the shimmering heat of noon as it blazed in the surrounding sugarcane field. I could hear the buzzing quiet. There was not a soul in sight. The Captain woke up. We were to be put up at Reform estate and there was still a long drive ahead of us.

I came away with the feeling that it was something more than a coincidence when some weeks later I came across an article in *Fair Play,* a monthly publication of the nineteenth century, that told of Maxwell acquiring Philippine estate in 1874 for an astounding twenty-one thousand two hundred pounds! I wondered why he would want to buy that sugarcane estate.

"Of course," said the Captain, "of course he would want to own that estate. It was where it had all begun for the Philips, and I suppose as he became quite wealthy, he was in private practice, buying it became for him a responsibility. But I am just guessing. In those days they were bringing in the coolies in large numbers. It may have been a good financial move, for all we know."

THE FOLLOWING TUESDAY, we met as usual in his rooms to continue our work. Something I had read came to my mind, and I asked the Captain:

"Do you know that on the day St. Luce Philip was appointed to the Legislative Council as an unofficial member, he made a motion that ended apprenticeship in Trinidad?"

"Oh yes? That's really interesting."

"It was in August of 1838. I saw it in the Gazette."

"That sort of thing was remembered, and re-remembered, enlarged upon, which Maxwell inherited. Now, let's be realistic, in the first place, it was the governor of the day who put St. Luce in there and allowed him to move that motion. They gave that to him a consolation prize, like everything that is given to a colonial. After all, it was his brother J.B. Philip who had the laws altered in favour of the free coloureds, laws which ultimately benefitted the emancipated. So it was a case of the colonial government rolling with the punches, so to speak, and giving the devil his due."

"I saw that Maxwell was given the responsibility for the drafting of the law that annexed Tobago to Trinidad. There was initially much skepticism in the Leg Co about that."

"My father remembered that his speech was long and rambling, but the week after, when they met again, the motion was moved arguing on the grounds of Trinidad's self-interest. What else have you found?"

"The newspapers of the time describe Maxwell as the great legal lion of the day. It would appear that his knowledge of the old Spanish laws was exceptional. He spoke Spanish fluently as well as Hindustani! His versatility actually amazed people. Judges complimented him. One judge, I forget who, said that his presentation evoked the Old Bailey. Then there were several sensational trials. I read the report on a case of a man called Brunton, a Diego Martin planter, a coloured man who was accused of murdering a priest. I found that utterly fantastic—a black man kills a white priest who was having an affair with his black wife, and Maxwell gets him off. I never heard of anything like that before."

"Yes, that was a sensational one. People still talk about it."

"Many of his court appearances were reported in detail, pages and pages in the Gazette. When you read his obituaries, there is no doubt that he was seen by the editors of those papers as a champion defense lawyer, one writer even remarking that any criminal defended by Maxwell was bound to get away."

"He also served as mayor, which gives you an idea of his political popularity. For Maxwell to be elected mayor following the likes of Sir Louis de Verteuil and others like him who came from the French Creole establishment of Port of Spain, shows that the government of the day understood that it was now expedient to have a mayor who represented the interest of the masses."

"I saw that there was something of a scandal that concerned his mishandling of funds while he was mayor; he resigned over that. Did you know about that, Captain?"

"Yes yes, there was some bobol or the other."

"He wasn't actually implicated, per se, in any wrong-doing or chicanery. He apparently merely overspent the budget by a few thousand dollars."

46. THE PRODIGAL'S WAY

"Well, Maxwell in the end chose his own destiny, every man does; life is about choices. But he may well have become a hostage to fortune."

"A hostage to fortune? What does that mean?"

"You become a hostage to fortune through an act, commitment, or even a remark which turns out to be unwise, because it invited trouble or could prove difficult to live up to. If Maxwell ever declared, as he may have, that he would see this colony receive home rule status and, failing that, give up his role as a representative of the people's interest, he could be perceived as being a hostage to fortune. It was impossible for him in the first instance to live up to those expectations in a Crown colony like Trinidad, and I am sure he came to understand that and left it behind and got on with his life."

"The writers, I suppose the editors of the papers, obviously his supporters who produced the obituaries, all say that he was bitterly disappointed and died a heartbroken man, because it was his race that prevented him from getting the post of Attorney General. But I remember you saying that it was his political popularity among the ordinary people that compromised his position."

"Yes, as we discussed before, as A.G. he would have had to act as a member of the colonial government against individuals who would have been his political supporters. The Colonial Office may not have believed that he could do that fairly. He was too politically popular, perhaps active. It's the same with me. I could be mayor, but not A.G."

"Interestingly, as mayor, Maxwell made sure that his family name was remembered by naming Philip Street for his uncle J.B. and building the great arched gate to Lapeyrouse cemetery. But you know, Captain, what I have come to realise is that the governor of the period of Maxwell's rise was Sir Arthur Gordon, and it would appear from what I am seeing in the newspapers that he introduced significant reforms."

"That's interesting, Nello. So whereas Maxwell as a hostage to fortune could never have met the expectations of the people by himself, he may have influenced Gordon. What was the most important reform?"

"For me, introducing entrance examination exams that would allow black and coloured men to enter the Civil Service was very important. J.J. Thomas, whom we spoke about, was a beneficiary."

"Why don't you look up what Gordon did in more detail? You now seem to have access to all the newspaper files. Old Comma has let you into his most secret archives!"

OVER THE FOLLOWING WEEKS, the Teachers Training College being on vacation, I pored over the old newspapers in the Public Library's collection, which I must tell you were exceedingly eclectic. It would seem that Gordon's tenure, which lasted from 1866 to 1870, did see the implementation of profound changes in the colony's social landscape. Not the least of which was the removal of Charles Warner as Attorney General, a man who was portrayed in some of the newspapers as being anti-Catholic and generally against the very culture of the place. The Captain had thought of him as an enduring presence, representing forms of suppression, all alien to the so-called Créole culture of the colony, which was then considerably more French than it is today.

Warner, it would appear, was brought down by Governor Gordon when caught taking advantage of some orphans, depriving them of their inheritance or some such. At this period, a man called George Garcia was Solicitor General, and had been for over a decade. I didn't pay much attention to that matter.

What I found more interesting were the changes in the laws that affected the majority of the population, put in place by Governor Gordon. For example, the building of a new road linking Arima to Valencia and on to Manzanilla, thus opening up to the east coast of the island, which gave people new opportunities. Gordon also made Crown lands available in small lots at low prices to everyone. That, too, benefitted ordinary people enormously, especially

46. THE PRODIGAL'S WAY

the squatters, many of whom were Africans, literally the children and grandchildren of the former slaves, along with the mostly black Créoles who had settled in the central part of the island. This generous and very broad-ranging distribution of Crown lands laid the foundation for what would become this island's second-greatest treasure trove after sugar: the cocoa boom of the 1880s which made the small cocoa planter well off and of course the rich even richer.

It was purely by chance, as I gathered and tried to assimilate all of this information over several days, which I must tell you was distributed between many newspapers, all with their own interpretations and contradicting points of view, that my eyes fell upon Joseph's *History of Trinidad*, which was lying open on the table at which I was working. It was overdue and I was about to return it. I noticed a paragraph that read that on the 5th of January 1826 a "royal proclamation was published, which removed certain vexatious regulations respecting the free blacks and people of colour. . . . Their enactment was contrary to the letter of the Cedula of 1783, and the spirit of the 12th article of the capitulation."

Having read *Free Mulatto*, I knew that Joseph was referring to J.B. Philip. As I drew the book over to read it again, I could not help but feel, then and there, that what Gordon had accomplished was the culmination of J.B. Philip's work of forty years before. It made my hair stand on end as I wondered if Maxwell may have had any influence on all of this, being himself fully au courant with what his uncle had achieved for the free black and mixed-race people, an achievement that with emancipation benefitted the former slaves, and in the long run the entire population.

Leaving the library that afternoon, I could not help but wonder at the relationship of these two men, Gordon and Maxwell. All these reforms, enacted in four short years, had been at the very heart of every bone of contention for generations. Maxwell, upon his return home in 1855, was perceived as charismatic by some and as being the inheritor of the Philip family's legacy, which of course he could not possibly live up to. As the Captain had phrased it: a hostage to fortune. His support for the Catholic Archbishop, in fact for the Catholic Church itself, was expressed, mere weeks after his return, in a speech that was reported in most of the papers giving support to Archbishop Spaccapietra. All this popular support saw him flirt with the reformists. They would have him be a liberator, like Simon Bolivar or Toussaint L'Ouverture. This was the period when he was the star of the *Star of the West*, the popular Catholic paper.

I could not help feeling, as I made my way home, that I had come to the closing of a great and historic cycle. Plainly, Maxwell had not been a radical activist, it was not in his nature to be one. I was now inclined to see him as a histrionic personality. Shakespearian, dramatic in style, excitable. Flirtatious, surely charming, and I am sure, seductive. Did he manipulate the new governor? Surely not. Did the Colonial Office in London appoint a governor who, according to the *Encyclopaedia Britannica*, was liberal in outlook? Did "they" see the need to reform, to change the way the colony was run? End the Warner way of doing business? Did "they" understand the impact of a histrionic personality such as Maxwell's on a colony such as Trinidad, where the culture of resistance to British colonial rule was obvious and could become volatile? Most of the inhabitants of the colony didn't even speak English at the time, but French and Patois.

I have come to understand Trinidadians have always had an inclination toward resistance and cherish a charismatic leader, and the Colonial Office thought that Maxwell's charisma could be harnessed by elevating him, allowing him to become mayor of Port-of-Spain, the first man of colour to wear that golden chain. He was mayor apparently for one and a half terms. In 1869, Maxwell was made an acting unofficial member of the Legislative Council. In just about fourteen years he had built a lucrative practice and had garnered a following, certainly among the editors of the dedicated left. What else could "they" do? I couldn't help but see Maxwell playing to the gallery, a gay piper earning his pay.

The following week we met as usual, and after discussing at length the Captain's own political misadventures, he felt compelled to return to the topic of being a hostage to fortune.

46. THE PRODIGAL'S WAY

"Remember we talked about that the other day," he said. "I wanna tell you that there are other examples of that in the history of these islands. Take for example the Haitian revolution and Toussaint L'Ouverture, its leader. He led his people to victory and promised all sorts of things and they expected a lot from him, but it was inevitable that the ideal would fail. He was captured and taken away to France, where he died in prison, never having achieved what he wanted for his people."

"As you mention that. I came across a book in the library the other day. I started reading it, *Stella: A Novel of the Haitian Revolution*, written in the 1850s."

"You won't find much written on that subject locally. I was thinking, when you are finished with me, try to take a look at the life of L'Ouverture, explore the politics of that time. The Haitian Revolution. You could re-cast its history to serve the interest of today's labouring masses. You could show that the slaves were the forebears of the workers of today, and that they, the workers, are the inheritors of the atrocities of slavery. Hapless victims of economic greed, today's workers can be seen as the inheritors of a misery that must never be forgotten. As a young fellow, I had the opportunity to read some so-called 'banned literature'. Among these was a paper about the theory of permanent revolution. It made me think how the Haitian Revolution and the French Revolution were intrinsically intertwined throughout, and how Jacobinism could have inspired Toussaint and his inner circle. Think about it, Nello, you could put the slaves themselves centre-stage, as working people, boldly forging their own destiny against nearly impossible odds."

"Now that's interesting. You're saying that the working masses of today are trapped because they have inherited this situation from their ancestors? And yes, I could see how this view of inherited victimhood could energise today's political consciousness, certainly in the British West Indies."

"Because it has a highly personal dimension to it," said the Captain. "People will relate to that. They already feel like victims, and you could show them how they have inherited this feeling in the period of the revolutionary Atlantic."

I mentioned my doubts to Albert Gomes one evening at the Black Lion. In his typical laconic humour, he commented: "Naturally, Nello, it's happening inside your head, but why should that mean it is not real!"

As a socialist, as a student and a practitioner of that political ideal, the Captain had, without spelling it out, made something clear to me. Which was that black people, subject people, who were thinking people, all over the world, who had known nothing else but subjugation, exploitation and the most pernicious forms of racism, were turning to the ideals of socialism as the only intelligent, in truth scientific political response to imperialism and all that was implied by that system. I hardly had the words as yet to express those thoughts.

The Servant Of The Centurion

1870 - 1888

For tho' from out our bourne of Time and Place
The flood may bear me far,
I hope to see my Pilot face to face
When I have crost the bar.

Alfred, Lord Tennyson

Philippine • The Servant of the Centurion

Josèphe-Michel & Toinette Ventour's Children

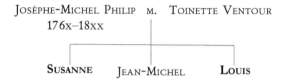

Josèphe-Michel Philip m. Toinette Ventour
176x–18xx

Susanne   Jean-Michel   Louis

Philippine Estate was originally owned by Susannah and her brother Jean-Baptiste-Louis Philip. Susannah sold her share to Marie Rénee Philip, née Fortin, in the 1790s. Susanne and Louis (see above) bought Philippine from Marie-Rénee and Jean-Baptiste-Louis around 1813. It was then managed by André Montrose Philip. After Susanne's death in about 1827 or '28, it was managed by her brother Louis, who now owned it. Susannah's husband William Robin, Frederick Maxwell and later Thomas Crosbie, son-in-law of Marie-Rénee and Jean-Baptiste-Louis, all managed Philippine at some point in time. Philippine was left to Michel Maxwell Philip in 1869 by Louis Philip. It was later acquired by the Lamont Family.

47. THE PIED PIPER

"To strive, to seek, to find, and not to yield"

Alfred, Lord Tennyson

PHILIPPINE ESTATE HOUSE, SOUTH NAPARIMA, TRINIDAD, B.W.I. 1929

LOYOLA COTTAGE, TRINIDAD 1870: After his cousin Louis's death in 1869 the rights, obligations, possessions and debts of Philippine estate, the last of his family's properties on the island, were left by Louis to Maxwell. Those debts amounted to well in excess of twenty thousand pounds.

In looking over Philippine's records, which were kept in several tin trunks, Maxwell saw how the estate had passed from hand to hand through the family as a very precious thing, to eventually come to him via his cousin Louis Philip. Being hopelessly ineffectual, and thank God he knew it, Louis relied on successive family members to manage the estate. This period saw some of the earliest indentured Indians in Trinidad at work in the cane fields of Philippine.

Louis had kept everything as he found it, the family Bible that contained their scattered genealogy going back to the 1760s being among the items that had come down through the years. Maxwell thought that perhaps he should bring this Bible up to date. Then there was the great bed, the old-fashioned silver Spanish candelabra, the great gilded mirror, a miscellany of furniture, countless *objets d'art*, paintings of his relatives and watercolours of bashful girls in floral settings, a great many books and of course the delightfully pornographic mezzotinted prints.

St. Luce and Claire, after the sale of Concorde estate, moved to Great Coram Street in London in 1858, where St. Luce died three years later. The news made him sad, inconsolably so, Eliza tried her best but Maxwell would weep every time he thought of his boy days at Concorde and his aunt Claire—the long twilights in the front gallery where she would read to him.

St. Luce and Claire's son Louis, with enough money at hand, had stayed behind in Trinidad—England, he declared, was not for him, adding that he was no one there, but here in Trinidad, he was everybody. Maxwell agreed; he too shared that view.

These upheavals all coincided with what Maxwell would later describe as the most fruitful, in truth the most successful, period of his public life, which began with the coming of Sir Arthur Gordon to Trinidad in 1865.

Gordon was a liberal politician, a past president of the Cambridge Union Society which prided itself of encouraging debate and the promotion of the notion of free speech. It was in this spirit of free speech that matters affecting the colony were discussed freely and openly, and not necessarily always in the public forum of the Legislative Council, but often in the privacy of the governor's residence, a charming house that was, until recently, the Peschier's estate manager's home. These conversations were mostly held with George Garcia and one or two others, people who Garcia trusted.

Garcia was then the colony's Solicitor General. He had served in that post, a highly influential position in the colonial government, for

47. THE PIED PIPER

some sixteen years and was something of a seasoned politician. His was the only voice of the so-called Catholic party in the Legislative Council ever since the retirement of Pierre Ganteaume. Garcia was in effect, if such a thing could exist in a Crown Colony, the leader of an opposition. Between 1851 to 1859, he acted on nine occasions as a Puisne Judge and on twelve occasions held the post of Chief Justice of the Colony.

They were enjoying the way the evening's light appeared to vibrate the radiance of the yellow pouis in bloom; the trees were sending their blossoms across the sloping lawn, creating a veritable carpet of gold. Garcia, taking this moment, remarked, "Your Excellency, with your kind permission, I would like to present to you the central figure in what could have easily become a farce, even a comedy of errors or, at worst, an uproar in the town."

"I believe I know to whom and to what are you referring, Garcia."

"I am referring, Your Excellency, to Mr. Maxwell Philip, Q.C., a Creole, a man of colour who is invested, as I am sure you are aware, by our at times very vocal press as the person who represents their interests. The comedy of errors that we narrowly avoided was an attempt to send about rabble-rousers, coming out of what we call the jamette society, and using the name of Maxwell Philip, they could have easily gotten enough people to create a disturbance. Luckily, his disassociation with their cause was all it took to calm the situation."

"Of course we know all about your famous Creole. There is quite a voluminous dossier on the Philip family at the Colonial Office, going back to a realtive of his in Governor Woodford's times. It has become something of required reading. Colleagues of mine have met your man in London at the Inns of Court, and we know of his connections through his family's investments to certain interest in the City's banking sector. No quixotic character, your man. He appears, by all accounts, a person dedicated to his *own* cause. I am sure it will be instructive to make his acquaintance."

"Indeed, Your Excellency. I have known Maxwell Philip ever since he was a boy, and have furthered his ambition as best I could. His manner, his way of comporting himself, would seem as sheer pomposity in another person—not in him! He is a brilliant practitioner. A man of the world, well read and conversant with affairs. It is somewhat in spite of himself that he is invested with such perceived powers by a segment of the population, and more due to his family history which you just mentioned and his oratorical charisma rather than to his own political inclinations, which, I can assure you, are much less than what is ascribed to him. However, in my respectful view, he would be of great use to you in your endeavour, and you may find in him a kindred spirit or at least a highly educated, well connected sounding board for some of the much-needed reforms that you have outlined in our discussions."

"If you say so, Garcia. I have long placed my confidence in your judgment."

It was thus that some days later, Maxwell Philip found himself invited to the governor's office in the Government Buildings in Port-of-Spain, where George Garcia had the pleasure of presenting his protégé to Sir Arthur.

It was a delightful meeting of minds, of shared interest and a growing confidence in each other's judgment. Sir Arthur and Maxwell had heard a great deal about each other, and finding that they shared a variety of interests, they conversed with the avidity of colleagues who had always been convinced of their commonly held points of view. They discussed liberal reforms that would allow for growth and development to take place in the colony, where the stagnation of the conservative politics of the Warner family had degenerated to the most obvious forms of nepotism, not to mention the sordid and corrupt nature of what had become known as "Warnerism". Their friendship was to endure throughout Governor Gordon's tenure in Trinidad.

As the decade of the sixties came to a close, Maxwell experienced a sea change, a series of transformations that would alter the course of both his personal and professional life. The most

47. THE PIED PIPER

alarming, in truth the most distressing, was an illness that was to overwhelm Eliza. A heart condition that would worsen, causing her to become increasingly bedridden. This was for them both a most disappointing, frightening and unfortunate happening, one that appeared to deprive them of a future together.

This was during Maxwell's last days as mayor of Port-of-Spain, which came with its own embarrassments in a manner so peculiar to this hybrid society, with everyone asking at the end of the day: "Where has the money gone?" Well, he hadn't lined his pockets, he had merely overspent the budget. Seeing the rising consternation, he resigned as mayor.

But even before this embarrassment came along a more vexing issue. It was about a coloured man, a person whom he knew, Dr. Maurice Saturnin, the scion of a family as well respected as his own. Dr. Saturnin had fallen into disgrace as a result of his mismanagement of the Leper Asylum, and Governor Gordon had given him the sack. Elements in the Créole community immediately pounced upon this as yet another example of black people in Trinidad always being the victims. At an overcrowded public meeting in Greyfriars Hall, Maxwell, then still mayor, spoke out in Dr. Saturnin's defence, but heeding Eliza's advice, one that stemmed from an intuitive faculty very similar to what came naturally to some female members of his own family, he was not hostile to and did not condemn Gordon.

The so-called radicals, a clique that had been in existence since before the days of Governor Woodford, now in their third or fourth generation after the passing of their founder St. Hilaire Begorrat and his creature Protein, were applauding those who attacked Maxwell for his reticence to challenge the new governor. This coincided with an attack by the Catholic church, whose interest was similar and whose tentacles reached into the most secret spaces, discovering that on top of everything, the hypocrite was a Freemason! It did not take any length of time for the discovery to be made that he had married Eliza in an Anglican church in England, and that not one but two Archbishops had been duped by him into being his daughters' godfathers. All for the purpose of the hypocrite's personal popularity among the Catholics, who were in the majority here in this colony. Someone commented on Maxwell's self-interest, his perfidy towards his own people, and remarked that the coloured community would hardly be pleased that a man 'with such antecedents and actual associations of his name, should be thought as a good enough representative for them.' Another went further and characterised him thus:

> 'So M****'s bought! For Honour? No, but pelf,
> And having sold the Doctor, sold himself.
> And what's his station now? I answer then
> The first of cits, alas! the last of men.
> He thinks he's won a prize, a voice in state,
> He's lost the people's love, he's won their hate.
> He'll wear his master's fetters, lined with gold
> He'll act as Councillor, til next he's sold'."

Maxwell's perfidiousness, his treachery, his deceit and duplicity were headlined in the *Star of the West*, the Catholic newspaper, widely read and influential well beyond the quality of its content. It editorialised the manner in which he had betrayed his race, forgotten from whence he came, the root itself which was shared ultimately with the majority of the population: the obscurity of illegitimate antecedents and the ignominy of slavery, not to mention their complexions. They said of him, "Watch him good, he tink he white because he is in the governor's company."

But then there were the substantial reforms that advanced the quality of life of the population that were being brought forward by the Gordon administration, not a few of which had their origins in the many conversations between the governor, George Garcia and Maxwell, where a fellowship of enlightened interest had been formed. The opening up of entry to the civil service via exams, which gave non-whites, most of whom were Catholic, the chance to advance in their careers and live better lives; the disestablishment of the Church of England, thus putting Catholics and Anglicans on an equal legal footing; state aid for Roman Catholic primary schools, and

47. THE PIED PIPER

substantial funds to the new Catholic college—all these acts that favoured the majority of the population, the very people who, at another time, had been Maxwell's most ardent supporters. Gordon even invited an order of Dominican nuns to run the Leper Asylum, and the *Star of the West* could not find fault with that.

Eliza received a substantial inheritance from her relatives in England. Some of their London properties as well as their sugar interest in Antigua was sold and Eliza, knowing Maxwell as she did, graciously handed over what he needed to pay off all of Philippine's debts and to restart the estate as a going concern, worked by the indentured labourers who were arriving from India in increasing numbers.

Everything had now come to him. He opened the old Bible one morning when he was sojourning at Philippine, and his eyes fell on: "The first of the first fruits of your land you shall bring into the house of the Lord your God. You shall not boil a young goat in its mother's milk." A daunting thought, perhaps to some. But it did give him pause.

HE LOVED THE WAY THE EVENING LIGHT came through the ceiba pentandra up here on Cotton Hill. It was as though the sunlight, shattered, fell like shards of glass among the dry leaves. Then there was the breeze, which never seemed to leave the giant grove; somehow there was always a shifting, sighing sound coming from the great trees that crowded close.

That night in August 1869, Maxwell was awaiting the governor, they were on their way to George Garcia's newly built townhouse on Richmond Street. It was a farewell dinner party for Lady Gordon and Sir Arthur, whose term of office as governor of the colony was to come to an end in a few months hence. But his heart was not in it. Eliza was abed. Her heart, too, was not in it—in truth it was failing her, failing them both, because for fifteen years they had been as one.

Maxwell and Eliza had been invited by Gordon on more than one occasion to dine at the governor's residence, which was in truth the former Peschier estate manager's house that the English people in pursuit of charm referred to as 'the cottage'. Once, with quite typical spontaneity, they had returned the invitation and to their surprise, and to the dismay of the governor's staff, Sir Arthur and his wifewere pleased to accept!

That evening Maxwell had laid out the family's heirlooms, with just six of the large silver plates as it was a small party comprising Sir Arthur, his wife Lady Rachel, George Garcia and his wife Mariquita. The old Spanish silver gleamed in reflected memory of other times, while the crystal goblets and decanters of another era sent a spectrum to glisten among the shadows. Plainly, they were not new. Gordon had not remarked on it, but Maxwell saw that he was impressed. The Garcias had of course seen it all before and even knew something of their heroic past.

The evening was indeed a significant event in itself, seen by some as the governor's endorsement, having put an end to local men being debarred from entry of the civil service, of a fresh égalité. Others were shocked that a governor of a British colony would sit down to dine with such common people, made worse because Maxwell was a Negro.

Travel writers visiting the colony found it quaint, with one remarking that in a place such as this it might have become a necessity, seeing that outside of the military there were hardly any gentlemen about. Another expressed astonishment that the governor of the colony, the son of an Earl, should live in a house that had until recently been an estate manager's dwelling. The simple truth was Maxwell and Gordon had taken to each other.

For Maxwell, Gordon's arrival in Trinidad four years before had been as the poet wrote: "The evening beam that smiles the clouds away and tints tomorrow with prophetic ray." This governor's tenure, to him, had been much more than prescient, although it did correctly point the way that his future would eventually take, but more importantly, it demonstrated to him that he had been always right. He knew full well that he was useful to the colonial regime:

47. THE PIED PIPER

he wanted to be an able servant of the Crown, and when Gordon appointed him an unofficial member of the Legislative Council it helped to neutralise some of the discontent among the educated mixed-race and black people. They had co-opted him, and both he and Eliza were only too glad to abandon his popular politics of the 1850s and early 60s.

The opportunity to receive a coconut estate called Créole from the Devenish family just east of the St. James Barracks as payment for services rendered brought in a handsome income. Coconuts, which bore fruit throughout the year, were a staple ingredient in a wide variety of foods, and even more valuable as copra from which an edible oil was produced, which was also made into soap.

Now, awaiting Gordon, the August evening's gloaming unfolding gloriously in the distant west, a verse from Byron's *The Corsair* came to him, causing him to declare to the slowly departing sun:

> "Oh, who can tell, save he whose heart hath tried,
> And danced in triumph o'er the waters wide,
> The exulting sense – the pulse's maddening play,
> That thrills the wanderer of that trackless way?"

Yes, he and Eliza had been like happy wanderers. Not a day had passed when they had not laughed, sometimes at each other, most times at what had transpired in the High Court, in the Legislative Council chamber, or at harmony in Royal Prince of Wales Lodge, where he once was Right Worshipful Master. And now he was losing her.

"I hear you, Philip, quoting Byron to the setting sun! I have one for you!"

He had heard neither the governor's carriage nor his escort coming up the hill. Gordon was early, he often was because there was always something to talk about before they set out.

"I'll give you this one, Philip, bet you can't guess from whence it comes. 'You don't love a woman because she is beautiful, but she is beautiful because you love her. Never underestimate the power of love. The way to love anything is to realise it may be lost.'"

"Something from *Childe Harold's Pilgrimage*, what! Your Excellency, Lady Gordon, a pleasure, and there is Daly with rum punches. I'll close that stanza for you if I may: *'The heart has its reasons that reason does not know at all. Music is love in search of a word.'*"

To which the other continued: "*'There is pleasure in the pathless woods; there is a rapture on the lonely shore; There is society, where none intrudes, by the deep sea, and music in its roar.'*"

"Bravo!" they both exclaimed simultaneously, and laughed, as Maxwell took Lady Rachel's hand in his and raised it to his lips. They were so well met one would think that they had known each other all their lives.

After an enjoyable dinner at the Garcias, dulled somewhat by Eliza's absence, they repaired to the verandah, the ladies included, as it was an informal evening and the easterly breeze was especially lugubrious this night. Settling into the comfortable wicker chairs, with the lamps turned low to allow the heavens to illuminate the night, and with the ever trembling white-dusted-hair butler, left to George Garcia by his father as a part of his inheritance, in close attendance, Garcia steered the conversation from one amusing topic to another.

"Maxwell, your name was in the papers again!" exclaimed Garcia's wife Mariquita, her jewellery tinkling, winking one of her expressive eyes.

"Ah well," said Maxwell, smiling at her charming profile. The scent of Lady of the Night, coming into bloom, seemed to match the rising moon as it crested the Laventille hills. He saw that it was throwing elongated shadows of the trees across the lawn. "It's not to be avoided sometimes, even though one may wish to."

She laughed, as did the others. Maxwell, chuckling along to the laughter of the others, thought: 'That's what being in the public eye brings, one has to have a thick skin, as Mrs. Garcia knows well enough, being married to a man who was so often the final arbiter.'

"I read a letter to the editor, which hailed Philip's nomination to the Leg Co as satisfactory," said Gordon. "Colonel Pocock

47. THE PIED PIPER

showed it to me, and it stated that none who believed in reward for merit, not privilege, could take umbrage at your appointment, and declared that you had an honourable name, that you had earned yourself respect throughout the society. Yet another letter advised the coloured community to show their appreciation of the appointment by rejecting any slanders against me as governor, who had made it, and against the persons in whom I have placed my confidence. I must say, for such a small population of readers, there is great variety of opinion in the Trinidad press! Be that as it may, and taking all newspapers cum grano salis, I would like to take this opportunity to make an announcement. In as much as our learned friend, Garcia here, has accepted the position of Attorney General, succeeding the late much esteemed Justice Knox, who stepped into the breach after the sudden departure of Mr. Warner, it is with pleasure that I offer you, Maxwell, George's previous post, that of Solicitor General—in an acting post to begin with, to be confirmed by my own successor next year. We cannot imagine any person more suited to hold this position than you. With it comes a seat on the official side of the Legislature, a seat that through tradition represents the Catholics! One that you would think would put the pens of all those newspaper scribblers to rest. But no, not here, not in this island of such independent thinkers!"

"Congratulations," smiled Garcia.

"Congratulations, Maxwell," said Lady Rachel. "This would have been made perfect if Eliza was on her feet, as she is very much a part of what we mark this evening. Please give her our fondest regards."

"If I may, I would like to thank you, Sir Arthur, for what you have brought about in just a few years, your perspicuity, the fresh wind that you brought with you...." Here, Mariquita became lost for words, but nevertheless continued, "Your Excellency, you could not have selected a better matching pair, my George and Maxwell. Let's raise a toast, and after, Sir Arthur, please, tell us what comes to mind this evening!"

Sir Arthur was already formulating the thoughts that would describe the crafting of a new era in Trinidad. He saw a fresh frontier, an opening up of this so charmingly called Land of the Hummingbird, where opportunity would meet ambition and these folk, so diverse, even original in their backgrounds, would succeed each other to positions of authority in this most unique of colonies. He was on his feet and looking about him, his glass held high.

Maxwell beamed with pride for his friend and affection for his mentor. Looking at Garcia through tear-filled eyes, he could imagine this man in any of his many manifestations, reincarnations even. 'That he, they, whoever they were, should have selected me when I was hardly more than a child. I must have been a very bright boy.' He smiled or wept or both as he remembered going to Garcia's father's house that Sunday morning. 'I was small and left to wander around the place. There was no other house appointed in such a manner in Port-of-Spain. To me, it was the most fantastic house in the world, it was full of white archways, long cool corridors, stained glass wonders with castles and prancing lions. It had a chapel. There was a church inside this house! Silent, so still that even your breath echoed in there. The red eternal light was burning over the altar, which meant for me that the Holy Presence was here, God was here. I never had seen anything like that in anybody's house. It was as though this house somehow contained a town. It was not until many years later, when I visited Lodge Les Frères Unis on the occasion of the visitation of the Supreme Council to Trinidad, that I saw another place that was as superbly appointed, both in such original ways.'

He realised that they were applauding. He could not remember a thing he had said except at the end, where he heard himself say, " . . as your most humble servant standing here before you, Your Excellency."

"A toast," called Mariquita, raising her glass.

Among the well-wishing and toasting, Maxwell, being glad for the honours bestowed on him, could only think: 'I have to tell Eliza this. I have to tell her that . . . I have to tell her you are right, my

47. The Pied Piper

lovely, right about everything. As Solicitor General, I will be able to continue my private practice, as the remuneration for that post is low. But I hear that I will soon be appointed Counsel for Venezuela. As for the governors, they will always call the tune. And me! On the official side where uncle St. Luce sat. Interesting times ahead, Eliza! Interesting times, my girl. Ah . . . and at last we appear to be leaving . . .'

48. A Lie that is Half-Truth is the Darkest of all Lies

"Once in a golden hour
I cast to earth a seed.
Up there came a flower,
The people said, a weed."

Alfred, Lord Tennyson

C.L.R. James, Port-of-Spain, Trinidad, 1929. "Ah, Mr. James, I can hear from the confidence in your step that you have discovered what lies beneath the woodpile." Mrs. Broadway was talking to me even before she could see me. "I find that it took you rather long!"

That was amazing! I had only just discovered a newspaper article written in March 1912, which concerned a high court matter that showed that Maxwell Philip had started another family after his wife Elizahad died. And here was Mrs. Broadway, standing at the table in the billiard room, with the very same *Port of Spain Gazette* from 1912 in front of her, open on the page with the article that I had read at the library the day before.

"Take a seat, Mr. James, would you like some lemonade? There's ice."

I must have nodded as there was the tinkling sound of ice in a glass. "Thank you, it's quite hot. . ."

"So you have finally found it. Mr. James, were you shocked, surprised? I can see all of that frozen in your expression," she said, and laughed falsely. "You started at the beginning of time like the good little schoolboy you will always be. But what you should have done to get the real picture of my father was start at the end"—here she tapped her fingertips on the newspaper—"here, and you would have found the nigger in the woodpile."

48. A Lie that is Half-Truth is the Darkest of all Lies

Woodpile or not, the article had actually left me with more questions than answers, which I hoped to get from Mrs. Broadway. It referred in a somewhat roundabout way to an old court case from 1889, and stated that Philippa Anderson, née Philip, had been about eight years old when her father, Maxwell Philip, died. She had two younger sisters, Christina and Jane, all the natural children of Maxwell Philip and their mother, Dora Dookie. Philippa, it would appear, had lived with her father at Loyola until he sent her to the Convent in Port-of-Spain, but when he died she was taken out of the school and returned to Loyola.

A Mrs. Latour who, Philippa was later to discover, was her half-sister—in fact, Ethel Broadway's sister Catherine whom I had met earlier, and who had married a Latour—was said to be her guardian. Eventually, she was again taken out of the Convent, this time went not to Loyola, but to Cocorite village to live with her mother and sisters.

It would appear that they became quite indigent, as a servant of her father, the very same Mavaline Shemuerl who was still in Mrs. Broadway's employ, would bring them various necessities. The article went on to say that Philippa could not recall if a Mr. Iles, the executor of their father's first will, ever gave them any financial support. She never, so the article said, received anything whatever under the will made by their father. However, when it was discovered that they were the offspring of Maxwell Philip, there was a public outcry. This led to the Port-of-Spain Council becoming involved along with several prominent persons in an effort to assist them.

"Yes, yes, we knew all that. We don't live with our heads buried in a book." Mrs. Broadway was, somewhat to my surprise, obviously quite prepared to tell me about her father's second family. "What you don't know is that my father made two wills."

Well now, that started to make sense to me, if there had been two wills. Mr. Iles, the executor, obviously was no stranger to Philippa, since she remembered seeing him coming to Loyola, and to Maxwell's coconut estate in Cocorite. At some point in time, when they were obviously much older, Philippa and her sisters approached Mr. Iles and asked him for an account. He said that her father had left nothing for them as they were bastard children.

"That was actually not true, Mr. James," commented Mrs. Broadway when I asked her about it. "In his second will, my father actually left everything, lock stock and barrel, to his illegitimate children. As the newspaper states quite correctly, father's old steward at Loyola, Frederick Daly, was called into his bedroom. In the final stage of his illness, Father then dictated this codicil." She pointed to a large, handwritten document that lay next to the *Port of Spain Gazette* on the table. Daly, who later made a clean copy of the will afterwards, stated according to the newspaper article that he could not recall if Mr. Iles, the court appointed executor of the first will, was present when the will was dictated to him by Maxwell. It was signed by Maxwell and attended by two witnesses, Mr. Hunter, a merchant who lived in the neighbourhood, and Dr. de Boissiere of the Rookery. Daly also recalled that Maxwell gave a priest, Father Thomas Greenough, a stocking with what appeared to him to be a large amount money and told him to keep it for his three Indian children.

"Mr. James, when the editors came seeking information to write the obituaries, I was the one who told them all they needed to know," said Mrs. Broadway, a stern look in her ancient eyes. "Oh, how it touched their readers, when they learned how father was treated by the government! People just love to be made to look like they are victims. I simply left the rest to their overheated imaginings. I'm sure their papers sold more with those obituaries and orations. You know, father was loved by many, Mr. James. They all wanted to be his best friend, but very few ever came to know him."

Yes, I could well imagine that Ethel would never have told any of those people about Miss Dookie, her father's common law wife and their three daughters and in any event even if they knew, out of respect for him it would not have been printed.

48. A Lie that is Half-Truth is the Darkest of all Lies

Sliding the will across the table to me and turning it around, she pointed at the date, I saw that it was signed on 19th June, 1887, the year before he died.

"This is the clean copy of the new will. Well, Mr. James, there is no fool like an old fool, and my father, in some mad displacement of his sanity, not to mention his dignity, created a relationship with this person. He of course could not marry her. He couldn't take her anywhere. She was just a fat coolie woman, in an orini, the protégée of some pundit that he had done legal work for. She may have been given to my father as a gift, a part payment! She would never have been able to fill my mother's shoes. He couldn't take her to government house. He could not possible be made Attorney General! That was the great disappointment. In the minds of some people he was meant to succeed George Garcia! His fall from grace was used to further their agendas. Those absurd obituaries are his memorial, Mr. James."

"Oh, I see," I said, taken aback a little by the vehemence with which she spoke.

"You don't see anything at all, Mr. James, because you have no idea what you were looking for in the first place. You were in search of a popular hero, the young black who would turn the colonial tide. But in the end, it was nothing but an old man's twaddle. This will in front of you here was an absurdity. He left only our mother's painting to Catherine, while at the same time making her the guardian of his three illegitimate daughters, who were only four, six and eight at the time of his death and to whom he bequeathed everything—this house, all his estates, all his furniture and personal and real estate. He evidently had fallen in love with Miss Dookie, and now he wanted to share the entire family fortune with them."

The sun was setting and she got up, and I took that as my cue that I should be leaving. But no. There was more to be revealed. Turning on the electric lights in the billiard room, she continued in a more constrained voice.

"You know Mr. James, there was not much difference between this piece of rubbish and the old, the original will. My father was both wealthy and generous. The difference was that suddenly, we had to share our lives with all these people! Which was unthinkable, completely unfair, unjust, and as it turned out, it could not stand up in court."

Taking back the will and adjusting herself so the lamp shone on it, she continued: "Listen, Mr. James, to my father's generosity. As I said, what follows here is not much different from the first will. He gave fifty dollars each to his body servant Joseph, whom we used to call Canon, to his nurse Françoise Crichlow, to Miss Mary Evelyn, a servant, and to Mrs. Shermuel whom you have met. He also left three hundred dollars to his goddaughter Catherine Philip, the daughter of Rebecca Gittens, late of Tranquility Boulevard, who was deceased at the time he died. Catherine may have been another bastard of his for all we know! His old coachman Samuel Crichlow got fifteen dollars a month during his life, and so did Dora Dookie herself. Apparently she was the adopted daughter of Babagee Ramchand, a pundit who lived in Mucurapo, long dead by that time as well. He gave them our family name, Philip, he brought them to live here and made them beneficiaries of his will! Can you imagine that, Mr. James? He left them his coconut plantation Créole, you know it. It lies between the Diego Martin main road and the sea. Even this house, Loyola, where my sister and I had grown up. Our childhood home, Mr. James, left to three small children! This travesty of a will reads"—she stabbed the paper with her forefinger—"'I give all my furniture and plate, carriages, horses and other animals and things in Loyola aforesaid and within the four corners of its grounds to the said Philippa Philip, Christina Philip, and Jane Dora Philip'. And to add insult to injury, he bequeathed that 'the portrait of my late wife is to be delivered to Catherine Latour', my sister. Only that portrait was to come to her, nothing else! And nothing at all to me. Except the residue of his personal effects, they were to be divided equally among his five daughters—imagine that, he put me and Catherine on an equal footing with those three little Indian waifs."

48. A Lie that is Half-Truth is the Darkest of all Lies

"But if I may ask, Mrs. Broadway," I interrupted when she paused for breath, "this will was never implemented, correct?"

"Of course not. Of all the men who were supposedly the executors and witnesses to this absurdity, only Vincent Brown was seen by me as respectable, he was my father's protégé. The others merely went along with the sentiments of an old man in his dotage and indulged him in giving away my and my sister's inheritance. We took the will to court, and won the case. The court confirmed Mr. Iles as the executor of the first will. He made sure that this will was never implemented."

We sat in silence for a while. She sighed. I glanced at her. She seemed crumpled, bereft of the considerable energy that she had put into the last half hour, and appeared worn out sitting in the large winged chair, her hands, her fingers, I noticed for the first time, disfigured by arthritis.

"So now there you are, you have sucked me dry like an orange. Every time I see you, I know you are looking for some sort of scandal. Dr. de Boissière—not the one from Rookery Nook, but the white one who lived at Champs Elysées, to whom we owe the land on which Loyola stands—who was a friend of my father's mentor George Garcia as well as a member of the Leg Co, raised a motion in the Council that Maxwell's Indian children should be given a modest pension, which they were awarded, seeing that they were left quite destitute after my father died. They did receive it and went on in life. Philippine was eventually sold to John Lamont to cover the mortgages that had been accumulated. And everything else came to me and Catherine. So here it is, the scandal, this is the nigger in the woodpile. Of course we knew. Everyone knew about it all. Yet no one knew and if they did—ah well, it was just Maxwell, a born Créole. But at the end of the day, we are still here. So now get out of my house and you can write whatever you want."

So Ethel Broadway, in her usual style, had managed to once again tell me off at the end of the day. But after discovering all of this, I felt that the personality of this 'hero of the people' had been shaped for others and me by the obituary writers in the newspapers, who had all in a way been activists in the cause of the Captain's 'barefoot man'. Now I realised that what they had written about Maxwell, portraying him as a populist politician betrayed by the white peopl,e was mostly their wishful thinking—and obviously Ethel Broadway's edited version of her late father's life.

I now think that the truth about Maxwell was that he enjoyed being a civil servant, just like he enjoyed being a barrister. He was a man who enjoyed himself. What he definitely was not, was my Toussaint L'Ouverture, a revolutionary hero. So it came to me that I would give my article about him for the *Beacon* a bit of an entertaining, slap-dash quality, a bird's eye view if you like of his professional life, with some well-told blandishments of a personal nature. He did enjoy the swish of a skirt, and to add glamour to the already glamorous, I would raise a query concerning his birth, which I will say may be revealed in his book *Appadocca*, and suggest that this was an autobiography, portraying him as illegitimate and rebellious as described in many stories of mulatto life as one of outcasts, shunned from society but with a difference. The worm turns, his hero seeks revenge.

Mrs. Broadway was on to something when she talked about Trinidad people loving to be portrayed as victims, because it absolves them from responsibility and gives them the right to feel entitled. It chimed in with what the Captain and I had talked about when we discussed this idea of politicising victimhood for the cause, to energise the people. It will work better if Maxwell is seen as a victim, like the hero of his buccaneer story who overcomes victimhood.

I got on my bicycle and coasted down Cotton Hill, my fingertips on the brake, the headlamp barely showing the way. In my mind's eye, I could see Maxwell Philip, now an older man, a bit overweight, breathless, as he mounts the steps to the verandah with the maidenhair ferns. There are three small Indian girls crowding around him. In the penumbra of my imagination I glimpse the figure of a woman half shaded by the lace curtains standing in an upstairs window.

49. Captain Cipriani: A Time Bomb or a Time Capsule

"The old order changeth yielding place to new
And God fulfills himself in many ways
Lest one good custom should corrupt the world."

Alfred, Lord Tennyson

The Captain, Arthur Cipriani

Capt. Arthur Cipriani, Port-of-Spain, Trinidad, 1929. The breeze has quickened. This straightaway sends the schooners to rising and falling in an almost comic disorder; it also brings the smell of tar and goods and the voices of men, their accents echoing this vast archipelago that stretches from the Gulf of Paria to the Gulf of Mexico. It is one of my favourite places, especially on a Saturday afternoon. Returning the salute of the many who recognise me, I am standing at the black-and-white striped rail that marks the end of the Lighthouse Jetty, to listen to the splash of the sea and to wonder at the voyages made by those at anchor.

There is no doubt about it—these islands are standing on the cusp of change, their own wonder voyages.

James arrived this morning, quite early, in a state of nerves. He had written the *Beacon* piece and he wanted me to read it. But first there was new information, startlingly so, in a newspaper article of 1912 that he had found, which described a court case involving Maxwell's 'other' family.

"You showed this to Mrs. Broadway?" I was surprised.

"Yes," he answered, going on to say, "And she, as if waiting for it, for me, produced her father's will—his second will, which was, according to her, quite different from his first, which would have been more conventional I suppose. This new will left everything to his new family, which, it would appear, he brought to Loyola to live with him. Can you imagine that? I'm not sure who was living there with him after his wife had died, Mrs. Broadway and her husband maybe."

I listened with mounting astonishment as James in great detail described the content of the new will. Had Maxwell gone mad? But then, he had been still too young to be overtaken by senile decay.

"Come, Nello," I said eventually, "Let's get some coffee and you can tell me all about it. I still have an hour before I am meant to be at the Princes Building for the meeting of the City Council Workers Union."

As we went downstairs, Nello continued excitedly: "Well, Captain, it came to me first during this business with the second will. Even though *Appadocca* may not have been autobiographical at the time that Maxwell wrote it, a passage in the book becomes part of Maxwell's life much later on."

"Now that's interesting, Nello. Is that so? That's a weighty thought, my word, you must have been up all night." James did not catch the 'fatigue' but just continued.

"I know you have not read the book, but in a nutshell, Emmanuel Appadocca's white father says that Emmanuel is only his son 'of a

49. Captain Cipriani: A Time Bomb or a Time Capsule

sort', and since he was illegitimate, he, the father, had no obligations towards him. Maxwell, the author, apparently objected to this attitude by a father of bastard children. He lets his main character, Emmanuel rail against it, by saying that—one moment, I have it in my notes here—'certain creatures who are branded and repudiated by society'—such as bastard children like Emmanuel himself—'are beings who possess feelings, and who claim the same measure of justice as is meted out to all'. You see, Maxwell was training to be a lawyer, and he saw the legal dimension of a moral issue: illegitimacy, mixed-race descent, the cult of the will."

"All right, go on. Maria," I called to one of the girls in the kitchen, "two hot arepas for my friend here, and I hope you still have some of that nice accra and float."

"He may have been thinking about this for years, decades, Captain. Maxwell, in his dealings with the three daughters of his mistress, Dora Dookie, mother of his children, who was of a different race than him, and his three daughters with her, did assume full paternal obligations by bringing them to live with him at Loyola and by writing a second will in the full favour of his three illegitimate daughters. He wanted to ensure that the girls would not be stigmatised by society and he gave them his last name, Philip. By making them the main beneficiaries of his last will and testament, he righted a wrong that his literary hero had observed, and instead acted in full cognisance that the girls possessed feelings and that it was important that they were justly treated just like his two older daughters. So while *Appadocca* may not have been autobiographical at the time of writing, the hero of this, the first novel ever written by a Trinidadian, expressed early on the opinion of the author, and later on, the author's life imitated his own art! And as a postscriptum, the three Indian daughters suffered exactly the fate that Maxwell had Emmanuel decry: they were 'branded and repudiated'—certainly by their half-sisters and the executor, Mr. Iles—and did not get the 'same measure of justice' as Maxwell's legitimate daughters, as is evident in the newspaper article."

"The author's life imitated his art! Nicely said, Nello. Now let's have a look at that *Beacon* article."

James passed me some typewritten pages and I began to read. I didn't get further than the second page, where James had written that all through Maxwell's novel, *Appadocca* shows the powerful effect with which the misfortune of his—Maxwell's—birth weighed upon his mind.

"Nello, you can't be serious! The 'misfortune of his birth that weighed upon his mind'? But you know that Maxwell was not illegitimate, or a child of a slave and a white man like the character in his novel. His parents were married and both came from quite well-off and well-respected free coloured families. There was no misfortune. We had gone over this. After all the work we have done, you write this rubbish!"

James just shrugged and continued to eat his breakfast quite nonchalantly. "You know, Captain, I thought about this. I know that it's bending the truth to say that *Appadocca* is autobiographical. But in that second will, I saw that there was indeed a connection between Maxwell and the hero of his novel. And the real life Maxwell came up a little short on the hero front with his lack of political enthusiasm and his illegitimate children. So by saying that *Appadocca* mirrored his own life, I took some artistic license and made him more relevant to my readers, more political."

I began to understand. The main reason why James is 'bending the truth' about *Appadocca* being autobiographical is that he, James, instinctively is trying to change the future by portraying Maxwell as a victim. Nello really has become a politician! This was definitely a political decision in his writing, and the *Beacon* piece will be either seen as a time capsule, relegating Maxwell Philip's life to the past, or as a time bomb, which could alter political thinking in these islands going forward.

THE END.

In Memoriam Gérard A. Besson
1942–2023

When for the last time
You close your mouth
Your words and soul
Will belong to the world of
No place, no time.

(Rumi)